AF652567

Calcutta
The Stormy Decades

Some Books from Social Science Press and Aurum Books

Persistence of Poverty in India (HB)
Edited by Nandini Gooptu and Jonathan Parry

German Writings on India and South Asia
'Everywhere is Becoming the Same'? (HB)
Nicole Mayer-Ahuja

French Writings on India and South Asia
Tocqueville in India (HB)
Jean Alphonse Bernard

Savage Attack: Tribal Insurgency in India (HB)
Edited by Crispin Bates ad Alpa Shah

The Year of Blood: Essays on the Revolt of 1857 (HB)
Rudrangshu Mukherjee

The Autobiography of a Revolutionary in British India (HB)
Kali Ghosh

German Writings on India and South Asia
Cultural Encounters in India
The Local Co-Workers of the Tranquebar Mission, 18th–19th centuries (HB)
Heike Liebau

French Writings on India and South Asia
Scholars and Prophets: Sociology of India from France in the 19th–20th centuries (HB)
Roland Lardinois

The Politics of the Pharmaceuticd Industry and Access to Medicines: World Pharmacy and India(HB)
Edited by Hans Löfgren

Economics and its Stories (HB)
Amal Sanyal

Everyday Nationalism: Women of the Hindu Right in India (HB)
Kalyani Devaki Menon

4 Victoria Terrace: Memoirs of a Surgeon (HB)
Subir K. Chatterjee

Rebels from the Mud Houses: Dalits and the Making of the Maoist Revolution in Bihar (HB)
George Kunnath

Behind the Backlash: Muslim Americans after 9/11 (HB)
Lori Peek

Windows into a Revolution: Ethnographies of Maoism in India and Nepal (HB)
Edited by Alpa Shah and Judith Pettigrew

German Writings on India and South Asia
'When the war began we heard of several kings': South Asian Prisoners in World War I Germany (HB)
Edited by Franziska Roy, Heike Liebau and Ravi Ahuja

Unruly Hills: Nature and Nation in India's Northeast (HB)
Bengt G. Karlsson

Telecommunications Industry in India: State, Business and Labour in a Global Economy (HB)
Dilip Subramanian

The Many Worlds of Sarala Devi: A Diary
Translated by Sukhendu Ray and

The Tagores and Sartorial Styles: A Photo Essay (HB)
Malavika Karlekar

Reflections on Cambridge (HB)
Alan Macfarlane

The Everyday State and Society in Modern India (PB)
Edited by C.J. Fuller and Vêronique Benei

'Good Women do not Inherit Land': Politics of Land and Gender in India (PB)
Nitya Rao

Cultural History of Medieval India (PB)
Edited by Meenakshi Khanna

Cultural History of Modern India (PB)
Edited by Dilip M. Menon

Delhi: Ancient History (PB)
Edited by Upinder Singh

Literature and Nationalist Ideology: Writing Histories of Modern Indian Languages (PB)
Edited by Hans Harder

Religious Division and Social Conflict: The Emergence of Hindu Nationalism in Rural Inc (PB)
Peggy Froerer

The Enigma of the Kerala Woman: A Failed Promise of Literacy (PB)
Edited by Swapna Mukhopadhyay

Nature, Culture and Religion at the Crossroads of Asia (HB)
Edited by Marie Lecomte-Tilouine

Social and Economic Profile of India (HB)(In full colour)
Peeyush Bajpai, Laveesh Bhandari and Aali Sinha

India and China in the Colonial World (PB)
Edited by Madhavi Thampi

Viramma: Life of a Dalit (PB)
Viramma, Josiane Racine and Jean-luc Racine

Lived Islam in South Asia: Adaptation, Accommodation and Conflict (PB)
Edited by Imtiaz Ahmad and Helmut Reifeld

Forthcoming

Dalit Women: Honour and Patriarchy in South India (HB)
Clarinda Still

Aurum Books

Sabotage (PB)
Anita Agnihotri, Translated by Arunava Sinha

Opium Poppy (PB)
Hubert Haddad, Translated by Renuka George

Forthcoming Aurum Books

Mahatma Gandhi: Anti-biography of a Great Soul (PB)
Michael De Saint Cheron, Translated by Asha N. Spaak

Revolutionary Passions (PB)
Hamit Bozarslan, Gilles Bataillon, and Christophe Jaffrelot, Translated by Indranil Chakroborty and Soma Dutta-Gupta

Calcutta
The Stormy Decades

Edited by

Tanika Sarkar
Sekhar Bandyopadhyay

SOCIAL
SCIENCE
PRESS

Published by
Esha Béteille
Social Science Press
69 Jor Bagh, New Delhi 110 003

© Tanika Sarkar, Sekhar Bandyopadhyay 2015

All rights reserved. No part of this publication may be reproduced, stored in a retrieval system, or transmitted, in any form or by any means, without the prior permission in writing of Social Science Press, or as expressly permitted by law, or under terms agreed with the appropriate reprographics rights organization. Enquiries concerning reproduction outside the scope of the above should be sent to Social Science Press, at the address above.

You must not circulate this book in any other binding or cover and you must impose this same condition on any acquirer.

Distributed by
Orient Blackswan Pvt. Ltd.
Bangalore Bhopal Bhubaneshwar Chandigarh
Chennai Ernakulam Guwahati Hyderabad Jaipur
Kolkata Lucknow Mumbai New Delhi Noida Patna
www.orientblackswan.com

ISBN: 978-93-83166-07-7

Advisory Board
T.N. Madan
Dipankar Gupta
Jonathan Parry
C.J. Fuller
Veena Das
Bibek Debroy
Kaushik Basu
Abusaleh Shariff
Alaka Basu
Pratap Bhanu Mehta

Social Science Press is grateful to Anandabazar Patrika for permission to use their archival photographs in this book.

Social Science Press gratefully acknowledges the generous financial support from Nine Dot Nine Mediaworx Pvt Ltd towards the publication of this book.

Set in Sabon 10/13.1
Typeset by Eleven Arts, Delhi 110 035
Printed by Summit Advertising
Tel.: 011-45011844, e-mail: summit_advt@yahoo.co.in

For
Professor Soumyendra Nath Mukherjee
who pioneered the history of Calcutta

Contents

COMMUNAL RELATIONS: SOLIDARITIES AND VIOLENCE

POSTCOLONIAL TRANSITION

Acknowledgement

This book attempts to capture a most critical period in the life of Calcutta in all its complexities. The two decades—1940s and 50s—threw up myriad representations in contemporary media, literature and in visual and performative arts. Yet, so far, there is no history of Calcutta that looks at the city as a whole at this precise point of time. We have tried to bring in as many aspects of urban self images of those times as possible. We have also tried to look at the two decades as a unified yet contradictory historical experience. In doing so, we have incurred many debts and we would like to take this opportunity to acknowledge all the generous help that we have received.

We want to acknowledge, first of all, the contributions of all those who have written various chapters or translated poems for this book. Some of them are established scholars; but many of them are young, budding historians, who either have just finished PhD or are still continuing their doctoral research. These young scholars bring in refreshingly new ideas to this book. We would like to thank them for their interest, enthusiasm and active co-operation.

We are particularly thankful to Anandabazar Patrika for the amazing photographs of the period. These photos of various landmark events described in this book make the written narratives much more meaningful and enhance the value of the book.

Finally, we gratefully acknowledge the active encouragement and support of Esha Béteille and her editorial team at Social Science Press. Without their warm enthusiasm and co-operation, this book would never have seen the light of the day. We cannot thank them enough.

If any error still remains despite our sincere efforts, we remain responsible for that.

Tanika Sarkar
Sekhar Bandyopadhyay

Contributors

Anna Sailer is currently completing a PhD on labour relations in the jute industry of colonial Bengal, at the Center for Modern Indian Studies, at the University of Göttingen.

Anwesha Roy is a PhD research scholar at the Centre for Historical Studies, Jawaharlal Nehru University, Delhi.

Anwesha Sengupta is a Doctoral Candidate at Centre for Historical Studies, Jawaharlal Nehru University, Delhi.

Debjani Sengupta teaches literatures in English at Indraprastha College for Women, University of Delhi.

Gargi Chakravartty is a former faculty member of the Department of History, Maitreyi College, University of Delhi.

Ishan Mukherjee is pursuing his PhD at the University of Cambridge and is affiliated to Trinity College and the Faculty of History.

Janam Mukherjee is an Assistant Professor of History at Ryerson University in Toronto.

Nariaki Nakazato retired as professor of South Asian history from the Institute for Advanced Studies on Asia at the University of Tokyo. He is now Emeritus Professor, The University of Tokyo.

Partho Datta teaches undergraduate history in Zakir Husain P.G. Evening College, University of Delhi.

Rajarshi Chunder is presently pursuing his PhD in History at the Centre for Historical Studies, Jawaharlal Nehru University, Delhi.

Sanjukta Ghosh completed her doctoral thesis from the School of Oriental and African Studies on agricultural knowledge transfers, with a fellowship from the Association of Commonwealth Universities, UK. Her post-doctoral academic and participatory research is on decolonisation, transnational politics of food relief and its legacy on contemporary food rights movement.

Sekhar Bandyopadhyay is Director of New Zealand India Research Institute and Professor of Asian History at Victoria University of Wellington in New Zealand.

Siddhartha Guha Ray is presently an Associate Professor in History at Vivekananda College, Kolkata.

Sohini Majumdar is preparing for PhD admission and she has completed her MPhil from Centre for Historical Studies, Jawaharlal Nehru University, Delhi.

Sukanya Mitra is a Junior Research fellow, Nehru Memorial Museum and Library, Delhi.

Sumit Sarkar retired as Professor of History, University of Delhi.

Swagata Mazumdar is an independent translator.

Tanika Sarkar is Professor, Modern History, Centre for Historical Studies, Jawaharlal Nehru University, Delhi.

Uditi Sen is an Assistant Professor of South Asian Studies and History at Hampshire College, USA.

CHAPTER
one

Introduction Calcutta in History and Historiography

Sekhar Bandyopadhyay

Whether or not we consider the arrival of Job Charnock in Sutanuti in 1690 as the beginning of the modern metropolis of Calcutta, the city nevertheless celebrated its tercentenary in 1990, and this created an unprecedented interest in and a market for the city's history. The two-volume tercentennial history of Calcutta published that year is a testimony to that heightened interest in varied themes related to the city's past as well as present—highlighting the continuities in its lived experiences, resurrecting the idea that Calcutta is a living city as it always was.[1] The city ever since has not stopped attracting scholarly interest of historians, both professional and amateur.

Serious academic research in urban history of Calcutta had however started in the late 1970s with pioneer scholars like Soumyendra Nath Mukherjee and Pradip Sinha. Mukherjee[2] had looked at the early social history of Calcutta in the nineteenth century when in its native quarters the *dals* or factions of high caste Hindu elite operated to control its social and political life. He showed how their leadership was composed and how their influence extended beyond the urban limits of Calcutta. While Mukherjee

I wish to thank Ambalika Guha for providing research assistance that helped me write the Introduction.

[1]Sukanta Chaudhuri, (ed.), *Calcutta: The Living City,* Vol. I, The Past; Vol. II, The Present and Future (Calcutta: Oxford University Press, 1990).

[2]S.N. Mukherjee, *Calcutta: Myth and History* (Calcutta: Subarnarekha, 1977).

concentrated on the social life of early Calcutta, Sinha[3] discussed its physical environment, its overall setting of dualism between the white and the black town, the ethnic composition and the occupational pattern of its population, the fortune makers and family founders, and their role in social change. For retrieving the story of its physical growth and administrative development, Calcutta owes a great deal to its resident Malayali scholar, P. Thankappan Nair, whose wide-ranging scholarship explored practically every aspect of the history of this metropolis, from the seventeenth to the nineteenth century—touching on the origin of its name, a history of its streets, the beginning of its press, the story of its High Court and its police system, and its more modern south Indian diaspora.[4] Thanks to these pioneering scholars, we now have a fairly clear idea of the development of this colonial metropolis. And some of these themes, like its physical development, the changing nature of its urban space, its evolving modernity and its image as a city of nightmares, have all been further explored in recent years in the works of Swati Chattopadhyay[5] and Partho Datta.[6]

So far as its cultural life was concerned, ever since Raja Rammohun Roy set foot in the city in 1815, Calcutta became the centre of a unique cultural efflorescence, which goes by the name of 'Bengal Renaissance', and a rich literature now exists on this theme.[7]

[3]Pradip Sinha, *Calcutta in Urban History* (Calcutta: Firma K.L.M., 1978).

[4]P. Thankappan Nair, *Calcutta: Origin of the Name* (Calcutta: Subarnarekha, 1985); *Calcutta in the 17th Century* (Calcutta: Firma K.L.M., 1986); *Early History of Calcutta High Court* (Calcutta: Bannerjee Book Company, 1987); *A History of the Calcutta Press: The Beginning* (Calcutta: Firma K.L.M., 1987); *A Tercentenary History of Calcutta: A History of Calcutta's Streets*, Vol. 2. (Calcutta: Firma K.L.M., 1987); *Calcutta in the 19th Century: Company's days* (Calcutta: Firma K.L.M., 1989); *South Indians in Kolkata* (Kolkata: Punthi Pustak, 2004); *Origin of the Calcutta Police* (Calcutta: Punthi Pustak, 2007).

[5]Swati Chattopadhyay, *Representing Calcutta: modernity, nationalism and the colonial uncanny* (London, New York: Routledge, 2005).

[6]Partho Datta, *Planning the City, Urbanization and Reform in Calcutta c. 1800 to c. 1940* (Delhi: Tulika Books, 2012).

[7]For a detailed historiography of Bengal Renaissance, see Brian A. Hatcher, 'Great Men Waking: Paradigms in the Historiography of the Bengal Renaissance', in *Bengal: Rethinking History, ed.* S. Bandyopadhyay, (New Delhi: Manohar, 2001), 135–166.

If this high culture is rightly criticised as elitist, Sumanta Banerjee's work[8] has further highlighted the dualism within this culture of the black or native town of Calcutta. He shows how the lower orders—the artisans, labourers and menials—who were the early settlers of the black town, were gradually marginalised and driven out of the precincts of the city as the urban development gained in momentum. With this the popular cultural forms were marginalised too by the new urbane values of the Calcutta *bhadrolok* and their better technology. The elite culture in Calcutta developed under the western influences and in an environment of loyalty to colonial rule. The perceptions of the lower orders as regards colonial rule and protest against it also came to be coloured largely by those of the elites. The folk culture in Calcutta, Banerjee argues, evinced an awareness of the basic contradiction between the rulers and the ruled, but it had not been able to develop an idiom necessary to overthrow that oppressive order. Some of these themes have been enlarged further in Anindita Ghosh's work on print culture and publishing in Calcutta, focusing on aspects of debate and identity formation through cultural encounters with colonialism in the nineteenth century.[9]

This brings us to the political culture of Calcutta. The city perhaps had lost its national significance ever since the imperial capital was shifted to New Delhi in 1911. But it continued to witness an inexhaustible variety of political activities that attracted the interests of historians. While it is possibly only Rajat Ray who has written a focused history of city politics in the late nineteenth and early twentieth centuries,[10] a number of other studies have explored how nationalist politics have been played out within the precincts of this provincial capital, but we need not go into that discussion here. An ensemble of such themes concerning urban politics can

[8]Sumanta Banerjee, *The Parlour and the Street: Elite and Popular Culture in Nineteenth Century Calcutta* (Calcutta: Seagull, 1989).

[9]Anindita Ghosh, *Power in Print: Popular Publishing and the Politics of Language and Culture in a Colonial Society,1778–1905* (New Delhi: Oxford University Press, 2006).

[10]Rajat Kanta Ray, *Urban Roots of Indian Nationalism: Pressure Groups and Conflicts of Interests in Calcutta City Politics 1875–1939* (New Delhi: Vikas Publishing House, 1979).

be seen in the book edited by Pradip Sinha in 1987,[11] dealing with such varied political experiences ranging from those involving the *bhadrolok* to those participated by the working classes, from early association politics to non-conformist youth movements of the 1960s, from the activities of elites like Ramkamal Sen or Mahendra Lall Sarkar to those of the modern day *bustee* (slum) dwellers, from the general political culture of Calcutta to the specificities of women's participation in the Swadeshi movement.

All these urban historical writings on Calcutta usually span long periods and either look at stable forms and experiences or trace their makings over a considerable period of time. The present book however puts together a set of essays that, in sharp contrast, focus on a thin slice of time, a little more than a decade—from the early 1940s to the early 1950s—a decade of profound and radical change, rare in the life of most cities. It was a decade that saw the effects of a world war, the severest famine in the history of the subcontinent, the worst communal violence that looked like a civil war, massive anti-colonial and left movements, labour strikes, Independence and Partition, mass refugee influx and migration of its own religious minority—in short, urban disorganisation on a vast scale, accompanied by significant deaths, and the birth of a new nation state and a new democracy. These were the best and the worst of times, occurring in crowded sequence, churning up catastrophe and exhilaration in equal measure and ruthlessly compressing vast, unprecedented, indeed, unimaginable changes in the urban landscape and demography within a span of a little more than ten years. The city that was forged in and by these years was a very different Calcutta. This book seeks to capture the processes of change that marked the transition from the colonial to the postcolonial period in the life of this historic metropolis from the writings of scholars, both established and young, who are opening up some new dimensions in Calcutta's recent past. It thus focuses on urban history with a difference, a history of a moment in time as much as of place. It focuses on some elements of continuity, but more on some cardinal changes that have not marked previous histories of Calcutta.

[11]Pradip Sinha, (ed.), *The Urban Experience: Calcutta. Essays in Honour of Professor Nisith R. Ray* (Calcutta: Riddhi–India, 1987).

These momentous changes of the 1940s took place against the backdrop of a significant spatial reconfiguration of the city between the 1930s and the outbreak of World War II in 1939. Following on the works of Nair, Partho Datta shows how these development plans were undertaken by the Calcutta Improvement Trust, which had independent funding to modernise the city to make it a business-friendly twentieth century metropolis. This meant construction of wide roads criss-crossing the city, clearing of slums to make provision for public parks and impressive commercial and residential buildings. This modern city, as Rabindranath Tagore once lamented, seemed to be losing its 'organic' character. This new development further marked out the social differentiation within the city, which Sinha and Banerjee had observed in an earlier period. As working classes and slum dwellers lost out and were huddled into congested areas on the outskirts of the city, the new middle class, the rentiers, the businessmen and their organisations embraced the new modern look of the city. So the nationalist elite soon endorsed the development project that had started as a colonial enterprise. Therefore, as Datta argues, in a way the city's organic character was indeed renewed, as the old dichotomy between the 'white' and 'black' towns now gave way to the new class differentiation between the 'south' and the 'north' 'Calcuttas'. This consolidation of power by the middle classes and business groups became meaningful when turmoil set in the city in the early 1940s.

This social dichotomy between the elite and the wider 'public' was manifesting itself in a variety of ways in the quotidian life of the city. And it became even more apparent when something out of the ordinary happened. Rajarshi Chunder shows this by exploring the popular outburst of emotions at the death of Rabindranath Tagore in August 1941. The death of the national icon was the city's first encounter with a tragic situation after a long time, and the people reacted with an unseemly expression of raw emotion, which violated the aesthetic sensibilities of the genteel elite society, which preferred the poet's last journey to be a private and solemn affair. The division between the city's civil and political society was thus being clearly reflected in the cultural and emotional registers of the city.

However this dualism—this class and cultural divide and the urban spatial separation—all those demographic and physical boundaries in the life of the city were transgressed when a series of crises began to shake it through its foundation. First, as World War II broke out, the city experienced the first Japanese bombing on 21 December 1942, resulting in two people being killed and fifteen injured. This led to widespread panic and large-scale exodus from the city. As Ishan Mukherjee argues in his essay, this was because of a deep distrust in the colonial government reflected in wild rumours about air raids and the Japanese. It was difficult to pin down the sources of these rumours, as they spread across class and cultural barriers, reflecting a deep-seated anxiety and disapprobation of the colonial state, its racist attitudes and its inability to protect its subjects. And all these became further apparent a year later when the Japanese bombed the Kidderpore dock on a massive scale on 5 December 1943, killing at least 335 dock labourers, whose bodies lay unidentified and un-enumerated, and were later disposed off without any individual record. The treatment of the corpses, as Janam Mukherjee argues in his essay, exposed the prejudice, indifference and dehumanization that underpinned the colonial administration's attitudes to the poor. As long as their bodies served an important economic or political purpose, they were considered essential to the colonial state. As soon as they ceased to be of any utility, they came to be treated as a 'security risk' jeopardizing the war effort, adding to the burden of administration and generating rumours.

This neglect of the poor was equally matched by closer wartime collaboration between industry and the state, particularly where British capital dominated, and at a time when capital-labour relations were deteriorating. As Anna Sailer shows in her essay, organisations like the Indian Jute Mills Association, operating from Calcutta, arrogated to itself some of the functions of the state in securing steady supplies to meet the war needs at the 'home front' and acting as mediator between the government and the mills. It also established, monitored and oversaw the Air Raid Precaution scheme (ARP) in Calcutta and its industrial hinterland. But its more important concern was to secure a steady supply of labour for the jute mills of Calcutta by preventing a mass exodus of workers that was being fuelled by rumours and accelerated by the Japanese air raids. To accomplish this, it recommended an increase in wages, initiated a propaganda campaign and introduced a food rationing system. All this was done not just to ensure wartime production, but because the managers were apprehensive that in a situation of stress, labour conflict might be triggered any moment.

Siddhartha Guha Ray's essay traces the story of one such protracted conflict between the tram workers of Calcutta, under the organisational banner of the Calcutta Tramways Workers' Union (CTWU), and their British employers and their imperial backers. He locates the presence of the tram workers in the broader socio-political anti-colonial activities throughout the 1940s. Within the general context of the war their struggle took on a wider political dimension and did not remain solely confined to demanding war allowance or asking for casual leave or immediate payment of provident fund. They made their influence felt strongly during the anti-imperialist struggle. For instance, during the demonstrations against the Indian National Army (INA) trials of 1946, the tram workers lent support to the Communist Party of India in organising a strike to protest against the indictment of the INA soldiers. They lent similar support to rallies organised against the trial of rebel naval men following the mutiny in the Royal Indian Navy (RIN). Equally notable was their role in providing shelter to the victims of the famine in1943 or resisting the communal violence of 1946.

In many other ways too, the war remained structurally related to the famine that accompanied it and the communal violence that followed. The establishment of the Mahila Atma Raksha Samiti by the women of Calcutta—both middle class and slum dwellers—was a response to the Japanese aggression during the Second World War and the rising propaganda against Fascism and Hitler. As Gargi Chakravartty shows, fashioned after the model of the Soviet Women's Anti-Fascist Campaign, the Samiti however focused more on fighting on behalf of the poor women because the adverse consequences of rising prices had begun to affect the city's poor. The famine of 1943, which resulted in close to three million deaths, threw the most serious moral and ethical challenge to the city's middle classes, who faced large-scale influx of non-cultivating destitute migrants begging for food on the streets of their city. The everyday spectacle of hunger and death thus created a major dilemma for their social conscience. As Sanjukta Ghosh shows in her essay, while some still remained engrossed in their shameless display of consumption cultures perpetuated through their control over the distribution system, others through their cultural productions responded creatively to the everyday survival strategies of the hungry millions. Famine literature and art remain testimony to that moral crisis of Calcutta, at a time when the colonial state showed no qualms in sacrificing the well-being of its subjects in the interests of its war efforts.

Although the famine itself did not result in any food riots in the city, the distrust and antipathy towards the alien government and the pent up anger generated by hunger and death eventually burst into an insurrectionary upsurge in November 1945, and then again in February 1946. As Sohini Majumdar shows in her essay, it was triggered by the trial of the three INA prisoners at Red Fort in New Delhi, when the students and workers organised protest marches and openly confronted the British law enforcement machinery in open violent battles on the streets of Calcutta. The popular upsurge caught the established political parties off guard and they all rushed to support it, as the Congress, Muslim League and Communist flags were used side by side by the protesters. Calcutta witnessed similar outbursts again in February 1946, as Captain Rashid Ali of the INA was convicted. It was started by the Muslim League students, but was soon joined by others, thus showing remarkable Hindu-Muslim amity at the barricade lines. However, as Majumdar argues, the leaders of the established political parties were not prepared to allow these revolutionary movements to progress any further. The result was to be seen in a few months' time.

From the morning of 16 August 1946, the city of Calcutta witnessed an unprecedented scale of communal violence. In five days of frenzied madness—that has gone down in history as the 'Great Calcutta Killings'—an estimated 4,000 people were killed and another 10,000 were injured. As Nariaki Nakazato shows in his essay, with a biased government—structurally weakened by split authority and divided control over the machinery of law and order—the citizens had little chance of protection and security from the state. At this time of exceptional crisis, bordering on civil war conditions, the existing civil society networks like trade unions or *para* (neighbourhood) networks proved to be remarkably ambivalent, as multiple layers of social and territorial loyalties were reduced to a mono-dimensional religious polarity. As the city turned into a site of fratricidal strife that spared no one—neither the *bhadralok* nor the underclass—the crisis deeply affected the quotidian lives of the poor as well as the middle-class joint families and their gender relations. As Debjani Sengupta argues, this moral crisis of the rioting city is amply reflected in the Bengali novels written on this period of Calcutta's history. They represented a deep pessimism that even the euphoria of Independence was unable to heal, as this scar was created by an abysmal divide in the social psyche of a city.

Yet, possibly even the riot of 1946 was not capable of completely dehumanising a city's social and civic life. As Anwesha Roy's essay shows, the peace initiatives taken by the common people, trade unions, voluntary organisations and the political parties to end communal violence and promote social harmony possibly demonstrated the limits of this communal divide. There were also remarkable scenes of communal amity when freedom arrived on 15 August 1947. But sadly, despite all those positive initiatives, something had indeed changed more profoundly in the structures of community relations in the city. The essay also brings into focus the impact of Gandhi's intervention when he resorted to fasting during the fresh outbreak of riots in September 1947. The riots stopped out of a sense of reverence for the Mahatma. But it was a transient miracle, as it failed to end communalism that was to sweep the city again in 1950, as Anwesha Sengupta describes in her essay. But before that, of course, the arrival of Independence had brought in a remarkable sense of optimism to the troubled life of this city.

After a series of calamities and catastrophes, a decade of pain, death and destitution, the country's Independence came as a piece of good news to the beleaguered city of Calcutta. Its inhabitants celebrated it in an exuberant manner. But as Sekhar Bandyopadhyay's essay seeks to demonstrate, India's Independence did not represent a dramatic break with the colonial past, but rather it was more of a symbolic transfer of power. Many of the problems plaguing the city in the last few years of colonial rule—such as scarcity, inflation, epidemics, industrial strife, communal violence—all continued well into the immediate postcolonial era. Even the Congress party, which took charge of the government after Independence, had not yet evolved any concrete policies, strategies or political consensus to cope with the challenges inherited from colonial times. Hence, it fell back upon the colonial mode of enforcing discipline. Yet, as the essay also argues, new ideas of liberation and new forms of politics also began to emerge at the same time, which were given more concrete shape in the next few decades.

Evidence of continuity, for example, was clearly discernible in the story of town planning in Calcutta in the immediate post-Independence period of the 1950s. As Sukanya Mitra's essay argues, the same CIT and its modernist models dominated the planning discourse in the Nehruvian era. Mitra uses a popular film *Suryatoran* as an entry point to look into the debates on urban space and housing problems in post-Independence Calcutta, and its growing dualism between the middle-class *bhadralok* and the vast underclass of slum dwellers that had become a prominent feature of city life since the 1930s. The unresolved debate between the modernist and indigenous schools of thought on town planning continued to lend to a fast-growing megalopolis, the unfortunate appearance of an unplanned growth, full of contradictions.

However, a new feature of Calcutta's urban landscape after Independence and Partition was the sprouting of squatter colonies set up by the refugees who arrived in thousands from East Bengal. The story of their displacement, their struggle for rehabilitation and their valiant effort to forcibly settle down in unoccupied lands in the city and establish 'squatter colonies' has been narrated by a number of historians. Their support for anti-establishment politics, rallying round the communist led organisations like the United Central Refugee Council and the valiant proactive role of their women have all become parts of a refugee mythology, which Uditi Sen has questioned in her essay. Through a micro-historical analysis of Bijoygarh colony in the southern outskirts of Calcutta, she shows how the educated high-caste *bhadralok* refugees, far from engaging in militant struggle against the establishment, used their social and cultural capital and political connections to negotiate with the state to secure legal status for their illegal occupation of land. It was by using these assets that these refugees, who arrived in the first wave of migration, were able to carve out a place for themselves in the urban life of postcolonial Calcutta. This rehabilitation trajectory was however unavailable to the second wave of lower caste peasant migrants, who arrived after 1950 with very little resources and virtually no social and cultural capital, and ended up in refugee camps in the districts or outside the state.

If the refugees captured the imagination and sympathies of the postcolonial citizenry of Calcutta, they completely forgot its Muslim population. As Anwesha Sengupta shows, in the post-Partition period, particularly after the riots of 1950, many of them—in their thousands—fled from the city, reluctantly and with much pain, or became internally displaced, living in refugee camps for security. Those who chose to remain in the city were gradually marginalised as a vulnerable minority. Their cultural symbols and resources were gradually erased from the city's landscape. They began to lose their graveyards and *wakf* lands, and were gradually ghettoized in specific *mohallas* of the city. While the city's East Bengali refugees are remembered, valorised and memorialised, its internally displaced minority is conveniently forgotten as their story does not fit into the dominant narrative of a secularist nation.

The story of Calcutta from the beginning of the 1940s till the beginning of the 1950s is thus a saga of momentous changes that shaped the subsequent trajectory of this historic metropolis. Rarely has any city in world history undergone such profound change compressed into one decade. Its unplanned and rapid growth, its refugee colonies, its evolving cultural and structural dichotomy, and the marginalisation of its religious minority that we witness in this period, also mark the life of what is modern-day Kolkata. It was a period, which Amalendu Sengupta has rightly described as the '*Uttal Challish*' (the roaring forties).[12] Yet, as the Postscript tries to show, this period also witnessed significant creativity and

[12]Amalendu Sengupta, *Uttal Challish: Asamapta Biplab* (Calcutta: Pearl Publishers, 1989).

cultural production in the sphere of literature, art, drama and films. This book seeks to capture some of these critical and contradictory developments that marked a turbulent time in the history of the modern postcolonial metropolis of Calcutta, chaotically and creatively emerging from its colonial past.

PART one

Ordering the Urban Space

Planning triumphant, Central Avenue, 1940s
(*Courtesy:* Partho Datta)

Informal spaces, Lower Circular Road, 1940s
(*Courtesy:* Partho Datta)

Rabindranath Tagore in a railway compartment at Howrah Station on his way to Santiniketan after illness 1940.
(*Courtesy:* Anandabazar Patrika)

Funeral procession of Tagore, August 8, 1941.
(*Courtesy:* Anandabazar Patrika)

CHAPTER two

The Flute (1932)

Rabindranath Tagore
Translated by Sumit Sarkar

Kinu Goala's Lane:
A single room with iron bars
Downstairs, on the alley.
Damp walls, swathes of mortar peeled away
Many stained patches.
A sticker from a roll of cloth
With Ganesh, Giver of Good Fortune
Stuck on the door.
Another creature lives here
Sharing my rented room—
A lizard.
(The only difference with me—
It does not worry for food).

The salary comes to twenty-five rupees a month
A junior clerk in a merchant office
I eat at the house of the Dattas
Where I teach their son.
I spend my evenings at Sealdah Station
To save on electric light.
Engines rumble and whistle there
Busy passengers rush around, call for porters.
..Half past ten ..
And back to my dark and lonely room.

My aunt's home lies beside Dhaleshwari river
A marriage was fixed between her niece-in-law
And my wretched self.
The ritual hour was auspicious, indeed,
For on its eve I ran away.
The girl was saved—and me, likewise.
She never entered my home but in my mind she comes and goes
A sari from Dhaka draping her, red *sindur* on her forehead.

Monsoon rages
I need to spend more on trams
At times, cuts in salaries too.
At edges of the alley
Garbage piles and festers
Mango skin, mango stones
Remains of a jackfruit
Fish fin, dead kitten-
And much other rubbish.
My umbrella springs lots of holes
Like my monthly salary, after many fines.
The office dress is always sodden
As is the mind of the pious Gopikanta Gosain.

Dark shadows of the rainy day
Lie still in my damp room
Like rat in a trap
Senseless.
Night and day, it seems
I am chained hand and foot
To a half dead world.

Kanta Babu lives at the corner of the lane
Well combed long hair, large eyes,
A man of taste.
He likes to play on the flute.
At times, a tune is heard
Wafted along by the poisoned air of the lane—

Deep at night, in the half shadow of early morning
In the twinkling light of evenings.
Suddenly at dusk,
Strains of Sindhu-Baroan float
And skies tremble with
The eternal pain of parting.
And suddenly one knows
The alley is a great lie
Like the mad ravings of a drunkard.
And suddenly I understand
The clerk Haripada is no different from Emperor Akbar
Torn umbrella and imperial canopy,
Both reach the same paradise.

The song comes true
At dusk, an hour meant for weddings
There Dhaleshwari flows
Deep shadows of Tamal trees shade the banks.
And in the courtyard
She waits,
Draped in her Dhakai sari
Red *sindur* on her forehead.

CHAPTER three

Calcutta on the Threshold of the 1940s

Partho Datta

This essay will briefly examine the spatial configurations that emerged in Calcutta city at the end of the 1930s.[1] War was declared in 1939 but Calcutta was affected only from the winter of 1941 when the city was bombed by the Japanese.[2] The war interrupted many state sponsored projects of a 'civilian' nature and the end of the 1930s is a good vantage point to take stock of changes that the city had undergone in the previous decades. One major actor in the 1920s and 1930s had been the Calcutta Improvement Trust (CIT, set up in 1911). A glance at the map of Calcutta illustrating the work of the CIT till the 1940s shows us, graphically, the changes effected by the Trust (Illustration 1). The Trust restructured large swathes of the city and gave it a new look. It profoundly affected politics and society in Calcutta. The image of a congested old city transformed by modern planning has been caught best by the novelist Bimal Mitra in his best-selling Bengali novel *Sahib Bibi Golam,* published in the 1950s.[3] The novel opens with an imaginative evocation of traditional north Calcutta

[1]This essay is based on my book, *Planning the City, Urbanization and Reform in Calcutta c.1800 to c.1940* (Delhi: Tulika Books, 2012). I have incorporated some additional material and revisions. An important new book that discusses the planning of Calcutta is Monidip Chattopadhyaya, *Paschimbangey Parikalpita Nagarayan: Utsa O Sandhan* (Calcutta: Shivam, 2013).

[2]Srimanjari, *Through War and Famine, Bengal 1939–45* (Delhi: Orient Blackswan, 2009), 1.

[3]Bimal Mitra, *Sahib Bibi Golam* (1952; reprint, Calcutta: New Age, 1970). I am grateful to the late Professor Partha Sarathi Gupta for drawing my attention to this novel. It was made into a film in Bengali by Kartick Chattopadhyay (1956) and in Hindi by Abrar Alvi and Guru Dutt (1962).

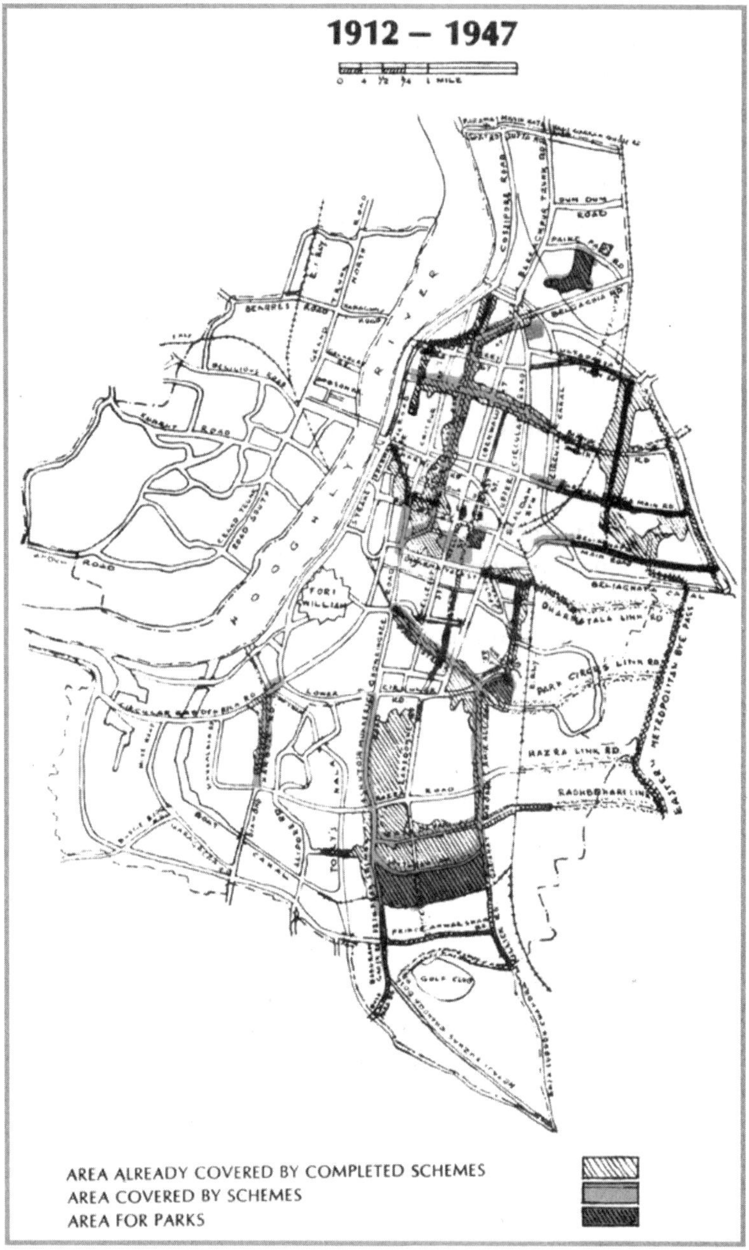

Illustration 1: The work of the CIT, 1912–1947.

of *shorpil golis* (serpentine lanes). The demolition of a moribund building by the CIT in the Bow Bazar area set the stage for the dramatic story in the novel. The theme of impending change can also be seen in a series of drawings of Calcutta that the well-known Bengali artist Mukul Dey produced in 1917. His nostalgic drawings of Chitpur, Jorasanko and Barrabazar were perhaps prompted by announcements that parts of north Calcutta neighbourhoods would be demolished by the CIT.[4] In 1927, the first Chairman of the CIT, C.H. Bompas, in a talk to the Society of Arts in London, mentioned that half a square mile of property had been demolished and not less than 50,000 people had been displaced in Calcutta since the Trust began work.[5] This is an astonishing figure which indicates the scale of the work, its impact, and the hidden violence of improvement. If there was any response to this displacement by the people most affected, i.e., dwellers in *bustees* and the labouring poor, then it was ignored. However, the response of the propertied to the issue of acquisition and compensation for land was vociferous, as was the response of the business classes, professionals, elected members of the Corporation and Legislature and nationalists of various hues to other aspects of the work of the CIT. The articulate response of the upper classes indicated their social power and laid bare the class structure of the city.[6]

Allister Macmillan who compiled a commercial guide (1928) on Calcutta could not help noticing the dramatic changes brought about by the Trust. He wrote that a visitor from 1900

> would today experience many visual shocks ... a few years after an improvement has been effected it is exceedingly difficult to recollect a locality as it appeared previously.

[4]Reproduced in Partho Datta, *Planning the City,* 220, 258.

[5]C.H. Bompas, 'The Work of the Calcutta Improvement Trust', *Journal of the Royal Society of Arts*, 75, 7 January 1927, 213.

[6]In an excellent essay, Indivar Kamtekar has investigated the class response of the *bhadralok*. During the 1943 famine, their response was muted since it affected them obliquely—the victims of famine, who died in thousands on the streets of Calcutta, were mostly the rural poor. On the other hand, the Great Calcutta Killings in 1946, in which the *bhadralok* were directly affected, led to a clamour for the Partition of Bengal. Indivar Kamtekar, 'A Different War Dance: State and Class in India, 1939–1945', *Past and Present,* No. 176, August 2002, 218.

Another new feature noted by Macmillan was that the

> expansion of motor transport and the consequent speeding up of traffic has necessitated the provision of traffic police, a need which has been attended to by the Commissioner of Police in a very noteworthy manner.[7]

In 1912 when the CIT began work, there were only 22 heavy and 1790 light motor vehicles in the city. The motorcar was relatively uncommon; the commonest vehicles were four-wheeled two or four-horse cabs, or the one-horse closed cab. Pedestrians predominated the streets of Calcutta.[8] More supporting evidence of dramatic changes comes from Kshitindranath Thakur, who, in a Bengali book (1930), wrote:

> Forget about those who left the city half a century ago, even those residents who went abroad ten or twenty years ago, if they came back now would find parts of Calcutta unrecognizable.

Although he grumbled about displacement and rising taxes, there was in his account something pleasurable about the new urban spaces that had emerged. Thakur could not help admiring the spanking new roads, where according to him even perambulating *phulbabus* (dandies) would not risk wearing down their delicate footwear.[9]

To understand better what had changed in the city by the 1930s we need to briefly dwell on both the character of the Trust as well as the condition of Calcutta in the early part of the twentieth century when the Trust began its work. Although the Trust had been set up in 1911, major projects became operative in 1919 after the First World War.

[7]Allister Macmillan, *Seaports of India and Ceylon: Historical Descriptions, Commercial and Industrial Facts, Figures and Resources* (London: W.H. & L. Collingridge, 1928), 46–48.

[8]E.P. Richards, *Calcutta Improvement Trust: Report by Request of the Trust on the Condition, Improvement and Town Planning of the city of Calcutta and Contiguous Areas* (Hertfordshire: Jennings and Bewley, 1914), 104–105.

[9]Kshitindranath Thakur, *Kalikataye Chala Phera, Sekal O Ekal* (Calcutta: By Author, 1930), 135. The title of this book made a deliberate gesture towards Rajnarayan Bose's celebrated *Sekal O Ekal* (Then and Now, published 1874).

Improvement Trusts were set up in India following the plague (1896), and were unique colonial institutions with no precedents in modern planning history. As autonomous bodies with independent funding, they could bypass elected municipalities. The Trusts were controlled by European bureaucrats and Indians had only a token presence. With powers to demolish and rebuild, access to land was crucial to the work of the Trust. In land acquisition and the politics around it, the Trusts had the full support of the colonial state, and for this reason they became a major force behind the restructuring of cities like Bombay and Calcutta in the early part of the twentieth century. Ostensibly, Trusts were not town planning bodies since they had no brief for zoning, but their sanitary schemes for improvement of localities and new roads made them the moving force behind planning. A full complement of plans, planners and consultants like engineers, architects and doctors assisted the Trusts in formulating the new look of cities.

According to the 1901 Census, the population of Calcutta stood at 8.5 lakhs,[10] which qualified it as the second largest city of the British empire after London. Steady growth of the city since the last decades of the nineteenth century was due to migrations and economic activity. The 1901 Census recorded that 55 per cent of the city's population had been born outside the city.[11] Business and trade in Calcutta had grown from Rs 91 crore in 1896–97 to Rs 153 crores in 1910–11, according to another estimate.[12] Calcutta and its suburbs also contained two-thirds of the industries, while the number of workers employed in its mills and factories constituted over half the total number for the whole of Bengal.[13]

[10]P. Thankappan Nair, *Calcutta Municipal Corporation at a Glance* (Calcutta: The Calcutta Municipal Corporation, 1989), Table 1: Calcutta, Area and Population, 1698–1984, 327.

[11]Atiya Habib Kidwai, 'Calcutta in 1901: Social and Physical Differentiation' in *Calcutta, Foundation and Development of a Colonial Metropolis,* ed. J.S. Grewal, (Chandigarh: Urban History Association, 1990), 31.

[12]*Calcutta Improvement Trust*, *Annual Report 1912–1913* (Calcutta: Calcutta Improvement Trust, 1913), 37. All CIT Annual Reports hereafter abbreviated as CIT *Annual Report.*

[13]A.R. Murray, 'Note on the Industrial Development of Bengal', *Indian Industrial Commission*, Minutes of Evidence 1916–1918, Vol. VI, Confidential Evidence (Calcutta: Government Printing Press, 1918), 107.

Jute and other mills stretched out along both sides of the river Hooghly, north and south of the city. Smaller establishments and workshops which included jute, cotton, rope, flour, oil etc. capped the northern portion of the city in a horseshoe fashion and were encroaching into residential areas as well.[14] However, the logic of colonial development was such that the presence of factories and workshops did not necessarily mean that Calcutta had become an industrial city. In the words of geographer Atiya Kidwai, Calcutta at the beginning of the twentieth century was 'a late pre-industrial city'. Only 27 per cent of the largely male working population was employed in the industrial sector. A quarter of the population was in domestic service or fell into the category of casual work, whose nature has been insufficiently documented.[15] The 1901 Census figures show that 38.8 per cent of the city's population lived in *kutcha* houses and 89.83 per cent had less than three-fourths of a room per head.[16] By these figures alone it is possible to imagine Calcutta as a vast slum, with congestion in its *bustees* stretching to bursting point. Overcrowding and the concomitant sanitation problems were the most apparent symptoms of the city's malaise, whose ramifications had implications for governance as well as for the economy. This was the state of the city when the CIT began work.

One of the first projects that the CIT executed was the improvement of the Surtibagan area in the north, an area bound by Kolutola Street, Harrison Road, College Street and Lower Chitpur Road. This was one of the 'most congested' districts.[17] A survey commissioned by the Trust in 1911 and undertaken by Dr Crake, a veteran at such surveys—he had published an important retrospective report on the plague epidemic in the city in 1908[18]—had identified this locality as dangerously insanitary with only 5 per cent

[14]Richards, *Calcutta Improvement Trust: Report*, 12.

[15]Kidwai, 'Calcutta in 1901', 31.

[16]J.R. Blackwood, *Census in 1901*, Vol. VII, *Tabular Statistics* (Calcutta: Bengal Secretariat Press, 1902), 2.

[17]*The Calcutta Improvement Trust, 1912–1945*, reprinted in *The Calcutta Improvement Act, 1911 and Allied Matters*, Vol. 1 (Calcutta: Calcutta Improvement Trust, 1974), 16.

[18]H.M. Crake, *Calcutta Plague 1896–1907* (Calcutta: Criterion Printing Works, 1908).

of the area occupied by lanes, and recommended that more than 30 per cent of the houses be demolished.[19] It was not accidental that the improvement of a locality in north Calcutta inaugurated the work of the CIT. From the middle of the nineteenth century, Indian neighbourhoods and buildings in the north had been identified as the source of all diseases by the colonial government. The projection of Central Avenue through north Calcutta was the next project—monumental in scope and reach—that attempted to address this problem more comprehensively. The project was accomplished in parts and throughout the 1920s and 1930s, work continued steadily. A beginning was made with the demolition of a mass of dwelling houses and shops in the corner of Dharmatalla and Bentinck Street inhabited by poor Anglo Indians.[20] Following the old alignment of Halliday Street between Machuabazar and Colootola, the new Avenue progressed northwards, reaching Beadon Street in 1931.[21] The Avenue, when it was finished, was a single track road, almost 3 miles long and 100 feet wide, which became the principal north–south route through the city. 'The great Central Avenue has broken through the clotted mass of buildings which was North and Indian Calcutta, and joined up with the broad avenues of the South City' claimed Shrosbree, the Chief Valuer of the Trust.[22] At the southern end of Central Avenue, two important roads, 84 feet wide, stretched from east to west, from Wellington Street to the Currency Office (east of Dalhousie Square). The total area encompassed by the Central Avenue projects was 201.1 acres.[23]

Barrabazar, located in the heart of the city and the most important trading and commercial centre, got two new roads. Bazaars, like neighbourhoods, were seen as centres of insanitation and they too

[19]*CIT Annual Report 1912*, Plate on Ward 8 (Colootola); CIT *Annual Report 1912–1913*, 8.

[20]T. Emerson, 'The Central Avenue: Calcutta's New Thoroughfare', *Bengal Past and Present,* XXVII, Part 1, 53, 1924, 73.

[21]*The Imperial Gazetteer of India*, Vol. XXVI (Oxford: Oxford University Press, 1931), Map of Calcutta.

[22]Albert de Bois Shrosbree, 'Constructional and Architectural Aspects of Calcutta', in *Port Cities of the World,* ed. Walter Feldwick, (London: Globe Encyclopedia Company, 1927), 266.

[23]*The Calcutta Improvement Trust, 1912–1945*, 16.

had invited regulation from the nineteenth century. After the plague, the problems of Barrabazar were seen as intractable and one scheme suggested that the whole area be razed to the ground and that the new railway station be built there instead.[24] Some of the schemes implemented by the CIT in the 1920s were the improvement of Kalakar Street, at the centre of Barrabazar. It was extended northwards from Harrison Road and widened from 20 feet to 60 feet, where it met the new 100-foot east–west Kali Krishna Tagore Street. Another important project was the new bridge which had been commissioned to replace the old pontoon bridge (1874) across the Hooghly river.[25] The steel scaffolding of the new cantilever bridge loomed over the Calcutta skyline and was visible from all corners of the city. It was completed in 1943. The bridge was the principal connection to the industrial suburb of Howrah and also to the railway station (built in 1906) across the river. A new 100-foot road (Brabourne Road) was projected, also connecting the railway station and the new bridge to the centre of the city.[26]

The scheme to improve the suburb of Maniktala across the Circular Canal to the east was also begun with the extension east of Grey Street. A new, broad north–south 100-foot road from Beliaghata Main Road to Ultadanga Road was projected through Maniktala.[27] Moving south, the Trust tackled the eastern end of Park Street, the neighbourhood known as Karaya Bazar. This densely settled area was cleared to make way for Park Circus, a focal point for six important roads: New Park Street, New Theatre Road, Syed Amir Ali Avenue, Dilkusha Street and Suhrawardy Avenue. The last one was projected northwards towards Entally.[28] Next came the

[24]Frank G. Clemow M.D. and W.C. Hossack M.D., *Report on the Sanitary Condition of Ward VII (Burra Bazar) Calcutta* (Calcutta: Caledonian Steam Printing Works, 1899), 63.

[25]*New Bridge between Calcutta and Howrah, Report of the Committee of Engineers*, Vol. 1 (Calcutta: Bengal Secretariat Book Depot, 1922).

[26]*The Calcutta Improvement Trust, 1912–1945*, 19.

[27]*The Calcutta Improvement Trust, 1912–1945*, 22–23; M.R. Atkins, *Calcutta Improvement Trust, Note on the Improvement of Manicktola* (Calcutta: The Edinburgh Press, 1923).

[28]*The Calcutta Improvement Trust, 1912–1945*, 17.

redevelopment of areas to the extreme south, a low-lying area dotted with deep tanks which could only be accessed through the congested locality of Bhowanipur. This area was redeveloped by making two important link roads, east to west, connecting the old Russa (the extension of Chowringhee Road) and Gariahat Roads. The new Rashbehari Road was 120 feet in width, and parallel to it and further to the south, was Southern Avenue, 150 feet wide which boasted of a dual carriageway.[29] These in brief were the improvements made by the Trust or projects which were in the process of being executed when war was declared in 1939.

These road alignments showcased the logic of improvement adopted by the Trust. The street mesh in Calcutta, as the surveys done by the Trust had found, was large, which meant that neighbourhoods had narrow lanes as the only means of communication. The goal was to reduce congestion and improve sanitation by intersecting such areas with wider roads and open spaces. The nature of this improvement was Haussmannian.[30] The larger goals of this sort of planning had an economic rationale favouring mercantile activity and business—a web of boulevards and streets would connect the city and make possible the efficient circulation of goods and services. The various plans projected for Calcutta (1913–14) and an early proposal for a metro network (1921) imagined a city united as an economic whole.[31] A corollary would be the stimulation of the market for real estate as moribund and insanitary areas would be upgraded through improvements and better connectivity. The resulting market for land would lead to commercialisation, and a turnover of property would in turn stimulate building projects, refurbishment of old buildings and raise land values.

[29]*The Calcutta Improvement Trust, 1912–1945*, 22.

[30]Norma Evenson, *The Indian Metropolis, A View from the West* (Delhi: Oxford University Press), 124–125; Datta, *Planning the City*, 212–217.

[31]James Maden and Albert De Bois Shrosbree, *Calcutta Improvement Trust, City and Suburban Main Road Projects, Joint Report* (Calcutta: Trust Engineer and Chief Valuer's Office, 1913); Richards, *Calcutta Improvement Trust: Report* ; Harley H. Dalrymple-Hay, *Calcutta Tube Railways, Report on the Tube Railways and Preliminary Estimate of Cost of Construction of Proposed Tube Railway between the East Indian Railway near Benares Road, and the Eastern Bengal Railway near Bagmari Road* (London: R.J. Cook & Hammond, 1921).

The Indian business classes in the city welcomed the change. They wanted the intervention of planning to stabilise and legitimate the existing economic order.[32] If Calcutta in the late 1930s had a new look because of the active intervention of the colonial state in the guise of the CIT, then it also had the full support and approval of a large section of the Indian elite in the city. It is possible to probe in more detail the views of the principal Indian business organisations like the Marwari Association and the Bengal National Chamber of Commerce since the CIT had sought out their views on improvement. The Marwari business class—prosperous Hindu and Jain merchants from Rajputana—were predominant in the piece-goods trade and were brokers of many other commodities.[33] Well before the First World War they had captured the potentially lucrative market for raw jute (*phtaka*).[34] The attraction of the kind of improvement sought by the CIT is dramatically borne out by some of the suggestions made by the Marwari Association about the development of Barrabazar, where many Marwaris had offices and godowns. 'A hopeless congestion is ... the permanent condition of things in Barrabazar', the Association reported. The solution it offered was street widening and demolitions in the form of the extension of Old Court House Street northward through Barrabazar up to Chitpur Road and Strand Road to facilitate communication between the southern business quarters and Barrabazar on the one hand, and the residential areas up to Cossipore, on the other. The Association welcomed the large-scale clearing of *bustees* to the north of Barrabazar because it felt that expanding business was taking over residential land. 'As a matter of fact' it wrote, the 'people of Barrabazar are already acquiring lands, building big houses and moving towards Tarachand Dutt Street, Syed Salley's Lane,

[32]I have taken this argument about the economic function of planning from John D. Fairfield, *The Mysteries of the Great City: The Politics of Urban Design, 1877–1937* (Columbus: Ohio State University Press, 1993), 135.

[33]Amiya Bagchi, 'Work and Wealth in Calcutta, 1860–1921' in *Calcutta, The Living City: The Past*, ed. Sukanta Chaudhuri, Vol. 1 (Calcutta: Oxford University Press, 1990), 216.

[34]Omkar Goswami, 'Collaboration and Conflict: European and Indian Capitalists and the Jute Economy of Bengal 1919–1939', *Indian Economic and Social History Review*, 19, 2, April–June 1982, 143.

Machuabazar Street, Marcus Square, Muktaram Babu's Street etc.' It would facilitate matters, the Association asserted, if this process was formally incorporated as a CIT scheme.[35]

The Bengal National Chamber of Commerce, another influential body, represented the sizeable Hindu Bengali traders of Hatkhola, Kumartooly, Barrabazar, Beliaghata, Ultadanga and Chitpur.[36] As owners and managers, they ran a large number of printing presses, oil mills, bakeries, flour mills, and rice mills, and also owned small iron foundries, iron and steel works, leather and tanning works.[37] In 1911, during the debates on the CIT bill in the legislature their articulate Secretary, Sita Nath Ray, a prominent merchant, spoke up for this group:

> Living as we do in the midst of congested and most insanitary and unhealthy areas which are the nurseries of all epidemic disease, it is our earnest desire that prompt measures should be taken to remove all the insanitary areas, to remove congestion, and to provide streets and wide roads in the northern portion of the town.[38]

To the CIT, the Bengal National Chamber recommended the opening of new streets instead of widening old ones, which,

> if properly planned, would open out the insanitary areas and offer building sites at a far less cost. The Trust should, therefore, run wide streets through the congested quarters, North to South, East to West.[39]

These statements testify that the Bengal National Chamber like the Marwari Association had a stake in the improvement schemes floated by the Trust. However, their approach was more cautious, as the street widening they anticipated was more likely to disrupt smaller establishments like workshops etc., often located in residential areas.

[35] *CIT Annual Report, 1912–13*, 27–28.

[36] Rajat Kanta Ray, *The Urban Roots of Indian Nationalism: Pressure Groups and Conflict of Interests in Calcutta City Politics, 1875–1939* (Delhi: Vikas, 1979), 37.

[37] Bagchi, 'Work and Wealth in Calcutta, 1860–1921', 221.

[38] *Proceedings of the Bengal Legislative Council*, 15 August 1911, 352–353.

[39] *CIT Annual Report 1912–1913*, 36.

The traders in Radhabazar had successfully stopped a road scheme which would have disrupted their traditional businesses. And it was because of the Bengal National Chamber's determined opposition that the port commissioner's project of diverting the jute trade from Hatkhola to Kasipur had to be abandoned.[40] The Bengal National Chamber however urged the Trust to consider 'how far it can utilize the existing insanitary houses by rendering them fit for habitation', another interesting suggestion that would minimise demolition. They also wanted the 'provision of small open spaces in congested neighbourhoods (to) be tackled on comprehensive lines'.[41]

The middle classes and the rentiers were another broad group with a stake in the city and included zamindars, urban slumlords, professional classes, petty officials, etc., who displayed a range of political attitudes from collaboration with the Raj to opposing it politically. Their broad identity was Bengali Hindu from the upper and middling castes and they were united by a shared sentiment of citizenship, nationalism, and literary culture. Education was a hallmark and a large number were lawyers. The British Indian Association represented zamindars and wealthy land owners, who worried that the Trust's exclusive right to demolish and rebuild would hurt their economic interests as owners of property in the city. For this reason, the British Indian Association lobbied hard to get a seat on the Board of the Trust.[42] But the initial reaction of this group to the Trust was cautious, and an essay in the nationalist journal *Dawn* even commented that it was in the 'right direction'.[43] A more determined opposition however came to the fore once the authoritarian and autonomous nature of the Trust became clear to Indian legislators. Led by veteran nationalist Surendranath Banerjea, public meetings and debates erupted in the city. In one public speech, he was reported to have said that rate payers 'paid the piper but had not the right to call the tune'.[44] Banerjea was joined

[40]Ray, *The Urban Roots of Indian Nationalism*, 74–78.

[41]*CIT Annual Report 1912–1913*, 36.

[42]*Proceedings of the Bengal Legislative Council*, 15 August 1911, 363.

[43]P.C. Dutt, 'How Bombay City has been Improved: Lessons for Calcutta', *Dawn*, VII, n.s. No. 6, June 1911, 62.

[44]*Amrita Bazar Patrika*, 1 April 1911.

by another veteran Bhupendranath Basu in the legislature. A few years later Chittaranjan Das leading the newly formed Swarajist opposition tried to block the work of the Trust in the legislature. He organised a protest when the proposed alignments of the Central Avenue at its north end threatened to clear an old bazaar near Raja Rajballab Para.[45]

The long debate in the legislative assembly and outside in the local press succeeded in winning important concessions for the propertied in the city. There was a 15 per cent solatium, i.e., compensation over and above the market price on all acquired property which included houses and slums, a right to appeal to the High Court if arbitration failed and increased representation of Indians on the board of the Trust.[46] Surendranath Banerjea had said that he was against the 'revolutionary provisions'[47] of the Trust and once these had been settled, the Indian propertied classes were happy to go along with modern town planning. The British Indian Association commented that:

> some of the ***bustees*** as well as sites to be acquired are too valuable on account of their centrical (sic) situation to be utilized for the construction of dwelling houses for the working classes to be displaced.[48]

Statements such as the above testify that the Association was sympathetic to the logic of commercial development of land in the city and was willing to overlook the problem of re-housing for the displaced labouring population. On the other hand, patriotism made the British Indian Association sensitive to the urban ecology of Calcutta. In their testimony to the Trust they put forward a model that addressed the varied and mixed land-use pattern in the city. Their plans taken from Ebenezer Howard's Garden City Association

[45]Comment by Sir Hugh Stephenson, in C.H. Bompas 'The Work of the Calcutta Improvement Trust', 218. The information on Chittaranjan Das's support for the traders of Raja Rajballab Para, I owe to Professor Partha Chatterjee, Kolkata.

[46]Bompas, 'The Work of the Calcutta Improvement Trust', 202; *Amrita Bazar Patrika*, 23 April 1911; Ray, *Urban Roots of Indian Nationalism*, 72.

[47]*Amrita Bazar Patrika*, 1 April 1911.

[48]*CIT Annual Report, 1912–191*, 27–28.

of England, put forward a model of graded traffic circulation: wide avenues would connect the centre to the suburbs, narrower streets would be made for ordinary traffic, while narrower and less expensive roads within residential areas would serve local needs. Small parks were to be built on land at the back and not on the expensive front parts of built up areas.[49] Such recommendations attest to the circulation of ideas about conservation and modern town planning among the Indian elite.

What these testimonies reveal is that despite the state of alert that the elite and business classes displayed and their willingness to make concrete suggestions for improvement, they failed to generate any viable critique of the goals of the Trust. Their arguments remained very much within the vocabulary of modern reformist schemes for improvement and sanitation, thus in effect speaking the same language as Trust officials. The work of the CIT went ahead as planned and large parts of the city were cleared of slums and many areas demolished to make way for new streets. Appreciation and enthusiasm replaced dismay and anger. One Bengali commentator said:

> Mr Bompas (the first Chairman of the CIT) was taken for a murderer at first, but in the course of a few years people forgot what they had previously called him and in the course of another few years came to the conclusion that he was an angel, and the people wanted more improvements in Calcutta.[50]

Another typical contemporary Bengali account noted:

> Thanks to the valuable services rendered to the city by the Improvement Trust of Calcutta, the town has been opened out in some of its most congested and unhealthy quarters and large roads and public squares have been provided for in many parts of the city, but for which, it would have been impossible for the Corporation of Calcutta, within another half a century, to bring to the door of the citizens the sanitary conveniences and comforts which they now enjoy.[51]

[49] *CIT Annual Report, 1912–1913*, 45.

[50] Comment by S.N. Mullick in C.H. Bompas, 'The Work of the Calcutta Improvement Trust', 216.

[51] Chunilal Bose, *Health of Calcutta* (Calcutta: By Author, 1928), 4.

The most extraordinary statement of appreciation was written in 1930 by Bipin Chandra Pal, the well-known nationalist, who wanted the 'City Fathers' (i.e. the British) to turn Calcutta into the 'City Beautiful' (the reference here is to the movement for refurbishing towns then in vogue in the USA):

> The Improvement Trust has done a lot in this direction, particularly in the southern area. The extension of old Chowringhee Road to the very borders of Tollygunge, is certainly a noteworthy achievement of the Calcutta Improvement Trust. When the road was being reconstructed, we thought it would be something like the boulevards of Paris, lined on both sides with beautiful gardens.[52]

This growing appreciation was anticipated and acknowledged by the Trust officials and C.H. Bompas noted that

> I don't believe that there is a city in the Empire where work of this character would have been received not merely so resignedly but with such cheerfulness, good sense and good temper.[53]

For this reason the Trust was careful not to trespass on possibly volatile areas such as communal sentiment. E.P. Richards' plan (1914) for proposed changes in the city carried the following reassurance:

> At the present moment in Calcutta, a large section of the public appear to need re-assuring that town-planning requirements will be strictly subordinated to their religious feelings; and that no temple, thakur bari, or mosque will be interfered with or removed, except with the free acquiescence and agreement of those concerned.[54]

The old Putiya Kali temple (near Sovabazar Rajbati) built in 1894, which fell in the way of the proposed alignment of Central

[52]Bipin Chandra Pal, 'Civics and The Spiritual Life', *Calcutta Municipal Gazette,* 20 December 1930, reprinted in *The Calcutta Municipal Gazette, Anthology Number,* 17, eds. P.T. Nair et al.

[53]Bompas, 'The Work of the Calcutta Improvement Trust', 213.

[54]Richard, *Calcutta Improvement Trust, Report,* 80. It is possible that this caution was prompted by the Kanpur Mosque incident (1913) where protests and riots were provoked by the demolition of a mosque by the local authorities.

Illustration 2: Aesthetic appeal, Putiya Kali temple on Central Avenue.

Avenue in the north was allowed to stay and the nationalist architect Sris Chandra Chatterjee was asked to redesign it (Illustration 2).[55] This patronizing policy also saved the house of playright Giris Chandra Ghosh, 'the Garrick of Bengal', which also fell in the middle of Central Avenue.[56] Among other concessions to Indian sentiment, the first part of Central Avenue beginning near Bentinck Street was named Chittaranjan Avenue, after C.R. Das who died in 1925. Das was the first Indian mayor of the city and as we have noted earlier, had opposed the Trust on many occasions. There was a certain irony in the naming. A concession to Indian nationalism, it set the final seal of approval on the work of the CIT.

However, the response of poets and authors in the city was more ambiguous. Rabindranath Tagore may not have been responding exclusively to the work of the CIT but in a message in 1933 to his friend Amal Home, who edited the influential *Calcutta Municipal Gazette,* he wrote:

> Cities are organic expressions of Culture. Uptil (sic) today our cities have grown up, as much of our exterior life has, classically. They have been imitation of Europe and their lives have flowed in channels which have been sometimes tangent, sometimes parallel to

[55]*CIT Annual Report, 1936–37,* 24; Prosenjit Das Gupta, *10 Walks in Calcutta* (Delhi: Harper Collins, 2000), 106.

[56]Emerson, 'Central Avenue', 74.

> our own. Now that India is slowly coming to her own our towns should mirror our national cultures and artistic sensibility. I would look forward to a Calcutta which would reflect this ideal.[57]

Tagore was wary of imitative urbanization in Calcutta and he was also repelled by the underside of modernity. Some of this tension is reflected in his tussle with younger poets who were often sceptical of Tagore's aloofness from the squalor of modern city life. In 1938, the poet Samar Sen wrote:

> Tagore, in a recent article, has ridiculed those young writers who think that to describe the dirt and the dustbins of the city is to be modern and progressive. City life is, on the whole, alien to Rabindranath.[58]

Sris Chandra Chatterjee, the nationalist architect, who had restored the temple that stood in the way of the Central Avenue (see above) and had also designed the Laxmi-Narayan Temple complex (based on ancient Gupta temples) popularly known as Birla Mandir in Delhi, was critical of the emerging form of urbanism and like Tagore was a votary of the indigenous and organic community life of pre-colonial India. In an introspective essay (1948), he wrote:

> It is suggested that as the most vital and immediate measure, the covetous enterprise and the anti-Indian activity of the practicing architects and civil engineers in the country have to be retarded, and gradually reformed, with the erection of economic, attractive, model structures in neo-Indian styles.[59]

[57]Fascimile of letter by Tagore dated 19/11/33, reproduced in *Calcutta Municipal Gazette,* Saturday, 13 September 1941, Tagore Memorial Special Supplement (reprinted Calcutta: Calcutta Municipal Corporation, 1986), 112.

[58]Samar Sen, 'Calcutta in Poetry', *Calcutta Municipal Gazette,* 26 November 1938 reprinted in *The Calcutta Municipal Gazette, Anthology Number,* 93, eds. P. Thankappan Nair et al.

[59]Sris Chandra Chatterjee, *Architect and Architecture Then and Now, An Essay on Human Planning* (Calcutta: University of Calcutta, 1948), 1. On Sris Chandra Chatterjee, see Samita Gupta, 'Sris Chandra Chatterjee, A Quest for a National Architecture', *Indian Economic and Social History Review,* 28, 2, 1991, 200.

Clearly, the change in the built environment of the city and the emergence of new spaces had provoked a degree of soul-searching and a sense of cultural loss among this elite.

Let us now examine the state of the city at the end of the 1930s. The population had more than doubled since 1901, with the 1941 Census recording a figure of 21 lakhs.[60] The increase in population would have put pressure on housing, but the CIT's policy of appropriating land and undertaking demolitions continued steadily, a policy that was based on recouping costs by the sale of improved land. By 1938–39, several large plots at the southern end of Central Avenue which had been created were taken up by investors. The CIT's return that year from these sales was half a crore of rupees, which indicated that the recoupment policy was a resounding success.[61] On the Bentinck Street crossing, two grand buildings came up in the 1930s—Victoria House (the offices of the Calcutta Electric Supply Corporation) and Statesman House (the offices of the premier English newspaper) (Illustrations 3 & 4). The imposing style of these buildings complemented the business establishments on Clive Street.

Illustration 3: Bentinck Street crossing, demolitions, 1920s.

[60]Nair, *Calcutta Municipal Corporation at a Glance*, Table 1, 327.
[61]*CIT Annual Report, 1938–39*, 9.

Illustration 4: Bentinck Street crossing transformed, 1930s.

The presence of the Royal Exchange, the offices of the East Indian Railway, the Chartered Bank, Lloyd's Bank, firms like James Finlay and Sons, Bird and Co., Gillanders Arbuthnot and Co., Balmer Lawrie and Co., the contractors Martin and Co., etc. had already established this area in the 1920s as the commercial hub of the colonial economy of eastern India.[62] These developments showcased the bid by the CIT to decongest the centre of Calcutta and develop a commercial and civic core with monumental buildings and grand thoroughfares. With restricted opportunities in the money market, due to the beginning of the Second World War, investment in the central business district and the southern areas intensified. Such was the demand for land in these areas that the CIT had to discourage speculators and restrict sale to only 'bona fide' purchasers.[63]

Plots on Central Avenue were bought up by Marwari merchants who had strengthened themselves in the economic boom during the First World War. Commercialization of areas like Barrabazar,

[62]Macmillan, *Seaports of India and Ceylon*, 267.

[63]*CIT Annual Report 1940–41*, 10.

in the wake of improvements by the CIT, meant that they were rapidly losing their mixed business and residential character. Many Marwaris chose to shift from Barrabazar to the new apartment blocks now available on Central Avenue and its contiguous areas.[64] This repeated an earlier trend from the late nineteenth century, when Marwaris rapidly bought up plots around the newly made Harrison Road,[65] which was a major thoroughfare connecting two important economic nodes—the railway stations Sealdah and Howrah. In 1928, Allister Macmillan, whom we have quoted earlier, noticed 'huge structures of four, five and six storeys' flanking Central Avenue.[66] These imposing buildings testified to the strong and confident presence of the Marwari community in north Calcutta. The stamp of the Marwaris was also marked in the style of the new buildings on Central Avenue, which sported architectural embellishments like *jaalis* and *jharokhas* from Rajputana. In the vivid words of Soumitra Das, this was as if 'Rajasthan meets Attica'.[67] The improvements in Barrabazar and the new Central Avenue prompted one official to comment, keeping the 1926 Hindu-Muslim communal riots in the city in mind, that it had become easier to control the congested northern parts of the city.[68] Thus the work of the CIT reconfirmed the strong links that town planning had with policing.

The merchants and professional classes gained in the long run. The older settlement of Bhowanipur in the south was improved by the CIT and residential land was offered on attractive terms to the middle class *bhadralok*.[69] The Russa Road improvement scheme, which won the approval of nationalist Bipin Chandra Pal, widened the old road to 100/120 feet and the tramway was realigned. The result eliminated a 'crowded and insanitary area' providing easy access to Tollygunge further south, 'with a street on which fine

[64]Soumitra Das, *A Jaywalker's Guide to Calcutta* (Mumbai: Eminence Designs, 2007), 117.

[65]Sukumar Mitra and Amita Prasad, 'The Marwaris of Calcutta' in *Calcutta, The Living City: The Present and the Future*, Vol. II, ed. Sukanta Chaudhuri (Calcutta: Oxford University Press, 1990, 1995), 110.

[66]Macmillan, *Seaports of India and Ceylon*, 47.

[67]Das, *A Jaywalker's Guide to Calcutta*, 115.

[68]*CIT Annual Report 1926–27*, 58.

[69]*CIT Annual Report 1920–21*, 21.

buildings have been, and are being erected, combining, as is usual in Calcutta, dwelling quarters above and large shops below.' The whole district now appeared 'more prosperous and its inhabitants more healthy because of the greater freedom of movement the work in question has enabled them to enjoy.'[70] In the 1920s, private enterprise was also active in developing upper-class residential areas. Places like Ballygunge had already attracted private developers and it helped that the approach road to this area from Lower Circular Road was widened. Reshee Case Law, who had been active in the affairs of the CIT, developed Ballygunge Park and areas west of Gariahat through his Hindoostan Cooperative Society. Seth Apcar built Queen's Park, also in Ballygunge.[71] He was following in the footsteps of the powerful Armenian builders and real estate managers since the late nineteenth century, like Johannes Carapiet Galstaun and Thaddeus Mesrope Thaddeus who had developed areas like Rawdon and Pretoria Streets, Lansdowne Road and Park and Free School Streets.[72] Private firms like Mackintosh Burn and Co. built Minto Park in Bhowanipur, and reclaimed and developed large swampy areas south of Alipur. The port commissioners built Portland Park for their officers.[73] There is no doubt that private developers extended the sort of town planning envisaged by the CIT. The thrust to the south opened up access to 'the great playgrounds of Calcutta Society'—the two golf courses and the Tollygunge race course.[74] The Mudiali dumping ground disappeared, and was replaced by the handsome Southern Avenue fronting the newly created Dhakuria Lakes.[75] The presence of the Marwari business community in this area also is attested by the existence of the Marwari Rowing Club.[76] In time, this residential area came to be associated primarily with bourgeois westernized Indians.

[70]Macmillan, *Seaports of India and Ceylon*, 46–47.

[71]Phelp, 'Forty-five Years in Calcutta, Councillor Phelp's Reminiscences', IV, *Calcutta Municipal Gazette*, 19 May 1928, 6.

[72]Anne Basil, *Armenian Settlements in India: From the Earliest Times to the Present Day* (Calcutta: Armenian College, 1969), 144–146.

[73]Phelp, 'Forty-five Years in Calcutta, Councillor Phelp's Reminiscences', 6.

[74]Macmillan, *Seaports of India and Ceylon*, 46.

[75]*CIT Annual Report 1934–1935*, 8.

[76]*CIT Annual Report 1933–1934*, 8.

By the 1930s, the stamp of the CIT was all over the city, even in areas it did not tackle directly. Commercial establishments, government offices and residential areas were emerging as distinct spaces. The investment in design, lay-out and street furniture by the Trust—parks, playgrounds, trees, footpaths, setbacks, railings, street lamps etc., exuded an aesthetic appeal.[77] Calcutta became famous for its restaurants, theatres and departmental stores. Unlike the exclusive clubs of the city which catered to the white ruling class only, these places were open and indicated the emergence of a new, consuming public. Satyajit Ray remembers being taken as a child (in the 1930s) to Whiteway Laidlaw, the department store on Chowringhee, to see the special Christmas display.

> At the time the British were still ruling our country. Whiteway was owned by them. The sales people, as well as most of the customers, were white. My eyes were dazzled by these glamorous people. We were supposed to go up to the first floor. But where was the staircase? There were no stairs immediately visible, but there was a lift. That was the first time I saw a lift. It is likely that the lift installed by Whiteway Laidlaw was the first one in Calcutta.[78]

The upper classes did well from the work of the CIT. The propertied in Calcutta had their ancestral houses demolished, but were compensated. Many made the move from mixed neighbourhoods in the north to inhabit newly developed and more exclusive enclaves in the south. As a result, the old stereotype of 'Black' and 'White' towns was displaced by a new one—'South' Calcutta in sharp class contrast to the 'North.' The ideology of improvement was attractive to the propertied, but it muddled the neat divide of colonialism and nationalism. A nationalist like Bipin Chandra Pal could oppose the colonial government politically and yet feel at home in a modern westernized Calcutta. Surendranath Banerjea too had mellowed with time and he wrote in his autobiography, in 1925, that the 'splendid

[77]Albert de Bois Shrosbree, *Calcutta Improvement Trust, Note on the Lay-Out of Main Roads by the Chief Surveyor and Valuer* (Calcutta: Estates and Valuation Department, 1916).

[78]Satyajit Ray, *Childhood Days, A Memoir,* Translated by Bijoya Ray (Delhi: Penguin Books, 1998), 19.

work begun by Mr Bompas which has harmonised important sections of our great city, has been continued with unabated vigour and undiminished efficiency'.[79] An interesting story which circulated widely in the 1950s was about the new road (see above) connecting Wellington Street to Dalhousie (completed in 1939, now Ganesh Chandra Avenue).[80] It was widely believed that this alignment had been made to facilitate Dr Bidhan Chandra Roy's (Congress politician in the 1930s, mayor of Calcutta and post-independent Bengal's popular chief minister, 1948–61) daily morning drive from his residence in Wellington (after seeing patients) to Writers Building, his office.[81] Whatever the truth of the story, it demonstrates that the CIT had shed its colonial image and had been indigenized. It also indicates that by the early 1940s, power in the city had shifted to the nationalists.

The working classes and the labouring poor were at the receiving end and had to confront displacement, as new public spaces in the form of streets and parks made their appearance in Calcutta. The axe of improvement fell on the people without title to property, the inhabitants of the *bustees*, tiled huts, and makeshift masonry houses, who were the majority and who had to crowd into neighbouring wards or shift to less developed areas on the fringes of the city. Their response, if any, was muted and there is no official record of their opposition. In any case, the *bustee* dwellers, by virtue of paying no taxes, were not entitled to have a say, and the absence of their voice in the official records is testimony to just such an attitude. For the working classes, the CIT claimed, 'the utilization of highly improved lands for *bustee* purposes is not an economic measure'. Some attempts at re-housing were made with the erection of cheap dwellings in 1913, in the Wards Institution Area in Maniktala.[82] The attempt to make these economically viable proved a resounding failure and they were rented out to clerks and students.[83] The

[79]Surendranath Banerjea, *A Nation in the Making, Being the Reminiscences of Fifty Years of Public Life* (1925; reprint, Bombay: Oxford University Press, 1963), 327.

[80]P. Thankappan Nair, *A History of Calcutta's Streets* (Calcutta: Firma KLM, 1987), 352–353.

[81]I am deeply grateful to Mr P. Thankappan Nair, Kolkata, for recounting this story to me.

[82]*CIT Annual Report 1912–1913*, 10.

[83]*CIT Annual Report 1916–1917*, 14.

displaced Anglo-Indians (see above) fared a little better. A block of tenement housing built for them contained 72 single-room, 36 double-room and 24 three-room apartments.[84] Off Central Avenue, this housing complex later became well-known as Bow Barracks.[85]

Finally, in the 1940s, the CIT had to declare that:

> Calcutta has been up to the present a city without a housing policy ... there is at present no organization for the re-housing of Calcutta as a whole. No data, no statistics, no financial basis of population, no settled policy and no organization exists to give effect to such policy.

It was found in the 1941 Census that congestion in some areas in the north had in fact *increased*. Overcrowding in the *bustees* had reached new heights and one *bustee* in the centre revealed figures of 1300 persons per acre.[86] Improvements in north Calcutta thus fell into a familiar pattern where road-building by demolishing insanitary property only managed to squeeze the population into adjacent areas. If the goal of planning was to decongest the city, then the work of the CIT was having the opposite effect. In no time, therefore, the benefits of such improvements threatened to run aground. Willy nilly, therefore, the 'organic' character of Calcutta survived: *bustees*, lanes, squalor and traditional neighbourhoods. They formed a mix with *pucca* buildings, boulevards, sanitised spaces and planned areas. This was the state of the city when war was declared in 1939. Calcutta's enduring image of dramatic contrasts was thus formed during these decades.

[84]Bompas, 'The Work of the Calcutta Improvement Trust', 211.

[85]I owe this information to Dr Jayani Bonnerjee, CSH, Delhi. This neighbourhood has been the subject of a feature film *Bow Barracks Forever* (2004) by Anjan Dutt.

[86]*The Calcutta Improvement Trust 1912–1945*, 35–36.

CHAPTER four

A City in Mourning
7 August 1941

Rajarshi Chunder

> It's time for the bird to leave/the nest would soon be empty/it would fall off, song-less on the dust, with the rustling twigs/I would go from hence to the shores of the sunset sea, as do dried leaves and broken flowers....[1]

Rabindranath Tagore died on 7 August 1941, at his ancestral residence at Jorasanko in Calcutta. As the news of his death spread, the city witnessed scenes of intense mass frenzy on an unprecedented scale. Eyewitness accounts and newspaper reports have recorded expressions of popular grief in great detail and in interestingly different ways. The facts about the last day were strongly disputed and the ideal form in which the event of death should have been handled was equally a matter of debate.

Public mourning for illustrious figures was not unknown to Calcutta. When the great Swarajist leader C.R. Das passed away suddenly in June 1925, people poured into the streets to accompany the funeral procession. Das was a leader much loved by Calcuttans as he challenged the efficacy of Gandhi's political decisions at the time of the waning of the Non—Cooperation Movement.[2] The death of Jatin Das, the Bengali revolutionary who died after a sixty-three-day long hunger strike in protest against inhuman conditions in colonial prisons in 1929, was similarly mourned by a mammoth funeral

[1]Rabindranath Tagore, 'Prantik' (Poem No. 14), 1937, (Calcutta, Kartik, 1406 B.S.) 23. [Translation mine]

[2]*Amrita Bazar Patrika* Special Issue, 18 June 1925, 1.

procession. Bengal had been, from the early twentieth century, the hotbed of revolutionary activities and Jatin Das' death predictably led to widespread public demonstrations of mourning.[3] There was, then, already a form of public grieving that was familiar to the urban public. But mass frenzy was not a part of it.

Rabindranath Tagore's death was a different case altogether. He was no politician; he had always been critical about the nature of anti-colonial agitations and was distant from the established nationalist groups, both Gandhian and revolutionary. Although he was the most renowned Indian literary figure of his times, much of his novels and poetry was never as universally accessible to popular taste as were the writings of his contemporary, Sarat Chandra Chattopadhyay. Some of his novels—*Ghare Baire*, most notably—had been strongly criticised by Bengali nationalists for its transgressive social and political themes. His university and school were lampooned by the popular literary journal, *Shonibarer Chithi*. The Nobel Prize did make him a cultural icon for the whole country although, Tagore himself was unhappy that a foreign award ensured his iconic status. Yet at the time of Tagore's death mass grief took a wild and uncontrolled turn.

Calcutta society was visibly divided into civil society and others. This division was acted out in the way the city mourned the poet's death.

ABSOLUTE END OR NEW BEGINNING: RABINDRANATH TAGORE'S VISION OF DEATH

In September 1937, in the middle of a conversation with the inmates of Santiniketan, Rabindranath suddenly lost consciousness. His health had been gradually failing due to intense strain. Although this led to immense worry among those close to him, his condition improved within a few months. Being on the verge of death was a novel experience for Tagore.

For Tagore, death was at once painful—a parting with life—and also a new experience—a journey towards a new life. His first intimate contact with mortality happened early, when Kadambari Debi, wife of Jyotirindranath Tagore died in 1884. Tagore later wrote about the experience vividly in his memoir, *Jibonsmriti*.

[3]*Amrita Bazar Patrika*, 14 September 1929, 4.

> I did not know, till then what death meant. I took life to be all encompassing in its own right. When death tore apart this vale of surety, I was startled. The world around me remained the same and yet, she, who was no less real, had suddenly disappeared into oblivion. It was like a dream. That which was there and that which was not—how could these be joined?[4]

And yet this sense of loss was occasionally replaced by a deep relief, which even bordered on exultation. Tagore described this new feeling thus:

> Realizing the fact that life was not absolute, I was greatly relieved. That we are no prisoners within this earthly prison bred in me a certain joy. The person whom I had tried to hold forever slipped out of my hands—I was pained at this loss; but also, I was at peace when I saw it from the point of view of salvation.[5]

Tagore reminded himself that death was not a complete termination of life but a meeting of the individual self with the universal self. It was a journey towards a new beginning rather than an end in itself. He expressed this sentiment while remembering the death of his son Shamindranath (d. 1907).

> The day after Shami left, I was returning to Calcutta by train. As I looked outside the window I saw the sky was lit brightly by moonlight. There was not a sign of loss to the world. My mind assured me that nothing had been lost. Everything does exist even beyond our knowledge. I am also a part of that existence. I have to perform my duties.[6]

The idea that the dead were as real an entity as the living was central to Tagore's perception. Death was also the door through which every person would eventually pass through to God. The poems of *Prantik* as well as those included in the collections *Rog Shojjay* (In the Sickbed), *Arogyo* (Getting Well), and *Shesh Lekha*

[4]Tagore, 'Jibonsmriti' (1912) in *Prabandha Shamagra* (Calcutta, 2003), 1102.
[5]Ibid., 1103.
[6]Quoted in Prasanta Pal, *RabiJibani*, Vol. 5' (Calcutta, 1994), 387.

(Final Notes) express similar conceptions. Tagore believed the mortal body to be a divine creation which through death became one with God once more.

Thus when Tagore came to Calcutta for medical treatment in June 1941 and the doctors suggested an operation, he was absolutely against it. He requested herbal or homeopathic treatment instead, so that his body would not be violated in its final hours. As his untampered body was born from the hands of God, so he wanted to give it back to his Creator.[7] But the doctors, nonetheless, thought an operation to be the best course. The strain proved too much for Tagore.

It is clear that Tagore considered Death to be something solemn and sacred which should be honoured as a journey to meet the Absolute. It was a moment of quiet parting. Yet what happened on the streets of Calcutta with his mortal remains was a violent negation of his ideas. His notion of a beautiful, solemn and quiet end was upheld by those intimate to Tagore. They were prepared with a set of final rites—a mix of quiet worship and meditation—which would have been appropriate to Tagore's own ideas. They were shocked by the public violation of this private space which actually happened on the last day.

THE PREPARATION: 7 AUGUST 1941, MORNING

There are many first-hand reports of Tagore's death, recorded by persons close to him and who were prepared to document almost every moment of his last journey. One such memoir is by Rani Chanda. She was a student of Kala Bhavan at Santiniketan, and was much loved by Tagore. Later she married Anil Chanda, a close friend and associate of Tagore.

Rani Chanda[8] writes that on 7 August 1941 (22 Sravan 1348 B.S.), people had been coming to the Tagore mansion at Jorasanko since the break of dawn. Although they were close relatives of the family, common people also came in large numbers.

[7]Nirmal Kumari Mahalanobis, *Baishey Sravon* (Calcutta, Srabon, 1414 B.S.), 67. [Translation mine]

[8]Rani Chanda, *Gurudeb* (Calcutta, Magh, 1414 B.S.). [Translation mine]

> Morning came. Amiyadi arrived with a handful of champaa flowers and put them at the feet of Gurudev. At about seven, Ramanandababu [Chatterjee] prayed at the bedside of Gurudev. Shastrimoshaai chanted mantras sitting at his feet.[9]

Oxygen was given to the patient continuously, but to no avail. At about 12:10 in the afternoon Rabindranath breathed his last. Chanda remembers that the crowd gathered outside the Jorasanko mansion was demanding a glimpse of Rabindranath. Yet the door was barred as the body was being prepared for its last journey.

> We draped him in silk, ... decked his brow with sandal paste, a garland of white flowers was put on his neck. White lotus and gladiolus were kept beside him. I put in his hand a freshly blooming lotus. As we saw him, lying on the bed regally attired, it seemed that an Emperor was initiating his journey. We could not think of anything else.
>
> Everyone came and quietly paid their homage. Brohmosangeet [devotional songs] were being softly sung. In the inner courtyard, Nandada [Nandalal Bose] had been working since daybreak. He was designing a bed suitable for the last journey. Gurudev is nothing less than the king of kings; the last journey should suit his taste.[10]

And then,

> At about three o' clock suddenly the bier carrying Gurudev was taken downstairs. We watched from the western veranda and saw a boat of flowers disappearing in a wink, through an ocean of humanity.[11]

Nirmal Kumari Mahalanobis, wife of Prasanta Chandra Mahalanobis, perhaps the greatest confidant of Rabindranath, who had accompanied Tagore in his travels in Europe earlier, in her reminiscence, *Baishey Shrabon,* gives a more or less similar account of the day. In the account, one gets a more vivid picture of how the crowd behaved.

[9]Ibid., 168.
[10]Ibid.
[11]Ibid., 169.

> When we were bathing Gurudev, some men came upstairs and, breaking open the door, burst into the room. What an insult to this motionless form of the poet.... He lay there helpless, before the gaze of thousands of people. Surenbabu [Surendranath Kar, a student of Abanindranath Tagore, himself an artist] and others pushed them out of the room. Every door was being guarded. Although the doors were barred ... shouts could be heard from outside—open the door. We want to get a glimpse of him.
>
> We could hear the roaring of the impatient mass of people waiting downstairs....
>
> I remembered that Gurudev once told me 'If you are my true friend then see to it that my end does not come in Calcutta—amidst the maddening din of 'Hail to the World Poet' or 'Bande-Mataram'. Rather, I want to be cremated in Santiniketan under the open sky among the boys of my ashram. Men and nature there, would prepare the path of my last journey.
>
> At about three in the afternoon, some strangers entered the room suddenly. They snatched away the regally dressed form of the Gurudev from in front of us. We sat still, but from a distance could hear 'Hail to the World Poet', 'Hail to Rabindranath', 'Bandemataram'.[12]

Two points are worth noting. First, the emphasis on the solemn beauty of Rabindranath in death—a regal, near-divine figure. It constitutes an aesthetic of mourning. Persons close to Tagore and brought up according to his aesthetic sensibilities found the snatching away of the mortal remains an act of robbery from its rightful owners.

THE POET AND THE CITY: UNEASY ENCOUNTERS

The expression of public sorrow at the death of Tagore was all the more a shocking experience for the people close to him, because Tagore himself had few warm associations with the city of Calcutta which he cherished. In his childhood, he regarded the city as a prison. Whenever he got a chance to leave the city, he was overjoyed. His visits to Bolpur and the Dalhousie hills in 1873

[12]Mahalanobis, *Baishey Sravon*, 152–154.

were two instances of escape which he remembered fondly in his later memoirs.[13]

In later life, when he went to manage the family estates in Shelaidaha in 1891, Tagore got yet another chance to leave the city behind. The daily humdrum of a busy and soulless city was replaced by a rich and serene countryside which gave him the peace he craved.

Large sections of the Calcutta literati too did not have a high opinion of Tagore in his early years as a poet. This was what Kaliprasanna Kavyabisharod, himself an established poet and playwright had to say about Tagore's poetic pursuits.

> The long and the short of the matter is this—although I have not written anything about the beauty of the female body, about kisses and other such themes as featured in Kori o Komal (a volume of poems by Tagore) there would be no dearth of poems which are ethical.... And dear reader, you may recite these in front of your wife without feeling the least awkward.[14]

As late as 1909, when Tagore had already emerged as the most distinguished poet of Bengal, he was accused of corrupting both the Bengali language and the genre of poetry. Famous personalities like Dwijendralal Roy, poet and dramatist, and C.R. Das (through the journal *Narayan*) were the principal critics of Tagore. Attacks were both literary as well as personal. For example, Dwijendralal Roy, in an essay entitled *Kabye Niti* (Ethics in Poetry), published in 1909, accused Tagore of spreading immorality through his songs and poems. He wrote wryly that neither did Tagore's poems have originality (as these were lifted from the Vaishnava poets of Bengal, and were bereft of the spirituality which characterised the Vaishnava poems) nor did these have any moral pretentions. He sarcastically pointed out 'This Poet of ours does not have motherly affection for the womenfolk. He can only regard them as objects of desire'.[15]

[13]Tagore, 'Jibonsmriti' (1912) in *Prabandha Shamagra*, 920–929.

[14]Quoted in Prasanta Kumar Pal, *Rabi Jibani*, Vol. 3 (Calcutta, Poush, 1417 B.S.), 114.

[15]Quoted in Prasanta Kumar Pal, *Rabi Jibani*, Vol. 6 (Calcutta, Phalgun, 1409 B.S.), 124.

Later, his principal detractors were associated with the popular journal, *Shonibarer Chithi* whose editor, Sajanikanta Das, led a campaign against him.

Tagore was aware of such 'moral criticism' and was often pained by it. This was one of the reasons why he avoided Calcutta. Sometimes he expressed his irritation openly, as he did in answer to the felicitations given by the Calcutta literati, when he received the Nobel Prize (1913). Mostly, he remained silent.

Tagore's unease about Calcutta increased in his old age. He preferred living in Santiniketan, closer to nature rather than in the concrete jungles of the city. In November 1937, he wrote to Hemantabala Debi, one of his admirers and critics,

> I am forced to come here [Calcutta] for a medical check-up. Back in Santiniketan, the sky is bright with sunshine. Flowers are blooming in my garden; the birds are dancing about in the morning.... I rest reclining on my couch under the open sky. I don't like leaving [Santiniketan] to come here.[16]

All these discomforts about the city had made Tagore request Nirmal Kumari Mahalanobis not to perform his last rites in Calcutta; Santiniketan was, in his opinion the ideal place for it.

THE JOURNEY: 7 AUGUST 1941, AFTERNOON

Let us now turn to the actual happenings on that fateful day. In order to reconstruct the event I have looked into newspapers like *Anandabazar Patrika* and *The Statesman*; the monthly *Shonibarer Chithi*; memoirs of persons close to Tagore and his admirers which include Sushovan Chandra Sarkar, Tapan Raychaudhuri and Bijoya Ray. The varied descriptions would bring out the contrast in outlook of two distinctive groups within the civil society of Bengal—one reared by 'Rabindrik' aesthetics upholding the importance of privacy for an occasion like the death, and the other who wanted to extend the space of a private mourning and turn it into a public one.

[16] *Chithipatra*, Vol. 9 (Calcutta, Baishakh, 1404 B.S), 356.

After having been prepared for the last journey, Rabindranath's bier started for the Nimtala burning *ghat,* in north Calcutta, carried by thousands of people, complete strangers to the Tagores. The *Anandabazar Patrika*' reports:

> The journey to the cremation ground started from the home of the poet and slowly moved through upper Chitpur Road, Vivekananda Road, Chittaranjan Avenue, Kollutala Street, College Street, Cornwallis Street, Grey Street and Batakrishto Paul Avenue. As the procession moved, those who had gathered on the roofs of the houses, beside those streets, showered flowers, rose water and parched rice on the poet. Some threw garlands. College Street and Cornwallis Street were the most crowded. The road from College Square to Hedua was packed to the brim.... Such unprecedented show of respect to the renowned poet is something to be proud of.
>
> The procession roamed around the city for about two hours, and covering a distance of about five miles, eventually reached Nimtala burning *ghat* at about 5.40 pm ... [The spot of cremation] was surrounded by a wall and was situated on the banks of the Ganges. In order to control the crowd, men were placed in a row near the spot.[17]

The report then goes on to describe the scene at the burning *ghat.* From it, one gets an idea of the extent of mayhem which took place on that day.

> Long before the death procession reached Nimtala, thousands had congregated there. The roads leading to the *ghat* were all blocked....
>
> As evening approached, we saw an unparalleled scene of public grief at Nimtala. Trams, buses and motor cars came to the *ghat* carrying numerous men and women. Many came walking too—they seemed like ants. The river was full, with boats carrying many people, and these boats anchored at the shores so that the men could get a glimpse of the scene of cremation. Everyone tried to get a place of their own, so that they would miss not a single

[17] *Anandabazar Patrika,* 8 August 1941 in *Rabindra-Prasanga Anandabazar Patrika (22 March 1932–31 December 1941)* ed. Chittaranjan Bandyopadhyay, Volume 4 (Calcutta, 1998), 88–89. [Translation mine]

thing. The roofs of railway vans, trees, hoods of motor cars were all packed with people.

The crowd increased more, in the evening. The little space available at the burning *ghat* was not at all sufficient. There was a great commotion as everyone tried to get near the spot of cremation. The people were so eager to watch the cremation ceremony that they carried the biers of strangers in order to enter into the burning *ghat*. The crowd was so great that the gateway to the *ghat* collapsed, making way for the mass to push itself inside. Much effort was made to control the crowd. Long before the procession arrived, some ordinary corpses had been brought to the *ghat*, but these had to wait for long to get cremated. This was due to the excessive crowd. Due to the excessive pressure from the congregated masses, the wall surrounding the cremation spot collapsed, and it became quite impossible to stop the people from rushing in. This led to delay in the ceremony for two hours.

The cremation ceremony began at about 8:15 pm. It was performed according to the rites prescribed by the Adi Brahmo Samaj. Rathindranath Tagore, the son of the poet, could not perform the last rites as he was indisposed. The rites were performed by Subirendranath Tagore, the son of late Surendranath Tagore. [...][18]

It is evident that unprecedented chaos had ensued. *The Statesman*, however, somewhat underplayed the extent of commotion. One can also note conflicting elements in the report when we compare it with the *Anandabazar Patrika*.

Here is the relevant part of *The Statesman* report:

Remarkable scenes were witnessed in the afternoon when the remains of Dr Tagore were borne through the streets of Calcutta to the Nimtala Ghat for cremation.

Thousands of white-clad Indians besieged the Jorasanko House of Dr Tagore and later joined the funeral procession.

The procession with the flower covered bier started at about 3:30 pm and as it emerged from Dwarkanath Tagore Street into Chitpore Road, the huge crowd which had gathered there became tense with excitement.

With the greatest difficulty, progress being counted by inches,

[18]Ibid.

> the pall bearers struggled into the centre of the throng which immediately surged round the bier. There was a frantic rush to touch the bier and wreaths and bunches of flowers were showered on it. As the crowds swelled, until it looked like an army on the march.
>
> Similar reports are then given about the route taken by the procession. What it adds to the *Anandabazar Patrika* is that the procession arrived at the University Senate House in College Street where a brief halt was made to enable the Vice-Chancellor and the members of the University to pay their last tributes.
>
> Wreaths were offered by the Vice-Chancellor on behalf of His Excellency the Chancellor, the University and its various departments. Floral tributes were also offered by members of the Senate and the Syndicate and various other academic bodies.[19]

Then journey was resumed and the procession reached the burning *ghat* amidst a similar show of public veneration.

> The crowd was the densest at Nimtala and it was with the greatest difficulty that the bier was taken to the site which was selected for the cremation. The rush was so great that several people fainted. Touching scenes were witnessed as the body was placed on the funeral pyre. A hush fell in the vast crowd, while many broke under the stress of emotion.[20]

And then, after the necessary rites had been performed by his only son, Mr Rathindranath Tagore, and as dusk stole over the river, the pyre was set alight. Slowly the flames crept over the pyre and, gaining in intensity, they consumed the earthly remains of India's national poet.[21]

The Statesman does not mention the extent of commotion which took place in the Jorasanko House. Second, it notably downplays the intense chaos at the burning *ghat*. It does not refer at all to the breaking down of the walls surrounding the spot of cremation. Neither does it mention the collapse of the gateway due to the heavy pressure of the crowd. Third, it made an interesting comment that the

[19]*The Statesman*, 8 August 1941, 1.
[20]Ibid.
[21]Ibid.

last rites were performed by Rathindranath, while the *Anandabazar Patrika* mentions that these were performed by Tagore's grandson, Subirendranath. Perhaps, the reporter made a mistake about the latter and thought him to be Rathindranath. What is the most vital is the contrast in the outlook of these papers about the event itself. The *Anandabazar Patrika* found the chaos and the loud public mourning to be moving and frankly described it. It saw it as an unprecedented show of respect to the renowned poet which was 'something to be proud of'. The *Anandabazar Patrika* was a nationalist daily which had also painstakingly recorded the achievements of Tagore through the last two decades as a national achievement. Therefore it gave primacy to the grief of the people at the loss of a 'national icon'. *The Statesman* on the other hand constructed a more solemn image of mourning and as far as possible tried to describe the last rites of Tagore within that framework. It is interesting that it remembered 'Dr Tagore', an honour recently conferred on him by University of Oxford. It also records the tribute from the academic community which was left out by the *Anandabazar Patrika* as an insignificant detail while it dwelt on the unruly expressions of mourning as the true sign of popular grief.

We look at three memoirs by Sushovan Chandra Sarkar, Bijoya Ray and Tapan Raychoudhury. There is an element of similarity in all these accounts as all of them have spoken critically about the mayhem.

Sushovan Chandra Sarkar, noted historian and teacher at Presidency College, Calcutta, was personally close to Rabindranath. He was Prasanta Chandra Mahalanobis' brother-in-law. His wife Reba had been a much loved student at the Santiniketan School. Sarkar had also been a member of the governing body of Viswabharati. His work, *Prasanga Rabindranath* is by no means an uncritical account of Tagore. So it can be safely said that Sarkar did not, in any way exaggerate the happenings on the last day.

> 22nd Sravan, 1941. Rabindranath's condition had deteriorated considerably. So my wife and I went to Jorasanko early in the morning. But there was no hope then. Life was ebbing out slowly from the poet.... One thing disappointed me. Rabindranath was then, still living, and a bier had already been made for him. It may be that

> Rathindranath could not maintain his calm, and Prasantachandra (Mahalanobis) had been bed-ridden at his place in Baranagore.... In this situation everything was being managed by Sajanikanta Das and perhaps, Charuchandra Bhattacharya. They suggested that it would be advisable to cremate Rabindranath before sunset. Thus the bier was made.[22]

Sarkar comments that Tagore could have been easily moved to Santiniketan as was his wish. This was not at all impossible as one of his friends worked as an officer of the East Indian Railways. Thus the commotion which occurred during the last journey could have been avoided.

He continues,

> When Tagore breathed his last, B.M. Sen, the then Principal of Presidency College asked me to go and announce the news to the students and close down the college for the day.... As I came back to Jorasanko, news of the poet's had already spread. It seemed that the entire city was breaking down on Jorasanko. We could not enter at all and went to the ancestral home of Prasantachandra Mahalanobis, at 210 Cornwallis Street. The death procession, it was told, would go that way. It did go, but at such speed that we could not have a last glimpse of the poet. We rushed to Nimtola *ghat,* but it was impossible to get in there....

The tone of annoyance is clear. He also sees the members of the Tagore family as no less responsible for letting the situation go out of hand. He, too, had a firm conception of a 'private' death mourned quietly by those close to Tagore, at a place which Tagore loved the most. This is interesting because Sarkar was a committed Communist and believed common people to have an autonomous identity. Yet his conviction about a private mourning suggests that in this particular instance he prioritised the aesthetic ideas of Tagore rather than his own political commitments.

Tapan Raychaudhuri, noted historian and a person who admired Tagore's work since childhood, was then a student in the

[22]Sushovan Chandra Sarkar, *Prasanga Rabindranath* (Calcutta, 1989), 24–26. [Translation mine]

Scottish Church College, Calcutta. He remembers the day in his autobiography:

> On one hot afternoon in July, 1941, we were attending a class taken by Mowat [Professor of English].... Suddenly there was a commotion outside. Poet Tagore ... had been sick for some time and there was great anxiety regarding the state of his health. Mowat asked me to go and find out what the commotion was about. It was as I had feared. Tagore had died. I came back to the class bringing the sad news. A great scream of bewildered misery went up and the students rushed to the door. I shall never forget the expression on Mowat's face: 'This is how you mourn your great men', he seemed to say without uttering a word.... To him their [the Bengalis'] noisy response to great tragedy was only further proof of their barbarism.[23]

In the Bengali original, of which the above is an English translation, Raychaudhuri is sharper:

> I had not imagined that I would have to witness such scenes of pure barbarism. There was a great commotion—everyone was screaming and pushing one another. The iron gate of the Jorasanko mansion collapsed due to excessive pressure from the mass of people congregated outside. The crowd was so great that we were, it seemed, being carried through it rather than having to walk. Suddenly, the poet was carried outside by the people—his majestic form was seen on the bier. Many were plucking his hair and beard. We could see the remains of the poet for a second.[24]

Bijoya Ray, wife of the filmmaker Satyajit Ray, records the event in her memoirs of her husband. Satyajit Ray was the son of one of Tagore's close friends Sukumar Ray. His grandfather Upendrakishore Ray was also close to Tagore. Ray himself had been a student of Kala Bhavan, Santiniketan, for two years (1940–41). As a film maker, Ray made three feature films based on Tagore stories (*Teen Kanya in 1961; Charulata in 1964; Ghare Baire in 1984*). Incidentally the

[23]Tapan Raychaudhuri, *The World In Our Time* (New Delhi: Harper Collins, 2011), 137–138.

[24]Tapan Raychaudhuri, *Bangalnama* (Calcutta, 2007), 97. [Translation mine]

documentary which Ray made about the life and works of Tagore, *Rabindranath Tagore* (1961) opens with the scene of the public mourning on the day of Tagore's death. Here is the relevant portion of Bijoya Ray's memoirs.

> I still remember clearly the death of Rabindranath. He was one of the greatest geniuses of the world, and was always outside public gaze. But the way in which the people played about with his mortal remains, after his death, is unimaginable.
>
> I was then working in the Bethune School. As soon as the news of his death reached us, the school was closed for the day. Bulada (Bula Mahalanobis, younger brother of Prasanta Mahalanobis) was waiting for me outside and with him, I went straight to Jorasanko. There, everyone was waiting on the spacious varandah ... we could see him—all was quiet. Ramananda Chatterjee, Suniti Kumar Chatterjee and others were sitting on the floor of his room.
>
> We all went to Bulada's Cornwallis Street residence [ancestral home of Prasantachandra Mahalanobis]. We were told that the death procession would go that way, and we could get a glimpse of it from the terrace. But what we saw made me wonder if the remains could reach the burning *ghat* properly.
>
> The bier was being carried by many a known personality. But to our utter disappointment, we saw that thousands of men were doing whatever they liked by getting the remains of the poet to their avail. Some were pulling at his limbs, others were plucking his hair and beard. It seemed that everyone had lost their mental poise in grief. Instead of serenely paying obeisance to a person of such stature as Tagore, what the people did was unmitigated barbarism. Tears were raining down my eyes.... Returning home I saw that Manik [Satyajit Ray] had also come back. 'I could not stay', he said ... 'I thought that I would accompany them to the *ghat*, but there was such a crowd that I could not manage to get near him. So I returned.'[25]

We can easily identify the common points in the three narratives. First, there was unmitigated commotion; second, there were attempts to tamper with the mortal remains of Tagore which is evident from the pulling at his limbs or plucking his hair and beard; third, the reason for this, as Bijoya Ray suggests, was because Tagore, during

[25]Bijoya Ray, *Amader Kotha* (Calcutta, 2008), 71–72. [Translation mine]

his life time was beyond the reach of the public. The accounts reaffirm the idea that the event was seen in terms of stealing the body by an unruly and unsophisticated mass.

In the section dealing with the news of recent events, the editor of *Shonibarer Chithi* describes the death of Rabindranath and the commotion which ensued.

> The sun had set in Bengal, on 22nd Sravon last, Thursday, 7 August, at 12.13 pm. He was eighty years of age when he breathed his last.
>
> We did not, initially, intend to write more on this. But some of the intellectuals and members of the literati and editors of journals are spreading baseless rumours about the tragic event. We have heard that there had been scurrilous acts with the mortal remains of Rabindranath. Some have noticed in this, conspiracies of particular men or institutions. Still others are pained to note such 'demonic' outburst of mass grief.
>
> We inform the public, from firsthand knowledge that no such thing ever happened. Nothing was done to dishonour the dead poet. The rumours are totally baseless or intentional. The show of public grief, which some have interpreted as showing disrespect to Tagore, was totally unintentional. Everything that took place did so because of natural tendency of the people.[26]

The editor then goes on to comment on the points of accusation brought up. These were, first, when Tagore breathed his last, the people broke open the gates of Jorasanko and created intense commotion. Second, some of the outsiders, who were eager to fulfil their own motives, took control of the mortal remains of Tagore and planned the route which the procession would take according to their wish. Third, many did not get the opportunity to get a glimpse of Rabindranath, as the last journey started before everybody could congregate. Fourth, the progress of the procession had been too rapid, which had made it impossible for many to pay homage to Tagore. Fifth, the remains of Tagore were tampered with in many ways at the burning *ghat*. Sixth, Rathindranath, the son of Rabindranath was not allowed to enter the *ghat* in order to perform the last rites. And finally, as there was a majority of Hindus at the

[26]*Shonibarer Chithi* (1941): 716–722. [Translation mine]

ghat, the last rites could not be performed according to Brahmo ritual. The editor goes on to refute every accusation.

First, he said, rumours had spread that Rabindranath had passed away, before he actually did. Even City College, one of the pioneer educational institutions of Calcutta, had closed down for the day because of the rumour. So it was quite natural that the common people would lose their calm. They congregated at the Jorasanko mansion since early morning. When they came to know that he was still living, many of them left, while many more waited patiently. The latter were allowed to go near Rabindranath in order to get a glimpse. When the news of his death was broken by the doctors, there was a huge crowd waiting outside. Some of the more fortunate men had been waiting outside the room where Tagore was lying. Commotion started there. Those who were waiting downstairs demanded to have a last glimpse of Rabindranath too. But they were not allowed entry.

According to the editor, in this situation the members of the Tagore family should have allowed the people entry into his room. If it had been the case, they would have quietly come upstairs, paid their homage and gone away. The gate had collapsed on its own, due to the combined pressure of all congregated outside. However, those who were standing near the gate had to pay the price for the incident. The editor points out that the reason for such an act was the intense eagerness of the people to see Tagore for the last time. No one had any intention of dishonouring Rabindranath.

Secondly, the editor insists that the way in which Tagore was carried to the burning *ghat* was another example of love and respect. Complete strangers carried the bier and no particular group had anything to say in the matter. All had the right to carry Tagore to his last destination and that was exactly what took place. It may be said that the people of entire Bengal shared this responsibility, and the members of Jorasanko, or the Vishwabharati or the Adi Brahmo Samaj had nothing to say in this matter. According to the editor this had been absolutely legitimate and a matter for rejoicing.

Third, it had been the wish of Rathindranath, that the journey should not be delayed in any way. The police authorities too had made the same request. This was because of the black-out in

Calcutta. It was feared that delaying the journey would lead to accidents in the dark. By that time, Tagore's associates were too tired to think rationally. They easily lost control over the proceedings and the masses took over. This was an unprecedented incident in the history of the city and something to be proud of.

Fourth, the route of the procession had been decided earlier. The procession was to reach the burning *ghat* before evening. But with the crowds pushing the bier on the way, it was going very fast. It was impossible to control the pace. As the procession could not reach the burning *ghat* within the specified time in the evening, there was complete mismanagement at the *ghat*. The Calcutta Corporation, which had been responsible for the event management, failed to perform its task successfully.

The incident of plucking the hair and beard of Tagore was dismissed by the editor of *Shonibarer Chithi*. He held that no such incident had occurred and this was a deliberate attempt to tarnish the image of Bengalis in the eyes of the world. He pointed out that the mass of people had already congregated at the burning *ghat*, long before the mortal remains of Tagore arrived. There had been excessive pressure from the crowd and it was impossible to manage the crowd. The ground was also slippery and the people, in order to keep their balance, could have stumbled against the bier. There was no attempt to stamp on the remains of Tagore or collect relics from his body.

It had been decided earlier that Rathindranath, the son of Rabindranath would not perform the last rites. Even, Tagore's nephew Abanindranath knew about it. So the rites were performed by Subirendranath, the grandson of Tagore. If Rathindranath intended to perform the last rites of his father, he would have been definitely allowed entry. So the assertions were totally false.

ATTEMPTING AN APPRAISAL

Tagore's death clearly raised wider issues for the civil society of Bengal. The most important among them was the way in which the death of a famous personality should be mourned. The bone of contention here lies in the relationship between death and privacy. The group of intellectuals and intimates close to Tagore was influenced by his moral, civil and aesthetic values. They saw a great death like that of Tagore to be something solemn and private, an event for an intimate circle.

The other group led by Sajanikanta Das and his *Shonibarer Chithi* shared a completely different perspective on the event of mourning. He represented the urban crowds and wanted the mourning to be controlled by them. Although he was a political conservative, in this particular case he was in favour of giving the people autonomy to appropriate the body, dominate the streets and violate the private space of mourning turning it into a public event. On the other hand, a noted communist like Sarkar asked for a private death for Tagore and a solemn and quiet procession.

In the context of the nature of mourning an interesting parallel can be the earlier debate between Rabindranath Tagore and Nabin Chandra Sen, a contemporary poet. The issue was similar—how the death of a famous personality (in this case Bankim Chandra Chatterjee) should be mourned. Interestingly, Tagore was in favour of organizing a public mourning as the means of honouring a popular literary figure as Bankim while Sen refused to conform to this idea, insisting that 'celebrating' the death of a person through public mourning was a very 'western' notion which could not be transplanted in the Bengali (and also Indian) milieu. What Sen suggested was to make the birthplaces of such famous personalities, sites of pilgrimage where annual fairs should be held to honour their memory. Partha Chatterjee's article on this subject deals with the complexities of the debate.[27] Chatterjee makes a distinction between the civil and the political society. According to him the elite intellectuals of Bengal considered the domain of civil society to be exclusive, and the 'public' could not match up to the standards required by civil society. The function of the civil institutions in relation to the public at large was one of pedagogy rather than free association.[28] Chatterjee lays emphasis on the inevitability of

[27]Partha Chatterjee, 'Two Poets and a Death: On Civil and Political Society in the Non-Christian World' in *Questions of Modernity*, ed. Timothy Mitchell (Minneapolis: University of Minnesota Press, 2000), 35–48.

[28]Chatterjee, 'Two Poets and a Death', 45.

a divide between the civil and the political societies in the city. The autonomy of the latter was not recognised by the former.

Yet, contrary to Chatterjee's conclusion, in the case of Tagore's death and the tussle which ensued about what should be the form of mourning, civil society itself was split.Tagore's death thus displayed a divided city and an urban public that designed the last moments and the last journey in ways that were mutually incompatible.

PART two

War, Famine and Unrest

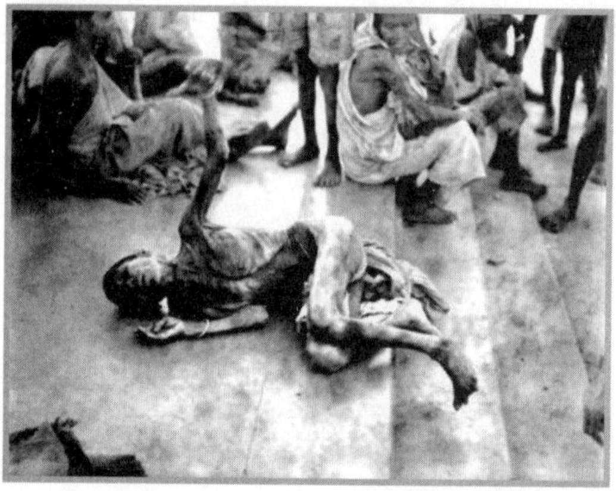

Famine scenes on Calcutta streets 1943.
(*Courtesy:* Anandabazar Patrika)

Japanese bombing in Calcutta, December 22, 1941. (glass splinters) (*Courtesy:* Anandabazar Patrika)

Famine scenes on Calcutta streets 1943. (*Courtesy:* Anandabazar Patrika)

Japanese bombing in Calcutta, December 25, 1941. (*Courtesy:* Anandabazar Patrika)

CHAPTER five

The Elusive Chase
'War Rumour' in Calcutta during the Second World War[1]

Ishan Mukherjee

At twenty past ten on the cold winter night of 21 December 1942, the air-raid sirens suddenly rent the air. The people of Calcutta[2] were not altogether unprepared, for they had been expecting something dramatic to happen for quite some time. Exactly after twenty-eight minutes, however, their worst fears were confirmed: Calcutta was being bombed by Japanese aircrafts.[3]

On being informed of the air-raids that claimed about two lives and injured about fourteen people that night,[4] Viceroy Linlithgow telegrammed the Bengal Governor's office with a cheerfulness that could perhaps come so spontaneously, as it did, only to an experienced servant

[1]Research for this paper began as part of my M.Phil dissertation titled 'War on the Horizon: Regimes of State Control in Bengal, 1939–45', submitted at Jawaharlal Nehru University, which was supervised by Prof. Neeladri Bhattacharya and Dr Sangeeta Dasgupta. Earlier drafts of this essay were read by Prof. Joya Chatterji, Dr David Washbrook, Prof. Janaki Nar, Prof. Tanika Sarkar and Dr Indivar Kamtekar. I gratefully acknowledge their suggestions and comments, though responsibility for all errors are entirely mine. I would also like to thank Neha Chatterji for discussing the essay at length and making valuable comments.

[2]Throughout the period under consideration and until recently, Kolkata was called Calcutta. The latter name will be retained throughout this essay.

[3]Message from the Governor of Bengal to the Viceroy, 21 December 1942, IOR MSS Eur F 125/42, Linlithgow Collection, India Office Collection.

[4]Ibid.

of an empire preparing for an epic war: 'Yours is the first capital city in India to suffer in the war a baptism of fire and her citizens have provided an admirable example of steadiness and fortitude. Well done Calcutta.'[5]

It did not take long for the Government to doubt its own optimism about high civilian morale as air-raids assumed increasing frequency in Calcutta and the general state of panic became far too obvious to miss. Within a day of the first air-raid, considerable exodus of people from Calcutta was noticed, together with some labour shortage in the dock areas. By the end of December, a series of labour strikes and absenteeism could be contained only after some extra war-time allowances and concessions were announced. Total exodus figures stood at 3,50,000 by government estimates.[6] Though the actual scale was obviously much larger,[7] even this conservative figure was not insignificant in a city with a population of 21,08,891.[8] Most embarrassing of all for the government was the news of a 'disappointingly large number' of absconding police personnel, constituting about ten percent of the lower ranks of the Calcutta Police force.[9]

Perhaps the most important reason attributed to this general state of panic was the circulation of certain kinds of war information doing

[5]'Telegram from Viceroy to Governor', 21 December 1942, Ibid.

[6]'Confidential Report on the Political Situation in Bengal for the Second Half of December 1942', L/P&J/5/150/1943, India Office Collection, British Library.

[7]Statistics of exodus by the railways collected by the Special Branch of Calcutta Police show just how patchy the data was. The data of population outflow through road was undoubtedly even more dubious given the lack of proper institutional mechanisms for collecting it. Such data collected at the bottom of the administrative machinery proves the shallow foundations of much of 'official statistics' so confidently quoted at higher administrative levels and so often assumed to be authoritative even by historians. See the following files in the Records of the Special Branch, Calcutta Police: File No.-P.M. 757/41, K.P.M. No.-01565/05, Year-1941; File No.-P.M. 757/42, K.P.M. No.-01566/05, Year-1942. A more systematic collection of data can be found in the following file: File No.-P.M. 757A/43; K.P.M. No.-01573/05, Year-1943. For the limitations that the police faced in collecting the required statistics from the railways, see File No.-P.M. 757/42 II, K.P.M. No.-01567/05, Year-1942, Part II.

[8]Census for 1941, quoted in *Report of the Health Officer of Calcutta for 1941–42* (Calcutta: Corporation Press).

[9]'Confidential Report on the Political Situation in Bengal for the Second Half of December 1942', L/P&J/5/150/1943, India Office Collection, British Library.

the rounds in the city that were deemed harmful for civilian morale and the war effort at large. Two specific categories were employed to describe these circulating information—'Anti-War Propaganda' and 'War Rumour'. This essay would principally concern itself with the constitution of these archival categories, unpacking what was designated specifically as 'War Rumour', the emergence of the latter in the official parlance of the local state apparatus and efforts at suppressing it through specific policing strategies.

I

The records of the Special Branch of Calcutta Police during the Second World War organized anti-British information it collected in two sets of files under two different headings. One set of files was entitled 'Anti-War Propaganda' while the other set was called 'War Rumour'. Through a careful reflection on this valuable archive, it is possible to trace the emergence of 'War Rumour' as an administrative category of classification, and its continuous reconstitution in opposition to what was labeled as 'Anti-War Propaganda'.

'Anti-War propaganda', specifically denoting *anti-British* war-propaganda (for it could, and did, include pro-'enemy' war propaganda along with those generally opposed to the war in principle and in spirit) was seen as a circulating piece of information with a specific, often political, objective, which included that of drawing support towards its own ideas and view-points as opposed to those of the colonial government. Consequently, the 'propagandist' was usually acknowledged within the text of the propaganda, whether written or oral in form. This could be an individual, a group or an organization, which explicitly accepted responsibility for producing the information.

Moreover, anti-war propaganda was thought to have a pre-determined target audience (either explicitly stated in the text of the propaganda, or easily identifiable in its mode of address and discursive structure). The propagandist wanted to garner support from a specific group or community. This community could be as large as the nation (in much of Congress nationalist propaganda, for example) or as small as, say, daily wage labourers of one specific jute mill.

In contradistinction to 'anti-war propaganda', 'war rumour' was understood as information without any clear, pre-determined or at least self-evident objective, except that of causing panic and confusion. It had no apparent intention of drawing support of any kind towards itself and consequently the identity of the 'rumour-monger' remained elusive, sometimes changing in the process of its circulation, despite the strenuous efforts and virtual desperation on the part of the city administration to identify one. This is precisely what rendered rumour policing an elusive and somewhat self-defeating project. Effective policing of rumour required the figure of the rumour-monger as an object on which its disciplinary regimes or its legal sanctions could be imposed. Yet, the difficulty of identifying the 'source' of a rumour with precision was being looked upon, in the very process of official classification, as its hallmark, a characteristic that set it apart from its counter-point (propaganda) in the first place.

Finally, a 'rumour' was characterized by the absence of a specific pre-meditated audience; it was not targeted at any well-defined social group or community. If it had any aim (and the police insisted it did), it was to cause general commotion and panic and encourage doubts on the ability of the colonial state to protect its subjects in situations of crises. This lack of a target-audience did not render it weak, however. To their dismay, the police realized that this was precisely what gave rumours the necessary flexibility and power to float across a heterogeneous socio-cultural and geographical terrain, sometimes cutting across specificities of class, gender, religious community and neighbourhood. And if the police personnel themselves were running away, the gullibility of at least the rank and file of the law-and-order establishment itself could not be ruled out altogether.

The characteristics of war rumours delineated above do not find any explicit canonical articulation in the archive, but can be derived through a careful analysis of the classifications and general descriptions of policing practices deployed to deal with the problem. This may be illustrated through a close study of the strategies deployed by the state (here, the city police) in specific instances of rumour-policing.

II

On 18 March 1942, Ms Clark, the Deputy Organizer of the Women's A.R.P. Section,[10] happened to visit A. Barry Bros., a shop in the New Market, at around fifteen past five in the evening. In this posh sprawling market in the heart of Calcutta, she immediately noticed unusual commotion and a flurry of panicky activities among the shopkeepers. The shops were hurriedly being shut down. The jewelers in the middle alleyway of the market were clearing out their shops and trying to dispatch their stocks elsewhere. On enquiry she learnt that a 'Memsahib' had been around warning of an air-raid before 7 o'clock and that the 'goondas' were preparing to rush in and loot the shops in the market. She had advised the shopkeepers to close down their shops immediately.

Without delay, Ms Clark went straight to the Superintendent of the market only to find that he was already out on his rounds. Not knowing what to do next, she came back and started requesting the shop owners not to close down business and that this was all nonsense. As she was in her uniform, the shopkeepers finally listened to her and a lot of them pulled up their shutters once again.

The following day she wrote to Mr Janvrin, the Deputy Commissioner of Special Branch of Calcutta Police, giving the details of what had happened the night before. The only information that Clark could gather about the lady in question, however, was that she was an Anglo-Indian.[11] An investigation was immediately commenced.

On being questioned by the police, The Superintendent of the market informed that at around 3 pm on 18 March 'there prevailed a great panic among the shop-keepers of the market owing to a baseless rumour that Calcutta will be bombed by the enemy planes ... sometime between 4 and 7 pm.' Some shopkeepers started closing down their shops while others rushed to the market office to verify the information. The office staff explained that it

[10]A.R.P. stood for Air Raid Precaution.

[11]Letter from M. Clark, Deputy Organizer, Women's A.R.P. Section, to J.V.B. Janvrin, Deputy Commissioner, Special Branch, Calcutta Police. Records of the Special Branch, Calcutta Police, File No.-P.M./757/42 II, K.P.M. No.-01567/05, Year-1942, Part II.

was completely baseless, following which some of the shops were opened again. The Superintendent confessed that the origin of the rumour was unknown.[12]

Another apparently unconnected incident simultaneously caught the attention of the police during the course of its enquiry. Market Sergeant E.G. Marshall informed the investigating officer that in the morning of the same day his bearer[13] took his ten year old daughter to the Loreto Day School at Dharamtala Street close to the New Market. One of the lady teachers of the school told the bearer that the girl must be taken back home before 1 pm as there was going to be an air-raid in the afternoon. On hearing this, Mrs Marshall, the Sergeant's wife, rushed to the school and brought the girl back home at about 2 pm.

19 March was a holiday, and so the police went to the Sergeant's house and found his daughter, Miss Marshall, at home. On being examined, the girl told the police that it was Miss Rose, a teacher in her school, who told her that there could be an air-raid in the afternoon, that her mother had already arrived in the school to take her back, and that she must go home at once.

Mrs Marshall and the bearer were not found in the house and thus the police went in search of the school teacher. It was discovered that Miss Rose was an elderly Anglo-Indian lady residing in 13 Corporation Street who had been teaching in Loreto Day School for the past thirty years. On being questioned by the police, she narrated a completely different story. She said that she knew nothing about the air-raid rumour till it was Mrs E. Marshall, the Sergeant's wife, who went to the school to bring her daughter back at around two in the afternoon. Mrs Marshall told her that she had been informed over the phone that there was to be an air raid at 2:30 pm and so she must take her daughter home. This caused considerable panic among the teachers and students of the school and when another teacher, Mrs Hrey, (who was also a part time worker in the Fort),[14]

[12]Re: Panic in the New Market on 18/3/42, dated 19.3.42, ibid.

[13]The word 'bearer' refer to a male domestic servant.

[14]'Fort' probably refers to the Fort William, which meant that Mrs Hrey was closely connected with the Government and she had an insider's knowledge of information circulating in Government circles.

contradicted Mrs Marshall, the latter entered into an argument and asserted that she was a Sergeant's wife and thus she had better knowledge of what was going on. Finally Mrs Rose sent for the girl and allowed her to go home with her mother.

While the episodes relating to the Sergeant's family and the teachers of the school were getting shrouded in a web of allegations and counter-allegations, the actual incident that sparked off the controversy was getting sidelined. Now the police came back to investigate what exactly had happened in the market. They began with the shop that Ms Clark visited the day the incident took place—A. Barry & Bros. There the police learnt that the people heard the rumour from a European lady customer of a shop by the name of M.E. Naskar & Co. but when enquiries were made at the other shop, everyone denied that any of their customers had anything to do with the incident.

Further questionings followed and one Shahabut Ali, an employee of R.S. & Co., cloth and dressmakers, gave a new story. He explained that Kartik Chandra Samanta, an employee of an oilcloth store adjacent to his, had told him that the enemy 'wireless' had announced that Calcutta was to be bombed on 18 March between 4 pm and 7 pm. On hearing this, Ali went to the Corporation Market Office to ascertain whether there was any truth in what he heard. On being told that the information was false, he questioned Kartik once again; the latter confessed that he had no personal knowledge of the enemy wireless broadcast and that he had only heard of it from others. Upon investigation, Kartik was found absent, but the rest of the employees of the shop told the police that all of them had only *heard* of an enemy broadcast that threatened to bomb the city on that day, but nobody knew who had actually listened to the radio.

An enquiry among the staff of the market office produced yet another version. Mr Kundu, one of the employees of the office, told the police that Shahabut Ali reported that it was one 'Mr Wallis', a customer, who had spread the panic. Shahabut Ali, on being re-examined, explained that he had only referred to the 'wireless' and that the office staff must have misunderstood him and presumed he was referring to a customer by the name of Mr Wallis.

Thoroughly puzzled by the various conflicting narratives and unable to fix responsibility on anyone, the police ultimately decided to close the case. To their relief, they found that the panic had subsided. Many shopkeepers, especially jewellers and silk dealers, were packing up and sending their stocks to places outside Calcutta for safety. But the good news was that the shopkeepers dealing in foodstuffs were not shifting their merchandise.

The police decided to question Sergeant Marshall and his family for a second time.[15] Mr Marshall narrated the same story: that on hearing the rumour from the bearer he and his wife got nervous and brought the child back home. Mrs Marshall, supporting the version of her husband, denied having heard any rumour over the telephone and also that she ever told Miss Rose or any of the school teachers about any possible air-raid. As proof of her statement, she pointed out that they had no telephone connection at home.

But another fact came up during their interviews at the Marshall's. The bearer who took their daughter to school that day, reported Mr Marshall, was a temporary employee in their house who had been engaged only about ten days before the incident took place and that he had disappeared since the morning of 19 March, the day after the panic in the market, without even taking his salary. Questioned about the bearer, the Marshall family replied that they did not know his name or his address, and that they simply called him 'boy'.

Having found a run-away menial at last, the police wasted no time in concluding that this bearer must have been responsible for the entire chain of events. They could hardly establish any logical connection between the incidents at the school, the Marshalls' house and the market, but the police, by then, had realised that the investigation was becoming a wild goose chase.

The above narrative demonstrates that what the police found particularly exasperating in their attempts at tracking rumours was the inability to arrive at a consensus regarding the source of the rumour or the identity of its perpetrator. They could identify no apparent motive behind its propagation other than creating a general

[15]Further report regarding panic at the Municipal Market on 18.3.43, dated 21.3.42, ibid.

state of panic. The rumour-monger, in this case, appeared first as an unknown Anglo-Indian lady, then it mutated into a school teacher, followed by the sergeant's wife. The blame was then transferred onto a wireless broadcast, which in another version became Mr Wallis, a customer, until the police settled on the servant at the house of the Marshalls.

It also shows the power of a rumour to circulate across socio-economic and cultural boundaries. It affected cloth and dress makers, jewellers and silk-dealers as well as shopkeepers dealing in foodstuffs. It reached Shahabut Ali, a Muslim, as well as Kartik Chandra Samanta, a Hindu; it affected daily activities of market officials; it scared members of a British Sergeant's family; it alarmed the teacher's of a girls' convent school.

The strategies of investigation and the problems it encountered in the process will be discussed later. It is pertinent here to first outline the kinds of rumours that the police came to confront.

III

Apart from periodic air-raid panics such as the one described above, war rumours recorded by the Calcutta Police can be divided, very broadly, into two basic categories. The first group of rumours arose from the fear of civil evacuation and adoption of a scorched-earth policy that was allegedly to be pursued by the colonial administration. The second category of rumours, on the other hand, dealt with themes of racism intrinsic to British rule shamelessly exhibited even at the peak of its war-induced vulnerability, its inability and unwillingness to protect the interest of its colonial subjects, and even the desirability of Japanese occupation that could, in fact, emancipate India from the clutches of British imperial dominance.

The fear of large-scale civilian evacuation produced a series of rumours in Calcutta as it acquired enormous strategic importance as the military headquarters of the Eastern Front of the Allied forces in India. It was thought that military requirements might require them to leave their homes and hand over their property to the government at very short notice. For example, from the area around the Bankshall Street Police Courts, it was reported that there prevailed a rumour among few 'intelligent and educated sections of the public' that the residents of the entire area south of Hazra Road were to be evacuated at forty-eight hours' notice in order to facilitate military operations.[16] Slightly later, the police reported a rumour among the 'educated public' that some portions of South Calcutta were to be evacuated for military purposes since an air-base was to be built in Ballygunge Maidan.[17] Later in the month, there was another rumour, circulating again among the educated public of South Calcutta, that the military authorities would take control over the Grand Trunk Road from Calcutta to Patna and that the owners of all the houses lying within seven hundred feet on either side of the road would have to evacuate on twenty four hours' notice.[18]

There was also a pervasive fear that once the city was evacuated, it would be completely destroyed in order to prevent its use as a Japanese base for further advance into India. Not surprisingly, a spurt of rumours regarding a planned destruction of Calcutta was reported all across the city. In the beginning of March 1942, for example, 'half-educated Bengalees' in North Calcutta reportedly believed that powerful explosives had been planted in the Cossipore Gun and Shell Factory so that when it was blown up as per the scorched-earth strategy, most houses in the Cossipore area would also collapse leading to enormous loss of civilian lives.[19] Similarly, on 3 March 1942, the police reported a prevalent rumour among labourers of the Oriental Gas Company at Beliaghata that dynamite had been placed in the factory to blow it up when necessary. Again, the merchant community in the Barrabazar area believed, it was reported, that arrangements were complete to blow up Howrah and Sealdah railway stations so as to prevent the railway line from falling into Japanese hands.[20] The same rumour underwent slight reformulation by 13 March 1942, when a section of Muslims in Zakaria Street and Phears' Lane was thought to believe that the Government had placed dynamite at Howrah and Bally bridges and

[16]'War Rumours', Monthly Serial No-2, Records of the Special Branch, Calcutta Police, File No.-P.M./757/42 Part II, K.P.M. No.-01567/05. 1942.

[17]War Rumours, Monthly Serial No-3. Ibid.

[18]War Rumours, Monthly Serial No-6. Ibid.

[19]War Rumours, Monthly Serial No-2. Ibid.

[20]War Rumours, Monthly Serial No-3. Ibid.

at Howrah and Sealdah railway stations to destroy them. They also apparently believed that before retreating from Rangoon, the British troops set fire to the whole city, including the houses of civilians, and that a similar procedure would be adopted in Calcutta in case they had to withdraw from it as a result of a Japanese invasion.[21]

The second set of rumours concerning British injustice and the desirability of Japanese occupation of Calcutta had several layers to it. First several rumours reported that the British were practicing unabashed racism even after their defeat in South East Asia. Far from protecting their colonial subjects, they were themselves running away, leaving non-Europeans to their fate. It was feared that they would do the same if a similar situation arose in Calcutta. As ships containing evacuees from South-East Asia touched shore in Calcutta, all the passengers had stories to tell about the horrors of their journey and how they were discriminated against during evacuation. On 4 March 1942, for example, passengers of an evacuee ship complained that while they were left to starve throughout the journey, the Europeans travelling with them were being lavishly served the best meals and that they were throwing crumbs of bread at the sea-gulls. When the Indians on board complained of this discrimination, they were brutally caned. They were also displaying their wounds and swellings to the public as proof of their sufferings.[22]

Rumours about the horrors suffered by Indian evacuees were gaining credibility from testimonies of important Indian personalities evacuated from South-East Asia. These were being reported in the Calcutta press. *Forward*, for instance, reported Mr Jamnabhai's speech at the annual meeting of the Federation of Indian Chambers of Commerce held in Delhi on 8 March 1942, where Jamnabhai, who was the President of the Indian Merchants' Chamber of Singapore, recounted the extreme horrors and agonies suffered by Indian evacuees because of rampant racism they faced at every step of the evacuation process designed by the British Government in Singapore.[23]

[21]Ibid.

[22]Miscellaneous-4.3.42, War Rumour. Ibid.

[23]Report of the Central Intelligence Officer, Calcutta, dated 19 March 1942. Ibid.

In contrast to the racist anti-Indian bias of the British administration, the Japanese were seen as positively helpful and benevolent towards Indians. The Japanese were brutal indeed, but apparently their brutality was directed exclusively towards the British and their Indian collaborators. On 17 February 1942, the police noted a rumour that the Japanese had looted a post office in Burma. The Japanese soldiers found out that the Post Master, who was an Indian, was hiding under his table whereupon they dragged him out and enquired whether he was pro-British. When the Post Master answered in the negative, he was given some money and asked to leave. The rumour went that the Japanese demonstrated their sympathies towards Indian nationalist aspirations by asking every Indian they held captive if they were either 'Gandhi-man' or 'Bose-man'.[24] In either case, they gave those Indians money and invited them to settle down peacefully in Burma.[25]

On 24 February 1942, the police reported a rumour that after the Imperial troops had withdrawn from Moulmein, the Japanese soldiers entered a hospital and shot down all the wounded British soldiers. When a Bengali doctor, who was on duty, protested against this barbarity, the Japanese Officer-in-charge plainly told him that it was none of his business as long as wounded Indian soldiers remained unharmed. He was given money and a pass to leave Moulmein.[26]

Even though the Japanese were seen as friendly towards Indians, a few rumours warned against testing the patience of Japanese soldiers too much. According to a rumour in South Calcutta, an Indian doctor of a Military Hospital in Burma was once ordered by the occupying Japanese army to shoot all 150 British patients admitted at the hospital. When he refused to comply, the Indian doctor was kicked so hard that he reportedly lost several of his teeth. Thereafter, the Japanese soldiers killed all the wounded British soldiers with their own revolvers.[27]

[24]By 'Gandhi-man' and 'Bose-man' the Japanese apparently referred to the followers of Gandhi and Subhas Chandra Bose respectively.

[25]'Memorandum on 17.2.42', Records of the Special Branch, Calcutta Police, File No.-P.M./757/42 Part II, K.P.M. No.-01567/05. 1942.

[26]Note on War Rumours on 24.2.42, ibid.

[27]Ibid.

In general, however, the Japanese were seen to be keen on cultivating Indian support for their regime. Indians who served in the government under the British were not only allowed to stay back, claimed one rumour, but they were being reinstated in their offices with double their previous salary.[28] According to other rumours, the Japanese were appointing Indians to high administrative positions, which they were never allowed to hold under British rule. It was rumoured that an Indian had been appointed Governor of Penang after the Japanese conquest, though there was confusion whether he was a Bengali Barrister or a Tamil from Madras.[29] Symbolic racial hierarchies that colonial rule had till then perpetuated was reportedly being reversed by the Japanese. A high-ranking British military officer in Singapore, according to one rumour, was forced to pull a rickshaw mounted by an ordinary Indian.[30]

Contrary to anti-Axis propaganda about anarchy in occupied territories of South-East Asia, the Japanese were believed to be keen on restoring order, fostering peace and resuming business as usual. They were honouring all bank drafts and other contractual obligations with Indian businesses in Hong Kong and Singapore, reported one rumour, while attracting huge financial capital by offering five per cent interest on fixed deposits and two and a half per cent on current accounts.[31] Some rumours spoke about tokens issued to employees of Japanese firms in Calcutta while they were winding up their business at the onset of the war. They were apparently assured that if these tokens were produced upon a future Japanese occupation of Calcutta, all their losses would be repaid and they would be given preferential treatment under the new regime. Many erstwhile employees of Japanese firms in Calcutta were said to be in possession of these tokens.[32]

The most alarming were those rumours that spoke about how Indians were actively helping the Japanese or had enthusiastically started preparing themselves for a future Japanese occupation. On

[28]War Rumours, Monthly Serial Number 2, ibid.

[29]Ibid.

[30]Ibid.

[31]Miscellaneous, 13.3.42, War Rumours, ibid.

[32]'Letter from Special Branch, C.P. and Berar to J.V.B. Janvrin, Deputy Commissioner of Police, Special Branch, Calcutta, dated 27 March 1942. Ibid.

4 March 1942, there was a rumour that the Japanese were employing captured Indian sepoys and pilots to fight against the British on much higher salaries. In fact, it was believed that at the first blitz on Rangoon in December 1941, Japanese planes brought down by anti-air-craft guns had Sikh pilots from Punjab.[33]

Another sensational rumour held that the Bengali youth had already started learning the Japanese language so that they could serve the needs of their prospective rulers. Command over Japanese was apparently seen as the key to securing well-paid jobs after the occupation, as a result of which Japanese primers were out of stock in the Calcutta market. The attention of the police was drawn to one popular Japanese primer written by someone called Saito, which was reportedly selling like hot cakes.[34] This must have reminded British officers of the early history of their own regime when it was precisely this class of young Bengali men who actively took to learning English to serve the needs of the Company administration some two centuries back. This rumour, therefore, was found particularly unsettling for the police and they immediately commenced a thorough investigation into the matter only to discover that Japanese primers were indeed hard to find. The police found out that Saito's book was particularly popular as it was the prescribed text in the Japanese language syllabus of the University of Calcutta. It was in any case difficult to proscribe a University textbook. But, more importantly, any attempt at censorship, it was thought, would only encourage rumours and may have tempted more people to learn Japanese. Thus, the matter was quietly dropped. The only solace for the British officials was that the books could not be acquired any more as these were already out of stock in the market.[35]

Evidently, war rumours were symptomatic of deep uncertainties about the future. People in Calcutta were living in constant anxiety about the fear of Japanese bombings. As these fears materialized, they were left to wonder what lay next. Forces directing the course of the war were world-historical forces, profoundly affecting everyday lives of ordinary beings utterly powerless to influence its

[33]Miscellaneous, 4.3.42, War Rumours, ibid.

[34]Miscellaneous-4.3.42, War Rumours, ibid.

[35]There are various notes on the issue of Japanese primers. Ibid.

course. These widespread uncertainties and vulnerabilities found expression in one interesting form of 'rumour-mongering' that involved astrological predictions regarding the course of the war and the fate of Britain and its Indian empire. These deserve some description. The police noted with some nervousness on 18 February 1942, that Calcutta astrologers with some following such as Bijoli Banerji of Shalimar and Rai Bahadur Kailash Chandra Jatisarnava had been engaged in astrological calculations trying to determine the fate of Britain in the war. They had predicted that the British forces would have a terrible time till 2 March, but the stars would turn in their favour from 3 March and would lead to their ultimate victory. Reaffirmation of ultimate Allied victory, though, rescued these astrologers from charges of sedition.[36] Not all forecasts were favourable for the British though. 'Forecast by a Great Indian Sadhu', a pamphlet that an I.B. officer discovered in a tram in the night of 29 March 1942, made 18 predictions which included forecasts of a revolution in India in April and May 1942, that was to lead to complete independence by 25 November, with the help of Axis military intervention. Both Germany and Japan were to advance towards India from both sides while Japan was to bomb some areas in the eastern fringes of British India. It predicted that Britain itself would be invaded between 15 and 30 April 1942, and that the war would come to an end by 15 August, of the same year, bringing about complete defeat of British and Allied powers. Calcutta, the 'famous' astrologer reported, was not to be bombed any further, though it would soon be declared an 'open city' by the British as the administration would be wound up and shifted to some nearby town.[37] The source of this pamphlet could not be determined, no other copy of it was discovered and the police was forced to close the issue. But there were other mediums through which 'seditious' astrological predictions could circulate, such as personal letters, which could be tracked better. One such letter from Sree Kumar Das of Benaras to his friend Anil of 5 Deshapriya Park, Calcutta,

[36]Records of the Special Branch, Calcutta Police, File No. P.M./757/42, K.P.M. No. 01566/05, Year 1942.

[37]Records of the Special Branch, Calcutta Police, File No. P.M./757/42 II, K.P.M. No. 01567/05, Year 1942, Part II.

described his meeting with a 'world famous astrologer' who had travelled the whole world, having visited Europe and America three times. He claimed to have seen the palms of many great men including that of Adolf Hitler, the impression of whose palm he produced as proof. On the advice of this astrologer he urged his friend to leave Calcutta before 24 *Magh*[38] for it was dangerous to live there after that date.[39] Another letter, this time addressed from Calcutta to Amritsar, spoke of astrological calculations made by the author himself, who predicted that the war would end very soon, though a 'Gas War', followed by the victory of Germany, would precede it.[40]

Various methods were devised to control the production of astrological forecasts, though the rate of success was abysmally low. Private letters could, to some extent, be intercepted and attempts were often made to trace the writers or the addressees of these 'seditious texts', but the sheer volume of panicky letters that the state was confronted with ruled out all possibilities of devising any full-proof method of stopping their circulation. It is time, therefore, to explore the range of strategies deployed by the urban administration to control the spread of rumours.

IV

Confronted with the onslaught of damaging rumours, the city administration took up the task of controlling and countering them. The New Market air-raid scare surveyed above was one among many instances that convinced the policing apparatus of the salience and intractability of such 'rumourous' war-related information, so that the hope of completely eradicating them was given up quite early on. But the task of keeping them under reasonable limits was not smooth either. At every step, the limits of state intervention was keenly felt

[38]*Magh* is the name of a month in the Bengali calendar that included dates from mid-January to mid-February approximately.

[39]Letter from Sree Kumar Das, Benares, to Anil Kumar Raha, Calcutta dated 24 January 1942. Records of the Special Branch, Calcutta Police, File No. P.M./757/42 II, K.P.M. No. 01567/05, Year 1942, Part II.

[40]Letter from Bandhu, Calcutta, to Krishan Kumar Kapur, Amritsar, dated 2 February 1942. Ibid.

as a result of many related factors: its own structural weaknesses both in terms of manpower and resources, lack of consensus within officialdom of what really constituted war-rumours, and, perhaps most fundamental of all, the deep suspicion among large sections of the public about the ability and willingness of the imperial regime to protect their interests, now that, more clearly than ever before, it was desperate to save itself from utter ruin. The swiftness of Axis triumph in South-East Asia did not leave either the British Indian state or its inhabitants in any illusion of the invincibility of the Empire where the sun was said to have never set.

Faced with the problem of controlling war rumours, the first response of the city police was what may be called ethnographic. It busily concerned itself with recording every piece of 'rumourous' war information that any official in the city came across, classifying, categorizing and profiling them in meticulous detail. This exercise in archiving matured over time. Slightly haphazard recordings of daily police notes slowly gave way to elaborate rumour collection forms that neatly broke up every such instance into six columns under six headings. The police, when confronted with any rumour, had to fill one of these forms and clearly take note of the nature of the rumour, the locality in which it was heard, the section of the population that seemed to have been affected by it, the approximate number of people who may have heard the rumour, its 'presumed' source and the general effect it seemed to have had upon those who had heard the rumour.[41] It is important to note that such dreary paperwork was far from a mere local innovation done at the behest of the city police. The generation of this mass of information was of interest at all levels of the colonial administration. For these forms, after being filled by the policeman on the spot, had to be forwarded to the Bengal Secretariat, which was then dispatched to the Central Intelligence Bureau so that the highest levels of the intelligence network of British India might keep a close tab on what was being discussed in the streets and bazaars of Calcutta.

The pattern of information collection underwent changes as the sheer volume of rumours became unmanageable. On 19 May 1942,

[41]These filled up forms can be found in Records of thee Special Branch, Calcutta Police, File No. P.M./757/42 Part II, K.P.M. No. 01567/05. 1942.

the Department of Information and Broadcasting of the Government of India instructed the Bengal government to discontinue the supply of its daily reports on rumours from Calcutta to the Central Intelligence Bureau and replace it with 'a weekly report based on a selective process, giving only such rumours as are important in indicating the general trend of gossip...'[42]

There was more to the story than just a growing lack of interest in rumours at the top of the bureaucratic hierarchy. These were also products of pressures from below, from the rank and file of the city police, who objected to the huge amount of wasteful labour spent on recording meticulous details about each rumour at a time when every personnel of the resource-starved and under-manned institution was being over-worked to their limits due to the wartime emergency. This growing sense of fatigue and irritation with cumbersome paperwork and red-tape becomes evident from a series of correspondences between the Home Department of the provincial government and the Calcutta Police.

Noticing the diminishing number of reported cases of rumours, a Bengal Home Department officer observed '... it would be interesting to know if this results from the fact that no rumours are now circulated, or none has come to the ears of the S.B. [Special Branch], or that the rumours are so numerous that all hopes of keeping pace with them has been abandoned.'[43]

J.V.B. Janvrin of the Special Branch of Calcutta Police identified two important reasons in his reply: first, many of the information previously recorded as rumours have eventually turned out quite prophetic. For example, the bombing of Chittagong and instances of assaults of villagers by the stationed Allied troops were actually confirmed by official sources after these were returned as rumours.[44] More significant was his second comment:

> It is I think very probable that whereas formerly officers used to report rumours they heard in the course of their day's work,

[42]'Letter from P.N. Thapar, Deputy Secretary to the Government of India, to the Chief Secretary to the Government of Bengal, dated 19 May 1942 Records of the Special Branch, Calcutta Police, File No.-P.M./757/42 Part III, K.P.M. No.-01568/05. 1942.

[43]Note from A.E. Porter, dated 9.6.42, ibid.

[44]Note from J.V.B. Janvrin, dated 13.6.42, ibid.

> now-a-days they do not unless the rumour is of particular interest. They find they have duties more immediate and important than to report rumours in the elaborate form now laid down. I would abolish the form. Forms may be useful in the compilation of reports, but the best intelligence officers who have to go forth and collect information are, I find, individualists who loathe forms. Regrettable but true.[45]

The pressure from within the police force was also echoed on 17 June 1942, in another official note from one A.E.A. Ray: 'Regrettable, but scouting for rumours is largely waste of time, results in a mass of paper reports, and diverts officers from more important duties.'[46] It suggested that it was 'better to insist on a careful appreciation of public opinion in which prevalent rumours might be mentioned'[47] rather than getting the personnel to fill up lengthy forms.

The rumour collection forms were eventually abolished. The volume of rumour reporting also thinned out over time, but it continued nonetheless till the end of the war. However, careful scrutiny of this mass of documents reveals another mechanism of control that the state held in high priority—the generation of its own war propaganda, celebrating Allied military prowess, demonizing the Axis powers (especially Japan in the Indian context) and asserting the strength of the British Empire to protect itself and its subjects against all external and internal threats.[48] Noting the myriad pro-Japanese rumours in circulation, an exasperated police officer insisted:

> The public should be repeatedly told the facts regarding conditions obtaining in enemy occupied areas. It is useless merely to say that the behavior of the Japanese is too atrocious for words. Quote

[45]Ibid.

[46]Note from A.E.A. Ray, dated 17.6.42, ibid. the official designation of A.E.A. Ray is not mentioned, but he appears to be a high-ranking police officer.

[47]Ibid.

[48]The various dimensions of this form of state initiative during the Second World War have been explored in Sanjoy Bhattacharya, *Propaganda and Information in Eastern India 1939–45: A Necessary Weapon of War* (Richmond, Surrey: Curzon Press, 2001).

> facts. Anti-British elements quote Jalianwalabagh etc. Anti-Japanese elements have been given practically nothing to quote. Pro-Japanese propaganda, chiefly over the wireless, is on the other hand so good ... that people are beginning to think whether it would not after all be a rather good thing if the Japs did come...[49]

Closely linked to this initiative of producing pro-British war propaganda, and articulated through the same forms of mass media, were the communiqués issued by the Commissioner of Calcutta Police through newspapers. This strategy was adopted in the backdrop of war-time lighting restrictions imposed on the city as an air-raid precautionary measure that fuelled rumours of aerial bombing as well as that of 'goondas'[50] who were apparently preparing to loot the houses of ordinary residents under the cover of darkness. Adopting the disposition of a paternalist disciplinarian, a communiqué issued on 29 April 1941, requested the co-operation of 'law abiding and innocent citizens' in tracking down 'rumour spreading criminals' who were 'guilty of a crime attempted against the whole city; a crime worse than murder.' The Commissioner of Police assured his citizens that 'every beat in the city is being patrolled every night by civic guards' who had the backing of 'the whole force and authority of Government' and who would assist the police 'at a moment's notice' in dealing with the criminals.[51]

Observing no signs of the 'goonda' rumours subsiding, the Commissioner assured the public once again in a communiqué on 2 May 1941, that every police station was maintaining a list of 'goondas and bad characters' and keeping them under surveillance. He further advised that people should remain calm, ignore all rumours of goonda attacks and inform the Deputy Commissioner of the Detective Department at the Lall Bazar police headquarters

[49]'War Rumours' Monthly Serial No. 3, Records of the Special Branch, Calcutta Police, File No.-P.M./757/42, Part II, K.P.M. No.-01567/05. 1942.

[50]For an account of what 'goonda' signified in the policing practices of Calcutta, see Suranjan Das and J.K. Ray, *The Goondas: Towards a Reconstruction of the Calcutta Underworld*, (Calcutta: Firma K.L.M., 1996).

[51]Communique issued by the Commissioner of Police, Calcutta, on 29 April 1941. Records of the Special Branch, Calcutta Police, File No. P.M./757/41, K.P.M. No. 01565/05, Year 1941.

of any 'goonda' from whom they apprehended trouble in their immediate locality.[52]

However, the communiqué issued after about a month was a complete turn-around from the earlier position of the city police. Instead of encouraging the public to report against goondas of their localities, the Commissioner asserted that expressing fear of goondas itself amounted to rumour-mongering. 'It appears that certain interested persons are spreading rumours regarding the occurrence of street robberies since the beginning of the period of lightening restrictions in Calcutta', he observed, warning that anyone found spreading such rumours 'shall be severely dealt with.'[53]

Behind this desperate shift of positions and trial-and-error strategy of rumour control adopted by the police is a deeper history of war-time institutional failures. The much valorized civic guards of the communiqués, for example, who were responsible for bringing the goondas to book, was a new voluntary institution created by the colonial state to meet the man-power shortages of its formal police force. Many of the recruits to these civic guards often themselves turned out to be local strongmen, often known to the local police as neighbourhood roughs and goondas, precisely those who were feared by the respectable householders who were to be protected by the police. These quasi-police forces were among the most unpopular war-time administrative innovations of the colonial state. A pamphlet issued by the Communist Party of India, for instance, described the civic guards as 'Vibhisan Vahini', a band of traitors who were betraying their own countrymen by supporting British imperialism.[54] The pamphlet reads:

> ... Civic Guard is a band of treacherous force ... They have defeated the paid Police and the Military Force for the sake of bread ... Civic Guards are more treacherous than the Police and more detestable than the Goondas. They are being beaten by the Dhangars and the

[52]Communique issed by the Commissioner of Police, Calcutta, on 2 May 1941. Ibid.

[53]Communique issued by the Commissioner of Police, Calcutta, on 23 June 1941. Ibid.

[54]Vibhisan was an allusion to the mythical character from Ramayana who colluded with Rama to betray his own brother, Ravana, in the epic battle of Lanka.

> methors in all localities still they have no shame and sense in them. Beware of them ... Leave the Civic Guards who are the enemy of this country. People of the country! Boycott the Civic Guards.[55]

There are also some literary allusions to the general unpopularity of the Civic Guards. Ratnamayee, a pious Brahmin widow in Bimal Kar's novel, *Dewal*, for instance, reflects upon the Civic Guards once her useless and unemployed son decides to join the force:

> Everyone looks down upon this profession. And that the job is not a respectable one, the greatest proof lies in those who have joined the Civic Guards themselves. All the useless boys of the neighbourhood, disowned by their parents, who used to waste all their time in useless pursuits, the entire uneducated illiterate lot—all of them joined this group. Since then Ratnamayee had developed a bad impression of this profession...[56]

Rumour control strategies did not only suffer from institutional problems, however. It simultaneously encountered conceptual and definitional difficulties. It may be remembered how the Department of Information and Broadcasting of the Government of India had instructed the Government of Bengal to replace daily reports of rumours with weekly notes on 'gossip'. Again, A.E.A. Ray of Calcutta Police insisted that rumour collection forms should be replaced by 'a careful appreciation of public opinion'. But, at every step, the city administration found it impossible to reduce rumours to 'gossip', 'public opinion' or any other category due to the specific characteristics that set them apart from these other forms of circulating information. Yet, apart from a general sense that rumour had very specific characteristics, the precise contours

[55]Home-Political Department (Internal), File No.-37/104/40-Poll(I), National Archives of India. Translation in original. It is possible that the civic guards were also employed as black legs in labour strikes during the war. Specific reference to Dhangars and methars may indicate the use of civic guards to break strikes of Calcutta Corporation workers that were going on during that time and in which the communists were deeply interested. Of course, this position of the Communists vis-à-vis war-time policing institutions were to change very soon with the Party's adoption of a pro-war stance in the coming months.

[56]Bimal Kar, *Dewal* (Calcutta: Ananda Publishers, 2003), p. 46. [Translation mine]

of this specificity remained undefined throughout the period while rumours were being policed. Nowhere did this manifest more clearly than the censorship strategies of the Calcutta police.

The war was, ultimately, a time of great social turmoil and uncertainty. Families were separated as women, children and older members were sent off to safer places. Individual migrants to the city, who had come from the countryside in search of employment or education, had to stay back despite anxieties about their loved ones in their country homes and their own safety in Calcutta. Friends and lovers were separated, husbands from their wives, parents from their children, giving rise to an atmosphere of general social anxiety. It is not surprising, therefore, that in the age when postal services were at the centre of social communication, the war-time anxieties found ample expression in personal letters of all kinds: letters exchanged with family members in the villages, detailing the conditions in the city; wives alarmed by rumours of devastations in Calcutta enquiring about the wellbeing of their husbands; anxious lovers confessing their love, warning each other of the impending calamity, before losing all contact once the postal system was dismantled. It was this form of social communication that the police wanted to clamp down upon as it formed the most potent route for the circulation of rumours.

Unsurprisingly, the sheer volume of personal letters that they were required to filter soon overwhelmed the censorship machinery. Officials expressed their alarm as two thousand panicky letters containing rumours were intercepted by the police in Calcutta in just two days—31 December 1941 and 1 January 1942—and confessed that there were many others they found impossible to take note of.[57] But, much more than the volume, what was perhaps more troubling was the lack of consensus regarding what, in fact, was a rumour, its definitional contours and the method of its identification. Many letters were deemed objectionable after they were delivered to the addressees without any censorship. When a home department officer, for instance, annoyed at the non-interception of 'objectionable' letters and the more widespread practice of keeping copies of some of them before delivering the original, demanded that originals of

[57]Note on War Panic, dated 6.1.42, Records of the Special Branch, Calcutta Police, File No.-P.M./757/42, K.P.M. No.-01566/05. 1942.

doubtful cases be forwarded to his office, the Deputy Commissioner of the Special Branch retorted: 'If you want letters of this kind in the original I will have them sent to you, but could you please give some kind of definition of what you want?'[58] This was as late as May 1942, and the police was still operating without any definite idea of what they really were after.

Colonial rule justified itself through its claims of establishing a 'rule of law'. This was what supposedly distinguished it from pre-colonial regimes that, in the colonial imaginary, represented the ultimate form of despotism. In controlling rumours, however, the police found it very difficult to stick to any semblance of legal procedures. This was undoubtedly the result of the elusiveness of the 'rumour-monger', the impossibility of identifying one specific individual or organization that could be held culpable and the consequent difficulty of bringing them under trial in a court of law. Time and again, the figure of the 'rumour-monger' appears in the police archive, only to slip away into oblivion. In the New Market panic case, for instance, the police had to be content merely with identifying a domestic servant as the offender and refrained from proceeding further to bring him to trial. This seems to be a typical pattern of police investigations into incidents of panic caused by rumours. Yet despite the unwillingness, indeed the inability of the police to pursue rumour cases through its courts, the elusive chase was seldom abandoned.

In cases of panic letters, the police adopted a range of strategies to build a strong case against the rumour-monger. The intercepted correspondences often formed the pretext for conducting house-searches and interrogations of the authors of the letters or their addressees. Every attempt was made to link them with subversive activities or groups so that they could be brought within the purview of law, but more often than not, there were no evidence to support a legal trial. When, as in most cases, legal procedures were found to be untenable, the police officers themselves indulged in practices that could hardly avoid charges of despotism—threatening their 'culprits',

[58]Notes on the letter dated 22.5.42, from Kanu to Mrs Sulochana Das Gupta. Records of the Sprcial Branch, Calcutta Police, File No.-P.M./757/42 III, K.P.M. No.-01568/05, 1942, Part III.

interrogating them for hours and, in numerous cases, forcing them to sign 'statements of regret' where the accused confessed to his 'crime', rendered an apology for their conduct and promised never to repeat the same. Rumour policing adopted practices that were para-legal at best and thoroughly despotic at its worst.

V

Since the time historians turned away from a narrow focus on official documents to look for alternative archives, attention has increasingly been directed towards oral sources—both as narratives recovered through field interviews as well as traces of orality embedded within textual forms.[59] This was accompanied by a closer dialogue between historians and anthropologists, practitioners of both disciplines reflecting critically upon their methodologies,[60] and historians arguing for a closer scrutiny of textual archives with greater attention to narrative strategies, slippages, marginalia and so on. The search for oral narratives that these new methodological orientations entailed often prompted historians to study rumours in different contexts and periods.[61]

[59]These impulses have given rise to what came to be known as 'Oral History'. For critical interventions in oral history, see, for example, Alessandro Portelli, *The Death of Luigi Trastulli and Other Stories: Form and Meaning in Oral History* (Albany: State University of New York Press, 1991); Luisa Passerini, *Fascism in Popular Memory: The Cultural Experience of the Turin Working Class* (New York: Cambridge University Press, 1987); Ronald Fraser, *Blood of Spain: An Oral History of the Spanish Civil War* (London: Pantheon, 1979). Oral History occupies an important place in Indian history writing. Influencial works in this genre include, among others, Shahid Amin, *Event, Metaphor, Memory: Chauri Chaura, 1922–92* (Berkeley: University of California Press, 1995); Urvashi Butalia, *The Other Side of Silence: Voices from the Partition of India*, (Durham, N.C: Duke University Press, 2000).

[60]Cohn's works remain perhaps the most powerful statement of the need for an active collaboration between historians and anthropologists. See Bernard Cohn, *An Anthropologist among Historians and Other Essays*, (Delhi and New York: Oxford University Press, 1990); Also, Bernard Cohn, *Colonialism and its Forms of Knowledge: The British in India* (Princeton: Princeton University Press, 1996).

[61]For a comprehensive summery of the variety of ways in which rumours have been studied, see the introduction to Anjan Kumar Ghosh, 'Partial Truths: Rumour and Communal Violence in South Asia, 1946–92', (Ph.D Thesis, University of Michigan, 1998). This is also an important monograph on rumour studies in South Asia.

In Indian historiography, rumours were often looked upon as a fertile ground that could yield alternative histories, producing narratives that could stand apart, question and challenge 'elitist' readings of official documents and high literature. This was linked to the wider project of democratizing the discipline, making it more inclusive and recovering hitherto submerged voices of the 'subaltern' masses.[62] Rumours, in this frame of reference, became an index for charting out popular understandings of historical events at variance with official versions that had till then dominated historiography.[63] In this intellectual milieu, study of rumours, even when recovered from the official archives, read 'against the grain', had little to say about statecraft or practices of governance.

Even in the study of rumours during the Second World War in British India, it has been used as a source for recovering alternative popular interpretations of larger world-historical events, throwing light on the fears and anxieties of ordinary people and their reactions to the experiences of the war. Rumours, in this understanding of its importance in historical analyses, could enable the historian to go beyond the enterprise of merely recording 'what happened' and explore what 'the people thought was happening'; it was to be used as an index for mapping 'popular consciousness' that could 'contest the imperial image.'[64]

While acknowledging the contributions of the 'history-from-below' approach in enriching our understandings of the past, this essay argues for much greater attention to the modalities of knowledge production embodied within the colonial archive, moving

[62]For a programmatic statement of the 'subaltern school' in Indian historiography, see the introduction in Ranajit Guha (ed.), *Subaltern Studies Vol I: Writings on Indian History and Society* (Delhi: Oxford University Press, 1982). Also see Ranajit Guha, *Elementary Aspects of Peasant Insurgency in Colonial India* (Delhi: Oxford University Press, 1983).

[63]For the use of rumour within the subaltern studies frame see, for example, Shahid Amin, 'Gandhi as Mahatma: Gorakhpur District, Eastern U.P.', 1921–22 in *Subaltern Studies Vol. III: Writings on Indian History and Society*, Ranajit Guha (ed.) (Delhi: Oxford University Press, 1984); David Hardiman, *The Coming of the Devi: Adivasi Assertion in Western India* (Delhi: Oxford University Press, 1987).

[64]Indivar Kamtekar, 'The Shiver of 1942', *Studies in History*, vol. 18, no. 1, n.s., 2002, pp. 81–102.

beyond a merely 'extractive' enterprise towards an 'ethnographic' approach, as 'sites of state ethnography' and articulations of colonial power.[65] Moving beyond 'against-the-grain' readings, it attempts to proceed 'along the archival grain' as well,[66] to unpack its systems of classification and categorization, to uncover the assumptions integral to such classificatory procedures of recording information and the ideas of 'truth' and 'fact' inherent in such assumptions.

This essay draws attention to how war rumour, as it emerges from the Calcutta Police archive, may be a valuable source to understand the everyday practices through which the colonial state and its agencies exercised control over society in situations of crises. It sought to explore the processes through which 'war rumour' crystallized into a bureaucratic category, enabling the law-and-order machinery to take cognizance of the phenomenon and deploy specific strategies to counter them. Rather than taking rumours as a reflection of the popular mind in any pure form, it urges the reader to recognize the nature of archival mediation through which 'war rumour' has registered its historical presence and inscribed itself within the official archive. To the extent that it illuminates specific strategies of governance and deployment of specific modes of statecraft, rumours may also be seen as a reflection of the official mind.

Official 'mind', in the singular, does not entail a reductive exercise, homogenizing the myriad practices of the everyday state into a monolith. It must, indeed, be conceptualized in its plurality, its multi-vocal resonances and contestations. But it does seek to provoke the reader by suggesting a unity of basic disposition towards problems of colonial governance that informed much of the practices of the local state apparatus in its everyday functioning, including the specific problem of controlling war rumours discussed in this essay.

It is also not the contention of this essay that the colonial state confronted rumour as an administrative problem for the first time

[65]Here I am borrowing some of the arguments outlined in Ann Laura Stoler, 'Colonial Archives and the Arts of Governance', *Archival Science*, vol. 2, 2002, pp. 87–109. Also, Ann Laura Stoler, *Along the Archival Grain: Epistemic Anxieties and Colonial Common Sense*, Princeton: Princeton University Press, 2010.

[66]Ibid.

during the Second World War. Rumour policing certainly had a longer history, though detailed case studies of earlier instances in India are hard to come by. However, there is no ground for doubting that rumours of the scale and type discussed above may have been particularly unnerving for the colonial state at a time when its legitimacy and its aura of invincibility was being globally challenged at multiple fronts. Also, the greatly expanded war-time administrative apparatus, resource-starved and overworked though it may have been, could have facilitated a certain degree of meticulous collection and categorization. But, more important is the question of its legacy: whether this knowledge concerning rumours that was produced during the war years had any lasting influence upon the future practices of statecraft, the extent to which it informed administrative practices of the colonial and postcolonial state. Pioneering studies of British colonial rule in India have emphasized the deep impact that ethnographic enterprises of the state, such as legal codifications[67] and census operations,[68] have had on the production of colonial knowledge about the subjugated society as well as on the self-representations and power relations within the society itself. Did this meticulous recording and classification of war-related information, production of categories such as 'anti-war propaganda' and 'war rumour', have any such lasting impact upon colonial (and postcolonial) knowledge production? Answers to these questions need to wait for further research.

[67]I am thinking of Bernard Cohn's works, especially his essays on law in *An Anthropologist among the Historians and Other Essays*.

[68]Nicholas Dirks, *Castes of Mind: Colonialism and the Making of Modern India* (Princeton: Princeton University Press, 2001); Also Bernard Cohn, 'The Census, Social Structure and Objectification in South Asia' in *An Anthropologist among the Historians and Other Essays*.

CHAPTER SIX

Japan Attacks

Janam Mukherjee

Analysis of the social, economic and political impact of World War II on India, as Indivar Kamtekar has rightly pointed out,[1] has often been relegated to footnotes in the history of modern India. With attention more frequently focused on the macro-politics of nationalism, the Pakistan movement, and negotiations for self-rule, the extent to which *war* shaped priorities, national alliances, and imperial policy in India during the 1940s has been largely overlooked. And yet, whatever were the concerns, contentions or calamities that confronted the Indian population during the period; the imperatives of the colonial state remained deeply enmeshed in a calculus of Total War. Defence, mobilization, security, and morale remained the primary mantras of authority in India—and particularly in Bengal—throughout the first half of the decade, and the exigencies of war allowed an authoritarian resolve that served to accentuate and, in fact, accelerate the entrenched predatory dynamics of colonial rule—even as the Empire itself was crumbling. In this sense, and as Kamtekar has argued, 'the state's new burst of energy and activity [with the outbreak of war] provides a flare of light enabling us to see its features more clearly.'[2]

The spotlight of war was nowhere in India as bright as it was in Bengal. Since the onset of war—and even before—governmental priorities in the province were consistently established in direct

[1]See the introduction to Kamtekar's 'A Different War Dance: State and Class in India, 1939–1945' in *Past and Present,* 176 (August 2002): 187–221.

[2]Ibid., 189.

relation to overarching concerns of 'defence'. After the fall of Burma in the spring of 1942, Bengal became the front in the Allied war against Japan, and Calcutta became the primary staging ground for the push east against a formidable enemy. By 1943, as many as 300,000 Bengalis had been recruited into the Air Raid Protection service (A.R.P.), the Civic Guards and the Home Guards, to form an ad hoc provincial native police force under the ambiguous banner of 'national defence.' In a disastrous scorched earth policy—officially known as 'The Denial Policy'—transportation facilities throughout the delta had been destroyed and all stores of putatively 'excess' food grains had been seized. Colonial manipulation of provincial politics had destabilized the organs of self-rule, and commercial firms, reaping record profits in war-related industries continued to scour the countryside to appropriate supplies of rice, both as speculative commodity and as 'dearness allowance' to conciliate restive workers. And, finally, famine had arisen out of the mix of wartime inflation, commercial and governmental myopia, and administrative chaos—devastating the province and creating social, political, and economic ruin that would haunt Bengal for generations to come.

It was under this dark cloud of famine, on 5 December 1943, with hunger-stricken bodies still accumulating on Calcutta's streets, that the city's dock complex at Kidderpore was bombed in broad daylight by two consecutive waves of Japanese aircraft. I have found nothing in my extensive historical research on the period that mentions the Calcutta bombings as anything but peripheral. Yet, as I will illustrate below, it was an extensive attack that caused considerable material and economic damage. It was also a uniquely revealing 'flare of light' that shone on the nature of administration in Bengal at that time. Much of the prejudice, indifference and dehumanization that lay at the foundation of colonial ideology was crystallized, in microcosm, during this particular calamity, and much of the rhetoric of concern for Indian welfare and security, which had justified an intensified authoritarianism in British India, was revealed to be entirely shallow. In this sense the realities of war in Bengal are related, on a deep structural level, to both the famine that preceded it and the continuing violence that followed.

THE PORT OF CALCUTTA

The Calcutta docks are situated on the west side of the Hooghly River, little more than a mile downstream from the city centre and 100 nautical miles upstream from the mouth of the river at the Bay of Bengal. Established in 1780, the complex at Kidderpore were the first deep water docks in Calcutta, built to accommodate the East India Company's fast-growing trade in Bengal. Throughout the 19th century, however, as Bengal was increasingly de-industrialized, and the extraction of large quantities of raw materials—particularly opium, cotton, coal, jute, indigo, oilseeds and tea—became the economic engine that fuelled colonial profit, the dock capacity at Kidderpore was fast proving insufficient. In 1870 a Board of Port Commissioners was appointed to oversee the development of the docks to meet increased needs. Locks at the mouth of a greatly expanded basin protected the inland dock area from tidal fluctuations, and an extensive network of storage sheds, mechanical cranes, and 27 deepwater berths were added to accommodate larger seagoing vessels. The King George Docks at Garden Reach, with 10 more deep sea berths, 3 dry docks and heavy cranes serving another enhanced complex of warehouses were added in 1929, and the Port of Calcutta was now on par with any other dock system in the world. Ten years later, on the cusp of World War II, shipping traffic through the Calcutta Port amounted to nearly ten million tons a year.[3]

As the docks grew, the area around them developed into a thriving commercial/industrial hub, with textile factories, jute and cotton mills, coal depots, iron works and tea warehouses lining the banks of the river around the port, and Calcutta's expanded 'docklands'[4] had developed into a sprawling industrial quarter of the city. The adjacent, densely populated neighbourhoods of Kidderpore, Watganj, Mommenpur and Metiabruz became thriving, if poor—and mostly Muslim—residential districts. The Hooghly River, to the north of the docks, had extensive moorings and remained lined with ships waiting to enter the locks at Kidderpore all year round.

[3]Ibid. (Ghosh's figure is 9,965,911 tons).

[4]The docks at Kidderpore and Garden Reach, together with the industrial and residential complexes that surrounded them, were referred to in Government and A.R.P. reports as 'the Docklands.'

To the south, a channel led out to 'Tolly's Nullah,' linking the docks to an extensive canal system that connected the port to the rice and jute-rich regions of eastern Bengal along 1,127 miles of navigable waterways. The docks of Calcutta, in this sense, were also a critical strategic target for Japan.

During the war, labourers associated with the docks, in particular—as of labour in Calcutta more generally—were officially understood as 'essential'[5] and as such, were—ostensibly—both protected and provisioned by numerous wartime acts.[6] Rhetoric about the welfare of the industrial labour-force in Calcutta was, in fact, central to an ideology that justified various schemes of appropriation and differential distribution of rice, which, in turn, contributed significantly to the acute impoverishment of the Bengal countryside, and ultimately famine.

But, as the bombings make clear, the 'priority' associated with labour during the war proved to be highly contingent. Just who was, in the last analysis, 'essential', and who disposable, was often a matter of expediency rather than principle. In the end the fate of poor, disenfranchised, and ultimately replaceable dock labourers meant very little, indeed, to a colonial administration at war. Even the exact numbers of labourers associated with the docks is not easy to ascertain with any degree of certainty. The Bengal Chamber of Commerce, for one, in its report on the bombings put the number of dock labourers at 11,000,[7] while Port Commissioner, Sir Thomas Elderton (I.C.S.), in his separate report, put the number at 18,000.[8]

[5]The Essential Services [Maintenance] Ordinance of 1941 had made it a criminal offence for any worker engaged in 'essential' war-related industries and enterprises from abandoning their station of employment without 'reasonable excuse,' under penalty of imprisonment. The rhetoric of 'essential' workers, moreover, became a mantra of the colonial administration during war. See S. Bhattacharya, *Propaganda And Information In Eastern India, 1939–45: a Necessary Weapon of War,* (Richmond: Curzon, 2000), 41.

[6]Representatives of the Bengal National Chamber of Commerce boasted at the Famine Enquiry Commission that 'there was not one single case of death among industrial laborers from famine.' (Nanavati Papers, p. 1089.) This presumption, I am here arguing, is highly misleading as the relative 'security' of industrial laborers in Calcutta was highly contingent.

[7]WBSA, Home Confidential, file W-30/43 (III).

[8]Ibid.

This discrepancy is puzzling, but more puzzling is that Elderton himself subsequently informed the Governor of Bengal that as many as '*30,000* workers enter the dock area every day.'[9] To make matters still more complicated, eminent historian Suranjan Das, in his analysis based on Intelligence Branch records notes that in December of 1942, there were 60,000 dock labourers in Kidderpore.[10]

It seems then that very many workers on the docks were contract labourers, or 'coolies'—lowly paid, unskilled, mostly immigrant workers who toiled long hours, sometimes in intense heat or driving monsoon rain, for poor wages, many without any provision for housing or messing, uncounted for by the Chambers of Commerce and unrecognized by the colonial state. Without, in short, any of the wartime 'priority' cited by governmental and industrial interests to rationalize their relentless campaigns to appropriate rice in the countryside, putatively to feed industrial Calcutta. J.W. Stanworth, of the British Merchant Navy, passed through the Kidderpore Docks during the war and witnessed a typical sight. His vessel was sent to load 10,000 tons of coal for export from Bengal to Shanghai, and, he recounts:

> This was all loaded by hand. Long planks of timber were placed from the quay to the deck of the ship and an endless belt of human misery ran up one plank with a basket of coal, threw the coal down the ships hold and ran down the other plank. Some people were filling the baskets and partners of two lifted the baskets on the shoulders of the endless belt of men. It was stifling hot on the ship as the port holes had to be closed to keep the coal dust out as much as possible. No one could sleep as the coal was being loaded 24 hours a day, non-stop, so after consultation we were taken to the Seamen's Club where we could bathe and sleep in cool rooms.[11]

Labour conditions even for those who enjoyed company 'benefits' as permanent employees, were anything but luxurious.

[9]Casey's Diary, p. 152. [Emphasis mine].

[10]Suranjan Das 'Nationalism and Popular Consciousness: Bengal 1942.' *Social Scientist,* Vol. 23, No. 4/6 (Apr.—Jun., 1995), 62.

[11]BBC oral history project 'WW2 People's War.' J.W. Stanworth at www.bbc.co.uk/ww2peopleswar/stories/36/a6021136.shtml (Last accessed June, 2010, 5:25 PM).

Working hours were long, environmental conditions harsh and housing arrangements insufficient. Of the regular workers, only 39 per cent were provided with housing at all.[12] The vast majority of dock laborers—both regular and contract—lived in the 'coolie lines,'—privately constructed, congested, slum-like encampments, with rows of corrugated tin or bamboo-mat shacks built haphazardly in empty lots close to the factory doors. They were notorious for their poor ventilation, lack of clean drinking water, insufficient sanitary arrangements and dangerously cramped quarters.[13] These encampments were also often run by unscrupulous local strongmen, who demanded exorbitant rents and lent money to the perennially indebted 'coolies' at similarly extortionate rates. Furthermore, even while industries were logging record profits,[14] due to wartime inflation the real wages of already severely impoverished[15] industrial workers *fell* by as much as 30 per cent.[16]

Apart from the labourers who inhabited the docklands, there were now Allied soldiers of every stripe. With major operations planned in Southeast Asia, the American presence, in particular, was mounting throughout the fall of 1943, and a large American Army depot had been constructed and heavy mechanical cranes added to the docks at Garden Reach. The British Army had a depot of its own on the docks, and barracks for soldiers of both nations, as well as those of many other Allied nations, were scattered throughout the area. As a member of the Calcutta Police who was stationed in the area remembers:

> the docks boiled with activity (and crime) as vast amounts of military ordinance poured in, and the Burma front and Nationalist China (via the Ledo Road) were kept supplied by troop and 'military special' trains through the Herculean efforts of the East Bengal and Assam-Bengal Railways. Soldiers, sailors and airmen from all the Allied nations wandered the streets in search of 'rest & recreation' which

[12]Arjan de Haan, p. 159 (The figure given for factory housed workers in 1946 is 39 per cent).

[13]Ibid., pp. 158–9.

[14]Kamtekar (August 2002), p. 203.

[15]Mitter, p. 526.

[16]Kamtekar (August 2002), p. 210.

usually consisted of a feed, a fight and sex (in any order) inevitably necessitating much police intervention.[17]

JAPAN ATTACKS

On Sunday, 5 December 1943, Calcutta awakened to its ongoing tribulation of famine. Three of the six A.R.P. 'corpse disposal' vans, originally commissioned to the Government of Bengal for air raid casualties, were making their rounds collecting 'sick destitutes' in various stages of starvation from the streets of Calcutta and removing them to 'repatriation camps' outside the city.[18] The irony of removing the *dying* from the streets of Calcutta in vehicles commissioned for the removal of the dead is telling. That tools allocated to deal with war were busy with famine 'relief,' is similarly instructive. Two more of these vans were with the Hindu Satkar Samiti and the Anjuman Mofidul Islam for the removal of Hindu and Muslim famine corpses, respectively. The sixth van, in a state of disrepair, was with the Calcutta Corporation awaiting re-commissioning. In the face of famine, disease and despair—as well as profit, political intrigue and indifference—the war with Japan had faded into the background, both in popular and official imagination. Nearly a year had elapsed since Calcutta had last been bombed, and the momentous events of that year had greatly attenuated popular concerns about Britain's war.

Calcutta was still, however, very much critical to its pursuance—even if the actual defence of Calcutta had failed to become a real priority. The Indian Command had been requesting better equipment to defend the city for some time, but military preparations had evolved little since 1941.[19] After the first bombings of Calcutta, in December 1942, elite 'Beaufighters' had been rushed in from the Middle-East, and as recently as November of 1943, three squadrons of highly effective 'Spitfires' had also been sent to the region. But

[17]Peter Moore, 'Policing War-time Calcutta,' at http://www.oldmartiniansassociation.co.uk/memories.html (Last accessed May 4, 2002, 1:45 PM), p. 2.

[18]WBSA Home Confidential, '8th Raid,' file W-30/43 (Note by Secretary of the Government of Bengal, E.W. Holland on corpse disposal).

[19]Stephens, p. 217.

by mid-1943 both the Spitfire and Beaufighter squadrons had been shifted to advanced positions for offensive maneuvers, and Calcutta was left defended by nothing more than a handful of obsolete 'Hurricanes,' together with a few batteries of equally out-of-date anti-aircraft guns.[20] Meanwhile, the Allied war in Europe was going well, and with increased American involvement in South-East Asia optimism was running high.

When the air raid sirens began to wail at 11:15 am, there was little excitement. Interrupted from his morning work, *Statesman* Editor, Ian Stephens, remembers feeling 'no more than a vague annoyance.'[21] A.R.P. drills were still a regular part of life—however insignificant the war seemed in relation to the monstrous difficulties Bengal faced. Moreover, the possibility of Japan mustering the audacity to launch a daylight raid seemed remote. At 11:27 am, however, the sirens began to sound the 'red alert,' which meant that an attack was imminent. Within 20 minutes the sky filled with the rumble of Japanese bombers; as many as 250 planes in all, stepped up at three levels and descending from a cruising height of 20,000 feet down unto the docks of Calcutta.[22] The bombers had launched from central Burma and had angled south across the Bay of Bengal, completely avoiding Allied defenses, which were bunched along the Burmese front at Chittagong and Shillong. By 11:45 am, out of a clear blue sky, a massive, broad-daylight attack on Calcutta was underway.[23]

The Japanese bombers, meeting no opposition, streaked in low and picked targets at will, as heavy explosive and anti-personnel bombs began pounding the docks. A series of heavy explosive bombs hit the coaling berths on the western edge of the south basin of the Kidderpore docks, igniting the coal and turning the wharf into a blazing inferno that spread to the adjacent goods' sheds rapidly. The concussions from the heavy explosive bombs,

[20]Ibid., p. 224.

[21]Ibid., p. 215.

[22]Ibid., p. 216.

[23]The sequence of events described below is all taken from the A.R.P. reports contained in WBSA, Home Confidential, file W-30/43. '8th Raid.' A map is also included in the file, which pinpoints the locations of the bombs. A chronology of events is given in the Calcutta Fire Brigade's report in the same file. Where relevant, reference will be given to the specific documents from this file.

which left impact craters 12 feet wide and 6 feet deep, also blew out the overhead electric lines and disabled communications. A second primary target, the Bengal Nagpur Railway (B.N.R.) depot, a few hundred yards north of the coaling berths, was also under heavy attack. Anti-personnel bombs—which burst into high velocity fragments of steel and shrapnel immediately on impact with the ground—rained down on the depot, piercing steel rail webs at ranges of up to 30 feet and destroying the railway's mainline. Fifty railway wagons, one engine and the goods yard were struck and partially or totally destroyed—as was the quarters of the 'lower paid staff' of the railway. A heavy explosive bomb was also dropped on the offices of Bird and Company, sandwiched between the coal berths and the railway depot. The Hooghly Jute Mill was hit by seven bombs and suffered extensive damage. Barges waiting to load or unload, anchored in the dock basin, were targeted as well, with the resulting fires jumping from barge to barge quickly. By 11:57 am—only twelve minutes after the bombing had begun—at least 11 barges were 'blazing furiously' on the water.

Anti-personnel bombs were also raining down on the 'coolie lines,' and the fires from the coaling berths and goods sheds spread throughout the workers' hostels. The sweepers' quarter of the B.N.R. was demolished, and the river dock of the Government Timber Depot was destroyed. Damage from anti-personnel fragments spread out in a 300 yard radius from the site of the bomb blasts, and as such, shops, private residences, and small factories outside the dock gates suffered collateral damage or were struck directly by misguided bombs. The Clive Jute Mill in Garden Reach was also hit and heavy explosive bombs fell in residential areas of Watganj and Kidderpore. A petrol pump, the A.R.P. barracks, a 'coolie market,' the Tramway Depot Drivers' Quarters, and a ration shop were also directly hit. Bombs also fell outside the general dock vicinity, with reports of heavy explosions in Bhawanipur and Alipore, more than a mile away. Along the docks and in the attached B.N.R. yard, 'coolies' took cover wherever they could find it, many going 'to ground in or under any form of structure which had the effect of hiding them from overhead. Corrugated iron sheds, wagons and latrines were all used and were, of course, entirely useless.'[24] Anti-personal bomb fragments ripped through the walls of these same structures killing many instantly. In its A.R.P. report, however, the Railway noted that those who died without sufficient shelter were, in fact, 'mainly non-B.N.R. employees.' The difficulty in the dock area, the report cited 'was that there was not always shelter for the *outsiders* who were present in the goods yard.'[25] At the Hooghly Jute Mill, immediately adjacent to the main dock, the shelters provided by the company were 'extremely defective,' lacking any proper covering wall, and even inside these shelters, workers were killed by flying fragments.[26]

The luckiest of the workers, perhaps, were those who successfully escaped the dock area once the shelling began. These labourers, it seems, may have been following the lead of military personnel in the area, who made great haste for the dock gates when the bombs began to fall. The Commissioners for the Port of Calcutta penned a complaining note to P.D. Martyn, Secretary of the Government of Bengal, a few days after the bombings, testily requesting that 'orders be issued that soldiers working in the Dock area must take cover in the Dock area. We want coolies to do this,' he added, 'but they certainly will not as long as men in uniform rush for the gates immediately when they hear sirens.' The 'behavior of the American Negro troops,' the Commissioners noted in particular, 'was disgraceful.'[27] The report of a Kidderpore Fire Brigade worker, stationed near the dock gates, was careful to assigned blame to American troops more generally:

> While reporting to control on the siren from the chummery, I happened to be near the above entrance. There was in front of me a jeep and American truck proceeding towards the dock. As soon as the dock siren was audible the truck immediately stopped and turned in the opposite direction, away from the dock, and in turning I went passed and saw a man lying in a precarious condition on the road, where the truck had backed and turned.[28]

[24]Ibid., B.N.P. Final Report.

[25]Ibid., Note from B.N.R. General Manager to Government of Bengal, Home Department. [Emphasis mine]

[26]Ibid.

[27]Ibid., Port Commissioners to Bengal Secretariat.

[28]Ibid.

British soldiers appear to have 'stood to' with more fortitude, but contributed considerably to the panic. A Military Police Security Control Officer on the spot describes the scene near the coaling docks as chaotic. Military lorries parked too close together relayed the coal berth fires across to the warehouse sheds. Other lorries had flat tyres and blocked emergency vehicles from entering the area. Troops poured in from ships and adjacent areas and 'using their own stretchers, gathered the casualties together, sending them off to Hospital in army lorries.'[29] In other places British soldiers 'seized Port A.R.P. stretchers, vehicles, etc., blocked roads by parking vehicles haphazardly, and generally speaking made it impossible for the Port A.R.P. to function in an organized fashion.'[30] Both the Port A.R.P. Controller and the 24 Pargana Controller also complained that the military had grossly interfered with their operations.

This subordination of the A.R.P to military personnel during the bombing—after four years of training, exercises and pay-rolling—is a telling demonstration of the true level of confidence that had been invested in this organization of local loyalists. The A.R.P. had been widely utilized by Government as a vehicle of propaganda, co-opting influential Hindu citizens into the 'war-effort.' Their 'drills' had been planned to instill a sense of 'emergency' in the population. They had been used to police the urban populations of Bengal during disturbances and they had been posted in front of control shops to 'keep the peace' when citizens of the city were clamoring for rice. During the 'food drive,' they had been deputized to seize supplies of rice from private citizens, and once famine victims began to fill the streets of Calcutta, they were sent out to round them up, by force if necessary, or to cart off their dead bodies to the nearest crematorium or burial ground. Now that bombs were falling and decimating the docks, however, the Air Raid Precautions services were unceremoniously pushed aside. In what would become a highly controversial report a Military Police Control Officer stationed on the docks observed that 'during the period between the first bomb and the 'all-clear,' Civil Defence Departments were conspicuous by

[29]Ibid., M.P.S.C.O.'s Memorandum 21/sco/80 to the Chief of the General Staff
[30]Ibid.

their absence; the entire fire fighting, first aid, and rescue work being done by the fighting services.'[31]

Finally, at 1 pm, after two waves of heavy bombings, the all-clear signal was sounded and the docks lay in almost total ruins. The coal berths had been razed by fire, along with as many as 15 of the 29 storage sheds lining the perimeter. The B.N.R. yard had suffered extensive damage, with at least 50 wagons and one engine destroyed in the attacks, and the tracks leading out from the yard were heavily damaged by anti-personal shrapnel and heavy explosive bombs. In the basin the burned out hulks of 11 barges, 3 ships (the SS Matheson, SS Nauchung and the SS Irtria), 1 dredger, and 4 tug boats smoldered on the water, and large sections of the 'coolie lines' along the Eastern Boundary Road had been devastated by fire. The area was also strewn with hundreds of corpses—human and animal—untended and unclaimed, that had already begun to rot in the afternoon sun. To make matters worse, the gates of the docks remained unmanned and hundreds of curious onlookers entered the area to survey the damage and collect 'souvenirs,' with 'crowds... allowed to collect around the [dead] bodies, resulting in very exaggerated rumors.'[32] Confusion, chaos and disorganization, as well as an administratively expedient rewriting of events, continued for many days to come.

At the same time, a steady flow of traffic *away* from the dock and industrial areas was picking up pace. Along Garden Reach Road, the main axial roadway running through dockland, a column of approximately 7,000 workers was reported moving towards points unknown. Along the Grand Trunk Road, the main highway into the surrounding districts, another group of an estimated 2,000 'coolies,' with bullock carts loaded down with personal belongings, was fleeing the city. From Bird and Company's dock complex as many as 10,000 contract laborers 'absconded immediately after the raid,' leaving the firm with less than half of its force, and workers employed by the Port Commission also fled in large numbers, with only 1,800 of the enumerated 11,000 laborers remaining. From the Hooghly Jute Mill, 80 per cent of workers quickly decamped or otherwise 'disappeared,' and the survivors of the B.N.R.'s heavily bombed

[31]Ibid., Memo 21/SCO/80.

[32]Ibid., Port A.R.P. Report.

out sweepers' quarters also 'ran away' in mass. What percentage of these same workers had actually been killed in the bombing is a question that is extremely difficult to answer.

For those that remained 'morale' was carefully monitored and engineered—by force where possible. The post-raid A.R.P. report from the B.N.R. noted that 'an attempted exodus on the part of *outsiders* by the Shalimar Ferry [which would have taken them across the river to relative safety] was checked.'[33] Under what authority and by what means the B.N.R. was able to arrest the movement of laborers who were not in their direct employment is not specified. Nor is it mentioned by what means and under what conditions these same workers were detained within the dock complex. The Port A.R.P., for its part, noted that stevedores and other essential dock hands were being 'housed in camps under military control.'[34] In this context a note from the Port Commission that several hundred of its own 'essential labour' had been 'accommodated in a warehouse shelter as a measure to instill confidence,'[35] also hints at a rather coercive 'accommodation.'

If the living remained of certain concern, however, the dead did not. As night fell, corpses still littered the docks, unclaimed, unidentified and untended. Within a few hours the crowds of 'sightseers' were replaced by crowds of looters who stepped over the dead bodies to ransack the docks for any unburned coal or other commodities left behind by the bombs and fires.[36]

DAMAGE CONTROL

In the morning many of the corpses still remained where they had fallen, while front page headlines in *The Statesman* relayed the official report from the Government of India that 'a number of bombs' had been dropped on 'the Calcutta area,' but that the damage had been 'slight.'[37] The scenario may have been much

[33]Ibid., B.N.R.'s Post-Raid Report. [Emphasis mine]

[34]Ibid., Port A.R.P. Report.

[35]Ibid.

[36]Ibid.

[37]*The Statesman,* 'Jap's First Daylight Raid on Calcutta,' 6 December 1943.

more grim, the government communiqué went on, had the defence of the city not been so stalwart: 'Our fighters intercepted the enemy aircraft and a heavy and effective barrage was put up.'[38] No further information was given. The report was, in fact, an exemplary model of vague and misleading understatement—in close keeping with official orders. In April of 1943, after the earlier air-raids on Calcutta, a Defense Circular was sent to all Provincial Governments outlining the official protocol for reporting on raids, stressing 'the vital necessity for the most careful wording [of post-raid reports].'[39] No mention should be made of the specific target of the bombing, instead, the circular read, 'this will be in general terms, i.e. "Calcutta area",—not "Docks of Calcutta."'[40] The extent of the destruction should also be left indefinite: 'where necessary to publish any mention of damage the general terms "slight," "moderate," and "heavy" or synonyms of these will be used. *These terms will have no relation to any specific numbers of casualties.*'[41] As to the number of casualties, the instruction went on, 'an underestimate is better.'[42]

Such obfuscation, however, failed its first test. The discrepancy between the information officially and unofficially circulated created resentment and only served to heighten anxieties. Rumours quickly began to spread about extensive damage to the docks and heavy casualties. Dock workers were in a state of 'extreme nervousness as a result of the casualties which took place among them,'[43] and the fear that they carried with them out of the docks was contagious. It was well known, moreover, that damage to the dock area had been anything but 'slight,' with plumes of smoke and ash from the attack being seen as much as two miles away.[44] Additionally, the hundreds of 'sightseers' and looters who had surveyed the wreckage and seen

[38]Ibid.

[39]WBSA, Home Political, file W-296/43.

[40]Ibid., (emphasis in the original).

[41]Ibid. [Emphasis mine]

[42]Ibid.

[43]Ibid., 'Bengal Chamber of Commerce Labor Conditions'.

[44]Ian Stephens, in *Monsoon Morning,* remembers that clouds of smoke and ash could be seen emerging from the dock area shortly after the bombing began. Stephens was at the Statesman building, approximately two miles distant from the docks.

corpses still littering the docks had carried these impressions back home with them. Even labour managers complained of an 'almost complete lack of [accurate] authoritative information,' which made it impossible to rally 'morale.'[45]

The claim that the attack had been effectively countered by the Royal Air Force (R.A.F.) and anti-aircraft fire also rang extremely hollow. None of the A.R.P. reports had mentioned this. Rather, the report from the B.N.R. was typical in citing consternation at the fact that 'so many planes were allowed to fly over targets in perfect formation and drop bombs with no apparent opposition.'[46] *The Statesman* accused the armed forces of complacency and speculated that perhaps 'the well known British disposition for relaxation over the week-end' (the attack had come on a Sunday) might explain the manifest lack of opposition with which the Japanese attack was met.[47] The Calcutta A.R.P. report outlined more general sentiments:

> Indian opinion is strongly critical of the R.A.F.'s failure to protect Calcutta; the success of the raid has caused some to think that the stories of R.A.F. successes elsewhere are exaggerated; others think that the British cannot defend Calcutta from air-attack. British opinion is even more strongly critical and is indignant that Calcutta, stacked with war materials, its docks full of ships, should be left unprotected.[48]

Boosting morale was a hard sell. On the third day after the bombing, less than 20 per cent of the dock labour showed up for work. The attack had been devastating; very little warning had been given, no defense had been mounted, shelter had been inadequate, the official line on the attack had been patently specious, rumors were spreading unabated, and, to make matters worse, dead bodies, uncollected and unidentified, still littered the docks—even on the third day—decomposing in the December sun.[49]

[45]WBSA, Home Confidential, file W-30/43.
[46]Ibid., B.N.R. Report.
[47]*The Statesman,* 'Sunday Morning,' 6 December 1943.
[48]WBSA, Home Confidential, file W-30/43.
[49]Ibid.

BODIES

In many ways 1943 could be considered the 'year of the corpse' in Bengal. In the latter half of the year, in particular, the corpse had become a ubiquitous and *material* 'social fact.' That there were as many as 1.5 million lives lost to famine in 1943, also meant that there were as many as 1.5 million corpses that remained behind and had to be dealt with—or not. The tremendous *weight*—in both material and socio-political terms—of these corpses put an enormous strain on Bengal society and administration. The management of corpses represented a recurrent moral riddle that had to be solved. Some famine corpses had been retained in 'constructive possession' of the state, others had been turned over to religious organizations for removal, and still others had been unceremoniously tossed into rivers and canals. Many others remained untouched where they had fallen and became a feast for wild dogs and vultures. Overall, the relationship of the corpse to 'the king' during famine was dependent on its differential relation to power. Corpses that proved compromising to colonial power—primarily those in Calcutta—where 'unclean' and had to be removed promptly and through official channels. Corpses that did not impinge on the functioning of the state were left to fate.

The treatment of the corpse, in this sense, provides a clue to the value attributed, by the state, to the life that once resided in it. Because the corpse consists of *only* the material aspect of being, without the contingency of agentive contradiction or contest, it is a kind of *tabula rasa* upon which the script of power is most clearly inscribed. The corpse, in this regard, represents the limits of essentialism: a stark and eerie ideological map to the psychological terrain of power.

The removal of air raid corpses was understood to be a central responsibility of the Civil Defence Services. The A.R.P. had its own corpse disposal squads, which had been drilled and trained in accordance with the A.R.P. Services Ordinance of 1941.[50] These teams had gained extensive experience removing corpses from

[50]WBSA, Home Political, file W-112/43 'Constitution of Mortuary Services under the A.R.P. Services Ordinance, 1941'.

the streets of Calcutta during famine. Their lorries, in fact, were still removing starvation victims from the city's streets when the 5 December bombing took place. The A.R.P. also had hundreds of beds in local hospitals reserved for air raid casualties only.[51] When the bombing actually took place, however, it appears that neither the A.R.P. corpse disposal squads, nor the A.R.P. hospitals served their prescribed purpose. Instead, the earliest reports from the A.R.P. Controllers of the Port and the B.N.R. noted that the R.A.F. interceded in casualty recovery efforts at every juncture, and began loading bodies onto *military* transport vehicles, almost immediately, and removing them to unknown destinations.[52] Seth Drucquer, the Office-in-Charge of the Post Raid Information Services (P.R.I.S.), responsible for gathering casualty statistics, noted on 6 December, that the removal of 'large numbers' of casualties by military personnel to military hospitals had severely hampered efforts to count the dead and injured. Bodies had also been shifted to several other non-A.R.P. hospitals, and had even been moved between unauthorized medical facilities without explanation or official documentation.[53]

When Drucquer received word through unofficial channels that bodies had been taken to the Indian Military Hospital, he visited the hospital to collect statistics. There he found only considerable 'irregularities in the situation.'[54] No list of persons admitted had been kept, no record of treatments administered existed, and no attempt to identify the casualties had been made. The Deputy Supervisor of the Port precinct also visited the Indian Military Hospital and reported that the Military Officer in charge could not even tell him the exact number of casualties brought in, nor how many were dead or alive. The treatment given to the injured was also rudimentary, 'nothing but tincture iodine being applied in many cases.'[55] Many were housed outside the hospital in army tents, throughout the cold December night 'without adequate clothing or blankets.' They had

[51]Casey's Diaries, 338.

[52]Ibid., first reports from the Port A.R.P. and the B.N.R. A.R.P.

[53]Ibid., Civil Defence Information Office, Final Report.

[54]Ibid.

[55]Ibid.

not been given food and no proper sanitation had been arranged. In effect, conditions starkly analogous to those prevailing throughout the famine-stricken province were recreated in microcosm at the Indian Military Hospital. The evidence pertaining to casualties of the raids taken to the British Military Hospital is still less documented. When Drucquer paid a visit to this hospital he was simply 'refused admittance.' At the private, Campbell Hospital, Civil Defence Information Office staff were similarly denied access and hospital administrators 'refused to give any details regarding the dead bodies collected there.'[56]

Those bodies not taken into military custody were the subject of considerable uncertainty as well. The police, the A.R.P., and the Calcutta Corporation were confused about their 'respective responsibilities.'[57] The Bengal Nagpur Railways A.R.P. Controller, in his report, complained that no clear instructions on removing dead bodies had been given. The Port A.R.P., for its part, followed the famine model, making over bodies to the Hindu Satkar Samiti and the Anjuman Mofidul Islam, ensuring proper funeral rites to the dead according to perceived religious community. The B.N.R. A.R.P. also recorded the religious community of the dead that were collected under its auspices, but little else. In his initial report, the A.R.P. Controller for the B.N.R. noted that A.R.P. 'sanitation sweepers' had assisted R.A.F. personnel and 'other European officers to lift bodies onto R.A.F. lorries, but admitted later that it had lost track of many casualties in the process.[58] The police, for their part, removed an unspecified number of corpses to the nearby Mominpore morgue, where the bodies lay for several days in tight 'files,' again without identification or enumeration.

Obviously, under such conditions, even a rough estimate of the number killed during the bombing of 5 December, 1943 becomes extremely difficult. In his final report, Drucquer—on a line penciled in and rough with erasure marks—reported the total number of dead, 'as revealed,' at 335. (To put this in perspective, during the first air

[56]Ibid.

[57]Ibid.

[58]Ibid. For the assistance of sanitation workers see B.N.R. Initial Report, for losing track, see Final Report.

attack by the German Luftwaffe on England during the 'blitz,' 436 Londoners were killed, and it was considered a catastrophic event.) The number killed on the docks, however, remains highly inconclusive. The Secretary to the Home Department of the Government of Bengal, remained skeptical. He reported to the General Secretary that the Port A.R.P numbers were 'very doubtful,' and warned that government would have to 'explain that the removal of large numbers of casualties to a military hospital had made the compilation of accurate statistics virtually impossible.'[59] The Secretary replied that he would issue the necessary caveat about the dead removed to military hospitals, and also noted that a 'considerable number of casualties... occurred on board ships and on freighters and barges,'[60] though their numbers, as well, were unknown. Similarly, there was little attempt made to estimate those bodies that had been consumed by fire. Fires in the congested 'coolie lines,' in particular, raged unabated for several hours and large portions of the encampments lay in complete ruins by late afternoon. A Military Security Control Officer had noted in his report that during the bombings he had seen '*nothing* being done by Civil Defence Services [in regards to fires in the coolie lines]. It is understood,' he continued, 'that the fire fighting services were busy elsewhere, but the coolies, who were a high percentage of the casualties, received no help from First Aid, Rescue, or Ambulance Squads until after the 'All Clear'.[61]

The pervasive disregard, disrespect and even disgust, with which the bodies of these (poor) labourers were treated reveals important aspects of the colonial mindset at the time—aspects which contributed significantly to the mentality of debasement, erasure and *de*-prioritization that led to famine. While these bodies served any economic or political purpose, they were touted 'essential.' Once their utility had been negated—as corpses—they became a 'security risk,' endangering the war effort (by registering the success of Japan's attack), encumbering the administration (by the awkward presence of their corpses), and generating rumours that threatened efforts at damage control. Their bodies, for the most

[59]bid., Kitchin to Martyn.

[60]Ibid.

[61]Ibid., Secret Letter 56/SCO/31.

part, had to be whisked away from public sight, denied, obscured and, ultimately, forgotten. Far from being protected or prioritized, they had been defiled, degraded, or entirely neglected once their utility had been—violently—revoked. This fact exposes the myth of patriarchal concern for the industrial labour of Calcutta that consecutive programs of appropriation, 'denial,' and militarization all banked on, and reveals the emptiness of the rhetoric that justified much of the official policy that precipitated mass starvation in Bengal. Ultimately, during the air-raid, these 'essential workers' fared little better than poor villagers during famine. Their violent deaths, except for the risks to 'security' that was entailed, meant next to nothing to the colonial state. Despite claims to the contrary; they were expendable, insignificant and very easily dehumanized

Of the 335 corpses officially counted in the Post Raid Information Service's Final Report, 260 were thus recorded as 'unidentified.' Seth Drucquer, in his report, attributed this shortcoming to several different causes. Non-A.R.P. hospitals, he complained, had made no attempt to gather information on the bodies brought to them and the police had not gained access to many of the bodies until several days after the raids. Although 'there [was] a provision for the Police to photograph unidentified dead bodies after raids,' he noted, 'by the time the Police arrived, they were too much decomposed for such photographs to be of any value.'[62] In a hand written and parenthetical addendum, Drucquer added that 'probably the Police, like the Post Raid Information Service (P.R.I.S.), were not informed of the whereabouts of casualties until it was too late.'[63] The Police Commissioner himself defended the record, reporting that their primary concern had been solely 'to have the dead bodies removed from sight as early as possible.'

Although the corpses accounted for were thus disposed of without name, physical description, or any personalized record that would facilitate future identification, there *was*, in the last analysis, one single mark of classification assigned to most of the bodies. Given that these same bodies had been left to rot, had been denied care, and had been all but systematically erased, the trace of 'identification'

[62]Ibid.
[63]Ibid.

that *was* recorded has to be understood as the state's most 'essential' distinction of all—one that would adhere to even an anonymous body, deprived of all social connection, dignity or recognition. That last trace, interestingly enough, was religious affiliation. How exactly such a determination was made, particularly of bodies in advanced stages of decomposition, is difficult to comprehend. The Officer-in-Charge of the P.R.I.S. remained silent. In his Final Report to Government, he explained:

> The labels which the Police tie on to unidentified dead bodies and of which a copy is given to P.R.I.S. contain a column for marks of identification on the body. A very large number of labels received did not have this column filled up, only one word being entered, such as; 'Muslim,' or 'Hindu.' This is of no use at all in establishing identification subsequently.

As during the Great Bengal famine then, the sole distinction made by the state often enough was in terms of religious identity. This simple binary distinction had become so ingrained in administrative thought that it was understood, by this time, to be the only necessary categorization—for even a corpse. The colonial state was, in this sense, reifying religious affiliation, by means of corpses, that would parallel the political distinction that was being used to 'divide and rule.' The idea that Hindu-ness or Muslim-ness adhered to the very body of the population, moreover, was a subtle license to violence against the *bodies* of the 'other.' The way those bodies were handled during and after the air raids was both an example of all that had been learned during the Great Bengal famine—and was also an indication of what was to come. It is a chilling fact that in the dehumanizing darkness of war and famine, this one simple and explosive distinction was all that was required in demarcating the disposable citizens of Calcutta. It is furthermore, a similarly telling and chilling foreshadowing of the darkness still to come.

SETTLING ACCOUNTS

The Essential Services [Maintenance] Ordinance of 1941 had made it a criminal offence for any worker engaged in 'essential' war-related industries and enterprises from abandoning their station of employment without 'reasonable excuse,' under penalty of imprisonment. 'The fact that a person apprehends that by continuing in his employment he will be exposed to increased physical danger,' it was noted, 'does not constitute a reasonable excuse.'[64] The threat of imprisonment it was understood, however, would do little to assuage the fears of current workers and might actually discourage labor recruitment. The War Injuries Insurance Ordinance, promulgated in the same year, was, in effect, a companion—and counterbalance—to the Essential Services Ordinance. Under the War Injuries Ordinance any individual 'gainfully occupied' in war-related industries was entitled to compensation in the case of injury 'caused by the impact on any person or property [by] any enemy aircraft.'[65] Reparation was to be worked out in accordance with the Workers' Compensation Act of 1923, and as such, the risks of war were associated with the occupational risks of employment. In the case of death, compensation would be made to the nearest of kin according to the same payment scheme. The War Injuries (Compensation Insurance) Act of 1943 reinforced the provisions of the earlier ordinance, clarifying that the liability of compensation was to rest on employers, who were subsequently to be reimbursed under the provision of the (mandatory) War Risks Insurance Ordinance.

In the days following the 5 December air raid, both the central and sub-area offices of the P.R.I.S. were swamped with relatives of dock workers who had gone 'missing' during the attack. The agency, however, was only able to satisfy a 'very limited number of enquiries... owing to the large number of unidentified cases.'[66] Applicants missing relatives had come not only to locate the whereabouts of their kin for sentimental reasons, but also to file insurance claims against the deaths of their family members—in extremely hard times. It was the responsibility of the P.R.I.S. to assist 'relatives of persons killed in filling up forms for claims under

[64]Bhattacharya, p. 41.

[65]War Injuries Ordinance, 1941. At: http://bdlaws.gov.bd/print_sections_all.php?id=192 (Last accessed July 8, 2010; 12:32 pm)

[66]WBSA, Home Confidential, file W-30/43, P.R.I.S. Final Report.

the War Injuries Scheme.'[67] However, its Chief Officer informed his superiors, the lack of identification of the majority of corpses had made it 'impossible to enable claims to be filed.'[68] It is likely that this state of affairs saved the capital interests operating in the dock area the inconvenience of having to formally declare that the enumerated dead found on their premises after the raids, were, in fact, 'outsiders.'

The exculpation of the Civil Defense Services from charges of inaction was a much more delicate bureaucratic affair. A memo by one particular Military Police Security Control Officer, forwarded to the Chief of the General Staff, stated in paragraph 7 that, 'during the period between the first bomb and the all clear, Civil Defense Departments were conspicuous by their absence—the entire fire-fighting, first aid and rescue work being done by the fighting services.'[69] This memo created quite a stir. The Chairman of the Port Commissioners, Sir Thomas Elderton—a well connected man and also the A.R.P. Controller for the Port—took sharp issue with the charges made by the military officer. He wrote an indignant memo to the Bengal Secretariat deploring the accusations, and ensuring the Secretary that Civil Defense forces in the Port had acted swiftly and courageously. The Bengal Secretariat, in turn, issued a note to the central Civil Defense Department of the Government of India, 'to record its most profound disapproval of the action of the Military Security Control Officer.'[70] The Additional Secretary to the Government of India assured the Bengal Secretariat that 'suitable steps [would be] taken to impress on the officer concerned the unfortunate repercussions which may result from derogatory comments on the Civil Services.'[71] The officer concerned, however, put it on record that his report had been 'based entirely on personal experience,' and, as such, could not be retracted. In the end, however, the now infamous paragraph 7 of his report was changed to read: 'During the period between the first bomb and the all clear there

[67]Ibid.

[68]Ibid.

[69]Ibid., Memo 21/SCO/80.

[70]Ibid.

[71]Ibid.

was delay in getting the Civil Defence Services into operation in some areas. When they started to function, however, they worked satisfactorily.' E. R. Kitchin of the Bengal Secretariat sent an apology to Sir Thomas for the 'injustices of the M.P.S.C.O.'s comments,' and Elderton sent him back an appreciation for his good work, noting that 'anyhow the man who made the mis-statements is no longer here.'[72]

The question of the removal of bodies by British military personnel—rather than the A.R.P.—was similarly tricky to resolve. The same Military Police Security Control Officer had alleged in his controversial memo that 'not one Indian civilian gave help or dared to touch a casualty,' and that the R.A.F. had done all the removal of bodies themselves. Alone, this allegation may have been dealt with in a similar fashion as the first. However, both the B.N.R. and Port A.R.P. reports had complained of military interference with the removal of bodies, suggesting that their stretchers and ambulances had been commandeered by the military. Of special concern was the B.N.R,'s response to question 15 (i) on the A.R.P.'s 'First Report' form: 'Who did the actual handling and removal of corpses?' The seemingly innocuous answer was initially given: 'R.A.F. and other European Officers volunteered to lift and remove bodies to mortuary in lorry loaded by the R.A.F.'[73] In subsequent days, with the number of 'unidentified' bodies generating public and administrative unease, and reports of military interference with Civil Defense operations causing consternation, the question of corpse removal simmered. Finally, more than two weeks after the bombing, the record was summarily 'clarified.' The A.R.P. Controller for the Railways sent a memo asking the Home Department to 'kindly correct' query 15 (i)—in answer to who had moved corpses—to read: 'Volunteers from among the B.N.R. officials, and Indians, including a Sikh, 2 Brahmins, and Indian Christians of the B.N.R. Sanitary Staff... with the help of a lorry provided by No. 978 Squadron R.A.F..' Nothing remained of the R.A.F. but the lorry, and in the place of their personnel, now sat this somewhat comical 'rainbow coalition' of colonial Indian cooperation.

[72]Ibid.

[73]Ibid., B.N.R. A.R.P. 'First Report.'

Meanwhile, the R.A.F. had accounts to settle of its own. Reports in *The Statesman* and other media outlets that Calcutta had been left wholly unprotected severely disturbed the forces. Leslie Chippett of the R.A.F. remembers the accusation and its aftermath colourfully. Chippett's squadron had just returned to Calcutta from Chittagong, less than 24 hours before the bombing, and 'although far from being prepared [had] struggled to get some [obsolete] Hurricanes into the air.' To no effect.

> Imagine the anger of the squadron from CO to the lowest [rank] when on the following Monday the Calcutta newspaper was very scathing, 'Where was the RAF, do they have the weekend off?' It was decided to show these critics [who] sat at home with their gins that the RAF did exist. On the following weekend a particularly important race meeting was to be held at Calcutta racecourse. Imagine the members chagrin when as the race commenced Hurricanes appeared at naught feet 'beating up' the racecourse. Horses went everywhere and I believe the race was concluded in the slowest time on record. I saw no further criticisms of 67 or any other squadrons. Further to this there is a story about a camera gun, film or lack of it, and discrepancies regarding a 'kill' made in that raid, but I'll leave that for another time.[74]

Imagine, also, the effect on an already traumatized population of such bully hijinx.

In fact, apart from patently specious official assurances printed in newspapers, little was actually done to boost the all-important 'morale' of the Indian population. A concerned business owner in the area posted a letter of protest on 10 January 1944, in which he wrote:

> Over one month has elapsed since the air raid on December 5th, and in the vicinity of our factory on Hide Road [Kidderpore], the only repairs which have been carried out appear to be those undertaken by the Calcutta Electric Supply Co. to their substation... all the small shops and *bustees* still remain exactly as they were a few hours after

[74]Archived at BBC 'People's War,' http://www.bbc.co.uk/ww2peopleswar/stories/06/a4040506.shtml (Last accessed July 8, 2010; 2:29 pm).

> the raid. The ruins of a Key-man shelter which was destroyed in the Port Commissioners' Depot have not been cleared away and is not exactly a good advertisement for Air Raid Precautions. It occurs to us that at very small cost, and bearing in mind that in the War Risks Insurance Fund there is a sum of about 9 crores (900 million) rupees at the moment, all the necessary repairs to shops, buildings and dwelling houses in the area can be fully restored. The effect on morale and the propaganda which would be possible as a result needs no further elaboration.[75]

The Bengal Minister of Commerce, Labour and Industry investigated the situation and found that the War Risks Insurance Fund did not apply. 'Repairs to shops, buildings and dwelling houses damaged by air raids cannot be helped from this fund,' he wrote, 'a scheme for insurance against war damage to immovable property not covered by the [War Risks Insurance Fund] has been considered and rejected.'[76] By the end of the war the War Risks Insurance scheme had collected 4.2 billion rupees through mandated enlistment and had paid out less than 5 million.[77] The Secretary of the Home Department was disappointed. 'The wording of the Metal Box Company's letter may [have been] unsuitable,' he responded, 'but there is something in what they say, viz: that air-raid damage should not be left just as it is indefinitely for all to see... this is not very satisfactory; i.e. a general denial of responsibility all around.'[78]

AIR RAID DAMAGE

The house that my father grew up in, on Mominpore Road, was one of those dwellings that had been damaged in the raid, and was never repaired again. Apart from the cracks in the foundation that had resulted from close proximity to the bomb blasts on the docks, there was also *unseen* damage that seemed to linger on indefinitely. My father carried with him, for the rest of his life, a profound and deep seated terror and anxiety that had been imprinted on him by

[75]Ibid.
[76]Ibid.
[77]Bhattacharya, p. 40.
[78]WBSA, Home Confidential, file W-30/43.

this attack. Our family's connection to the docks and to the air raids themselves had been, to be sure, uncommonly extensive. His father, a retired policeman with dwindling accounts, had property along the docks in the *bustee* settlements of migrant laborers, whom he shook down for rent on most weekends. My father's older brother—who even at this time was more or less the head of the household at 24 years of age—was an A.R.P. warden in Mominpore. Under his jurisdiction the morgue, less than a mile from the house, also fell. The neighbourhood itself was inhabited mostly by underemployed and impoverished labourers associated with the docks and its concomitant factories, warehouses and workshops, and had been swamped after the bombing with terrified dock labourers 'lying up' in its by-lanes and bazaars. Flocks of 'sightseers' had also moved through the area to observe the damage—and had moved back out bearing witness. Nowhere in Calcutta, in fact, could the 'rumors,' panic and trepidation have been more pronounced.

Surely the complex of factors involved must have impacted my father's young mind profoundly. But it was simply, in fact, the actual visceral, terrifying and apocalyptic *sound* and magnitude of the blasts that had shattered his nerves and continued to haunt him throughout his life. He had already lived in midst of the Great Bengal Famine, with bodies pilling up on the streets day by day. And he would live through, after only a very short interval, events that one would imagine would be even more deeply traumatic. But, perhaps because of his age at the time, or perhaps because of his temperament, the impression left on him from bombing of the docks was the deepest and most damaging of all. He never described (and possibly could not have even processed at such an age) the details of the event. In fact, from listening to his stories, I was under the impression that Calcutta had been bombed almost every night—as perhaps he was. He only referred to the bombings as the shattering of windows, the cracking of the foundation, and the repeated ear splitting reports that made him feel that the world itself was coming to an end. It was a story without beginning or end. No time frame or outline of events seemed to punctuate his memories and make them chronological. The bombings, in this sense, were memory without context.

Several accounts that I have heard or read from people who were children in 1943 are similar . Though the bombings of Calcutta have been an almost unnoticed chapter in the modern history of India, or even Bengal, they do seem to hold a particularly prominent place in the memories of the children who lived through them. To give one example, below is the memory of one child at the time:

> I remember as a little girl aged 8 years old living in Calcutta during WW2 in our extended family. *The Japanese bombed the city every night* at that time as it was an important city and capital of the British Raj. At dark the air raid siren used to start and we all had to go into our basement room for safety. We often had to stay for two hours or more until the all clear was sounded. We used to have our dinner early to eat before the air raids. As a little girl I used to always get very frightened during the bombing.[79]

The idea that the bombings took place 'every night,' although Calcutta suffered nothing of the sort, may, indeed, have more to do with 'always being frightened' by the bombings that did occur, than with the frequency of the actual bombings. Undoubtedly there is a whole body of scholarship on the progress of post-traumatic stress in children, but that is beyond the scope of this present analysis. Suffice it to say that every time a city is bombed in recent times, and its citizens are 'shocked and awed' by the impact of weapons far more powerful than those that were in use in 1943, and I reflect that in that city (of perhaps millions) there are a large proportion of children, I think of my father—and also of my mother, who wore a pin in the 1970's, that read: 'war is not healthy for children and other living things.'

[79]'Childhood in Calcutta,' (italics mine) archived at BBC's 'People's War,' at: http://www.bbc.co.uk/ww2peopleswar/stories/34/a2780534.html (Last accessed July 8, 2010; 4:50 pm).

CHAPTER seven

When Mill Sirens Rang Out Danger

The Calcutta Jute Mill Belt in the Second World War

Anna Sailer

Reviewing the Bengal jute industry in 1939, P. S. MacDonald from the Duff group of mills, and then chairman of the Indian Jute Mills' Association (IJMA), was hopeful about the trade situation. After an extended crisis of overproduction throughout the 1930s, a new industrial boom seemed to loom on the horizon, when the Second World War broke out.[1] Jute, in times of peace, was mainly used as a cheap packaging material for trading goods. Now, in times of war, it was also required for sandbags, tents, camouflage material, or for packaging war-machinery. Memories of the First War, which had brought the industry enormous profits, seemed to support these rosy anticipations.[2] This time, the demand promised to outstrip even the earlier growth levels. Orders began to come in from February 1939, when the British Government asked for 200 million sandbags from the mills at the Hoogli. Between September and December 1939, 923 million new orders came in. In

[1]Indian Jute Mills Association (IJMA), Report of the Committee, for the year ending 31 December 1939, Calcutta, 1940, p. 4.

[2]In the course of WWI, the exports of jute products increased by 113 per cent, and the volume of exports nearly doubled from Rs 202,5 million to 402 million per year; Omkar Goswami, 'Collaboration and Conflict; European and Indian Capitalists and the Jute Economy of Bengal', 1919–39, in: *The Indian Economic and Social History Review*, Vol. XIX, No. 2, pp. 141–180.

1939 itself, about 75 per cent of the entire volume of demand in the First War had already been overtaken. By the end of the year the mills faced new record levels of more than one million tons of jute goods, exceeding the previous records, made about 10 years ago.[3]

But unsuspected difficulties lay ahead. Orders for war-related jute goods were highly irregular. After the sudden growth in demand in 1939, demand for sandbags and other materials fell in 1940, and recovered only in 1942. The industry had to struggle with problems of transport, as import- and export-routes got blocked. Mills also had to deal with unusually high labour turnovers, as well as with periods of labour shortage. Managers attributed this to the availability of more attractive employment on Government and military schemes, as well as to workers' fears of the approaching war.[4] Three years after the 'historic' record-demands in 1939, G.M. Garrie, another representative of the Duff-company, contrasted earlier expectations with 1942 and concluded that the latter will rank as the gravest crisis year in the annals of this industry.[5]

In the early years of the Second War, then, the industry was caught between boom and dip, very high demands and a near breakdown of production. Managers and managing agents had to find ways of organizing production to meet urgent orders. At the same time, they had to secure transport routes, and find ways of retaining their workforce. They needed to react quickly to fluctuations in demand in order to provide for a degree of flexibility. Extensive conflicts over regulation of production and hours of work among millowners—a feature of the industry for decades—now seemed an unaffordable luxury. Consequently, the IJMA managed to regulate the hours of work during the war largely without internal disagreement. Earlier, conflicts had aroused fears that managing agencies might leave the Association. In the war years, by contrast, the membership of the IJMA grew to engross nearly all jute mills in India.[6]

[3]IJMA, Report of the Committee, for the year ending 31st December 1939, Calcutta, 1940, p. 65.

[4]Managers' Reports to the Directors, Shamnuggur South Mills, 1943, Dundee University Archives (=DUA), MS 86/V/8/14/3, p. 53.

[5]Managers' Reports to the Directors, Angus Jute Works, 1942, DUA, MS 86/V/8/13/1, p. 1.

[6]Gupta, Bishnupriya, Why did Collusion Fail? The Indian Jute Industry in the Inter-War Years, in: *Business History*, Vol. 47, No. 4, October 2005, pp. 532–552, p. 549.

The IJMA achieved an unprecedented expansion of power, and a centralization of industrial control, production and supplies. Trying to counteract tendencies towards labour-shortage, it decided, for the first time in its history, on the implementation of wage increases for all workers. This included compensation for workers even in idle periods. It began an impressive propaganda campaign to persuade workers to stay in the mills, and instituted food-supply shops in 'coolie lines'. Air-raid precaution schemes were installed in mills throughout Calcutta's industrial hinterland, ringing out warnings and providing personnel for damage control and first aid services.

During the war, then, the Association seemed to acquire the position of an all-powerful cartel. Many scholars see this as a central feature of the industry's development. Others, however, disagree and point out that the managing agencies, assembled in the IJMA, were, for much of the Association's existence, at loggerheads, hindering its efficiency.[7] At the same time, power relations that governed the development of the industry seemed to shift to mill-towns. Subho Basu characterizes this mode of control as a *manager raj*.[8] The power of the IJMA was certainly exaggerated by the first approach, and its critique allows us to consider conflicts and hierarchies within the industry, as well as in different localities, as a crucial aspect of its history. However, it continued the older argument on one essential point: by assuming the formal role of the IJMA to be more or less stable. Shifting contexts and exceptional situations, accordingly, rarely find a place in either view.

I would like to move beyond this and develop my argument along two lines. Industrial fluctuations led to a centralization of industrial action under the IJMA, which effectively did turn into an all-powerful cartel running the industry during the war years. Its powers, however, were not equal to the task of securing mill production during the war. Secondly, I draw on the concept of the *manager raj*, arguing that the IJMA increasingly connected and

[7]De Haan, Arjan, *Unsettled Settlers. Migrant workers and industrial capitalism in Calcutta*, Rotterdam, 2004, pp. 126; Goswami, Omkar, *Industry, Trade, and Peasant Society. The Jute Economy of Eastern India*, 1900–1947, p. 238; Sen, Samita, *Women and Labour in Late Colonial India. The Bengal Jute Mill Industry*, Cambridge, 1999, p. 28.

[8]Basu, Subho, *Does Class Matter? Colonial Capital and Workers' Resistance in Bengal* (1890–1937), Oxford, 2004, p. 74.

centralized local centres of control, thus, acquiring state functions. The *manager raj*, then, turned into a *manager state*, under the leadership of the IJMA. The crisis of production, and the anticipated breakdown of industry were then counteracted by attempts to govern the industry and its local centres from the IJMA offices in Calcutta.

SUPPORTING THE HOME-FRONT ...

Britain's declaration of war in September 1939, acquired imperial dimensions, as the Government of India signed up immediately. This triggered an enthusiastic response among Scottish overseers and managers in the jute belt. In the months that followed the outbreak of hostilities, IJMA members were busy with hectic activities designed to support the 'home-front'. Forms of support ranged from the production of sandbags and other war-related materials, including ammunitions, to the enlisting of overseers, who volunteered to join auxiliary forces, and the introduction of precautionary schemes in Calcutta's industrial hinterland.[9] The mill belt, then, seemed to turn into an extension of the 'home-front' in distant Europe. As early as September 1939, mills expanded their production, overseers packed their bags to leave the area and mill sirens rang out air raid warnings in preparation for possible attacks.

The enthusiasm for a war in Europe, so remote from the Hoogli, entailed a hope that the expatriates could contribute to war-efforts back home. Praising the 'generous and patriotic manner' of managers and overseers, P. S. MacDonald reassured his colleagues that the mills in Calcutta and its surroundings were making efforts, as well as sacrifices, to defend their 'home-front'.[10] This underlined the fact that Scottish managers and overseers were migrants who had come only temporarily to the industrial area around Calcutta, leaving behind families and friends. Extending the home-front to Calcutta, then, implied an attempt to reduce the gap between their two worlds.

[9]IJMA, Report of the Committee, for the year ending 31st December 1939, Calcutta, 1940.

[10]IJMA, Report of the Committee, for the year ending 31st December 1939, Calcutta, 1940, p. 11.

Overseers wanted to leave the jute belt for a higher cause and large numbers left Calcutta as military volunteers. Military culture and traditions were neither new nor uncommon among Scottish employees in jute mills. Through the first decades of the 20th century, managers regularly granted paid leave to overseers who joined the armed forces for short periods. Such practices were also common in times of peace.[11] During this war, however, the number leaving jute mills soon rose considerably, and by 1940 about 24 per cent of the Scottish staff had gone. This was a specific form of labour shortage. The IJMA, therefore, had to stop the established practice of granting leave to their overseers, as it increasingly generated a dangerous fragility in the structures of control in the mills.[12] Some mills began to train Indians as overseers. This was not a long term solution, and mill representatives were optimistic that '[l]ater on, when the war is over, we shall be able to strengthen our organisation again with the best we can get from Dundee or elsewhere'.[13]

War efforts had aspects other than the enthusiasm and hopes of Scottish expatriates. Wartime production was an even more important element, since, as Indivar Kamtekar put it, India turned into a crucial 'supply-base' during the war.[14] Very blatantly defining India's role as a mere supplier of raw materials and finished goods, P. S. MacDonald explained:

> The War has mobilised the economic unity of the British Empire and re-inforced all its material resources. India, in this world upheaval, stands in the favoured position of being a supplier of many important, raw and finished, articles so necessary for the conduct of the War.[15]

[11]Directors' Minutes Books, Champdany Company, 1912–1921, Glasgow University Archives, USG 91/7/1/2/1/2, p. 125.

[12]IJMA, Report of the Committee, for the year ending 31st December 1941, Calcutta, 1942, p. 11.

[13]Letter from P. Thomas to E. Benthal, 22 September 1941, Centre of South Asian Studies (University of Cambridge) (= CSAS), Benthall Papers, Box 14.

[14]Kamtekar, Indivar, A Different War Dance. State and Class in India, 1939–1945, in: *Past & Present*, 2002, pp. 187–221; p. 190.

[15]IJMA, Report of the Committee, for the year ending 31st December 1939, Calcutta, 1940, p. 29.

India's status as a crucial supplier of resources and goods in wartime gave industrialists in the colony a central place in defending their home country: especially if these industries were categorized as, 'key' or 'semi-key' industries, producing essential commodities for the war.

... AND PRODUCING THE GOODS

The Association played a crucial role in regulating production and trade, as well as in mediating orders and deliveries between government authorities and individual mills. The co-ordination of production and trade was particularly important, since with the outbreak of war unprecedentedly large orders had been placed by the imperial administration. A list which was received from various British imperial departments in the first three months of the war gives us a good indication of the magnitude of such demand:

> 712 million sandbags for the U.K.,
> 10 million sandbags for New Zealand, Iraq, South Africa, Aden, Burma and the Indian Arsenals,
> 40 million yards of standard Hessian Cloth, chiefly for the U.K., for camouflage purposes,
> 5 million yards of various kinds of Sacking Cloth, all for India and a considerable quantity of Canvas, Jute Webbing and Jute Twine for the U.K. and India[16]

These orders were received in very quick succession. Considering the scale and speed of production this required, the previous crisis of the industry proved to be of some advantage. Due to a threat of over-production, the mills of the IJMA had been working on a short-time agreement in any case. As recently as August 1939, they had agreed to a restriction of the weekly hours of work from 45 to 40. At the same time, about 20 per cent of their looms had been sealed, further curtailing production. With the sudden rise in demand in September, then, the mills around Calcutta had sufficient capacity to meet new orders, without having to restrict their regular production

[16]IJMA, Report of the Committee, for the year ending 31st December 1939, Calcutta, 1940, p. 10.

of goods. Within the first two months of the war, hours of work were increased to 45, then to 54, and, eventually, to 60 hours per week, and sealed looms started working again.[17] Workers who had been dismissed in August were re-employed, and new workers were hired as well.[18] By the end of the year, the workforce of the jute mill industry had increased by about 2,200 workers since 1938.[19]

The politics of regulating production according to demand and price levels was not in itself new. What *was* new was the absence of serious conflicts over the question of working-hours. The IJMA, thus, was suddenly able to decide on increases and restrictions of working-hours, or the sealing and unsealing of looms in comfort. In the course of the war, however, this efficiency of industrial control, paradoxically, turned into a problem. The cycles of rise and fall in demand for war-related goods, proved to be even more unreliable than 'regular' demands. The working hours of the mills of the IJMA between 1939 and 1943 demonstrated a very high degree of flexibility which characterised the rhythms of work:[20]

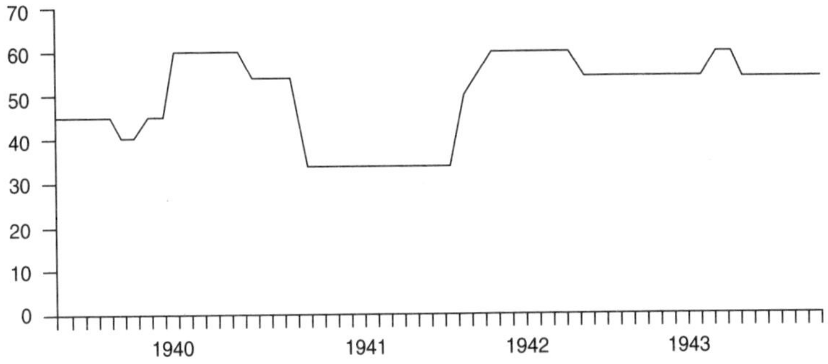

[17]Annual Report of the working of the Indian Factories Act in Bengal and Assam for the year 1939, 1940.

[18]For instance in the Titaghur Jute Mill No. 2, 57 looms were sealed on July 1939, which led to the dismissal of 150 workers, and to the eventual re-employment of workers in September, when looms were unsealed again; Managers' Reports to the Directors, Titaghur No. 2. Mill, 1939, DUA, MS 86/V/8/10/4, p. 50.

[19]Annual Report of the working of the Indian Factories Act in Bengal and Assam for the year 1939, 1940.

[20]Data compiled from: Director's Report to the Shareholders, Titaghur Jute Company Limited. 1939–1943, DUA, MS 86/III/5/5.

Between 1944 and 1945 statistics on the hours of work were not even available any more. Due to a coal shortage, a number of mills were not able to start their engines, and the question of the actual working hours of the IJMA mills was uncertain. The high flexibility of hours throughout the period indicated, on the one hand, that the growth the industry had hoped for was more unstable than it expected. On the other hand, as we will see in more detail later, the unreliable length of working-hours (and, thus, of wages), was one factor that contributed to the high labour-turnovers that became apparent in the years to come.

To return to 1939, however, after increasing working hours and (re-)employing workers, the IJMA reorganized the eventual production of goods. The Association acted, more precisely, as a mediator between governments' demands and mill production. Orders for sandbags and other materials had already been placed with it, instead of with individual mills or managing agencies. After negotiating prices for raw materials and finished goods, the IJMA delegated the orders to its members. In order to enable a 'neutral' share of profits, the size of the delegated orders was determined according to the number of looms installed in mills.[21] In a second step, the IJMA purchased the finished goods from the mills, and organized the transport and export of the bags. In order to fullfill its new functions as a central mediator between government and industry, the IJMA opened an office at the Esplanade in Calcutta, in co-operation with the Government of India. Here, orders by the Indian Government, the British Government, 'Empire Departments', and, 'His Majesty's Allied Governments and, in some cases, Neutral Governments', were recieved and delegated. P. S. MacDonald himself headed the office, in which, further, three controllers and 'a considerable clerical staff' were employed.[22]

Calcutta mills also began producing essential parts for the production of ammunition, such as shell base plates or anti-tank mine contacts. More precisely, engineering workshops, which were

[21]IJMA, Report of the Committee, for the year ending 31st December 1939, Calcutta, 1940, p. 66.

[22]IJMA, Report of the Committee, for the year ending 31st December 1939, Calcutta, 1940, p. 9.

usually attached to jute mills, began producing the parts in co-operation with Government ammunition factories in the area.[23] Their normal purpose in times of peace was the operation, control and repair of machinery, as well as the installation of new machines. For the duration of the war, however, the tasks of mills' workshops increased suddenly. Like the production of jute goods for the war, the production of amunition parts was regulated by the IJMA. In order to co-ordinate orders and deliveries of goods, a new office, the War Munitions Supply Section, was founded. The reports of the IJMA, as well as of managing agents, however, are largely silent about the ways in which the production of amunition parts was organized and controlled. Due to the specific kind of product, according to MacDonald, the IJMA was not allowed to give any further information on the subject. The production of ammunition parts, however, appears to have been a booming activity of the Hoogli mills, and by 1941, the chairman of the association reported proudly that orders for 1 ½ million component parts had been placed with the mills in the course of that year. He added appreciatively that 900.000 of the pieces ordered had already been produced.[24]

The quick introduction and centralization of war-related production in Calcutta, under the leadership of the IJMA, was on the one hand enabled by the structures of control which had already been established, and, on the other hand, by the presence of managing agencies in the city. Managing agents and owners of mills in Bengal, after all, employed representatives in Calcutta, who organised sales and supplies of 'their' mills, intervened in strikes and labour conflicts, and negotiated with local authorities in various matters, if necessary. They were also working in various functions in the IJMA, participating in the Association's different departments and its various meetings. Even the head of the IJMA usually came from this group, and MacDonald, for instance, was the representative of the Duff group of mills. The new structures of

[23]IJMA, Report of the Committee, for the year ending 31 December 1939, Calcutta, 1940, p. 11; Managers' Reports to the Directors, Shamnaggur North Mills, 1942, DUA, MS 86/V/8/13/2, p. 59.

[24]IJMA, Report of the Committee, for the year ending 31 December 1941, Calcutta, 1942, p. 11.

production established in co-operation with various governments, then, deployed forms of economic and industrial power which already existed in Calcutta. So too did the regulation of non-jute products such as ammunition parts. With the outbreak of hostilities in Europe, the IJMA, then, was able to extend the quantity and widen the range of production, coordinating and centralising the jute mills' war contribution in Calcutta.

This new-found efficiency of production, however, could also turn into a threat to the support for the home-front. The volume of jute goods now in production at the Hoogli, in combination with a general increase in production all around, suddenly led to a big rise in the demand for shipping space, which soon caused serious transport problems. The problem was intensified by new Government of India regulations on the export of war-related materials. Mills now needed to apply for permits to export jute goods. Government authorities, however, were not prepared for the large amount of goods waiting for export, as early as the first months of the war. The result was, as the IJMA reported, 'that there was much congestion at the docks, a certain amount of cargo was shut out from the some steamers and some steamers which were ready to sail were held up'.[25] Due to the combination of government regulations and shortages in shipping space, finished jute products, scheduled for shipment in October or November, could not be transported till late December, and deliveries scheduled for December and January had to wait till July 1940. In an attempt to relieve the pressure on transport routes and government authorities, the IJMA agreed to reduce the rate of production of sandbags, so that the mills would not deliver more than 50 million bags per month (irrespective of the urgency of orders).[26]

Restrictions on production eased the problem only for a while. Difficulties in securing sufficient shipping space persisted, while new regulations on trade created ever new difficulties. In an attempt to cope with the situation, the mills of the IJMA began to coordinate the import of supplies (such as new machinery) and the export of

[25]IJMA, Report of the Committee, for the year ending 31 December 1939, Calcutta, 1940, p. 80.

[26]IJMA, Report of the Committee, for the year ending 31 December 1939, Calcutta, 1940, p. 10.

goods on a more general basis, also covering regular production. Trying to ensure a steady supply of goods, the IJMA introduced centralised mill stores in 1941 which stored essential pieces of equipment.[27] Working hours, already flexible due to constantly shifting demands, were further regulated according to the availability of shipping space, while the IJMA tried to co-ordinate their orders with river transport companies.[28]

Even after centralizing production, and installing co-ordinated programmes for the import and export of goods, the situation of the extended 'home-front' around Calcutta continued to deterioriate. With the advances of Japanese troops, shipping of goods became increasingly difficult, and by 1942, shipping routes were fully blocked. The result was increasing pressure on railroad routes transporting goods through Bombay or Karachi. Railroads, however, were heavily utilized by military authorities, and had been so ever since the war approached Indian borders.[29] A shortage in wagons and train-transport, thus, soon affected the industry, leading to a serious crisis. Not only was the export of goods increasingly difficult, but the supply of coal was affected as well. A tendency towards coal shortages had already been visible before the war. This worsened rapidly, and in 1941, the IJMA noted severe difficulties in the procurement of coal.[30] In the second half of the war, the situation saw a massive deterioration, and several mills throughout the jute mill belt were unable to start their engines for large parts of the year. Indicating the scale of the problem, the Angus Jute Mill reported that the mill had lost 2,738 working hours during 1944, and worked only for 1,298 hours.[31] The IJMA's problems did not end there: it was unable even to reduce wage costs commensurately

[27]IJMA, Report of the Committee, for the year ending 31 December 1940, Calcutta, 1942, p. 40.

[28]IJMA, Report of the Committee, for the year ending 31 December 1941, Calcutta, 1942, p. 120.

[29]Warren, Alan, Burma 1942. The Road from Rangoon to Mandaly, London/New York, 2011, p. 202.

[30]IJMA, Report of the Committee, for the year ending 31 December 1941, Calcutta, 1942, p. 108.

[31]Managers' Reports to the Directors, Angus Jute Works, 1945, DUA, MS 86/V/8/16/1.

with this loss of hours. Due to growing fears of labour shortage, the Mill Owners Association had decided that their members should compensate workers for the loss in wages which were caused by the siutation.[32] This is not to say that the loss of working-time was compensated fully, or that real wages were rising. Srimanjari has convincingly argued that the opposite was actually taking place in the wartime jute industry.[33] From the perspective of the industry, however, the payment of even minor amounts as compensation, for periods in which the mills had been shut, marked an entirely new policy departure.

This time, the crisis of supply could no longer be counteracted, as it had been in the past, by an intensified coordination of supplies by the IJMA. Pushing the boundaries of cartelization, the IJMA decided to socialize the losses created for individual mills by coal shortages. In 1944, then, it founded an 'industrial pool', into which each member paid at least 'two annas in respect of each loom hour worked':[34]

> The fund so accumulated by the Pool will be disbursed by payments to mills which through shortage of coal have been unable to work their full quota of hours and the payments will be made under the following heads:
>
> (1) Reimbursement of compensation payments made to workers idle through shortage of coal.
>
> (2) Re-imbursement of loss incurred in the sale of subsidised foodstufs to the above workers.
>
> (3) The purchase of loom hours of mills not working through shortage of coal, which loom hours will thereupon be regarded as cancelled.

The 'industrial pool', then, enabled the sharing of losses, preventing competition among mills over the increasingly rare supplies of coal.

[32]Director's Report to the Shareholders, Angus Jute Works, 1944, DUA, MS 86/IV/5/1(1–4).

[33]Srimanjari, Through War and Famine Bengal, 1939–1945, New Delhi, 2009, p. 88.

[34]Director's Report to the Shareholders, Angus Jute Works, 1944, DUA, MS 86/IV/5/1(1–4).

The pool, in one sense, finalised the economic power of the IJMA, which had turned not just into a coordinating agency for production and trade; but also into a sort of intra-industrial welfare association, which could, at particular moments, create a certain degree of equality among its members.

PROTECTING THE INDUSTRY ...

The activities of the IJMA in supporting the 'home-front' were not restricted to regulating the production of sandbags or of parts for ammunitions. Rather, the assumed status of India as a supplier of materials and goods seemed to imply a second field of support: the protection of, key- or semi-key' industries, which were specific targets of enemy attack. Anxieties that industrial areas, such as the hinterland of Calcutta, might be affected by the war, seem to have prevailed—and not just among managers and mill-owners. Soon after India's entry into the war, government authorities approached the IJMA, suggesting the formation of a 'Special Constabulary Reserve' in the mill areas. Most of the members of the Association supported the idea, and a scheme was worked out. Its objects were:

> to provide a reserve force in the mill areas which, in the present emergency, could on occassion assist the regular police to maintain law and order and prevent sabotage.[35]

This 'reserve force' consisted of mill assistants who had volunteered to participate. The scheme also involved the provision of cars and firearms in the ownership of each member-mill to local authorities throughout the jute mill belt, in case of an emergency.[36] The 'Special Constabulary Reserve', then, provided for man-power and equipment throughout Calcutta's industrial hinterland. Jute mills located in the city, in suburbs, and in mill towns; to the east and the west of the river; near transport lines and nearby fields; served as a dense network covering the entire area. Thus, mills, factories and

[35]IJMA, Report of the Committee, for the year ending 31 December 1939, Calcutta, 1940, p. 77.

[36]Ibid.

workshops in the area stretching across the districts of 24-Parganas, Howrah and Hoogli, were (potentially) protected by the jute mill industry, strongly supplementing the operation of state authorities at a time of military emergency.

The special position of the jute mill industry, however, was not only a result of the large number of mills located all along the river. Crucial in establishing this network was the central organisation of the scheme by the IJMA (by now boasting about 100 constituent mills), which negotiated the requirements of government bodies with those of individual mills. As with the organization of war-related production, then, the IJMA acted as a mediator between government and mills, enabling a centralized defence of the 'home-front'.

Probably due to this unique position of the jute mill industry, government authorities requested the IJMA to install Air Raid Precaution schemes (ARP). These involved the establishment of a system of air-raid warnings, which could cover the entire industrial area around Calcutta; measures for air-raid precautions, such as control of lightning restrictions; as well as arrangements for 'the evacuation of casualties' after potential attacks. Agreeing to participate in the scheme, the IJMA founded a sub-committee for ARP communications. It was connected to the 'Air Raid Precautions Committee for Calcutta and its industrial areas', which colonial authorities had assembled in order to organize the protection of the city and its industries in case of an enemy attack.[37]

In the city's industrial hinterland, several mills acted as 'A.R.P. group-centres', delegating information from the sub-committee of the IJMA to mills in their 'group'. Information also travelled the other way around, and the mills in the 'group-centre' provided the sub-committee with information on the performance of the mills during tests, in order to control (and improve) the efficiency of the scheme.[38] The co-ordination between mills and IJMA, thus, provided for a connection between Calcutta and its industrial areas. In case of a bomb warning being recieved in Calcutta, for instance, the warning could be transmitted via the IJMA to these

[37]IJMA, Report of the Committee, for the year ending 31 December 1939, Calcutta, 1940, p. 78.

[38]Ibid.

'group-centres' in various parts of industrial Calcutta, who would then deliver the warning to other mills in the area. Likewise, if an enemy plane had been sighted in the northern or southern parts of Calcutta's surroundings, the message could travel back along the same lines.

The resulting connection between Calcutta and its industrial hinterland, however, was not the only advantage of the scheme. While the Air Raid Precautions Committee for Calcutta was responsible for the city's industrial surroundings, the municipalities to which these industrial areas belonged had founded ARP committees on their own, in order to organize local warning systems. Competition between different state authorities created significant problems. As the chairman of the IJMA explained, while considering other attempts to organise precaution schemes:

> The lack of centralised direction and control has been keenly felt in most other industries in this work and individual units in industry—especially those placed by Government in one or other of the special categories for A.R.P. purposes—have been subject to instructions from a number of controlling bodies which have been varying in form and confusing in detail and in purpose.[39]

In a bid to avoid these confusions, the IJMA attempted to incorporate different committees into their own ARP scheme. Thus, while working with the ARP committee in Calcutta, the managers' association encouraged its members to co-operate with local committees and participate in them.[40] Due to the 'manager-raj' in jute mill towns, and due to the concomitantly strong presence of mill managers in municipal bodies, a co-operation between different committees, mediated by the IJMA and its members, was established soon and without apparent difficulty. The committee of the Titaghur municipality, for instance, comprised the Sub-Divisional Officer of Barrackpore, the Chairman and Commissioners of the municipality, and the jute mill managers of

[39]IJMA, Report of the Committee, for the year ending 31 December 1941, Calcutta, 1942, p. 53.

[40]Ibid.

all mills in the locality. The Titaghur Mill served as 'group-centre', interacting on behalf of local mills and municipality with the IJMA in Calcutta.[41]

The complex network of mediated control within the jute mill industry, thus, *itself* served as a mediator between different levels of state authority, united in industrial Calcutta. More concretely, the *manager raj* in mill towns and municipalities was co-ordinated by the IJMA, and, thus, provided for the essential structure within which state authorities could function in a co-ordinated and centralized way during the war. Government functions, then, were not only superimposed on to the structures of control within the IJMA, but the Government's authority itself was realized by networks of mediation that were principally based on the jute mill industry. Already having expanded its functions to the regulation of all economic matters within the industry, the IJMA thus also increasingly played a key role in enabling the (necessarily) increased work of government in a time of war.

While the 'Special Constabulary Reserve' seems hardly to have been required during the war, and while mill assistants did not act officially as police men, the ARP scheme played an important role in the course of the war. Already in 1939, the possibility of enemy attacks was, paradoxically, constantly present in industrial Calcutta. While the war was still far away from Calcutta, test warnings rang, and ARP staff and the 'general public' were invited to various training programmes.[42] At the same time, mills began to train European overseers, as well as clerks, sirdars, mistris and durwans as ARP staff. Members of ARP staff were organised in squads, and deployed as air-raid wardens, first aid helpers, or fire fighters, but also for demolition works and for rescuing people after an attack. In courses on first aid or on damage control, conducted mostly within the premises of mills, members of the ARP staff were informed on how to fullfill the concrete tasks they were given in

[41]Managers' Reports to the Directors, Titaghur No. 1 Mill, 1939, DUA, MS 86/V/8/10/4, p. 4.

[42]IJMA, Report of the Committee, for the year ending 31 December 1939, Calcutta, 1940, p. 79.

case of an attack.[43] A number of courses, however, were at the same time offered throughout industrial Calcutta, organized by different authorities. Probably due to the memories of WWI, even seminars were offered at the Police Training School in Calcutta, in order to teach air-raid wardens as well as the general public of how to react in case of gas attacks.[44]

The number of ARP workers in the jute mill belt grew steadily in the following years. Several mills requisitioned not only the services of European overseers, clerks, or durwans as ARP staff, but also began to employ full-time ARP workers.[45] In 1941, after Japan entered the war, the IJMA specified the scheme further, improving workshops and training programmes, and improving the co-ordination between different levels and committees. The chairman of the IJMA, thus, reported proudly that

> I think I shall not be challenged if I say that this Industry has been in the forefront of A.R.P. works; its vital importance was early realised and work completed on a model scheme issued to you at the beginning of 1941. Since then a vast amount of labour has been involved in creating organisations and undertaking important protective measures.[46]

The impression of an imminent attack, threatening the jute mill belt in 1939, was increased by a series of test warnings. Jute mills, participating in these tests, used their mill sirens, deploying the sounds usually given off in case of a fire alarm, in order to give a 'warning', and, subsequently, an 'all-clear' signal. These first tests were not too successful. In some mills, the sirens did not sound as arranged; in other cases, the signal did not carry far enough. Another

[43]Managers' Reports to the Directors, Victoria Jute Company Limited, 1939, DUA, MS 86/V/8/10/6, p. 5; Managers' Reports to the Directors, Victoria Jute Company Limited, 1940, DUA, MS 86/V/8/10/6 p. 3; see also: Srimanjari, Through War and Famine Bengal, 1939–1945, New Delhi, 2009, p. 48.

[44]IJMA, Report of the Committee, for the year ending 31 December 1939, Calcutta, 1940, p. 79.

[45]Minutes of a Partners' Meeting held on Monday, 12 March 1942, CSAS, Benthall Papers, Box 15.

[46]IJMA, Report of the Committee, for the year ending 31 December 1941, Calcutta, 1942, p. 14.

problem occurred in electrically driven mills, which were not able to raise a sudden alarm on weekends or on holidays, when their engines were shut.[47] Essential questions concerning the actions during an actual air raid warning were, at the same time, still uncertain. For instance, if mills should allow their workers to leave the mills during an actual alert, or if they should keep their gates shut. It was only in November 1940, that it was decided 'if an air attack was imminent, engines should be closed down and workers allowed to evacuate themselves'.[48] It was also unclear if the mills' sirens could be used for summoning workers or for indicating the end of the working day, when an actual air raid warning had been issued. This step would have prevented confusion between the every-day signals of the mills, and the warning sounds. Managers, however, feared, that a silencing of these signals could lead to 'bad time keeping' among workers, and, therefore, to a loss in working time.[49] With the approach of Japanese troops in 1941, however, managers had to accept that, in case of an actual warning, mills would have to stop the every-day sounds of their mills for the time being.

The IJMA's new functions—connecting and mediating between various bodies of state control, and, at the same time, running protection schemes, then—developed pre-emptively. The Association's growth in political power was not so much a result of an actual crisis, in contrast to its gradually increasing power over industrial pursuits. Its new role was rather the effect of an anticipated conflict. In both fields, the economic and the political, the Mill-owners' Association acquired new functions within a few months, building on existing networks of control in the industry, as well as in mill-towns.

... AND PERSUADING WORKERS TO STAY IN THE MILL

Another set of problems, which became apparent (in managers' accounts) in the course of the first air-raid trials, were the reactions

[47]IJMA, Report of the Committee, for the year ending 31 December 1939, Calcutta, 1940, p. 78.

[48]Managers' Reports to the Directors, Shamnuggur South Mills, 1940, DUA, MS 86/V/8/10/6, p. 3.

[49]Ibid.

of workers. While managers tried to keep workers in the mills during test-warnings, workers tended to flee mills and mill towns. Managers interpreted this as signs of panic and fear, which were spreading among them. Thus, in the aftermath of the first tests, several mills could not start their engines, or at least only work parts of their looms. Reporting on incidents surrounding the test trials in the Titaghur Jute Mills, a representative of the mill wrote:

> We regret to report that these Mills [Titaghur Nos. 1&2] were closed during the morning shift on Thursday, 28th ultimo, solely as a result of the first A.R.P. 'try-out' in Calcutta and the surrounding industrial areas which took place between 11 and 11.15 A.M. During the past week or so, Titaghur district has been full of ominous rumours and labour generally has been very unsettled. Large numbers of workers left the district, while many others simply disappeared into the jungle through sheer fear, and actually all the female workers left our coolie lines during Wednesday night and Thursday morning. At the 6 A.M. start we had overhead only a small percentage of total complement at each Mill with practically no women, so it was impossible to start. In the afternoon a fair start was obtained at 1:30 and by 3 P.M. we were running to full complement again. Khardah Mill was also closed during the morning shift, while the other mills in this district, although also affected, were able to run part of their establishment.[50]

Trying to understand the reasons, representatives of the Bird Company concluded that Indian workers were generally afraid of the 'unknown', and, therefore, panicked in reaction to the unfamiliar war situation.[51] Most reports, however, pointed to 'false rumours' instead, which appeared as the principal reason for the flight of workers in Titaghur.[52] These, according to this assumption, created a false picture of the test trials as well as of the war situation, and

[50]Private official letter from Calcutta to Dundee, DUA, MS 86/V/7/6, 3.10.1940.

[51]Letter from P. Thomas to E. Benthal, 6 January 1942, CSAS, Benthall Papers, Box 15.

[52]Managers' Reports to the Directors, Victoria Jute Company Limited, 1940, DUA, MS 86/V/8/11/6/Managers' Reports to the Directors, Titaghur No. 1 Mill, 1941, DUA, MS 86/V/8/12/4, p. 70; IJMA, Report of the Committee, for the year ending 31 December 1939, Calcutta, 1940, p. 79.

the 'illiterate' workers believed these rumours easily, thus getting scared and fleeing the mill areas.[53] The IJMA tried to counteract 'false rumours', by pushing the mills in their membership to 'explain the experiment to their workers', and to 'issue general instructions as to the action which would require to be taken by mill labour in the event of a genuine warning being received'.[54] If workers were better informed of the tests and their purpose, so the hope went, then their anxieties might be relieved.

In considering workers' reactions and managers' interpretations, a striking ambiguity appears in the relationship between rumours and the role of information. While the battles in Europe were still far away in 1939, and while Japan had not even entered the war as yet, the circulation of rumours in workers' neighbourhoods apparently created the impression that enemy attacks were imminent. Managers, however, were unusually vague about the source of these rumours. The usual suspects—'outsiders', 'agitators' or 'mischief-mongers'—were never blamed, and it seemed unclear how these rumours had come up in the first place. Considering, however, the vast amount of information circulating through mills and neighbourhoods in the form of notices, or training programmes for sirdars, clerks, durwans, mistries, etc., it seems quite likely that these cautionary measures were themselves a source of rumours. The sudden and hectic activities of mill authorities, who were, after all, trying to protect the jute mill belt, hardly suggested that the possibility of enemy attacks reaching Calcutta in September 1939, was unlikely. A new notice posted by managers would, in this situation, barely have made a difference, and perhaps even made things worse. Rumours and information did not contradict so much as support each other. With the necessarily active involvement of large parts of the workforce in the schemes of mill protection, managers had, in a way, lost control over the 'information' which could leave the mill: so it became a 'rumour' in the bazaar.

[53]Managers' Reports to the Directors, Titaghur No. 1 Mill, 1941, DUA, MS 86/V/8/12/4, p. 70.

[54]IJMA, Report of the Committee, for the year ending 31 December 1939, Calcutta, 1940, p. 78.

Workers' responses to the precuations against enemy attacks, however, did not only result in 'temporary labour shortages', as managers and mill-owners put it, but also raised concerns among industrialists over increasing labour conflicts. In a way, then, workers' fears caused managers to panic. After the general strike in 1937, the number of labour conflicts in the jute mill industry had been comparatively high. Among the 36 strikes, counted in 1938, there had been serious mobilizations for another general strike, and in 1939, 25 strikes were counted, some of which were among the most militant in the history of the industry.[55] Demands included wage increases or the re-instatement of dismissed workers.[56] Another source of conflict was the recent introduction of employment bureaus under the guidance of the IJMA. They were established to regulate the employment of regular and daily workers, and were designed to reduce the authority of sirdars and clerks in the every-day working of the mill. Regular workers were registered, photographed, and in some cases even fingerprinted. Further, daily workers were recorded in a separate register, and categorized according to the amount of time they had worked on a daily basis in the mills.[57] For a few years after their introduction, these surveillance measures, and the attempt to abolish the sirdar system of intermediation, provoked resistance. With the onset of war, however, staff shortages rendered the new system temporarily unworkable in some mills.[58]

In this situation of general unrest and of change, fears among workers triggered by the air-raid trials, appeared to threaten the fragile peace between workers and employers even more. It was from this perspective that a representative of the Bird company explained:

[55]Managers' Reports to the Directors, Shamnaggur North Mill, 1938, DUA, MS 86/V/8/08/2/Managers' Reports to the Directors, Shamnaggur North Mill, 1939, DUA, MS 86/V/8/09/2; IJMA, Report of the Committee, for the year ending 31 December 1938, Calcutta, 1939; IJMA, Report of the Committee, for the year ending 31st December 1939, Calcutta, 1940; S.W. 630 1938—Jute Workers, 24-Parganas

[56]Ibid.

[57]Managers' Reports to the Directors, Shamnaggur North Mill, 1939, DUA, MS 86/V/8/10/3/Bengal Chatkal Mazdor Union, 1938, Special Branch of the Police, Calcutta: SW/630–1938.

[58]Managers' Reports to the Directors, Shamnuggur North Mill, 1941, DUA, MS 86/V/12/2

'Labour generally is our main uncertainty'.[59] Managers, thus, feared that 'agitators' might seize their chance to 'exploit' workers' anxieties over the war situation, in order to launch a new series of strikes.[60] The production of goods for profit and for the 'home-front' seemed at risk, due to anticipated labour conflicts. For managers and managing agencies, this was, in a way, a new situation. In the 1930s, when overproduction was a constant tendency, and when mills worked reduced hours, the time lost due to strikes could usually be made up, or the production of goods could often be delegated to another mill in the group of a managing agency. During this war, however, when the hours of work were already highly irregular, being co-ordinated with shifting demands and changing transport possibilities, strikes could suddenly lead to a loss of working time. Reactions of workers also highlighted a sudden shift in the balance in industrial relations, going alongside India's imputed role as a supplier of goods: in contrast to the 1930s, when labour had generally been in excess of demand, managers now needed their workers to stay in the mill and to work their full hours.

Yet another source of concern was the overall employment situation in Bengal which now seemed to offer plenty of other job opportunities. Between 1939 and 1940, the inspector of factories for Bengal and Assam registered an increase of 30,000 new workers in the province.[61] At the same time, managers noted an increasing shortage of 'badli' workers, who were employed in jute mills on an irregular and daily basis.[62] But among skilled workers, too, they noted a growing shortage. Trying to understand the problem, they pointed in particular to government factories, which not only paid higher wages, but also offered more regular employment than what

[59]Letter from P. Thomas to E. Benthal, 6 January 1942, Centre of South Asian Studies, CSAS, Benthall Papers, Box 15.

[60]IJMA, Report of the Committee, for the year ending 31 December 1939, Calcutta, 1940, p. 17.

[61]Annual Report of the working of the Indian Factories Act in Bengal and Assam, 1939 + Annual Report of the working of the Indian Factories Act in Bengal and Assam, 1940.

[62]Managers' Reports to the Directors, Titaghur No. 1 Mill, 1941, DUA, MS 86/V/8/12/4, p. 70.

workers could find in the jute mills with their constant changes in working-hours.[63] In the course of the war, military camps were set up in Calcutta and in its industrial hinterland, increasing the number of jobs offered. Here, the wages were not only higher than in jute mills, but conditions of work were also said to be better. Trying to prevent an intensified crisis of labour supply, the IJMA started negotiations with the Government of India and with military authorities, in order to restrict wages in government factories and in military camps. While the responsible authorities seemed to be willing to establish a maximum wage, such attempts were not too successful.[64]

Another, and eventually more important, field of activity was the regulation of wages in the jute mill industry. In September 1939, when the mills of the IJMA increased their hours of work, the Association also decided on wage-increases of 10 per cent, to be implemented in all its member mills. At the same time, a war-allowance was decided on, which workers received along with their regular wages.[65] The new policy of the IJMA, however, included more than only wage-increases. Trying to reduce the impact of the industry's flexibility in production and working-rhythms, the IJMA also instituted a food-allowance for periods in which workers had not actually worked. This was to be paid even when mills were shut due to transport problems, air-raid warnings, or other difficulties.[66] Trying, further, to bind 'badli' workers to the mills, an allowance was introduced which workers, who had registered themselves as 'badli', received for every week they appeared at the mill without having been employed. The IJMA thus introduced a form of unemployment-insurance for their workers. These practices, however, as managers pointed out, were based on extraordinary

[63]Report on an Enquiry into the conditions of Labour in the Jute Mill Industry in India, Labour Investigation Committee/Government of India, Calcutta, 1946, p. 6.

[64]Ibid.

[65]IJMA, Report of the Committee, for the year ending 31 December 1939, Calcutta, 1940, p. 18.

[66]Managers' Reports to the Directors, Angus Jute Works, 1940, DUA, MS 86/V/8/11/1, p. 45.

war-payments, and were not supposed to turn into a regular feature of the industry.[67]

The regulation of wages and other payments, however, did not seem enough to counteract workers' fears. One important reason here was certainly that wage-increases implemented by the IJMA could not make up for the rising costs of living.[68] From the perspective of managers, however, who claimed that workers earned more than ever, the problem, rather, was based in workers' fears, which had been triggered by the hectic air-raid trials. This seemed to increase when Japan entered the war. Requests for long leave reached record levels in the following months, proving the problems of a shortage of 'badli' workers even more forcefully.[69] Trying to counteract the flow of 'false information' outside the mills, the IJMA started an unprecedented propaganda campaign, in order to bring information of the war situation to their workers and to neighbourhoods. One part of this campaign was constituted by a series of pamphlets. In 1940, mills began to distribute a weekly paper called *Indian News Letter*, which explained 'the international situation in Europe'.[70] The paper was printed in English, and was handed out to 'influential workers', such as sirdars or clerks, 'who in turn explain the situation to the illiterate workers'.[71] Another paper, called *Talking Points*, was distributed in a similar way.[72] In an attempt not to rely solely on mediators, however, the IJMA also distribtued a monthly pamphlet for workers, called *War in Pictures*. This tried to explain the 'international situation' mainly through illustrations. It also

[67]Award In the matter of Industrial Disputes in the Jute Textile Industry in West Bengal between the employers of 89 specified jute mills and their workmen, Calcutta, 1948, p. 40.

[68]Srimanjari, Through War and Famine Bengal, 1939–1945, New Delhi, 2009, p. 88, p. 91.

[69]Managers' Reports to the Directors, Titaghur No. 1 Mill, 1942, DUA, MS 86/V/8/13/4, p. 45.

[70]Managers' Reports to the Directors, Titaghur No. 1 Mill, 1940, DUA, MS 86/V/8/11/4, p. 61.

[71]Ibid.

[72]Managers' Reports to the Directors, Titaghur No. 1 Mill, 1941, DUA, MS 86/V/8/12/4, p. 70.

contained written explanations in Hindi, Urdu, Bengali, and Telugu. In contrast to the two English publications, managers reported regularly that workers appreciated the *War in Pictures*, which was handed out to them with their wages.[73]

A second part of the propaganda campaign was the broadcasting of news and radio programmes in coolie lines. In 1940, a number of mills installed wireless-sets, with the support of the IJMA, in order to test this method of propaganda. Through these sets, war news in Hindi and Bengali was broadcast from Indian radio stations each evening, as well as musical programmes in Hindi or Bengali which were broadcast at irregular intervals. This new method, combining propaganda and entertainment, seems to have been received positively by workers as well. Even managers showed some excitement in their reports, not least because the 'microphone has been very useful in announcing instructions' concerning ARP precautions.[74]

Film screenings constituted the third part of the mill-owners' propaganda campaign. The IJMA, in co-operation with the Tea Cess Committee sponsored travelling cinema units, in order to deliver, at random intervals, a screen and machine to mills, for film perfomances. This seems to have impressed workers and managers alike. The manager of the Angus Jute Mill reported in 1941 that the shows 'were greatly appreciated by the workers and they were very impressed by the naval pictures in particular'.[75] His own appreciation of the film unit was also born out of the possibilities which this form of propaganda seemed to bear. Similar to the wire-sets (with microphone), the screenings could, after all, be used for informing workers about other topics as well:

> It is thought that this is a vehicle that could be used to 'put over' oblique propaganda such as Safety Films, films dealing with the

[73]Managers' Reports to the Directors, Victoria Jute Company Limited, 1941, DUA, MS 86/V/8/12/6, p. 70.

[74]Managers' Reports to the Directors, Titaghur No. 2 Mill, 1941, DUA, MS 86/V/8/12/5, p. 49.

[75]Managers' Reports to the Directors, Angus Jute Works, 1941, DUA, MS 86/V/8/12/1, p. 67.

> right and wrong methods of using stores, contrasts of conditions in other industries with our own, general educational films etc.[76]

One aim of the mills' manager, when repeatedly describing the many advantages of film screenings, was to persuade his managing agents to purchase a cinema unit for the Angus Mills.[77] This, however, did not happen, and the travelling unit of the IJMA does not seem to have circulated in the jute mill belt after the end of hostilities either.

Neither propaganda measures, nor wage increases, however, were enough to keep workers in the mills, when bombs actually did fall on Calcutta's industrial suburbs. In December 1942, Japanese planes dropped bombs in the Kidderpore Docks nearby Budge Budge, and in the north of Calcutta, hitting, among others, the Victoria Jute Mill and the nearby bazaar. After the first attack on nearby Budge Budge, the manager of the Shamnaggur North Mill reported:

> Labour was quite calm and contented until the third week of December when enemy Air Raids occurred at Budge Budge and Kidderpore Docks which caused the coolies from Kidderpore Docks to evacuate and for days and nights the crowds of evacuees treking up the Grand Tank Road on foot and in all sorts of conveyance was constant. This had a bad effect on the morale of the mill labour close to this throughfare as these evacuees, to justify their clearing out, told very exaggerated tales of what happened, causing local labour to be very fidgety.[78]

Managers tried, in the following days, to put pressure on local authorities to prevent the 'trek of coolies' from the south of Calcutta to walk along the Grand Trank Road passing their mills. Local authorities, however, saw themselves unable to intervene, or to change the route of evacuation, as the fleeing workers had not broken any laws.[79]

[76]Ibid.

[77]Managers' Reports to the Directors, Angus Jute Works, 1944, DUA, MS 86/V/8/15/1, p. 71.

[78]Managers' Reports to the Directors, Shamnuggur North Mill, 1942, DUA, MS 86/V/8/13/2, p. 58.

[79]Managers' Reports to the Directors, Angus Jute Works, 1942, DUA, MS 86/V/8/13/1, p. 72.

Given the anxieties of managers and mills' agents, these scenes must have appeared like a nightmare come true. Making matters worse, shop-keepers began to join the flight.[80] In contrast to earlier incidents of 'panic' among jute workers, the danger of attack was this time very real, and seemed to unsettle local structures of control throughout industrial Calcutta. The situation, however, got even worse, when Japanese planes raided the area again on Christmas eve:

> This caused quite a panic in the industrial area and a large proportion of the labour left the district. The fact that Victoria No. 1 Mill recieved a bomb through the roof into the Winding [department] while several other bombs did damage the Telinipara Bazaar had a very bad effect on the mill employees especially the imported labour. The up-country Hindus and Mohammedans and also the Ooriyas cleared out leaving so few that the mill could not be started up for some time owing to labour shortage and to others who were left being unwilling, through fear, to come to the mill lines from the jungle where many of them took shelter on the night of 24th December after the bombing took place.[81]

One result of the flight of workers was that more than 13 per cent of the industry was unable to work in subsequent days. A number of mills could, further, only work parts of their machines in the following weeks. Managers, by now in a panic themselves, tried to persuade workers to come back to the mill, and even began to write post cards to former workers.[82] It took till February to restore all the looms to work. But even then, work proceeded only with certain restrictions, as workers tended to refuse to work in double-shifts for the next couple of months, as this would require them to stay in the mill at night.[83]

While workers thus came back to the mills gradually, joined by new workers as well, the flight of shop-keepers in the aftermath of the bomb-raids posed a new set of problems, since food-supplies

[80]Managers' Reports to the Directors, Shamnuggur North Mill, 1942, DUA, MS 86/V/8/13/2, p. 59.

[81]Ibid.

[82]Managers' Reports to the Directors, Angus Jute Works, 1942, DUA, MS 86/V/8/13/1, p. 74.

[83]Managers' Reports to the Directors, Shamnuggur North Mill, 1942, DUA, MS 86/V/8/13/2, p. 2.

were hard to obtain. A petition of clerks working for the mills of the Bird Company illustrated the problem. In order to secure their own food-supplies, they requested a month's salary in advance, to stock up before a new attack hit the area.[84] The problem was not only the partial break-down of the network of food-suppliers, but, may be even more so, the possibility that this collapse might become absolute, if more bombs were to fall.

While the agents of the Bird Company refused to consider the petition, mill-owners took the request seriously. The company had been among the first ones to install food stores in some of their mills, in order to provide to workers at cheaper rates. Making use of these shops, in order to meet the growing difficulties in obtaining food-supplies, the agency's representative in Calcutta reported:

> Stocks of food in excess of present requirements are being bought and are being stored at Kinnison [Jute Mill, Titaghur municipality]. It is hoped that in a week or ten days we shall have sufficient to supply the normal requriements of the welfare shops for six weeks, although this of course does not mean that the full requirements of our labour force can be satisfied for that period. [...] There is no doubt that the feeding of labour generally during air raids is of the greatest importance, and it is hoped that the I.J.M.A. will make some centralised arrangement to supplement the arrangement which we have already been able to make.[85]

The advantages of storing food in the mills of the Bird company were quite clear. Not only could workers be provided with food, even in case of a further deterioration of transport and supplies, but the mills of the group would have been one of the few centres in the area where food could be received (or earned) easily.

The system, however, did not cover all the mills, even under the Bird Company. The Auckland Jute Mills in Jagatdal, for instance, were not among those who had recieved a food-shop. Here, however, food was exceptionally scarce. The situation was no better in the nearby Northbrook Jute Mills. In both mills, consequently, more

[84]Minutes of a Partners' Meeting held on Monday, 21 March 1942, CSAS, Benthall Papers, Box 15.

[85]Ibid.

weavers 'than could be accommodated have asked for long leave', trying to get away from the mill. Another result was that workers began to demand higher wages, in order to sustain themselves in the mill areas.[86] The hopes that the IJMA should support the 'arrangement' of food supplies, then, were well founded, at least from the perspective of managers, not least because this seemed the only way to prevent higher wages.

In the following months, the IJMA indeed started to extend the system of food-stores, which a number of mills had installed, and introduced a scheme of food-rationing throughout the mill belt. The IJMA requested all its members to start their own food-supply shop, where 'Rice, Dal, Atta, Mustard Oil, Sugar and Salt, were [to be] sold to the workers at prices under cost'.[87] The Mill Owners Association also installed a scheme for the delivery of food-supplies to the mills, with the help of the Bengal Chamber of Commerce. The actual supplies in the mills, were, however, organized by managers in the localities.[88] In 1943, when government shops opened up, supplying rationed food, the IJMA's system of food-supply was incorporated into the government scheme. Mill shops were registered as employers' shops, and 'became responsible for supplying the workers and their dependants'.[89] The delivery of supplies to the mill, however, was still organised by the IJMA and the Bengal Chamber of Commerce. One of the effects of the difference in channels of distribution was a considerable difference in the quality of food supplies, and managers complained that the food in government shops was better than in mill shops.[90]

Managerial fears that a break-down of production was pending if workers panicked, then, constituted a third dimension of the manager state. Triggered by workers' reactions, the IJMA regulated wages, introduced 'unemployment insurance', and launched

[86]Ibid.

[87]Managers' Reports to the Directors, Angus Jute Works, 1942, DUA, MS 86/V/8/13/1, p. 2.

[88]Ibid.

[89]Managers' Reports to the Directors, Titaghur No. 1 Mill, 1944, DUA, MS 86/V/8/15/4, p. 15.

[90]Managers' Reports to the Directors, Angus Jute Works, 1942, DUA, MS 86/V/8/15/1, p. 93.

extensive propaganda campaigns. The possibility of deepening crises after the bomb raids of 1942, as well as the already crippling food shortages, on the other hand, were a central incentive for the IJMA to install a food-rationing scheme. This scheme not only pre-empted the system of government shops, but, at the same time, perhaps laid the basis for the government food shops that were established in jute mills from 1943, as famine took hold of Calcutta, and Bengal.

CONCLUSION

In this paper I have traced the emergence of the IJMA as a *manager state* in the course of the war. This process was, on the one hand, based on the possibility of increased production and the protection of the 'home-front'. At the same time, however, the anticipation of a crisis of production, due to potential labour conflicts as well as to enemy attacks, was an important element in this process. The sudden increase in the Association's powers, then, was based on its capacity to regulate production and protect the mill belt; but, at the same time, it was also based on the crisis of transport and labour, which neither the cartel nor the manager-raj could tackle on their own. The manager state, then, was *just as much a result of the weakness of the IJMA, as it was a result of its strength*. While the Association had already developed means of regulating production, it suddenly had to invent ways to secure the possibility of production. A combination of centralisation, compensation-payments and propaganda was the result, which crucially shaped industrial relations during the course of the war.

At the end of WWII, then, the jute mill belt appeared like an entirely new area to managers. When talking about the end of the war at the annual conference of the IJMA, the head of the Association began by ironically giving voice to his colleagues' hopes that the industry could now, finally, return to the 'good old days'. The burden of the war, and the looming shadow of Indian independence, however, made this impossible. Thus, in the course of his speech, he also bore witness to the destruction of these hopes, as he concluded that such a 'return' was no longer an option.[91]

[91]IJMA, Report of the Committee, for the year ending 31 December 1945, Calcutta, 1946, p. 3.

CHAPTER eight

Protest and Politics
Story of Calcutta Tram Workers 1940–1947

Siddhartha Guha Ray

As a left-wing Bengali journal wrote in 1967, trams and tramwaymen have long occupied an important position in the public and political life of Calcutta since numerous political struggles have made them highly visible. 'Hence, whenever a political movement takes place in the city, the Calcuttans look forward to the tramwaymen, for their possible role in the event.'[1]

In fact, Calcutta tram workers had to travel a long way to place themselves in such an enviable position among the Calcutta working class. They not only fought for their own daily needs and wages but also got involved in broader political movements. The Calcutta tramways, being a public utility, were a major focus of public concern. As the Calcutta Tramways Company was a British Company registered in London, the people of Calcutta saw its workers' movement not as an isolated case of employees' agitation against the management, but as a conflict between the black servants and their white masters as well as a united struggle of the Indians against British imperialism. The first union of the Calcutta tramwaymen, the Calcutta Tramways Employees Union (CTEU), was formed in October 1920, in the wake of a spontaneous strike.[2] In 1927, the

[1]Bimal Mitra: 'Tram Companyr Naebi', *Kalpurush*, 9, 1967: 94. [Translation mine]

[2]Confidential Report on the Political Situation of Bengal for the First Half of October 1920, File No. 17/20. Home Department (Political Branch), Government of India, National Archives of India, (Henceforth, NAI).

CTEU was reorganized under a new name, the Calcutta Tramways Workers' Union (CTWU).[3] Bhupendra Nath Dutta, an early Marxist intellectual from Bengal was its founder president and Phanindra Kumar Sanyal was elected as secretary of the new organization.[4] The replacement of the term 'employees' with 'workers' and the names of the office bearers suggest the influence of the Communists in the reoriented organisation. In the same year the CTWU was affiliated to the All India Trade Union Congress (AITUC).

The reorganized CTWU wore a new look under the leadership of experienced organisers. The 1940s initiated an era of glorious struggles.[5] The present paper tries to locate the history of the tram workers in that decade. It also makes an attempt to discern how the Calcutta tramwaymen became an integral part of the political and social life of the city.

With the outbreak of the Second World War in September 1939, the Government of India, using the pretext of war, clamped down the Defence of India Rules. Civil liberties were suppressed and it was declared that any kind of working class protest would be dealt with stern punitive measures.

The changed political situation raised certain new questions before the working class. To make the workers aware of the new situation, the Communist Party of India (CPI) chalked out a programme to impart political education to the workers of different sectors. The tram workers of Calcutta played a leading role in implementing the programme. They started attending the Party classes from September 1939. At that time the CPI was a banned organisation. The classes were held generally at the underground office of the CPI at Kalighat near the Bashushree cinema hall, in Rajabazar, Park Circus and Belgachhia tram depots as well as in the Nonapukur Workshop of the Calcutta Tramways Company. Important CPI leaders like Naren Sen, Gopal Acharya, Sudhanshu Das Gupta and Saroj Mukherjee

[3]List of Labour Unions upto 1929 preserved by the Special Branch of Calcutta Police at Lord Sinha Road, West Bengal State Archives (Henceforth, WBSA).

[4]Ibid. See also *Royal Commission of Labour in India*, (Evidence), Vol. V, Part II (London, 1930), 61–62.

[5]For details see Siddhartha Guha Ray, *Calcutta Tramwaymen: A Study of Working Class History 1920–1967* (Kolkata: Progressive Publishers, 2007).

were entrusted with the task of acquainting the workers with the new political situation arising out of the war. The rank and file apart, politically more advanced workers of the Calcutta Tramways like Md. Zahir, Ket Narain Misir, Chatur Ali and Dhiren Majumdar used to attend these political classes.[6] The workers condemned the Second World War as an imperialist war. Bombay workers, led by the Communist Party, organized a tool down strike on 20 October 1939, which was incidentally the 'first anti-war strike in the world labour movement'.[7] The Calcutta tram workers accorded whole-hearted support to the strikers.

As the CTWU gradually emerged as a significant anti-imperialist force to reckon with, the government began to unleash terror and repression by using the Defence of India Rules. The early months of 1940, witnessed countrywide arrests of the Indian Communists. In June 1940, two important leaders of the CTWU, Md. Ismail and Gopal Acharya, were imprisoned and Somenath Lahiri, another important organiser of the CTWU was forced to go underground.[8] Despite such repressive measures, the Communist Party remained undaunted. In a leaflet entitled, *The Call of the Communist Party to the Transport Workers*, issued to the workers of rail, dock, tram and steamer, in 1940, the Calcutta District Committee of the CPI branded the war as an 'imperialist war—the war between the merchants'. Being 'the backbone of the British rule in the country', the transport workers—the leaflet suggested—could bring this 'imperialist war to a standstill and help the country in the fight for freedom more than others'.[9]

However, such a characterisation of the war did not last long. A significant international development brought about a change in the Communist stand. On 22 June 1941, Hitler's Nazi forces invaded the Soviet Union. R.P. Dutt wrote:

> The interest of the people in India and Ireland and of all the colonial peoples, as of all the peoples of the world, is bound up with the

[6]Saroj Mukhopadhyay, *Bharater Communist Party O' Amra*, Vol. 1 (Kolkata, 1985), 171.

[7]R.P. Dutt: *India Today* (Calcutta, 1979), 430.

[8]Author's interview with Gopal Acharya on 20 July 1982.

[9]Home Department (Political), Government of India, File No. 37/1/1940 (NAI).

> victory of the peoples against Fascism; that interest is absolute and unconditional, and does not depend on any measures their rulers may promise or concede.[10]

By November 1941, the imprisoned and underground members of the CPI began to rethink their strategy. In mid-December it was recognized that the imperialist war had become a 'People's War' with the Nazi attack on the Soviet Union. As the Soviet Union joined the war in support of the Allies, the CPI leadership advised its members and supporters to give 'unconditional' support to the British. Consequently the ban on the CPI was lifted and Communists were released from jail. Henceforth, the CPI worked conscientiously to encourage the workers and peasants to 'promote production'.[11]

STRIKES OF THE CALCUTTA TRAM WORKERS

The change in the Communist stand, however, did not bring about any change in the plight of the tram workers of Calcutta. The war led to a steep rise in the prices of essential commodities without a corresponding rise in the wages of the toiling poor. In Bengal, the cost of living had gone up by 200 per cent during this period, as compared to pre-war times. Apart from this general rise in prices, the Calcutta tram workers were confronted with severe problems in their living and working conditions. Latrines in the depots were dirty and arrangements for drinking water appeared inadequate. Conductors had to wait for about two hours or more after their regular duty hours were over, in order to deposit the day's collection and settle the accounts.[12]

Yet another new development began to haunt them. Japan's entry into the Second World War in the second half of 1941, seriously affected Indian workers employed in Burma. With the fall of Rangoon on 7 March 1942, Japanese forces reached very close to the Indian frontier. Before that, Indian workers in Burma

[10] *Labour Monthly*, September 1941.

[11] A Note from the Jail Comrades (Popularly known as the Jail Document—Home Department (Political), Government of India, File No. 44/32/1942 (NAI).

[12] *Rege Committee Report on Labour Investigation*, Delhi, 1946, 271.

leaving Rangoon walked through hills and forests and crossed rivers to reach India. They did not get their wages and other dues while leaving Burma and returned home empty-handed. This development seemed alarming to the Calcutta tramwaymen, particularly to the non-Bengali workers, as they were about to leave the city apprehending a Japanese attack and return to their native places in Bihar and Uttar Pradesh (UP). There was a spontaneous demand from the tramwaymen for payment of their provident fund money and other dues. But the management refused to clear any dues.[13] The *Capital*, mouthpiece of British business interest in India, however, did not attribute much importance to the genuine anxiety of the workers, as it editorially remarked that the tram workers were being 'unnecessarily influenced by the highly coloured stories from Rangoon'.[14]

In the last week of April 1942, the management of the Calcutta Tramways Company, as well as the labour commissioner, Government of Bengal, received a petition from the CTWU, demanding a war allowance amounting to 25 per cent of basic pay, full pay during sick leave, a fortnight's casual leave with full pay and immediate payment of 90 per cent of provident fund money.[15] Instead of giving a sympathetic consideration to the tram workers' demands, the management warned its employees that any 'unauthorized absence' on May Day (1 May) would be 'severely dealt with'.[16] In fact, the management apprehended a large-scale absence on that particular day as the Bengal Provincial Trade Union Congress (BPTUC) had planned to organize a May Day rally at Sraddhananda Park. Ignoring such intimidation, a large number of the tram workers participated in the May Day rally and remained absent from their work place.[17] The management retaliated by dismissing a conductor (No. 104) in the morning of 2 May, on the

[13]Interview with Gopal Acharya.

[14]*Capital*, 21 May 1942.

[15]Weekly Review of Labour Situation in Bengal—No. 18, 21 May 1942, Home Department (Political), Government of India, File No. 12/3/1942-Poll (1)—(NAI).

[16]Commerce and Labour Dept. (Commerce Branch), May 1942. Progs No. 615–621, Government of Bengal (WBSA).

[17]*Calcutta Municipal Gazette*, 9 May 1942.

ground that this particular worker took a leading role in organising the May Day rally.[18]

As the news of the conductor's dismissal spread among the workers, they organised a demonstration demanding his immediate reinstatement. Purssell, agent of the Company, told the demonstrators that after examining the full report of the case, he would give his decision on 4 May. But the workers stuck to their demand which was eventually turned down by the management. The tram workers of Calcutta resorted to a 'lightning' strike from 3.00 pm of 2 May.[19]

The transport system of the city collapsed due to the strike. According to an official communiqué, the tram workers, being 'excited by the tenor of speeches at the May Day meeting on the previous day, suddenly struck work'.[20] Immediately after the strike began, some important CPI leaders, including Bankim Mukherjee, approached the labour commissioner and assured him that they would try to bring the tramwaymen back to work by 4 May. Interestingly, in a meeting of the tram workers on 3 May 1942, Mukherjee requested them 'to withdraw their strike and resume work', just to provide a 'chance' to the government 'to mediate in this matter'.[21] But the workers refused to resume their duty unless their retrenched comrade was taken back. Dhiren Majumdar, secretary, CTWU and a tram conductor himself, supported the stand and the strike continued.[22]

The management agreed to reinstate the dismissed conductor in the evening of 4 May. At the same time the Government of Bengal assured the tram workers that their other grievances would also be sympathetically considered, on the resumption of their duty. The tram workers decided to call off the strike and tram cars began to ply through the Calcutta streets from 8.00 am of 5 May, much to the relief of the commuters.[23]

[18]Commerce and Labour Dept.(Commerce Branch),. Progs No. 615–62, Government of Bengal, May 1942 (WBSA).

[19]*Calcutta Municipal Gazette*, 9 May 1942.

[20]Home Department (Political), Government of India, File No. 18/5/1942 (NAI).

[21]*Calcutta Municipal Gazette*, 9 May 1942.

[22]Interview with Dhiren Majumdar on 10 January 1985.

[23]Home Department (Political), Government of India, File No. 18/5/1942 (NAI). Also *Calcutta Municipal Gazette*, 9 May 1942.

The grievances of the Calcutta tram workers were, however, not sympathetically considered by the management. The workers put pressure on the management to examine carefully their grievances but the management did not respond. To make things worse the management of the Calcutta Tramways dismissed four workshop workers on flimsy grounds.[24] The CTWU immediately threatened to go in for another strike. The situation compelled the management as well as the labour commissioner to meet the CTWU representatives. The CTWU was represented by Bankim Mukherjee. Mukherjee, on the evening of 19 May 1942, met the workers to convey the results of the tripartite meeting that was held among the management, the Government of Bengal and the CTWU. He told them that the management was ready to give certain concessions to them.[25] But the terms evidently failed to satisfy the rank and file of the Calcutta tram workers as the management refused to take back the four retrenched workers. The tramwaymen took an instantaneous decision to go on strike from the next day i.e. from 20 May.[26] Mukherjee tried to persuade the workers to wait for another day, but the request was turned down.[27]

The CTWU prepared a fresh charter of demands, claiming a 25 per cent increase in basic pay, one month's privilege leave and 15 days' casual leave, facility to withdraw up to 90 per cent of their money in the Provident Fund in an emergency, reinstatement of four dismissed workers, additional measures of service security and rest shelters for protection from possible air raids.[28] The last demand probably came in the wake of the shocking death of Golam Sharif, a dock worker at Chittagong, on 8 May 1942—who was incidentally the first victim of Japanese bombing in India.[29] The Calcutta tram workers presented this charter to the management and struck work on 20 May 1942.[30]

[24]*Calcutta Municipal Gazette*, 9 May 1942.

[25]Home Department (Political), Government of India, File No. 18/5/1942 (NAI).

[26]Ibid.

[27]*Janayuddha*, 30 May 1942.

[28]Monthly appreciation of Labour Situation in India, May 1942, Home Department (Political), Government of India, File No. 12/7/1942 (NAI).

[29]Mukhopadhyay, *Bharater Communist Party,* 18.

[30]Home Department (Political), Government of India, File No. 18/5/1942 (NAI).

At that time the Haque–Shyama Prasad Mukherjee Ministry was in charge of the provincial government of Bengal. Prime Minister Fazlul Haque assured two CPI leaders, Bankim Mukherjee and Gopal Halder, that the government would not resort to violence to break the strike.[31] It was at the initiative of the prime minister that a tripartite meeting was held on 22 May. The government had been represented by the Finance Minister Shyama Prasad Mukherjee and Labour Commissioner Hughes. The Calcutta Tramways Company was represented by its agent Pursell and Bankim Mukherjee and Sriprasad Upadhya were the representatives of the striking workers.[32] After a prolonged period of negotiations, it was decided that all four retrenched workers would get back their jobs and all the employees would be entitled to get two months' salary as bonus. The management of the Company further assured them that not a single striker would be victimized. The Government of Bengal, on its part, made it clear that the other grievances of the tramwaymen would be considered with 'care and sympathy'.[33]

The tramwaymen's strike of 20 May, was replete with far-reaching political significance. The decision to strike had been taken exclusively by the workers themselves. In their effort to get their grievances redressed, they did not hesitate to reject the proposal of their leaders to postpone the strike. After the withdrawal of the strike, a statement by Mukherjee was published, in which he categorically mentioned that 'all the credit for settling the strike should go to the ministers and the labour commissioner'.[34] A tram worker wrote an anonymous open letter in the pages of the *Janayuddha*, the official organ of the CPI, in which he vehemently criticised Bankim Mukherjee's statement. The tram worker wrote that the government definitely played a positive role in arriving at an amicable settlement, but the tram workers also shared some of the credit for this, which Mukherjee forgot to mention. Mukherjee, in his reply, in the same issue of the *Janayuddha* admitted that it was the unity of the workers which led to a settlement and without flexibility

[31] *Janayuddha*, 30 May 1942.

[32] Ibid.

[33] Home Department (Political), Government of India, File No. 18/5/1942 (NAI).

[34] *Janayuddha*, 10 June 1942.

in their attitude the deadlock could not have been broken. At the same time, he reiterated that had the leaders of the CPI been given one more day for negotiation the strike could have been avoided.[35]

In fact, evidence relating to both the strikes of May 1942, clearly manifest that there was a cleavage between the ordinary tram workers and the CPI leaders. Very obviously, Mukherjee's stand to either get the strike withdrawn or not go in for a strike at all must have been influenced by the CPI's new assessment of the Second World War and its consequent policy of not disturbing the war effort. In the wake of the Nazi attack on the Soviet Union, the vanguard of international Communism, the Imperialist War had overnight turned into a People's War. It was the decision of the CPI to cooperate with the British war effort as Britain was an ally of the Soviet Union.[36] The sudden change in the CPI stand was probably not in tune with the attitude of a large section of tram workers and hence, their dispute with the CPI leaders. The CPI programme of cooperating with the war effort appeared to many as a compromise, which definitely 'isolated and discredited' the CPI.[37] In fact, by distorting the essence of the People's War, the CPI turned itself into a passive ally of British imperialism for the time being, even at the expense of toiling people's interests.

The management of the Calcutta Tramways Company did not take any positive steps to redress the grievances of the workers. The decisions of the meeting of 22 May, were not even executed. In mid-July 1942, the Company issued an order that twelve workers of Rajabazar Depot would have to work for additional hours, beyond their normal duty of eight-and-a-half hours.[38] The workers were ready to comply with the order, but requested that the management provide them a half-hour recess to have their midday meal. But the request was turned down. The workers expressed their unwillingness to work for additional hours. The Company retaliated by suspending the twelve workers who refused to work. Aggrieved workers started

[35]Ibid.

[36]Jail Document—Home Department (Political), Government of India, File No. 44/32/1942 (NAI).

[37]See Sumit Sarkar, *Modern India 1885–1947* (Delhi: Macmillan, 1983), 411.

[38]*Janayuddha*, 22 July 1942.

an agitation in the Rajabazar Depot against the suspension order. The pressure of protest compelled the Company to withdraw the suspension order against eleven employees, excepting driver No. 727 (according to another source, conductor No. 717).[39] On 17 July 1942, the suspended man was finally discharged. The decision of the management was greeted with a lightning strike by the workers from that afternoon. Within a span of just two months, Calcutta faced the tremors of yet another tram strike.

The Government of Bengal, invoking the Essential Services Maintenance Ordinance, 1942, declared the strike illegal. There were severe police atrocities against the striking tram workers and arrest warrants were issued against two prominent CTWU leaders, Md. Ismail and Gopal Acharya.[40] As requested by some CTWU leaders, Fazlul Haque, the prime minister of Bengal, issued a statement on the evening of 19 July, that all the arrested tram workers along with their leaders be immediately released and not a single striker be victimised. He further added that the government's declaration regarding workers' grievances would come out soon.[41] On the prime minister's assurance, the tramwaymen decided to withdraw their strike and resume duty from the morning of 20 July 1942.

A press communiqué released by the Government of Bengal on 22 July, stated that the principal demands of the strikers relating to bonus, leave, provident fund and security of service would be settled by the labour commissioner. The communiqué added that such strikes were illegal, and their recurrence would henceforth be severely dealt with.[42] But the issue of the dismissed worker (Driver No. 727 or Conductor No. 717) did not find a place in the press release, and also did not carry a single word condemning the unlawful retrenchment of workers by the Company.

The decision to launch this strike rested solely with the workers. The CPI did not accept the decision with good grace as the Party's

[39]*People's War,* 2 August, 1942; that the dismissed man was Driver No. 727, whereas Home Department (Political), Government of India, File No. 18/7/1942 (NAI) informs about the dismissal of Conductor No. 717.

[40]*Janayuddha*, 22 July 1942.

[41]Home Department (Political), Government of India, File No. 18/7/1942 (NAI).

[42]*Calcutta Municipal Gazette*, 25 July 1942.

stand on the People's War again stood in its way. At a later stage of the strike, the CPI dominated CTWU, however, gave unstinting support to the strikers. The CPI organ, the weekly *Janayuddha* wrote, 'The workers would do better if they tried for an amicable settlement through the Union, instead of resorting to a strike. But the high-handedness of the Company broke the patience of the workers.'[43]

Towards the end of 1942, Calcutta faced Japanese bombing, causing panic among the people of the city.[44] A large number of tram workers were about to leave the city, throwing the transport system into complete disarray. In this situation, the management of the Calcutta Tramways Company announced certain concessions for the workers on 24 December 1942, which included distribution of essential commodities like rice, pulse, flour and kerosene at a concessional rate and enhancement of dearness allowance by Rs 2 at a flat rate.[45] In response, the workers assured the Company that they would keep the trams running, despite the fear of aerial bombing. [46]

In early 1943, the workers found that a section of the supervisory staff, who were in charge of the distribution of rations at a concessional price, were involved in corrupt practices, depriving the workers of their legitimate share. The CTWU pressed the management to take steps against the guilty officers. But the protest went unheeded.[47] The workers decided to intensify their agitation demanding the redressal of their long-standing grievances. The agitation ultimately forced the government to set up an Adjudication Committee under the chairmanship of R. Gupta, a government official, in early 1944, to examine the grievances of the tramwaymen.[48]

The recommendations of the R. Gupta Committee came in December 1944, and some of its awards regarding timetable, canteen facilities, and leave went in favour of the workers. But the Company

[43]*Janayuddha*, 22 July 1942.

[44]*Amrita Bazar Patrika*, 22, 23, 25, 26, December 1942.

[45]*Janayuddha*, 30 December 1942.

[46]Ibid.

[47]*Janayuddha*, 17 February 1943.

[48]Sisir Mitra, *A Public Facility: Its Management and Workers (*New Delhi: People's Publishing House 1980) 39.

unnecessarily delayed the implementing of the awards.[49] Yet, having committed to not disturbing the war efforts against the Axis powers, the tram workers were not inclined to paralyse the urban transport system with any strike, if avoidable. Meanwhile, some important developments took place in international politics, with the Soviet Red Army's historic triumph over German invaders and consequently, a decisive turn in the war situation in favour of the Allied powers. This brought a change in the tram workers' attitude as well, as they no more remained strike-shy. When they found that till the middle of 1945 not a single recommendation of the Adjudication Committee had been executed, they planned to intensify their agitation for an early implementation of the awards.[50]

The CTWU prepared a note highlighting the fact that the number of daily passengers had gone up from three-and-a-half lakhs in 1940 to eight-and-a-half lakhs in 1944, but that during this period, no new car had been introduced, nor were any extra hands taken on to reduce the workload. There was a steady rise in the Company's profits—Rs 31,18,000 in 1940 to Rs 64,60,695 in 1944.[51]

The War left an adverse impact on the Indian economy, and Bengal was very badly affected. A large number of people died of starvation on Calcutta streets during the vicious summer of 1943, as Bengal became the worst victim of a 'basically man-made famine'.[52] Following the famine, prices of essential commodities ran high, but without any corresponding hike in tramwaymen's wages. In the wake of the Calcutta Tramways Company's huge profits on the one hand, and soaring prices of essential commodities on the other, the Calcutta tram workers demanded Eid and Puja bonuses in August 1945. Even this modest demand was turned down by the Company.[53] The management further reacted in a bitter way by dismissing the cashier Ram Kamal Ghosh and conductors Ket Narain Misir and Wauzul, allegedly for fomenting trouble.[54]

[49]*Janayuddha*, 14 October 1945.
[50]Ibid.
[51]Ibid.
[52]Sarkar, *Modern India*, 406.
[53]*Amrita Bazar Patrika*, 6 September 1945.
[54]*Janayuddha*, 14 October 1945.

On 5 September 1945, the CTWU submitted a strike notice to the labour commissioner, Government of Bengal, claiming that the 'continuous refusal' of the Company to fulfill workers' demands had led them to decide 'to resort to a peaceful strike as their last weapon', starting 19 September. In the same notice, they placed a charter of demands:

(i) One month's pay as bonus for Eid and Puja every year from 1945.
(ii) Increase of dearness allowance.
(iii) Setting up a Wage and Accident Enquiry Committee, consisting of representatives of the government, the Company and the Workers' Union.
(iv) Legal recognition of the Workers' Union by the Company.
(v) Immediate reinstatement of the discharged workers.[55]

The government opened negotiations with both the management and the Workers' Union to avoid a strike, but the effort yielded no result. The strike of about 8,000 tram workers began on 19 September 1945, and not a single car left the depots. From the very first day of the strike, union activists were seen keeping a strong vigil at every depot to make the strike a total one.[56] The strike almost paralysed the city transport system, causing severe inconvenience to office goers. But public sympathy rested with the striking tramwaymen, and the clerks of the mercantile firms of the city donated Rs 6, on their own, to the strike fund.[57]

The government, after consulting Godley, the agent of the Calcutta Tramways Company, announced on 20 September, that the bonus issue would be settled by an Adjudication Board, but the discharged workers would not be taken back.[58] But the Central Strike Committee, after seeking the opinion of the ordinary workers, rejected the proposal. The CTWU reiterated that certain conditions should be fulfilled by the Company, such as non-discrimination in awarding bonuses, immediate reinstatement of the two discharged

[55]*Amrita Bazar Patrika*, 6 September 1945.

[56]*Amrita Bazar Patrika*, 20 September 1945.

[57]*Janayuddha*, 14 October 1945.

[58]*Amrita Bazar Patrika*, 21 September 1945.

workers, and withdrawal of charge sheets against the strike leaders.[59] The strike continued.

As the strike continued causing immense inconvenience to the public, the government announced on 26 September, that a Conciliation Board with a non-official chairman acceptable to both sides, would be formed to examine the grievances of the tramwaymen as well as to settle the issue. It was also declared that the Conciliation Board would include, besides the chairman, two members representing the workers and two nominees of the Company.[60] The Central Strike Committee, that same afternoon, organized a meeting of the tram workers at Wellington Square and decided to withdraw the strike from 28 September.[61]

The Conciliation Board met on the 2, 3, 4 and 5 October, to arrive at an amicable settlement. On the evening of 5 October 1945, the Board gave the following decisions:

(i) All the workers of Calcutta Tramways, who were in service on or before 31 August 1945, would receive one month's pay as bonus.
(ii) Conductors Misir and Wauzul and the cashier Ram Kamal Ghosh would be unconditionally reinstated.
(iii) All charge sheets against the striking workers would be withdrawn and not a single worker would be victimised.[62]

The strike of September 1945, meant a partial victory for the workers. The management of the Calcutta Tramways Company agreed to concede two major demands—those for non-differential bonus and reinstatement of the discharged workers. But another significant demand, that of giving legal recognition to their Union, remained unfulfilled. Furthermore, the tramwaymen's demands for an increase in the dearness allowance and formation of a Wage and Accident Committee also went unheeded. The importance of the strike, however, was acknowledged elsewhere. Indrajit Gupta, a prominent CPI leader as well as a veteran trade union activist,

[59]Ibid. *People's War*, 14 October 1945.
[60]*People's War*, 14 October 1945.
[61]Ibid.
[62]*Amrita Bazar Patrika*, 6 October 1945.

remarked in a press conference, 'For the first time the non-official's role in the industrial dispute was recognized in Bengal'.[63]

After the strike, some new facts came to the knowledge of the CTWU. In between the years 1942 and 1945, the Company showed an annual average profit of Rs 46 lakhs, after setting aside Rs 10.5 lakhs as repairment cost. According to an estimate made by the CTWU, the Company built up a huge Reserve Fund, amounting to about Rs 110 lakhs. But the company incurred very little expenditure for repairing the cars between the years 1942 and 1946. The CTWU alleged that the Company took an indifferent attitude to the improvement of the operational efficiency of the tramways in the 'interest of the travelling public of Calcutta' (a phrase used in abundance by the Company, as well as by the government, during the tram strikes').[64]

In the 1940s, the Calcutta Tramways Company amassed huge profits but spent very little either for the benefit of the workers or for providing better services to the commuters. Under such circumstances, the Calcutta tramwaymen pressed the Company to take measures for improving the condition of the workers. The tram workers invited the attention of the management to the fact that the disparity between their wages and the prices of essential commodities was gradually becoming wider.[65] Even an official report suggested: 'There is no one fixed principle of wage determination followed by the Company. Dearness Allowance was first introduced in 1942 and since then has been changed, mostly as a result of workers' demands.'[66]

The CTWU framed a fresh charter of demands and submitted it to the management on 27 November 1946. The demands included:

(i) Revision of basic wages.
(ii) Introduction of gratuity
(iii) Increase of Provident Fund contribution by the Company from 6.25 per cent to 8.33 per cent of basic pay.

[63]*Janyuddha*, 14 October 1945.
[64]*People's Age*, 9 February 1947.
[65]Ibid.
[66]*Rege Committee Report on Labour Investigation*, Delhi, 1946, 44.

(iv) Revision of leave rules.
(v) Payment of two months' pay as bonus.[67]

But this charter of demands had been totally ignored by the management.Deafening silence on the part of the management for six long weeks led the tramwaymen to prepare for an organized movement. On 3 January 1947, they decided through a ballot in favour of a strike. Out of approximately 7,000 workers, not less than 6,002 (about 85 per cent) participated in the strike ballot, and of them, 5,945 voted in favour of a strike, while only 41 opposed it and 16 ballots were declared invalid.[68] Accordingly, the CTWU served a 14 days' strike notice on the Company on 7 January.[69] The labour commissioner, Government of Bengal, immediately announced that the tramwaymen's grievances would be referred to an Adjudication Committee. But the CTWU stuck to its decision to strike from 22 January.[70] The Government of Bengal declared through a press note that the dispute having been already referred to an Adjudication Committee, the 'commencement and continuation' of the strike would be illegal.[71] In response to the press note, Md. Ismail, the president of the CTWU, made it clear that the tram workers were concerned with the modalities by which the wages should be adjudged and they looked forward to a properly ascertained wage level at which a worker and his family could 'meet their essential requirements at present day prices'. The statement of the CTWU president further revealed that the wages received by the Bombay transport workers, as recommended by the Divatia Committee, were significantly higher than those drawn by the Calcutta tramwaymen.[72]

There was very little response from the Company. Nobody came forward to put an end to the deadlock and arrive at an amicable settlement. In this situation, the Calcutta tram workers, remaining

[67] *Amrita Bazar Patrika*, 10 January 1947.

[68] *Amrita Bazar Patrika*, 7 January 1947.

[69] *Amrita Bazar Patrika*, 8 January 1947.

[70] *Calcutta Municipal Gazette*, 25 January 1947.

[71] Ibid.

[72] *Trade Union Record* (Monthly Bulletin of AITUC) Vol. VI, No. 9, May 1947, 100.

true to their earlier decision, struck work on 22 January 1947, to paralyse 'Calcutta and Howrah's main city transport'.[73] It was probably the longest strike in the annals of the tramwaymen's struggle. On 24 January, H.S. Suhrawardy, the prime minister of Bengal, warned that the strikers would have to face dire consequences, if they did not withdraw their strike.[74] When asked in the Bengal Legislative Assembly to make the house aware of the official measures taken to break the stalemate, Shams-ud-din Ahmed, labour minister of Bengal, in his lengthy speech, only condemned the strikers in unequivocal terms. He even went to the extent of branding them 'offenders' for bringing about a total disruption of urban life and blatantly encouraged the Company to take punitive measures against the strikers and 'employ new hands' to keep the trams moving.[75] Such threats, however, failed to pacify the workers and the strike continued. Encouraged by the rigid stand of the government, the management of the Calcutta Tramways Company reiterated that the workers must resume duties before expecting any negotiation.[76]

The Government of Bengal took stern measures to suppress the strikers. Important office bearers of the CTWU, including two prominent CPI leaders, Somenath Lahiri and Md. Ismail, were arrested. During the strike period, the police even raided different newspaper houses in Calcutta, including the *Amrita Bazar Patrika* and the *Swadhinata*, the CPI organ.[77] It was a deliberate attempt to muzzle the press to prevent them from publishing any statement of the CTWU.

Meanwhile, strong public opinion swept through Calcutta in favour of an early settlement. The Government of Bengal was vehemently criticized for its inept handling of the situation. Fazlul Haque, the former prime minister of Bengal, 'attacked the ministry's

[73]*Calcutta Municipal Gazette*, 25 January 1947.

[74]*Calcutta Municipal Gazette*, 15 February, 22 February 1947.

[75]*Proceedings of the Bengal Legislative Assembly* (First Session) 3 February to 28 February 1947.

[76]Mrinal Kanti Basu: *Smriti–Katha* (Autobiography in Bengali) (Calcutta, 1968), 369. Mrinal Kanti Basu was a pioneering trade union leader of Bengal in the 1930s and 1940s. He was the president of the BPTUC for many years.

[77]*People's Age*, 27 April 1947.

stand' for prolonging the crisis.[78] Kiron Shankar Roy, leader of the Congress Parliamentary Party, asked the labour minister to call a conference of the representatives of the workers and the Company to find 'a just and honourable Compromise'.[79] Sarat Bose, a prominent Congress leader of Bengal, also stated that the 'Government of Bengal and the Tramway Company should not lose a single day more in bringing about a settlement of the strike.'[80]

The strike received support from the workers of other sectors as well. Bus workers of Calcutta observed a token sympathy strike on 10 February despite stiff resistance from the government and the Bus Owners' Syndicate.[81] On 18 March 1947, the AITUC observed 'Demand Day' in support of the tram workers' demands. On 'Demand Day', middle-class employees of Calcutta, particularly those in the Ordnance Factory, the Supply Directorate, and the Post and Telegraphs held a meeting to pledge unstinting support to the striking tram workers.[82]

Throughout the strike period, tram workers of Calcutta remained peaceful and resolute; there was no theft or vandalism, which often springs from hunger and hopelessness. Many among the workers took up jobs as pedlars and hawkers for sheer survival, but never resorted to crime.[83] As the strike continued for a considerable length of time and the tramwaymen showed no signs of yielding to pressure, the Company and the government agreed to negotiate. A tripartite conference comprising the representatives of the workers, management and the government, was held on 9 April 1947, to explore 'avenues to a solution of the deadlock.'[84] Most of the CTWU leaders were either in prison or absconding to escape arrest warrants. Hence, Mrinal Kanti Basu, the president of the Bengal Provincial Trade Union Congress, was entrusted with the responsibility of representing the workers in the negotiation.[85]

[78]Ibid.
[79]*Calcutta Municipal Gazette*, 15, 22, 23 March 1947.
[80]Ibid.
[81]*Calcutta Municipal Gazette*, 25 January 1947.
[82]*People's Age*, 30 March 1947.
[83]Basu, *Smriti-Katha*, 369.
[84]*People's Age*, 27 April 1947.
[85]Basu, *Smriti–Katha*, 370

After the tripartite conference, the Company agreed to raise the minimum wage to Rs 30, with a flat interim relief of Rs 7.5. The management of the Company also assured the workers' representative that not a single man would be victimised for participating in the strike. The Government of Bengal also agreed to withdraw the declared Adjudication Committee and set up in its place an impartial tribunal under the Industrial Dispute Act, 1947, to publish its findings within a week on questions relating to increase in basic wages, bonus and pay during the strike period, together with other demands. The government also promised to 'release all the arrested leaders of the tramwaymen as soon as their strike was withdrawn'.[86] Immediately after the announcement on 16 April 1947, two absconding leaders of the CTWU, Dhiren Majumdar and Chatur Ali, who had so far been sheltered by the workers, appeared on the scene to inform the workers about the terms of the settlement. Workers expressed satisfaction over the decision and agreed to withdraw the strike form 18 April. Tramcars again plied through the Calcutta streets after eighty five days. All the arrested leaders were released.[87]

The government set up a tribunal with S.N. Guha Ray, ICS, as the chairman. The tribunal submitted its report within a week, which went in favour of the workers. The recommendations of the tribunal 'surpassed their own expectations'. The claim of a minimum basic wage was settled at Rs 40. After thoroughly examining the price index and comparing the wage structure of the tram workers with that of the other industries, the tribunal awarded Rs 67.50 as the minimum total emolument of a Calcutta tram worker, excluding the house rent allowance, which the tribunal fixed at Rs 5 per month. So, all inclusive, the minimum gross monthly salary for a worker came to Rs 72.50.[88]

The strike of 1947 was a remarkable victory for the working class. Notwithstanding the communal violence in the city on one hand and starvation due to abysmal poverty on the other, the

[86]*People's Age*, 27 April 1947.

[87]Ibid.

[88]Mitra, *A Public Facility,* 41.

Calcutta tramwaymen could clinch the issue in their favour. The government's threats and the Company's ploys failed to make them yield to pressure. Their well-earned victory against a British monopoly brought about a welcome message to the Calcuttans only a few months before Independence.

CALCUTTA TRAMWAYMEN AND ANTI-IMPERIALIST STRUGGLES IN 1945–46

A general anti-imperialist struggle struck the tottering edifice of British imperialism in late 1945 and early 1946, which has been described as 'the Edge of a Volcano'.[89] In fact, tension began to mount as soon as the government decided to hold a public trial of the Indian National Army (INA) prisoners. As the trial proceeded, tremors of a countrywide protest swept India. Calcutta became particularly turbulent in February 1946. The disturbance broke out in the wake of the sentence passed on Abdur Rashid Ali, a captain in the INA, for seven years' imprisonment. The people of Calcutta started an agitation for his release. At the initial stage, the agitation did not receive 'much support', but eventually, the movement gathered momentum with the advent of the Communists.[90] On 11 February1946, the CPI activists and the left wing students organized a procession to show solidarity with the INA prisoners, which entered the Secretarial area, 'in violation of a long standing prohibitory order'. The police behaved with unwarranted ferocity to bring the situation under control. The brutality of the police action only provoked the demonstrators, comprising workers and students under CPI influence, to enter into the prohibited area. 'They', to quote an official note, 'started an orgy of lawlessness'.[91] The Calcutta tramwaymen were active organizers of the rally.[92] To protest against the 'police atrocities', the CPI called a general strike

[89]Moon while editing Wavell's Journal *The Edge of Volcano*, cited by Sarkar, *Modern India*, 418.

[90]Home Department (Political), Government of India, File No. 18/2/1946 (NAI).

[91]Ibid.

[92]Gautam Chattopadhyay, 'The Almost Revolution' in *Essays in Honour of Prof. S.C. Sarkar*, ed. Barun De, 430.

on 12 February 1947. The tramwaymen, in their uniforms, played a prominent role in making the strike a success.[93]

No public transport plied on 12 Feburary due to the 'strike of their operatives'.[94] The day witnessed a series of violent actions, and the Government of Bengal called in the army to suppress the agitating mob. Calcutta remained tension-stricken up to 14 February. Even a government source admitted that the police and military firings had claimed as many as 38 lives. The same source revealed that the Communists 'exploited' the situation, 'in spite of persuasion' by senior Muslim League and Congress leaders to pacify the agitation.[95] Manik Bandyopadhyay, one of the most eminent Bengali novelists, was manhandled by the police for his close links with the CPI. Manik Bandyopadhyay retaliated by writing a novel *Chinha*, which immortalised the uprising of Rashid Ali Day (12 February 1946). This memorable account may also corroborate the fact that the Calcutta tram workers were active participants in the entire incident, as seen in the character of Osman, a tram conductor with the indomitable zeal of a fighter.[96]

Mob violence once more intensified with the news of the mutiny in the Royal Indian Navy (RIN) in Bombay and Karachi in early 1946. Students and workers in Calcutta 'came forward to sympathize with the mutineers'.[97] The CPI called for a 'General Strike' on 23 February 1946, to express solidarity with the mutineers, as well as to protest against 'police atrocities in Bombay and Karachi'. A massive rally of the Calcutta working class and the students paraded the Calcutta streets that day, which went upto Wellington Square to hold a meeting in support of the rebel navalmen. The tram workers took up the most prominent positions; uniformed in their khaki dress, they led the rally. Two vice-presidents of the CTWU, Somenath Lahiri and Chatur Ali, were the main speakers

[93]*People's Age*, 24 February 1946.

[94]Home Department (Political), Government of India, File No. 18/2/1946 (NAI).

[95]Ibid.

[96]Manik Bandyopadhyay, *Chinha* (A novel) (Calcutta, 1985).

[97]Home Department (Political), Government of India, File No. 18/2/1946 Poll (9) (NAI).

at the Wellington Square meeting. Somenath Lahiri described the mutiny as a 'rehearsal before the final big battle' for Independence. Chatur Ali denounced the 'imperialist insolence' against the Bombay navalmen in unequivocal terms.[98]

The Congress and the Muslim League did not support the strike call,[99] giving much relief to the government. It was stated in a government report that 'subversive elements' like the Communists were responsible for fomenting trouble and the incidents in Bombay and Karachi found little sympathy from the 'large parties like Congress, Muslim League and Hindu Mahasabha'. The same report branded the Calcutta tramwaymen as the 'most effective trouble-makers' because of their pro-CPI leanings.[100] On the day of the General Strike i.e. on 23 February 1946, mob violence broke out in several places in Calcutta, and police repression continued unabated throughout the day. Two tram workers were arrested for 'peacefully persuading the bus passengers, not to travel' during the General Strike.[101] The incidents bear ample testimony to the active role taken by the Calcutta tram workers in the post-war anti-imperialist upsurge of early 1946.

CALCUTTA TRAMWAYMEN'S FIGHT AGAINST COMMUNALISM

Ranen Sen, a prominent CPI leader of Bengal, since the Party's earlier days, wrote in his memoir that the communal holocaust during 1946–47 left a disastrous impact on the working class movement in Bengal. Toiling people of different sectors, on many occasions, fell prey to 'ugly' communal propaganda of the Hindu Mahasabha and the Muslim League. But according to Sen, the Calcutta tram workers stood out as the 'lone exception' to this general trend.[102]

[98] *People's Age*, 3 March 1946.

[99] Ibid.

[100] Home Department (Political), Government of India, File No. 18/2/1946, Poll (9) (NAI).

[101] *People's Age*, 3 March 1946.

[102] Ranen Sen, *Banglay Communist Party Gathaner Pratham Yug* (Calcutta, 1982), 151.

Let us begin with an interesting episode. In 1943, the CPI, with a view to helping the famine victims and also to contributing to the Strike Aid Fund of different industrial sectors, introduced a fund called the Lenin Day Fund. A large number of tram workers, with close links to the CPI, involved themselves in the programme to collect money from their fellow workers for the Lenin Day Fund. A tram worker at the Park Circus Depot on being approached by the collectors for donation, asked, 'Why should I pay? I am a member of the Hindu Mahasabha' one of the collectors retorted, 'You are a Hindu no doubt. But before that you are a labourer and that is your first and foremost identity. Communist Party is the party of the toiling people. Then why won't you pay to your own party?' The Hindu Mahasabha supporter was convinced and contributed one rupee to the Lenin Day Fund.[103]

In 1943, when a severe famine broke out in rural Bengal (the mention of which has been made earlier) millions of people stricken by hunger and disease, began to leave their land and come to Calcutta. Tram workers organised shelter for them in their mess houses. They also made arrangements to distribute food in their Dover Lane mess and Lake Road mess.

In September 1944, the tram workers of Calcutta had demanded bonuses for Eid and Puja for each and every worker. But the management, with a view to striking at the root of working class unity declared the bonus before Puja but after Eid. The sinister motive behind the move was clear to the workers and they reacted with an en masse refusal of the bonus. Next year, the strike of 1945, enabled them to get the bonus for all and in time.[104]

In August 1946, the worst-ever communal violence broke out in the city. The Great Calcutta Killings led to the loss of innumerable innocent lives. Asok Mitra, an eminent scholar and a civil servant at the time, gave a graphic eyewitness account of the Great Killings of 1946 in his memoir.[105] The Calcutta tram workers emerged as the front men in the fight against the

[103]*Janayuddha*, 8 September 1943.

[104]*Amrita Bazar Patrika*, 13 September 1945.

[105]Asok Mitra: 'The Great Calcutta Killings of 1946—What went before and after', *Economic and Political Weekly* (February 1990), 273.

'flames of civil war'.[106] The Muslim League had issued a call for Direct Action Day on 16 August 1946. The CTWU convened its Executive Committee meeting to take a firm stand on the issue. A resolution was moved to observe a strike on 16 August, as a protest against the Muslim League's call for 'Direct Action'. One of the Executive Committee members was a Muslim League leader of the Rajabazar area, who vehemently opposed the strike resolution. Ultimately, after long negotiations and deliberations, good sense prevailed and the resolution in favour of a strike was unanimously adopted. Next day, a general body meeting of the CTWU, held in the University Institute Hall, extended whole-hearted support to the strike decision taken by the Executive Committee.[107]

On 16 August, Calcutta wore a violent look and large-scale rioting broke out, turning the city into a happy hunting ground for criminals. A girls' college with hostel accommodation, situated opposite the Rajabazar Tram Depot became a target of attack by criminals on the morning of the Direct Action Day. As the news broke, tramwaymen of the Rajabazar Depot mobilised themselves near the college and hostel area. The Muslim League member of CTWU Executive Committee (mentioned above) took a leading role in protecting the girls' hostel along with fellow tram workers and local CPI activists. They kept a strong vigil over the area until late in the evening, when all the girls were brought out safely from the college hostel under armed guard.[108]

The tram workers of different areas escorted people from a minority community to a place where they formed a majority. There were instances when tram workers in their uniforms boldly passed through an area dominated by the members of another community. People in general and particularly men from poorer sections developed an unflinching faith in the secular credentials of the Calcutta tramwaymen. Towards the end of August, the situation improved and the city was slowly returning to normalcy. Trams

[106]*People's Age*, 20 April 1947; See Suranjan Das: *Communal Riots in Bengal 1905–1947* (New Delhi: Oxford University Press, 1991), 181.

[107]Interview with Gopal Acharya.

[108]Ibid.

started plying through the Calcutta streets. However, Calcuttans had not yet recovered from the nightmare. Hatred and malice against each other were still there in their minds. While travelling on trams, commuters would often make provocative and irresponsible remarks against about people belonging to another community. Tram workers, particularly the conductors, took a firm stand against such irresponsible remarks, which could foment communal tension.[109]

The consequences of the Calcutta riot of August 1946 were severe leading to communal frenzy and large-scale carnage in Noakhali, Tipperah in East Bengal and also in Bihar in October 1946. The tramwaymen of Calcutta again rose to the occasion and sent relief squads to the riot-affected areas of East Bengal and Bihar.[110]

There was a fresh spurt of violence in March 1947, as Calcutta once more experienced sporadic outbursts of Hindu–Muslim rioting. The situation further deteriorated on 26 March. During that period, the Calcutta tram workers were involved in a prolonged strike (the details of which have been given earlier). Shattered economically, because of their two-and-a-half-month-old strike, they nonetheless showed remarkable resilience in their fight against communalism. Wearing strike badges they paraded through different parts of the city to defuse communal tension.[111] Taking advantage of the violence, the Calcutta Tramways Company management tried to break the morale of the strikers. It spread rumours that trams would soon be out in the streets in the Muslim dominated areas, with the help of the Muslim blacklegs.[112]

The rumour hurt Muslim sentiments. The Muslim Women's Society in a meeting expressed deep concern and resolved that such blacklegging, if true, must be 'prevented at any cost', as it would be a 'slur on the entire Muslim community'. Muslim girl students decided to picket in front of the Park Circus Tram Depot, if blacklegs attempted to run cars with official connivance, violating the strike decision of the CTWU.[113]

[109]Ibid.

[110]*People's Age*, 9 February 1947.

[111]*People's Age*, 20 April 1947.

[112]*People's Age*, 27 April 1947.

[113]Ibid.

One of the most unique features of the tram workers' movements in the 1940s was the role of the outsiders. Educated middleclass leadership with Marxist ideology like Somenath Lahiri and Gopal Acharya worked hand in hand with the labour leaders from working class origin like Dhiren Majumdar and Chatur Ali. As a result of mutual cooperation between the two sets of leadership, the CTWU demonstrated remarkable solidarity either in times of strikes or in their political and social activities. In pre-1949, China also the Marxist intellectuals became the leaders of the labour movements who 'soon merged with the leaders of working class origin' and 'difference of origin was of little account in carrying through the task at hand.'[114]

The years between 1940 and 1947, may be easily termed as the period of highest prestige for the CTWU. Maintaining the rich heritage of their struggle against the management as well as against the imperialist Raj, the tram workers of Calcutta demonstrated an exemplary organizational sense and immense political maturity. Even after many decades, trade union leaders and Communist activists remembered those glorious days. [115] It was during this period that the day-to-day economic struggle became inextricably linked with political awareness and activity in the rich tapestry of the history of the Calcutta' tramwaymen.

[114]Jean Chesneaux: *The Chinese Labor Movement* (California: Stanford University Press, 1968), 403.

[115]Mrinal Kanti Basu, Ranen Sen, Saroj Mukhopadhyay along with others mentioned in their memoirs that the Calcutta tram workers played a significant role in the political life of Calcutta in the 1940s.

CHAPTER nine

Emergence of Mahila Atma Raksha Samiti in the Forties—Calcutta Chapter

Gargi Chakravartty

The city of Calcutta was the epicentre of a radical women's movement in the early 1940s, which soon spread across Bengal. It arose directly out of the war situation. The Second World War took a new turn when Japan entered into an alliance with the Axis Powers in December 1941. With the fall of Rangoon to the Japanese Army in March 1942, an invasion of India seemed imminent. India, consequently, faced an acute food crisis as rumours spread of the disappearance of rice supplies from Burma, and the British destroyed 'all country boats in the coastal belt, where agricultural activity was banned as part of British defence preparation'.[1] Profiteers began to clandestinely buy up rice all over Bengal. The price of rice rose from Rs 5 per maund to Rs 10 and there was mass evacuation after the fall of Rangoon.

> War industries had to be speeded up, but only in certain big concerns factory workers were given a dearness allowance from 5 per cent to 6 per cent. At the present time this has been increased to 15 per cent in many places, but the number of people who benefited by this—however inadequate it might be—are a very small proportion as compared to the vast population of Bengal that have been affected by the inflation in prices.[2]

[1]Renu Chakravartty, *Communists in Indian Women's Movement, 1940–1950* (New Delhi: People's Publishing House, 1980), 16.

[2]Memorandum submitted to Famine Inquiry Commission by Mahila Atma

With the Soviet Union pulled into the War after being attacked by Hitler, the Communist Party of India (CPI), which was illegal at that time, brought out pamphlets to explain the Party's redefinition of the War. The Party now no longer called it an Imperialist War but the People's War. P.C. Joshi, general secretary of the Party, wrote a document titled 'Foreword to Freedom' in November 1941, under the pseudonym of Hansraj, where he explained the new Party line.[3]

The first week of November 1942, was observed as National Unity Week by the Party. Even though the Party now opposed the anti-colonial movements of the Congress, and supported British war efforts, its mass fronts, including the embryonic women's front, campaigned for the release of Congress leaders, for unity of the Congress and the Muslim League, and for a national government to stall the Japanese threat. Twenty squads of women volunteers moved around Calcutta and started recruiting members for the new Mahila Atma Raksha Samiti (MARS). They collected around 3,000 signatures, as they went around explaining the need for a national government.[4]

Communist women had to face the charge of being anti-national when they opposed the Quit India movement as part of the CPI strategy of supporting the British war effort at a time when the Soviet Union was under attack. They also opposed the Forward Bloc which believed that Subhas Chandra Bose would soon 'liberate India' with the help of the Japanese Army. Politically isolated, it was an uphill task for Communist women to carry on their campaign against fascism and Hitler, and at the same time, struggle for the release of Gandhiji and other political leaders while urging for a national government for national unity.

Who were these women who came close to the CPI and to the anti-fascist front? Their history of activism can be traced back to 1939, when the *Chhatri Sangh* (the women students' group of the All India Students Federation, close to the CPI) was formed in Calcutta

---

Raksha Samiti (MARS) of Bengal, Nanavati Papers, Famine Inquiry Commission Report, Vol I—National Archives of India (NAI).

[3]Hansraj, *Foreword to Freedom (India in the War of Liberation)* (New Delhi: Anand Press, 1941), 13.

[4]Kanak Mukhopadhyay, *Nari Mukti Andolon O Aamra*, *Eksathe* (Kolkata, 2005), 38.

and branches grew outside Calcutta. They were inspired by the news of the historic victory of Stalingrad, and the self-sacrifice of Soviet women like Olga Kovalova, Zoya (Tania) Kosmodenskaya, Natasha and many others. The appeal by the Soviet Women's Anti-Fascist Committee issued at an Anti-Fascist Women's Conference held in Moscow on 7 September 1941, to the women of the world to build up an Anti-Fascist United Front also created stirrings among the women in Bengal.[5] In 1942, the Anti-Fascist Writer's Association was formed in Calcutta. Soon, 46 Dharmatala Street became a cultural hub to rally anti-fascist intellectuals and cultural activists. It mobilised a large number of well-known writers and intellectuals, Communists and non-Communists alike.[6] People's Defence Committees (Jana Raksha Samitis) were formed to counter impending Japanese aggression and a few Communist women came up with the idea of forming a Mahila Atma Raksha Samiti for women's self-protection. Sometime in April 1942, at an informal gathering at the residence of Ela Reid (who later became the first general secretary of MARS), they discussed the need for an organization for women 'to fulfil the task of self-defence in a situation where women's security was at stake'.[7] Manikuntala Sen, a founder member of MARS, recalls:

> We felt that the AIWC (the All India Women's Committee of the Congress, of which communist women had so long been a part) would not suffice anymore. We would form our organisation primarily with middle class and lower middle class working and peasant women.[8]
>
> Sitting in Eladi's house, the objectives of the Samiti and a memorandum were drawn up. What would the Samiti be called? Renu said, 'The men are doing "people's protection". Our *samiti* would be for women's *atma raksha* or self-respect.'[9]

[5]Mukhopadhyay, *Nari Mukti*, 33.

[6]For details see, Chinmohan Sehanavis, *46 No. Ekti Sanskritik Andolon Prosange*, (in Bengali) (Calcutta: Seriban), 2008.

[7]Chakravartty, *Communists*, 21.

[8]Manikuntala Sen, *In Search of Freedom: An Unfinished Journey* (Calcutta: Stree, 2001), 74.

[9]Ibid. The *Jana Raksha Samiti* was already set up at the initiative of the Communists to carry on relief work among famine-struck victims. Among them were

The Party's women's front was already formed in 1942, with Latika Sen, the first woman member of the Party, as its convenor.

On 13 April 1942, at the initiative of Calcutta's Communist women, an anti-fascist women's meeting was convened at the University Institute Library Hall. The Kolkata Mahila Atma Raksha Samiti (Calcutta Women's Self-Defence League) was formally set up. Ela Reid was the convenor, and the organizing committee included Manikunatala Sen, Jyotirmoyee Ganguly, Sudha Roy, Renu Chakravartty and Sakina Begum.[10] A report of this meeting was carried in Bengal's party journal, *Janayuddha*, of 1 May 1942. The meeting resolved to build up a strong women's organisation for people's defence (if necessary, women would have to take up positions along with men in offices, factories, and even on the battlefield), to teach techniques of self-defence like *jiu jutsu* and *lathi* wielding to women, and to establish solidarity with the Indian Army.

An eight-fold programme was issued. This included: 1) a propaganda campaign, 2) creating public awareness against the Fifth Column, 3) building civil defence, 4) collecting funds, food, and cloth for famine-displaced people, 5) helping in the evacuation of ordinary inhabitants from military-occupied places and ensuring that they get work as compensation and for their rehabilitation, 6) demanding government-aided fair-price shops run by district cooperatives, 7) organising women's defence groups with training in the use of *lathis*, martial arts etc., 8) assisting the farmers to grow crops and other grains.[11]... This was a joint appeal; along with Communist women there were others from the Congress, the Labour Party and so forth.

---

women, being sexually exploited and the need for *atma-raksha* for such women was therefore felt by the women members of the Communist Party. Ela Sen married to Alec Reid, a journalist working with *The Statesman* got associated with this group of Communist women. The couple lived on the second floor of *The Statesman* building, which became a meeting place of those women. Recalling those days, Manikuntala Sen in her memoir writes: 'It was in the home of Eladi that our first mahila samiti or women's society was founded. Renu, Eladi, Kamala, Shanti Sarkar, some other people and I were present.'

[10]Mukhopadhyay, *Nari Mukti*, 33.

[11]Ibid., 34.

In the first week of September, women activists organised a week-long campaign to explain the danger of Japanese aggression. Area-wise meetings, exhibitions, morning processions (*prabhat pheris*), plays, and cultural functions became their modus operandi. Calcutta was the main centre of this movement. Women volunteers of MARS worked in squads, spread over fifteen *bustees* or slums.[12] ARP training and dispensing medical aid in case of a bomb attack were part of the campaign. Women students of Calcutta colleges like Ashutosh, Victoria, Bethune, City and so on played a significant role.

Though MARS was formed as a broad front of women with non-Communist backgrounds, like Rani Mahalanobis, Leela Majumdar, Mira Dutta Gupta and many others, Communist women took the initiative and the leading role in planning and doing the organisational work. Manikuntala Sen later recalled the help these women received from P.C. Joshi, who said that women should not only struggle for their own gender rights, they should also lead class struggles. Their priority should be constructive work, especially the welfare of women and children. Other struggles would continue side by side: anti-fascist campaigns and the movement for the release of political prisoners.[13]

When a women's meeting had to be organised in a *bustee* area or a low income group locality, activists went campaigning from house to house, not once or twice, but many times. Renu Chakravartty's recollection of those meetings reveals how difficult and tenacious the work of the young activists was.

> As the meeting proceeded, some would lose interest and start a babel, talking amongst themselves. So we evolved the method of staging simple dramas to carry our message through the visual world. We, the organisers, worked in a multi-purpose manner. We arranged the meeting place, did the propaganda for the meeting among the women, went round collecting them, spoke to them of the issues which were of importance, and last but not the least, acted for them, sang and danced for them in order to convey what we were trying

[12]Ibid, 35.

[13]Sen, *In Search of Freedom*, 95.

> to say through a cultural form which caught their imagination. It was hard work, but in the end it was rewarding. Women started samitis in their areas. They could not move far from their homes—but could move in their *paras* (neighbourhoods). We began getting many active mahila samiti workers from among these local women.[14]

Women from the Ballygunge middle-class area were similarly mobilised, after door-to-door campaigns.

> An acute food crisis drew these women towards MARS. Demands for rationing and a ceiling on the price of rice and paddy became the agenda for women's agitations. The net result was the setting up of controlled—price shops which soon became centres of profiteering and graft. The black market was by now virtually legalised and hoarding by small householders, rich tradesmen, and profiteers was openly carried out and widespread. The situation in Calcutta worsened as the first exodus began from the rice-producing villages into the cities. The granaries of the villages stood empty and lonesome, the godowns of the merchants were full and overflowing, rice released for the consumption of the people was three-times too little as compared with the crowds that clamoured for it.[15]

The Bengal Famine was round the corner.

This was the beginning of the vast procession of hungry people who came from villages to Calcutta in search of food. It was a

[14]Chakravartty, *Communists*, 19–20.

[15]Ela Sen, *Darkening Days: Being a Narrative of Famine-Stricken Bengal* (Calcutta: Susil Gupta, 1944), 15; Ela Sen (Reid) in the preface to her narratives on famine wrote about the horrific situation prevailing at that time with the markets being under control of blackmarketeers and corrupt officials. 'Strange things began to happen that had never occurred before—a trade in gravel sprang up for mixing with rice and thus shortening the weight of the actual grains. No longer could people choose what rice they would eat. They had to take whatever was given to them, which was quite often a mixture of two or three types of grain. In many markets, goondas took over the distribution in Calcutta shops and appropriated one-third of the grain for black-marketing purposes. Graft became rampant from petty to high officials. The price of rice soared up to Rs 40 except in the controlled shops whose stocks gave out within a few hours. The streets of Calcutta resounded with the cry of people that were hungry.'

new scenario. In fact the first exodus from the villages started as the controlled-price shops began to function. They came to beg, boarding trains ticketless, or walking endless miles towards the city in search of gruel. The CPI immediately launched a countrywide campaign—*Bhookha Hain Bangal*—raising funds for the famine-stricken people through cultural squads organised by the Indian People's Theatre Association (IPTA). In his detailed account of the Bengal famine in articles in *People's War* which were later brought out in a pamphlet titled *Who Lives if Bengal Dies*, P.C. Joshi wrote:

> I was hardly five minutes in Calcutta when I was shaken up as I have rarely been by a voice through the window *'Ma Go babure!'* I had never heard such accents nor such a tone.[16]

Joshi brought the misery of Bengal onto the Party's and, more importantly, the nation's agenda.

> MARS activists had already started their agitation on the food crisis in the *bustees* and in middle-class *bhadralok* areas. A campaign for collecting two thousand signatures of women was launched by the Calcutta MARS and the All India Women's Committee and a deputation to the food controller was led by women representatives asking for more controlled shops. Their efforts led to the opening of a few shops but these were far short of popular needs and they were located too far away from the *bustees*. Growing hunger and our persistent agitation again put the women on their feet. How many homes could hope to cook their food with coal being sold at Rs 5 a mund? How many could buy rice at Rs 15 a mund? How many working women could stand in queues for five and six hours a day![17]

On 24 January 1943, a large number of *bustee* women flocked together to attend a Food Rally in the Calcutta Town Hall. Acute scarcity had shaken them so much so that they came to the rally along with their husbands and sons from Baghbazar, Maniktala,

[16]P.C. Joshi, *Who Lives If Bengal Dies* (Bombay: PPH, 1943), 1.

[17]*People's War*, 14 February 1943, Report on Calcutta by Renu Chakravartty.

Entally and Park Circus. This brought them in touch with middle-class girls and women; no other issue could do this in the past. Since August 1942, the Calcutta MARS had been holding meetings and forming *Mohalla* Committees. The demand for rationing of food was raised and put forward for the *first time* by these women.[18]

Mahila Atma Raksha Samiti workers supervised queues in front of Calcutta markets. When it was decided to open controlled-price shops, MARS recruited 200 volunteers who worked in eleven shops spread across all the big markets in Calcutta. 'Their mission was to try and prevent the manhandling of the women in queues and to help them collect their legitimate quota.'[19]... Manikuntala Sen vividly recalls those experiences:

> Long queues of women from the villages could be seen in front of the markets. They came to collect rice and our workers took turns to stay beside them. As a result of our pressure, a subsidised rice shop was started in Gariahat market. The party's cadres founded the Jana Raksha Samiti (People's Protection Society) and we worked in unison. Hundreds of men and women from the villages rushed into Ballygunge station by the 3 am train to collect rice. On hearing the clamour from our homes, we would get there at that time, make them stand in queues and when the shop opened in the morning, make sure that they obtained the rice. We had to fight with the shopkeepers on their behalf regularly.[20]

[18]Mukhopadhyay, *Nari Mukti*, 39; Food rallies or conferences were regularly organised by the *Jana Raksha Samiti* (the People's Protection Society) to pressurise the government to open ration shops. Kanak Mukhopadhyay, a founder member of MARS, recollects how at the initiative of the Calcutta MARS, around 300 women, both Hindus and Muslims, from 20 slum areas joined the massive food rally at Town Hall, where they sang along with others a famous song on this food crisis—*Ki Kori Upay Re Ki Kori Upay Chaaler Daam Bish Taka Mon, Kerosene Tel nai........* (What shall we do? Oh dear, what shall we do? Rice costs 20 Rupees a maund, as for kerosene—there is none...........)

[19]Memorandum by MARS, FIC Report, Volume 1, Nanavati Papers, National Archives of India (NAI).

[20]Sen, *In Search of Freedom*, 70–71. Recalling those harrowing experiences, she writes 'Dividing the time into shifts, some of us would stay near the queues. Procurers from the sex trade would hover around young women who had to be guarded. Some women would give birth while they waited and they would have to

Young MARS activists like Bela (Bandopadhyay, later Lahiri), Usha, Kalyani (Mukherjee, later Kumaramangalam), Kanak (Dasgupta, later Mukherjee) and many others became *didimunis* or elder sisters to slum people. They 'had not only conquered the *bustees* and the queues. They were winning over the whole of the locality itself.'[21] In the beginning, it had been more a political campaign about abstract, general issues like fascism, which was not an immediately felt crisis. 'The movement lacked reality'.[22] Within five or six months, everything changed as practical work for daily necessities began. A reporter of the People's War narrates:

> Bela was called '*Didimuni*' by all the thousands of women who came to the queues before Baithakkhana rice shops. They simply adore her—would do whatever she asked them to do.

However, there is no doubt that the larger initiative did not entirely belong to women activists themselves but the Party guided them in all matters. Though the Party leadership was predominantly male, the fact that it enabled a broad women's front to come into being at this time did however create a forum for the politicisation of women and for a multi-class solidarity to develop among them. In that sense, Joshi's advice to women to engage in constructive and nurturing work—providing food—was helpful, even though it also restricted them and kept them in their traditional roles. Extending women's domestic roles into the public arena, enabled domesticated women to work in public and political spaces.

A report placed by S.G. Sardesai on behalf of the Central Committee of the CPI held in Bombay in February 1943, specifically addressed women members of the Party.

> Women volunteers must be organised to carry as volunteers in women's queues. Women representatives ought to be included by

---

be looked after. Sometimes a woman would remain in the queue with a dead child in her lap, refusing to let go of her place, there were many such incredible sights. Day and night, our workers did not have a spare time.'

[21]*People's War*, 23 May 1943.

[22]Ibid.

> every possible effort on all food committees. *New women comrades* [Emphasis mine] must be encouraged to speak at women's meetings on the issue of food.[23]

He also added that women standing in the queues must be protected from molestation by *goondas*.

From January 1943, a monthly bulletin was brought out by the women's front. Within six months, the number of women comrades rose to 151 and that of sympathisers to 438. There were 5,957 MARS members, and eighty branches of the Mahila Atma Raksha Samitis were formed in Bengal....[24] Initially the women's front worked from the Bengal Provincial Party office at 249 Bowbazar Street. An All Bengal Women's Party Cell was formed with five members—Manikuntala Sen, Renu Chakravartty, Kamala Mukherjee, Juiphul Roy and Kanak Mukherjee....[25]

****

The Calcutta MARS, along with the Muslim Women's Self Defence League, organised the first hunger march to the Bengal Assembly on 17 March 1943. Five thousand women in their tattered clothes and with babes in arms marched from Calcutta *bustees* and from the suburban villages in the north and south of the city. Manikuntala Sen recalls that memorable march:

> We did achieve something important. It was impossible to save people on rice acquired by begging from the better-off and *khichuri* or gruel of rice and *dal* cooked in the canteens. The only way out was to bring down the price of rice and open ration shops. It would require a revolution and we got down to work. At that time, the Chief Minister was Fazlul Huq. We decided that one day while the Assembly was in session, a women's procession would surround it and place its demand for rice.[26]

[23]The report was later published titled 'People's Way to Food' by S. Sardesai, (Bombay: PPH), 1943.

[24]Mukhopadhyay, *Nari Mukti*, 38.

[25]Ibid.

[26]Sen, *In Search of Freedom*, 71–72; MARS activists decided to surround the

The hunger march had a tremendous impact.

> It was one of the first militant actions of women which stirred the city of Calcutta and the Government had to sit up. A new stage in the movement was reached—from a purely middle-class movement of women, the Calcutta MARS had moved out to the working class housewife and had spread its message to the village poor.[27]

Huq pleaded helplessness. But the women were insistent about needing more shops, proper supplies, specially in *bustee* areas, and reducing the price of rice to the controlled rate of Rs 13.25 per maund. Finally, the Chief Minister was forced to order a hundred bags of rice to be distributed to the demonstrators then and there. Eventually, eight more shops were opened in Calcutta, out of which six were reserved for women.[28]

Within a few weeks of this march, the first conference of the Calcutta MARS was held on 27 and 28 April 1943, with five hundred women delegates from *bustees* and lower-middle-class areas. Eleven area meetings had been organised earlier and four local conferences held in central, north, south, and east Calcutta for its preparation.[29] The famine threatened utter destruction of family life as it scattered people all over in search of food. This realisation also drew wider sections of women into the political movement. It was felt that a 'National Crisis is a crisis in the kitchen and so was "National Unity, yet in embryo, a unity in and for the kitchen"'.[30] MARS

Assembly House while in session to place their demand for rice. A large group of women who came from all over Calcutta, assembled at the Town Hall and travelled without tickets in trams (thanks to tramway workers) and gathered at the gates of the Assembly House. Women leaders who managed to get the pass entered and 5000 women just followed them as the gates were opened. How the leaders got the pass cards has been narrated by Manikuntala Sen in the following excerpt: 'Fazlul Haq was a friend of my Dadu and he was very affectionate towards my father as well. I mentioned the names of my father and grandfather and arranged a meeting with him. When I asked for cards to enter the Assembly, he gladly supplied a few. Other cards were obtained by Renu, Gita Mullick, and Eladi.'

[27]Chakravartty, *Communists*, 30.

[28]Memorandum of MARS to FIC, Nanavati Papers, NAI.

[29]Chakravartty, *Communists*, 35.

[30]*People's War*, March 7, 1943.

now had 4,000 members in Calcutta itself. An executive committee was formed with eleven members. The noted writer of delightful children's fiction, Lila Majumdar, was president and Anila Devi was secretary. On 28 April 1943, at the open session of Calcutta MARS Conference, held at the Arya Samaj Hall, Mohini Devi, a veteran Congress leader, was asked to preside.[31]

> When Manikuntala returned to Calcutta from Barisal, she found Mahila Samitis had branched out all over her neighbourhood.[32] The Calcutta MARS decided that every unit would have to open a centre or two for constructive work. Milk booths and schools for children, handicrafts training centres for women and the elderly were started and most of the work began in the *bustee* area.[33]

Mahila Atma Raksha Samiti activists faced a number of challenges. A deputation of Beniapur and Entally *bustee* area led by them met the food controller asking for shops in their own *bustees*. These were located in residential areas for sailors and the men were away on ships. Nothing came out of the meeting and it was deeply demoralising for the women, who had expected much from that deputation. The Samiti activists explained that one conference would not settle the issue; this was, in fact, the beginning of a long battle. The mood changed soon as one working woman replied:

> Never mind, we shall still come for the meeting. And why shouldn't we come? We never dared stir out of our homes before. Today we walk a mile for rice and stand six hours in front of the 'Control'. We shall go wherever you ask us, show us the way.[34]
>
> Very soon, the women activists among MARS *could* mobilise a mass of women within a short time. The Mistripukur *bustee* at Chetla, the Hazra *bustee,* and the Garcha *bustee* became centres of mobilisation. Some of the women were terrified. One woman screamed out that white soldiers would shoot all those who joined

[31]Chakravartty, *Communists*, 35.
[32]Sen, *In Search of Freedom*, 95.
[33]Ibid.
[34]*People's War*, 14 February 1943; Report on Calcutta by Renu Chakravartty.

> the procession. But others were in no mood to listen to her. Sharp came Marium Bibi's cutting reply: 'We are prepared for everything: bayonets, bullets, everything. We are hungry as lions. We will devour everything that stands in our way, not excepting you too if you don't shut your filthy mouth.[35]

The first annual conference of the Bengal Provincial MARS was held in Calcutta on 7 May 1943, at the Overtoon Hall. By this time, the membership of MARS in Bengal had risen to more than 22,000 in 21 districts. Around 100 elected delegates and more than 400 observers attended the conference. The wide network of Mahila Samitis in different districts was put on a firm organisational footing and all local *samitis* were integrated with the Bengal Provincial MARS. *People's War* brought out a report of this conference, titled 'To defend Motherland Homes and Honour, Bengal's women organise Atma Raksha Samitis'. They came from 22 districts, from bombed Chittagong to cyclone affected Midnapore, from Rangpur in the north to 24 Parganas in the south. Mahila Atma Raksha Samiti now had a membership of 22,000.

The organisation was broad and representative. Indira Devi, the niece of Rabindranath Tagore, was its president. She had been active in the cause of women's social emancipation and fought for the removal of *purdah,* child marriage, and illiteracy. It brought Congress and Muslim League women, *bhadralok* ladies, and slum and peasant women together. The Calcutta unit of MARS had Mohini Devi, a renowned Congress activist, as its president. The most important resolution on food was moved by Gulbahar, a woman from the slum area. Slums and villages began to throw up a new category of women leaders.[36]

Along with campaigns for practical everyday needs, MARS activists also carried out door-to-door campaigns on national issues, elucidating the political line of the Party: the need for a national government and the urgency of a Gandhi–Jinnah meet, even if it failed. Renu Chakravartty later described this at a women's meet to celebrate the 50th anniversary of the CPI in 1975:

[35]Ibid.

[36]*People's War*, 23 May 1943.

> With a lot of patience and courage we went from door-to-door talking about political issues like Gandhi Jinnah must meet again. Going round in the area meant not going to known people but also to strangers. Following a lane and knocking at each door on both sides was a tedious job. Sometimes, we were chased away and abused in 1942 and even our houses were sought to be burnt down. However, many listened to us, discussed with us, gave money, became members and signed on the petition. 'Come again' was also the response from many—that was an incredible experience.[37]

Mahila Atma Raksha Samitis of Ballygunge, Tollygunge, and Sahanagar welcomed Gandhiji's efforts for unity and sent telegrams to Gandhiji and Jinnah urging them to resolve the deadlock in the League–Congress negotiations.[38] On 20 June1943, after another conference at the Town Hall on the food crisis, packed to capacity by women alone, the Calcutta MARS opened seventeen gruel distribution centres and eight free milk and medicine distribution centres in north, central, and south Calcutta.[39]

Where did the MARS get funds to run these centres? Kanak Mukherjee mentions the Bengal Relief Society, Marwari Relief Society, Bengal Women's Food Committee Corporation, Health Department, Standard Pharmaceutical, Indian Medical Association, Bengal Chemical, Calcutta Clinical Research Association etc.[40] Mahila Atma Raksha Samiti mobilised fourteen women's

[37]Renu Chakravartty's unpublished document—her speech in Bengali on the 50th Anniversary of CPI in 1975. [Translation mine]

[38]*Hindustan Standard*, 12 August 1944, IB Collection, File No. 1340/43, West Bengal State Archives (WBSA).

[39]Kanak Mukhopadhyay, *Nari Mukti*, 61; The Calcutta MARS carried out a massive programme at different places of distributing gruel (*khichuri*) to the hunger-struck people. Kanak Mukhopadhyay mentions the names of different areas of Calcutta where all those 17 relief centres were set up: 'In north Calcutta, Balram Ghosh Street, Gopal Mitra Lane, Panchanan Ghosh Lane, Harinath De Road, Banamali Sarkar Street; In Central Calcutta, Dickson Lane, Akhil Mistri Lane, Williams Lane, Pottery Road; in South Calcutta, Garcha bustee, Kankulia bustee, Charu Avenue, Indra Roy Road, Ramanath Paul Street, New Road, Raja Basanta Roy Road, Sah Nagar. Eight free milk distribution centres for children were opened at Nabakrishna Street, Harinath De Road, Durga Charan Doctor Lane, Bowbazar Street, Gariahat Road, Indra Roy Road, Hazra Lane, Raja Basanta Roy Road.'

[40]Ibid., 62.

organisations in Bengal for the Women's Food Committee, for the distribution of food, cloth, and medicine during the famine period. Within a short span of time, it collected Rs 75,000.[41] A leaflet was brought out titled 'A Call to Women' on 20 December1943, appealing for relief material and funds to people in and outside India. A Bengali translation, with photographs of famine-stricken women, men, and children, along with an introductory note on the relief work of MARS, was circulated in all the districts. The response was overwhelming. A letter from Perin Bharucha of the Punjab Women's Self-Defence League in Lahore, dated 27 January1944, to Kanak Mukherjee shows how inspiring this relief campaign was for other parts of India.[42] On 11 December1943, Calcutta MARS called a general body meeting of its members and sympathisers to discuss the question of rationing. The Calcutta MARS' second Annual Conference was held on 26–27 March 1944, with a membership of 3,080.[43]

By the end of 1943, the problem of rehabilitation of destitute women famine victims came to the fore. Taking advantage of the destitution and helplessness of women, some people tricked and exploited them and the Nari Seva Sangh was established in April

[41]Ibid., 61.

[42]IB Collection, File No. 1340/43, WBSA, Intercepted letter dated 27.1.1944: Communist Party's *Bhookha Hai Bangal* (Famine Stalks Bengal) campaign for fund collection spread to other parts of the country. Communist women took it up in their respective states. Once Perin Bharucha (later Ramesh Chandra) of Punjab Women's Self Defence League came to know from Somnath Lahiri, a Communist leader of Bengal about the initiative of MARS in relief operation, other than *Jana Raksha Samiti*, she decided to send the Lahore collection directly to the MARS. Hence she wrote from Lahore the following letter to Kanak Mukhopadhyay: 'Dear Kanak, I did not know till Com. Somnath told me that MARS had a separate fund. Uptil now we were sending our collections to People's Relief Committee. However our Lahore Collection, we shall send you separately from now onwards. We have just collected about 300 rupees and some medicines and almost two thousand clothes. (Warm ones also). I have written to your secretary asking her whether you want 300 in cash or you want me to buy out of it, powdered milk, glucose syrup, medicines or clothes or anything else. We are trying to get a free wagon to Dacca. Get Ela Reid to write immediately. This must be done fast. I have also written for two dozen copies more of your pamphlet—Perin'.

[43]IB Collection, File No. 1340/43, WBSA.

1944, by MARS and other organisations in order to counter that. The objective was to train them to start rehabilitation work in villages. Thirty women came to the Calcutta camp to undergo training in a four-month course, which taught them spinning, tailoring, needle-work, and how to make handicraft goods and handmade paper. Kamla Chatterjee and Renu Chakravartty of MARS took the initiative for this along with Sita Chaudhuri and Brahma Kumari Roy of the Bengal AIWC. By the end of 1944, an exhibition of handicrafts was held at Calcutta Presidency College which was inaugurated by Sarojini Naidu. She was deeply impressed with the quality of the exhibits and by the performance of Nari Seva Sangh.[44] From the beginning of June 1944, MARS took up the issue of the rehabilitation of displaced women very seriously. The week of 10–17 June 1944, was observed as Social Life Reconstruction Week (*Samaj Jibaner Punargathan Saptaha*). It was estimated that about 30,000 of Calcutta's 1,25,000 destitutes had gone into brothels.[45] The Samiti took steps to reclaim and rehabilitate them. The 'Fight Prostitution' campaign became one of the main planks of the MARS movement. 'Start Deserted Women's Homes' was the slogan.[46] Ela Reid, secretary of the Bengal Provincial MARS, issued a circular to all district secretaries to open shelters for rehabilitated trafficked women and other distressed women, instructing them to 'hold *baithaks* and mass meetings and send resolutions to the press and memorandum to the government'. The circular read:

> The government should be compelled to pass ordinance to put a stop to this, by opening at least one centre in each union and cottage industry to be started in towns and villages for the earnings of the distressed women.[47]

In the memorandum submitted to the Famine Inquiry Commission, MARS blamed the government for prematurely closing down relief kitchens.

[44]Mukhopadhyay, *Nari Mukti*, 73; For the entire speech of Sarojini Naidu in English see Chakravartty, *Communists*, 71–72.

[45]Memorandum of MARS, FIC Report, Nanavati Papers, (NAI).

[46]IB Collection, File No. 1340/43, WBSA.

[47]Ibid., Circular No. 12, 24 January 1944.

> Both non-official and official medical relief has been insufficient and inadequate. Thus it will be seen that malnutrition and disease [there were already epidemics] created in both men and women the feeling that the only means of keeping alive was by entering a brothel or by selling either wife or child. In this stage, some alternative occupation should have been found for both men and women or an extensive dole system should have been instituted for those medically certified as unable to work.

In this memorandum, the problem of acute milk shortage was pointed out and concrete suggestions were put forward to provide subsidised milk for mothers and children. It also asked for a temporary ban on the sale of ice cream and *chhana* sweets.[48] When Lord Wavell decreed that the streets of Calcutta must be cleared of garbage, left there by displaced people, fear shook the destitutes as they saw police vans, ARP vans with uniformed attendants picking up people at random and taking them away ... Mothers, weeping for their children, were forcibly picked up and carried away in these vans ... Thus husbands, wives and children were separated through official inefficiency to handle the situation and the general unwillingness to secure the cooperation of the public who had the confidence of the destitute.[49] Mahila Atma Raksha Samiti took up the issue of self-protection of such women.

The Samiti women tried to keep the organisation broad-based even though there was a campaign that it was merely the women's front of the CPI. The AIWC, the women's wing associated with the Congress, became resentful of the influence wielded by MARS from 1946. It denied that the latter had a broad, non-sectarian character and spread a smear campaign that its activities were simply a ruse by CPI women to infiltrate into AIWC ranks.[50] Earlier at the behest of Sarojini Naidu who addressed the Women's Student's Conference in Lucknow in 1940, a number of Communist women had indeed joined the AIWC. This was the time when the party was banned

[48]Memorandum of MARS, FIC Report, Nanavati Papers, NAI.

[49]Sen, *Darkening Days*, 21–22.

[50]IB Collection, File No. 1148/43, WBSA.

and it was difficult for them to work openly. They felt the need for an organisation which was not illegal and they regarded the AIWC as the best choice. Even after the formation of MARS, Communist women worked with the AIWC on issues like the Rao Committee Bill, property rights of women and right to divorce, and ban on dowry. Later, however, they felt the need for their own women's organisation with a frank socialistic and pro-Soviet creed. The division, however, began on the issue of lowering the membership fee of AIWC to 4 annas. It was difficult for poor women to afford Rs 3 as annual membership fee which was what the AIWC charged. Mahila Atma Raksha Samiti leaders were told that at sub-branches the fee could be lowered, but the annual membership fee of the AIWC would not be reduced. At the 19th session of the AIWC held at Akola (Berar) on 20 December 1946, MARS leaders fought for a general lowering but they were defeated. The AIWC leaders might have felt afraid that the 'Communists by this would swamp them out of the leadership'.[51]

In the post-famine period, things moved in a different direction. There were already differences, even among MARS leaders, regarding their association with the AIWC. It was clear from a letter dated 3 May 1946, written by Renu Chakravartty to Hazrah Begum, a renowned CPI leader of Kanpur, that some of the leading women comrades including Manikuntala Sen were 'unconcerned, uninterested and callous' about attending AIWC Executive meetings. Renu Chakravartty writes:

> We have got 5 office-bearers in the Calcutta AIWC but they neither work for the AIWC nor regularly attend its meetings. The general feeling is that we must now build up our own organisation, going more into working class areas, not wasting time in middle class organisation like AIWC. In fact, we are doing neither because upto the elections (of 1946) we just kept up MARS and the cooperative functioning in skeleton form and maintaining only its formal existence.[52]

[51]Chakravartty, *Communists*, 212.

[52]Letter dated 3.5.1946, intercepted by the police, IB Collection, File No. 1148/43, WBSA.

This was strong language against comrades. Renu Chakravartty wrote: 'all our comrades are scattered, muddled, each doing what they want'.[53]

A different national crisis, however, intervened at this time: communal riots that became a virtual civil war in 1946. Women could not operate on their own in the midst of such violence but assisted at relief centres. Mahila Atma Raksha Samiti secretary Anila Devi appealed for relief through a press statement from 93/1A Bowbazar Street:

> Although the MARS has not opened any separate centre for giving relief to the riot victims, yet individual members of the Samiti are giving every sort of service to the relief centres in their localities specially to the centre at Jasoda Mansion in South Calcutta and at Lake Hospital and Abhay Charan Vidyamandir where they were nursing the injured. Bina Sen, a committee member has collected a sum of Rs 400 for South Calcutta Congress Committee Relief centre. The Society appeals for help from generous public both in kind and cash. Contributions received by any member should be deposited in the office of the samiti.[54]

In September 1947, a Peace Squad (*Shanti Sena*) was organized by MARS along with Congress and League women. Kamala Chatterjee was the main initiator. Large numbers of MARS volunteers joined the huge procession which went round Beliaghata (where Gandhiji was staying) and other riot affected areas to bring confidence to the minorities in these areas and to cement the bonds of Hindu Muslim unity.[55]

Independence came to a truncated India. Bengal was divided and displaced people from East Pakistan migrated to Calcutta in massive numbers. Rehabilitation again became a central activity. The Calcutta MARS leaders established contact with refugee women who had been either members or sympathizers in East Bengal. With these contacts, they easily established networks in refugee colonies where displaced MARS activists were now herded. Manikuntala Sen writes in her memoirs:

[53]Ibid.

[54]IB Collection, File No. 1148/43, WBSA.

[55]Chakravartty, *Communists*, 108.

> After overcoming police repression, we set up units of our Samiti in almost every colony. We were on the move all the time. I began to find new friends in the colonies every day.[56]

Mahila Atma Raksha Samiti activists in Calcutta penetrated into 'every makeshift refugee household' and 'masquerade as a relief organisation'.[57] Against the backdrop of the communal propaganda of the Hindu Mahasabha and the general anti-Communist fervour, it was not easy for the Communist men 'to penetrate the thick wall of refugee resistance to the Communist ideology for quite some time'. Bijoy Majumdar, himself an important member of the CPI, visualised MARS as a 'Trojan Horse within enemy territory'[58] This was a difficult time. None of these new *samitis* in the colonies affiliated themselves to the MARS because they wanted to maintain their independent colony identity.[59]

[56]Sen, *In Search of Freedom*, 182.

[57]Prafulla Chakraborty, *The Marginal Men* (Kalyani, Lumiere Books,1990), 49; MARS women initially found it difficult to penetrate into the newly set up makeshift refugee huts in different colonies and camps, as they were linked with the communists, who were still detested for their anti-Quit India, anti-Subhas Chandra Bose stand and their position on minority question on the eve of the partition. There was an in-built resistance of the refugees to communists for quite some time. However MARS in course of time as a relief organisation could break that wall, and that has been lucidly explained by Prafulla Chakraborty in his seminal work on refugees of East Bengal.: 'Unlike the menfolk, the refugee women were more susceptible and more willing to talk against the Establishment to persons who soothed them with their women sympathy and brought them succour. They had to face the tantrums of the children when they were hungry. They had to go about food-gathering or borrowing money when the men folk returned home emptyhanded'.

[58]Ibid. 50.

[59]Sen, *In Search of Freedom*, 182–183: Different colonies had taken the names of national leaders of freedom struggle, like Bagha Jatin Colony, Nehru Colony, Netaji Nagar and so on and so forth. Mahila Samitis cropped up bearing the names of their respective colonies, eg., *Azadgarh Mahila Samiti*. According to Manikuntala Sen, who worked in these colonies, 'None of these new samitis affiliated themselves to the Mahila Atma Raksha Samiti; they wanted their independence.' MARS in late forties was looked upon as a frontal organisation of the CPI. However, when the National Federation of Indian Women was formed in 1954 as an all-India body with a broad non-partisan perspective to bring in progressive women from non-political and even from other parties, with prominent office bearers from non-party background, Bengal unit of the NFIW became acceptable to the colony mahila samitis, earlier reluctant to be affiliated to MARS. Many of them coalesced into the Bengal unit of the NFIW.

In the meantime, the Second congress of the Communist Party of India, held in February 1948, in Calcutta, gave a call for armed struggle with slogan: *Yeh Azadi Jhoothi Hain* ('This freedom is fake'), and replaced P.C. Joshi with B.T. Ranadive as its secretary. Under the new political line, the struggle for national liberation continued as it was felt that the national bourgeois leadership of the Congress had betrayed the people and compromised with British imperialism. Eventually, the CPI was banned and soon many Communist women, who were active in MARS, were put in jail or went underground. All the others faced intense police repression. At the Fourth Annual Conference of the Calcutta MARS, held on 19 June 1948, at the Chowringhee branch of YMCA, a decision was taken to divide the Samiti into West Bengal and East Pakistan zones. A delegation on behalf of the Calcutta MARS was sent to investigate police atrocities in Bara Kamlapur in West Bengal on 27 June 1948. It was led by Bina Roy Choudhury, headmistress of Beltala School, Shobha Hui, the president of Calcutta MARS and Asru Das, the secretary.[60]

At the end of 1948, from November 3 to 6, the first convention of toiling women of India was held in Calcutta, at the initiative of the Bengal Provincial MARS. It called for a new movement based on common struggles for land, bread, and freedom. The first task on the agenda was to protest against the Government of India's order banning the Asian Women's Conference called by the 80 million strong Women's International Democratic Federation (WIDF). In fact, a preparatory committee with many sympathizers and non-Party women was formed between 21 August 1948 and 7 December 1948. But the Indian government refused visas to the foreign delegates. As a result, the conference was later held in Beijing in China. The Party was now banned and MARS was considered by the government as a women's front of CPI.''Bans, slanders, and thousand other difficulties did not prevent the democratic women of India from joining the convention'.[61] A wide section of women from many parts of India, came to Calcutta and joined this convention. There were delegates from ten district branches of the Paschimbanga

[60]*Jugantar* (Bengali Daily), July 6, 1948, IB Collection, File No. 1340/43, WBSA.
[61]*People's Age*, 21 November 1948.

Mahila Atma Raksha Samiti, from the Parel and Shivaji Park branches of AIWC of Bombay, from the Janwadi Mahila Sangh of Delhi, from Kerala, from Assam, from the Benaras Mahila Mandal, from the West Bengal Central Government Employees' Union and from the teachers' association. There were also delegates from East Pakistan and representatives from girl student's association, IPTA, kisan and working class women. The presidium consisted of Parvati Bai Bhor and Jamini Dasi from the working classes, *kisan* leaders Atarbala and Baroda, and Manjusree Devi and Vimal Ranadive, leaders of middle class organisation[62] The new political line of the CPI was reflected in its report. The one year of freedom was not the sort of freedom of which women had dreamt—an end to poverty and want, security of jobs, healthy conditions for children.[63]

The convention was followed by an open rally culminating at the Indian Association Hall in Calcutta, where nearly one thousand women gathered in spite of the boycott of the press, and police repression under Section 144. Manjusree Devi inaugurated the rally and Anila Devi, Vimla Kapoor, and Perin Ramesh Chandra reported on the proceedings of the convention.[64]

Mahila Atma Raksha Samiti now drifted away from the AIWC. Around the same time, it got affiliated to the WIDF along with the Punjab Lok Istri Sabha, the Golden Rocks Nadar Sangam and Andhra Mahila Sangam. The AIWC too was approached by WIDF but it refused to get affiliated, presumably because of its fear of the Communist cast of the international body. According to police reports, MARS got affiliated to WIDF in the middle of 1946.[65] However, Ela Reid, general secretary of MARS, and Vidya Kanuga, a student representative, had already attended the first conference of WIDF held in Paris in 1945. WIDF members Simone Betrand of France and Morozova of USSR visited Calcutta in February 1948. They went to working-class and peasant areas to ascertain the condition of women and met members of MARS, AIWC, and other women's organisations in Calcutta, trying to affiliate Indian

[62]Ibid.

[63]Ibid.

[64]Ibid.

[65]IB Collection, File No. 1340/43, WBSA.

organizations to the international body. On behalf of MARS, Renu Chakravartty was deputed to look after the delegation and Sarama Das published a booklet in Bengali, titled *Viswa Nari Sangha* on 5 October 1948 to propagate WIDF messages.[66] Though the South East Asian conference could not be held in Calcutta, WIDF leaders invited an Indian delegation comprising women from all groups to attend the World Congress of Women to be held at Copenhagen in June 1953. Mahila Atma Raksha Samiti brought out a leaflet (undated): 'Build up Movement in support of political prisoners'. This leaflet mentioned the hunger strike of 600 political prisoners including 25 women; among whom were Manikuntala Sen and Kamala Mukherjee. It gave a call for a women's convention at the Indian Association Hall on 27 April 1948 to express solidarity with Communist prisoners who were on a hunger strike. The Samiti at this time was functioning from 13/1 Balaram Ghosh Street, Ground Floor[67] The Calcutta MARS now opened a MARS Cooperative Society functioning with many sympathisers as shareholders.[68] On 26 May 1948, fifty women led by MARS staged a demonstration in front of the Writers Building to demand the release of Manikuntala Sen and other political prisoners.[69] On 27 April 1949, a terrible incident occurred: police fired at a procession of women who were demanding the release of political prisoners. Mahila Atma Raksha Samiti leaders Latika, Pratibha, Gita and Amiya died in the firing.[70] After that, the day began to be observed as Women Martyrs' Day by MARS.

****

Mahila Atma Raksha Samiti left a far-reaching legacy on the future course of women's movements in Bengal. Women had already been front ranking activists in nationalist and peasant struggles. They had also joined revolutionary terrorist groups. But movements under the

[66]IB Collection, File No. 1148/43, WBSA.

[67]IB Collection, File No. 1340/43, WBSA.

[68]IB Collection, File No. 1148/43, WBSA.

[69]Ibid.

[70]Sen, *In Search of Freedom*, 202.

MARS had a different connotation. The political issues which they took up were enormously controversial in the national scenario: the danger of fascism, of Japanese invasion and the need for 'National Unity for a National Government'. These were by no means popular political slogans. But even at the height of anti-communist hysteria, MARS women could draw women of other viewpoints or opinions towards them with their commitment to the urgent needs of starving, dying, and threatened women.[71]

Women like Rani Mahalanobis repeatedly asserted that MARS did not belong to any political party. To strengthen her argument, she cited the examples of Nellie Sengupta who was the president of the Samiti in 1944, and also referred to the participation of Jyotirmoyee Ganguly, a leading Congress figure. In a press statement on 15 March, 1946, she said: I have mentioned before that the object of the MARS is to carry on its work with the help and active cooperation of all parties and all communities. Our aim is to give food to the hungry, to make the helpless self-supporting and to advance the welfare of the children. Should those who belong to the political party be not given any opportunity to participate in welfare work? Our only desire is to unite everyone in welfare work for women and children.[72]

Even as a mass front, however, MARS was definitely under the leadership of women affiliated to the CPI and they obeyed the Party line without any deviation all through its many radical changes and shifts. Eventually, however, they began to rethink the new political line initiated by Ranadive. At the same time, the impetus for such rethinking came from a changed international directive from the Soviet leadership: 'Democratic Movement of India would comprise the national bourgeoisie, the working class and both the rich and poor peasants, all taken together'.[73] The re-emergence

[71]'Letter from Suhana Devi 20 March 1946 to the Editor, *Nationalist*', File No. 1340/43, IB Collection, WBSA ; For details, see Lila Majumdar, *Pakdandi* (in Bengali), (Kolkata: *Ananda*, 2007), 307–308.

[72]IB Collection, File No. 1340/43, WBSA.

[73]Sen, *In Search of Freedom*, 211. Soon after independence in 1948, the CPI declared independence as fake, the slogan of the new leadership of the Party under its general secretary, B.T. Ranadive was *Yeh Azaadi Jhoothi Hai* (This Independence is Fake) and gave a call for an armed struggle. Eventually the Party was banned and many communist women along with men comrades were arrested. Political prisoners

of a non-insurrectionary multi-class national perspective meant preparations for the first general election to be held in 1952. Soon MARS leaders—Manikuntala Sen and Renu Chakravartty—were elected to the legislative assembly and parliament respectively in 1952. Mahila Atma Raksha Samiti also plunged into struggles for the regularisation of refugee colonies.[74]

*****

Mahila Atma Raksha Samiti had a far-reaching impact on other states as well—Punjab, Andhra, Bihar, Kerala, and so on. But a need for a separate organisation for women always remained a debatable issue among the party leaders even at a later stage. B.T. Ranadive and S.A. Dange opposed the idea and E.M.S. Namboodiripad and C. Rajeswara Rao were in favour of it, as Vidya Munshi conveyed to me in an interview on 15 March 2006. Many party leaders like Gangadhar Adhikari, S.G. Sardesai, Muzaffar Ahmed, and Bhowani Sen expressed in their writings the imperative need for a distinct mass movement among women.

The second interesting point was the relationship of the MARS with the AIWC. In spite of the fact that women within the Party distanced themselves from the political line of the Congress during the 1942 Movement, MARS continued working with the AIWC. It is interesting to recall that Sarojini Naidu came as a chief guest

began a hunger strike which continued for several weeks. Manikuntala Sen was also on hunger strike in jail. Towards the end of the hunger strike, she noticed a quotation in a newspaper and the quote was from a journal published in Bucharest, supposed to be the mouthpiece of the International Communist Movement, which mentioned the need for a democratic movement with the national bourgeoisie and other toiling masses, all taken together. This news made her rethink the efficacy of the political line of the party. And so she writes in her memoir: 'We had been told that workers and middle peasants alone were our allies. The rest were all enemies. But if I had to build a friendship with the very group that were described in that paper (a journal from Bucharest) then what had I been doing all these days? Why had I come to jail saying '*Yeh Azadi Jhoothaa Hai*' either? And why was I dying of starvation?'

[74]For details, see Gargi Chakravartty, *Coming Out of Partition* (New Delhi: Bluejay Books, 2005) Chapter 2.

to the All India Girls' Students' Conference, held at Lucknow in January 1940 at the initiative of the All India Students Federation and she continued to maintain close relations with these women, many of whom later became leaders of MARS. The Bombay session of the AIWC, held from 7 to 9 April 1944, elected a Standing Committee in which, in spite of the prevalent anti-Communist bias, two Communist women were taken in—Perin Ramesh Chandra from Punjab and Renu Chakravartty from Bengal. In the election for the Executive of the Standing Committee, Perin topped the list.[75] Within MARS, the section close to Sarojini Naidu tried hard to work with AIWC and they sustained this effort till early 1948. They also believed that they could turn the face of the AIWC towards working-class women, particularly in Bombay. Members of the Labour Party, the Bolshevik Party, or Congress sympathisers and even Congress women like Nellie Sengupta, who later defeated Kalpana Joshi, the Communist candidate in Chittagong in 1946, were associated with its activities, despite the fact that MARS was controlled by the Party and by Communist women within MARS.

Once it became legal, MARS consolidated itself and held its Sixth Conference in Calcutta from 3 to 4 May 1952. It soon changed its name to Paschim Banga Mahila Samiti (PBMS). The ideological struggle within the women's front, underwent an evolution with many of them asserting and taking a different position from the Party. At a meeting, sometime in November 1952, Communist women discussed threadbare, the politburo's document on, 'Task on the Women's Front'. While appreciating the call for a separate broad-based, multi-class organisation of women for equal rights, they disagreed with the Party for not addressing the issue of 'the double yoke of oppression'. They expressed their resentment that the Party document had failed to link the social with the economic demands of women. They were critical about the Party's formulations regarding working-class women as they did not address gender inequality.[76]

The constitution of the new National Federation of Indian Women (NFIW) was drafted by the section of the MARS that was close to the AIWC. It was given a federal structure, giving space to

[75]Chakravartty, Communists, 207.

[76]IB Collection, File No. 1340/43, IB Report, 25 November 1952, WBSA.

non-Party and non-political women's organisations and individuals, precisely to make it a broad non-sectarian front. Consequently, many non-Party women like Anasuya Gyanchand, Kapila Khandelwal, Aruna Asaf Ali, Pushpamoyee Bose and others from different states joined the organization and became its office-bearers. Their opinions were sought and given due weight, they were not just figureheads.[77] In West Bengal, fourteen different Mahila Samitis mostly from the refugee colonies and other places—who earlier had refused to be affiliated to MARS—now joined the West Bengal unit of the NFIW. Similarly, PBMS, which remained under the Party's control, became the most important constituent of the NFIW's West Bengal unit. The parallel existence of PBMS and the NFIW unit of West Bengal with other Samitis turned out to be a unique feature, reflecting the ideological struggle of the Communist women within the Party.

[77]Chakravartty, *Communists*, 225.

CHAPTER ten

Famine, Food and the Politics of Survival in Calcutta 1943–1950

Sanjukta Ghosh

> *Here in the city the goods of civilization are multiplied and manifolded; here is where human experience is transformed into viable signs, symbols, patterns of conduct, systems of order. Here is where the issues of civilization are focused: here too, ritual passes on occasion into the active drama of a fully differentiated and self-conscious society.*
>
> Lewis Mumford[1]

FAMINE VICTIMS IN THE CITY

In undivided Bengal, the famine of 1943 was the last major historical event of horrific deaths resulting from starvation and hunger-related diseases, that affected an estimated 1.5 to 3 million people,[2] with far-reaching effects on the neighbouring areas. Calcutta, as the microcosm of this human tragedy, continues to be inspired by its famine generation who were witnesses to a new kind of social construction of the city in the 1940s. The social memory of the event has contributed to numerous comparative speculations and allusions to a similar disaster in postcolonial India, during times of food insecurity.

[1]Lewis Mumford, *The Culture of Cities* (New York: Harvest Books, 1938; 1966; 1970 edition), 3.

[2]Amartya Sen, *Poverty and Famines: An Essay on Entitlements and Deprivation* (New York: Oxford University Press, 1981).

Food availability decline (FAD),[3] natural disasters such as the damage to the *aman* (kharif) rice crop both due to tidal waves and a disease epidemic, war and breakdown of legal entitlement are the key historical explanations of the 1943 Bengal famine. Bengal, as a key rice bowl of India saw a major decline in rice production by the 1940s and relied heavily on Burmese exports. The availability of cheap imported rice from Burma had prevented economic depression from spilling over into subsistence crises in either India or China. But this safety-net of food supply had created tensions among the indigenous farmers who struggled to produce rice for the market and maintain the stability of village subsistence-insurance mechanisms as well. The crisis was overwhelming in the post-war period with the onset of a man-made Bengal famine in 1943 that represented a crisis in food 'entitlement' among selective urban and rural groups.

War and famine created a complex situation of civilian response. Amartya Sen's study shifts the focus of the causes of famine from Malthusian food availability decline theories to poverty and 'entitlements'. The 'entitlement crisis' (one of the principle causes of famine in Sen's estimate), that implies the breakdown of the socio-economic conditions favouring the peasant's legitimate claim to food, was also the crisis point of Bengal's morality[4] to cope with the dramatic transformation of '*Sonar Bangla*' (bounteous Bengal). His analysis of famine was a trenchant critique[5] of the policies that led to inequalities in the mechanisms of food distribution, responsible for an uncontrollable situation of social and economic dislocation.

Commercialisation of agriculture led to myriad circumstances in which village relations were forged, and the agrarian relations were transformed, leading to a wide-spread loosening of patron-client ties. The works of Sen and Greenough show that market-generated ties in particular and obligations to dependents in general were severed rather quickly during periods of economic distress. Urban political

[3]Sugata Bose, in *Agrarian Bengal: Economy, Social Structure, and Politics, 1919–1947* (Cambridge: Cambridge University Press, 1986); 'Starvation amidst plenty: the making of famine in Bengal, Honam and Tonkin, 1942–45', *Modern Asian Studies*, 24, No. 4 (1990): 699–727.

[4]Paul Greenough, *Prosperity and Misery in Modern Bengal* (New York: OUP, 1982).

[5]Sen, *Poverty*, 1981.

mobilisation of the poor migrants in the post-famine period testified to this trend. It is now well-known that famine alters the terms of entitlement (legitimate claims) for the peasant and more recently it is argued that it alters the circumstances of enfranchisement (the degree to which the peasant can make a legitimate claim to subsistence) as well, particularly in its urban dimensions, as shown here.

War time market disturbances and famine-induced price controls led to shortage of rice, forcing a massive displacement of rural population. Greenough notes the collapse of patronage and nurture as direct causes of famine victimisation, brought about by migration into the city in search of food, work and basic provisions of living. Amartya Sen's analysis of the Bengal famine as a result of 'crisis in entitlement' draws attention to the fate of the non-cultivating group at the heart of famine resilience, as they suffer extreme deprivation, unable to either purchase food or exchange it for labour, being overwhelmingly weak. The moral economy based on the mutual benevolence of *annadata* (patron) and loyalty of *poshya* (dependent) proved to be inadequate in extreme cases of survival.[6] Large-scale destitution, begging and migration emerged, with evidence of loot and robbery as temporary solutions of living. In this essay, the definition of famine victims migrating to the city will apply to the amorphous group of non-cultivators who had no savings of any kind, such as the numerous petty traders, poor artisans, wage-labourers, servants, beggars and other displaced rural occupational groups. These groups migrated to the city of Calcutta on a vast scale, when expectations around traditional insurance mechanisms weakened, not only as a last resort of survival, but also due to changes in the circulation of food and other livelihood support structures.

This paper looks at the salience of new and hastily formed urban networks of food distribution mechanisms and other circumstantial exigencies to broaden the scholarly debate about fatalism in Bengali famine response. It shows how various, disparate strategies to survive hunger were often displayed as a dramatic mode of protest

[6]James Scott, *The Moral Economy of the Peasant: Rebellion and Subsistence in Southeast Asia* (London: Yale University Press, 1976); Arjun Appadurai, 'How Moral is South Asia's Economy?—A Review Article', *The Journal of Asian Studies*, 43 (May 1984): 3, 481–495.

that not only added to the rhetoric of human suffering, but was also represented in powerful cultural productions of the time with long-term implications. While famine had 'brutalized the consciousness' of the population,[7] migration in relation to it had subverted the meanings of existential structures associated with places[8] and emotions such as land, territory, community, home, hearth, family, subsistence, patronage that were exposed to many complicated and rapid layers of transformation. The everyday politics of survival encompassed various levels of emotional adjustments that justify a historical scrutiny of labelling famine victims as fatalistic, with inhibitions against 'snatching' food. Such an assumption has been immortalised in Manik Bandyopadhyay's novel *Chiniye Khai Ni Keno* ('Why did they not snatch and eat?'), that echoed the comments of Jawaharlal Nehru, with regard to the passivity of the famine victims.[9] This paper seeks to look at these transformative emotions in relation to struggle over food/rice, meanings of which changed in the context of new urban exigencies that emerged as a result of rural migrations into the city of Calcutta.

NETWORKS OF FOOD SUPPLY IN THE CITY

The search for rice in the city of Calcutta came in the wake of a gradual decline of several *haats* (small markets) in the villages that was depicted in contemporary novels such as Bibhutibhusan Bandyopadhyay's *Asani Sanket* ('Distant Thunder') and *Kreta o Dokani Shunya Haat* ('Vacant Village Market').[10] The absence of labour-intensive *dhenki* rice in the *haats*, and fluctuating market prices raised suspicions among villagers, who tried to overcome everyday scarcity by choosing to migrate to Calcutta. But these apprehensions about rice supply or limited access were linked to

[7]Suranjan Das, *Communal Riots in Bengal: 1905–1-947 (*Delhi: OUP, 1991).

[8]Janam Mukherjee, *Hungry Bengal: War, Famine, Riots, and the End of Empire 1939–1946* (PhD Diss., University of Michigan, 2011).

[9]Malini Bhattacharya, *Manik Bandyopadhyay: Selected Short Stories* (Thema: Calcutta, 1988), 197–198.

[10]Subrata Rayacaudhuri, *Kathasahitya, Manvantarera Dinagulite* (Calcutta: Pustaka Bipani, 2007), 94–95.

lower earnings, sale of gold stock, surplus land, and household utensils and other legitimate claims to livelihood.

Uncertainty regarding food supply, general inflationary pressures, the agitation of traders in Calcutta and repeated warnings of a Japanese invasion compounded to push up the price of rice in all the major markets to 37 rupees per *maund* (c. 82 lbs or 37 kg) in mid-August 1943.[11] The political threat posed by the proximity of the Japanese eroded faith in the government's ability to maintain order or even to defend Calcutta. The city had been bombed in late December and further sporadic attacks came in early 1943.

Calcutta was transformed into a military cantonment with blackouts and curfews amidst a chaotic urban spectacle of military trucks, foreign soldiers, trenches, paper window dressings, bomb shelters and a growing panic about everyday basic provisions. The musician and composer Jyotirindra Maitra reminiscences the event as: '...the blessings of military might drop on heads; weighed down under the lack of rice, lentil and clothes'.[12]

In this situation, the Bengal government decided to take a strong stand against the organized grain trade, when stocks in Calcutta and surrounding areas were sealed and police guards were posted. There was a prevailing tendency to play down real scarcity, for fear of public repercussion, as well as a lack of knowledge about the actual pattern of grain consumption. In public, the ministers responsible for food supplies gave ambiguous explanations for food shortage that continued to plague the relief ethos through the worst months of the famine.

Meanwhile, the government remained over-protective of Calcutta's 'priority classes' who kept up the city's vital war production. Food supplies were assured to officials and organised industrial work forces, including railway workers, officials, the army and other privileged groups, thereby not only swelling the wholesale grain market but also the quantity of food available in the city. In

[11]For the rise in prices of rice in other regions such as Burdwan, see Sir Azizul Haq, Evidence before the Famine Inquiry Commission, 1945, Vol. II, 426–438. For the price shifts in Calcutta see Sen, *Poverty*, 54.

[12]Quoted in Nikhil Sarkar, *A Matter of Conscience* (Calcutta: Punascha, 1998), 18.

May 1943, the whole eastern region became a 'free-trade' area, a scheme that succeeded in provisioning Bengal's cities, by extracting rice from Bihar and Orissa as well. The new policy resulted in the dominance and pervading influence of a new breed of food suppliers, including large-scale incursion of speculators, agents of big business, hoarders and small buyers from Bengal into all the markets. Bengal merchants and their agents went into the interior villages and offered fantastic prices, indulged in wild speculation, passing ownership of goods through various hands.[13]

The result of such chaotic internal trade was that more rice was transported into Calcutta than could be consumed by the metropolitan populace, through fair distribution. Towards the end of 1943, reports appeared about heaps of grain in the botanical garden shrouded with tarpaulins.[14] Simultaneously, a pervasive black market in rice sprang up in villages, towns, and cities, easily evading nominal price restraints.

The city of Calcutta witnessed different types of corruption in supplies, and rationing encouraged new kinds of administrative and political measures, mediated by ambiguous vocabularies of control. During the years of the Second World War, the functions of provincial governments expanded rapidly, incorporating new and ad hoc recruitment at a time when food rations were being rapidly organised.[15] There were no statutory controls to keep down prices by issuing licences to specific dealers and controlling the movement of commodities. The inability of the state to monitor and control trade with its limited resources encouraged abuses, black marketing, and hoarding of food. Food relief was therefore constrained by both, artificially created shortage of supplies and a preferential treatment towards feeding the privileged urban segment.

The politics of artificial price fixation, random favours to grain dealers, rapid and ambiguous arrangements of licences created a flux

[13]'Memo from the People's Relief Committee (CPI) to the Famine Inquiry Commission', Nanavati Papers, Vol. I, 2, NAI. Memo from the Bengal Rice Mills Association in 180.

[14]B.M. Bhatia, *Famines in India* (Bombay: Konark, 1963), 321–22.

[15]For an account of the wartime expansion in the government apparatus, see William Gould, *Bureaucracy, Community and Influence in India: Society and the State, 1930s–1960s* (London: Routledge, 2011).

in the distribution and access to rice, the shortage of which was already a source of moral panic among the city dwellers. Sharp fluctuations in grain prices led to newer recognition of public responsibility that was beginning to be redefined in the contexts of scandal and controversy over hoarding. A rapidly devised bureaucratic restructuring to meet the exigencies of war and the impending food crisis created different nodes of hierarchical controls, which stood between the local food administrators and the public campaign that brewed in the wake of secret price deals. Urban networks of new interest groups, comprising those dependent on rationed and controlled goods, all of the labourers involved in the movement, middle-class urban consumers, voluntary relief organisations and business groups were drawn into the everyday struggles of the urban poor in different capacities. The city was drawn into a complex bargaining network, whose members constructed various versions of food shortage by appropriating famine events to their own advantage.

Protest against urban relief failures was repressed by censoring political activism of the major nationalist party, while criticism of the government's food policy was discouraged in the state legislature for political security. Beyond all these immediate considerations to protect the vested interests of a war economy, a cultural assumption to prioritize the safety and integrity of a capital city, as an essential shelter, might have influenced the relief administration. Hence, for the famine victim, refuge in the city was the safest option, amidst all the chaos of food distribution and fledgling promises of the government. But wartime consumerism in the city brought out a sharp distinction between what was expected from relief and its constructed reality. This distinction foregrounds the cultural response to generic aspects of poverty, as well as to famine induced scarcity, hunger, and relief that was facilitated by various urban networks.

DISCURSIVE MEDIATIONS OF FAMINE IN THE CITY

At the time of war, the provincial committee of the Communist Party of India, forming an informal alliance with the ministers of the Muslim legislative parties,[16] remained committed to providing

[16]Greenough, *Prosperity and Misery*, 159–60.

food relief. But Calcutta's business community in conjunction with the bureaucracy had established control over several aspects of the province's governance. At the same time, many important economic and administrative decisions were adopted by the British governors in consultation with the military. It was in this anomalous political climate of rumour mongering, promises and secrecy of the administration, and press propaganda that the 1943–44 famine unfolded. Within this context urban networks were engaged in the production of wartime knowledge about famine and human suffering in the city. Famine was culturally embedded in the city's consciousness, the horrors of which evoked a battle of conscience in the bureaucratic circle. The moral tension was evident in the verbal struggle to agree on a descriptive nomenclature that would justify the exact magnitude of the city's food insecurities.

Wallace Rudell Ackroyd a member of the Famine Inquiry Commission, instituted in July 1944, found it hard to ascribe the year 1943 as a famine year. He was more at ease with the euphemism 'food shortage', but had also been alerted to the 'moral breakdown' of the city's administrative control of the food situation that was incidentally picked up by some press reporters.[17] Britain's Secretary of State for India, L.S. Amery made speeches in parliament using other euphemisms such as food 'situation', from a long cabled text avoiding words such as starvation, cholera, or corpse.[18] Ian Stephens wrote in detail in *The Statesman* about the shameful and deliberate efforts of the colonial government to conceal or underplay the facts of famine, implying the discursive control of famine in lieu of an objective and practical solution.[19]

The Statesman's campaign was instrumental in raising public consciousness about the situation, both in India and Britain. However, the government, by breaking into crude constructivism about the actual material conditions of the city, expected that it would be possible to control social protest by selective description and control of language. If politico-economic situations could be

[17]W.R. Ackroyd, *The Conquest of Famine* (London, 1976).

[18]L.S., Amery, and J. Barnes, *The Leo Amery Diaries* (London: Hutchinson, 1980).

[19]Ian Melville Stephens, *Monsoon Morning (*London: Ernest Benn, 1966), 189.

transformed through acts of language, so too could the materiality of food shortage. The speeches of Britain's secretary of state for India, L.S. Amery reveal this attitude, where the whole problem of famine was taken to be largely one of psychology. Hence, Amery asserted in favour of good propaganda in India, so that effective advertising of grain availability could induce hoarders to release grain.[20]

The government focused on food supply and rations, while Calcutta was dragged into a nexus of 'press propaganda' and 'oral rumour' that constituted crucial elements in the discursive management of famine. Hoarding had to be countered by 'forceful propaganda', including effective advertising of assured supplies but without revealing the quantitative data on actual amounts available for consumption. Press coverage on policy decisions, advertising and propaganda of food supplies were heavily relied upon, to a point where any counter opinion was treated with extreme suspicion. Criticism, such as *The Statesman's* pictorial exposes of famine horrors was attributed to a serious failure of the propaganda and publicity machine. Ian Stephens wrote in *The Statesman* that immediately after the first picture-page of the newspaper had come out on 22 August (1943), the Government of India's chief press adviser, Kirchner had warned that there were emergency rules to curb such actions. But Kirchner was equally baffled by the ambiguities of the emergency rules governing the use of graphic pictures in such circumstances.[21] *The Statesman* waged a relentless battle for eight weeks, feeding the urban readers with articles, letters, and photos, thereby embarrassing the authorities. Stephens recollected that the newspaper had enthusiastic backing from the public, 'British as well as Indian, Governmental and otherwise, in uniform and not'.[22] Hence, wartime exigencies involving a panic-stricken urban public were bound up with the particularities of the city's investment in the discursive management of famine victims.

The policing and control of the dispossessed revealed a sense of insecurity that was heightened by cases of local corruption. In urban constituencies, rumours were a key influential tool revealing the

[20]Ibid., 191.
[21]Ibid., 185.
[22]Ibid.

experiences of corrupt times. These constituted the anti-corruption narratives revealing the real and lived experiences of food shortage, rations, and war exigencies, in the form of propaganda literature of the literati and contemporary artists. The various claims of harassment and corruption coalesced into descriptions/narratives of fraud and scandals. During the 1940s corruption scandals in the city resulted in public outrage, escalating to anger and frustration towards the authorities.

Other than organised demonstrations of political parties, a spirit of urban activism fanned by a non-partisan style action against corruption was in place. Self-proclaimed residents' organizations claimed food relief, couching their demands in the new language of public service and citizenship. Their complaints about ineffective food distribution disguised a shift in emphasis from familial benevolence and the maintenance of philanthropic relations to a more general notion of citizenship and recommendations of service towards the nation. Wartime political instability and partisan clashes of the mid-1940s, the moral predicament of food insecurity, visible urban destitution and the sensitive accusations of wealth hoardings—all coalesced to give various aspects of corruption a richer meaning in public campaigns.

Campaigns against corruption with regard to food supplies could touch a whole range of social ills and its remedies were sought through different mediums and networks. The nature of urban migration and the protracted misery of the displaced population can be gleaned from a well-constructed sample survey of the famine affected areas, carried out in late 1944 to early 1945 by the Indian Statistical Institute (ISI). This study, funded by the Bengal government's Department of Relief, under the direction of P.C. Mahalanobis, interviewed 15,769 households covering all occupational groups, both cultivating and non-cultivating.[23] The survey revealed that 1.076 million persons were destitute after the famine year, whose survival depended solely on the charity of others. The plight of the destitute in the survey report, couched

[23]P.C. Mahalanobis, Ramkrishna Mukherjee and Ambika Ghosh, 'A Sample Survey of After-Effects of the Bengal Famine of 1943', *Sankhyā: The Indian Journal of Statistics*, 7, No. 4 (July 1946).

in authoritative statistics, demarcated those who existed in large numbers under newer official categories of victims who befitted the description of the 'starving ill'.[24] But the other more influential and emotive public images of the destitute in circulation at that time were of those who needed to be huddled together and removed from the city's pavement, whose rags smelt from a long distance, and whose children looked vacantly at the sky, almost dehumanized. Premendra Mitra described the new urban species as:

> Like men, or not quite like them,
> More like terrible grotesque caricatures.
> Yet they move and talk and
> Gather like garbage in the streets
> In a stupor in the piles of offal,
> pleading for the dregs of rice.[25]

FAMINE LITERATURE AND ART—CULTURAL BACKLASHES FOR SURVIVAL

The period between 1940 and 1950 saw a crucial transformation in Bengal's politics and culture, with a distinct contribution by Communist writers who were not necessarily influenced by the propaganda of their political party. Poets, theatre personalities, artists and novelists all rallied to provide a graphic testimony of the famine victims, whose pictures and experiences were repeatedly used as a metaphor to evoke emotional responses.The work of the Indian Peoples Theatre Association (IPTA), which involved the members of an earlier urban group called the Youth Cultural Institute, provided a critical impetus to the cultural front of the Communist Party in India.[26] Politically influential plays such as Bijan Bhattacharya's *Nabanna* ('New Harvest') (1944) staged by the IPTA acquired an

[24]Bernard S. Cohn shows how various categories of colonial knowledge were crucial to the colonial project of political and cultural control in Bernard Cohn, *Colonialism and Its Forms of Knowledge: The British in India* (Princeton: Princeton University Press, 1996).

[25]Quoted in Nikhil Sarkar, *A Matter of Conscience*, 20.

[26]Rudrangshu Mukherjee (ed.), *Art of Bengal: a vision defined 1955–1975* (Kolkata: CIMA, 2003).

iconic status in popular protests led by actors who were Communists and re-enacted with live improvisation during performances among the rural population. Apart from IPTA's portrayal of famine through stage performances, songs, banners and posters, several artists such as Zainul Abedin (1914–76), Somnath Hore (b.1921), Chittaprasad (1915–78), among others, painted stirring pictures in the same genre of realism.[27] In December 1944, the eighth annual conference of the All India Student's Federation saw the launch of an album comprised of famine art, by a young group of Calcutta artists, the sale proceeds from which were used to fund the famine relief work.[28]

Representing *samajbadi* (socialist and egalitarian) consciousness[29] the famine generated literati were able to communicate in their works elements of extreme pessimism, decadence, mistrust, and evidence of irresponsibility through images and texts. They distinguished between the outward manifestations of famine, and the inner contradictions among government officials and the social elite. The historical processes involved in assembling famine images and coding it for an audience, required configuring the famine artefacts—bowls of rice, half-eaten dead bodies, empty stores, shrivelled up breasts and so on, to provide a critique of wartime urban corruption and material greed. These were effectively cultural referents, adapted by critical urban constituencies to promote a social and moral struggle against famine.[30] Methodologically, I will use examples of these texts and art that represented famine as a transformative event in the lives of authors and their characters, shaping their relationships and personal values in both societal

[27]Rita Dutta, 'From Indian to individual' discusses the prints, sketches and bronzes of Somnath Hore, depicting the wounds of famine, in Mukherjee (ed.), *Art of Bengal*, 73.

[28]See the foreword by Sarojini Naidu in Arun Dasgupta, Kamrul Hasan (et al.), *Bengal Painter's Testimony*, December 1944 (IOL: P/V 1614).

[29]Tanika Sarkar mentions Sabitri Roy's socialist consciousness as concerns representing a structure of beliefs and sensibilities in social welfare that was non-partisan in its fundamental approach. See the Introduction in Chandrima Bhattacharya and Adrita Mukherjee, *Harvest Song: A novel on the Tebhaga Movement* (Stree: Calcutta, January 2006), vi.

[30]These cultural referents figure prominently in a postcolonial film of Mrinal Sen, *Akaler Sandhane*, 1980.

and familial settings. The temporal significance of 'famine texts', many of these being first hand oral testimonies, personal memoirs, photographs, genres representing real theatres cut across documentary and fictional narratives.

The multiple sites of confrontation in the city of Calcutta demonstrate the intertwining relationships between moral discourses, social practices, cultural referents and popular movements against food shortage and corruption of supplies in the basic provisions. Imageries of famine and mortality became a means by which people imagined and voiced their opinion as citizens, during a specific historical moment around decolonisation. Issues of food supplies affected by corruption, and rising to the challenges of anti-corruption were effectively debated in terms of the relationship between state and society, and other binaries such as the roles of the urban and rural gentry, privileged and displaced, communal tensions and disparate party ideologies.

Representing a suffering cityscape, Calcutta at the same time was host to various fluid symbols of famine protest: rice being a significant component in the food campaigns that were geared towards the production of poverty as 'popular' culture. In famine literature, the moral content of the idea of 'corruption' was linked to the specific supply and consumption of rice. A study of the semiotics of rice reveals the different scalar implications of poverty, modes of survival, social differentiation within the regimes of corruption, and how these distinctions were embedded in the cultural milieu. During famine, rice was seen as a special 'register' of consumption, associated with complexities of acquisition, which may or may not be a function of real scarcity, as there was evidence of hoarding and black marketing due to price restrictions or separate access for the elite. Rice as a scarce object acquired 'semiotic virtuosity' by signalling fairly complex social messages such as the moral sanctity of acquiring it through just means. It was also associated with specialised knowledge concerning the links between nutritional deprivation and its effect on the body and mind. The graphic pictures of starvation generated a high degree of linkage of consumption of rice to body, person, and social responsibility.

The usual picture of migrants relate to those who dragged themselves from the villages to Calcutta, dropping inert, perhaps in front of well-stocked food shops. Yet neither windows were broken, nor were shops looted. Their plaintive cries, '*phan dao go phan dao*' (begging for starch) echoed the city's lanes. *Phan*—the starch drained after boiling rice was all they would ask for. In the city, one heard the constant wailing for *phan* by the beggars who were chased out, when they moved from door to door in search of food, a visual that recurred in famine depictions. The cries for *phan* resonated in the city and descended into the general chaos of barking dogs, yielding an eclectic mix of emotion—disgust, empathy, vacant and repetitious acts that needed no direct attention. Although the disposable gruel satiated the hungry, it had neither any substantial nutritional value nor served as a symbolic gesture of charity. The serving of *phan* outside the house, from relief counters or by the roadside was seen as a routine way of averting an encounter between the privileged urban dweller and the visually horrific distressed. During his visit to Calcutta, P.C. Joshi (1907–80) the Communist Party general secretary remembered how the realities were extraordinarily different from the information available through the press, party and photographs. His personal encounter with a destitute was thought provoking:

> I have lived in slum areas as Communist organiser; I have worked in cholera infected areas as a youngster. But I had never seen such a sight before. My finger could hold the curtain no more, nor my eyes stand the sight.

Behind the curtains, Joshi heard a desperate voice '*ma go babure*' (pleading to the gentleman), but he could only see two 'cringing eyes over a face that looked blank, devoid of all human expression'.[31] The plaintive cries for *phan* from the destitute were however symptomatic of the inner contradictions of both the administrative management of famine and the civil responses to degrading material and moral conditions of urban Calcutta.

In these situations of desperation, 'entitlement' claims became more stark, when human emotions spilled over moral and prescriptive boundaries that underlined any passive form of peasant protest. In

[31]P.C. Joshi, *Who Lives if Bengal Dies* (Bombay: Peoples Publishing House, 1943) excerpt from *Khudartha Bangla*, ed. Madhumoy Pal (Calcutta: Deep Prakashan, 2013), 26.

desperate moments of hunger, Pradhan Samaddar as the anxious peasant and protagonist of *Nabanna*, loses his powers of reasoning in the city as he mumbles repeatedly in a soliloquy the pathos of losing a son, simply because he did not have enough rice. In Samaddar's soliloquy, one encounters a plethora of emotions that is not dictated by either legitimate claims to entitlement or issues of morality, but he turns to question the meaning of vacuous human life itself. A soul searching moment of critical humanism leads to silent suffering that represented emotions not just to tide over the temporal phase of famine, but also to consider a routine bout of domestic trauma such as accidental killings, murder, community infighting, hallucinations that pushed individuals to a point of exhaustion. Samaddar's anxiety exemplifies a range of famine victim's emotions that were disparate grievances, but could also add up to personal vengeance or lead to community clashes in contentious circumstances.[32]

The city networks involving mechanisms and agencies of rationing, refugee rehabilitation, relief and food control acquired an exemplary status in the literary and cultural production of famine propaganda. Calcutta was embroiled in the Leftist politics of image-making, news circulation, and reception through various means of knowledge production. Being a prominent leader of the Communist Party, P.C. Joshi was instrumental in transferring his direct experience and knowledge of surveying the famine districts to promote technical impressions of the famine victim. Joshi's partnership with the amateur photographer and a junior recruit to the Communist Party, Sunil Janah, became a critical source of technical representation of famine using photo journalism.[33] Janah was not only influenced by the city's artistic circle, including the close companionship of Chittaprasad, but also wrote personal memoirs and made technical collaborations with the likes of an itinerant American photographer Margaret Bourke-White, to create some of the stirring graphic-style images of

[32]See Sugata Bose, *Agrarian Bengal*, 1986, for a typical 'passive' approach of the famine victims who 'died without a murmur'. On a different note, Janam Mukherjee in *Hungry Bengal*, 2011, draws out the complex nexus between hunger and civil violence in the 1940s, by expanding the chronology of famine.

[33]Both Joshi and Janah provided detailed reports of the famine for the Communist Party's journal, while touring Chittagong and across Eastern Bengal. See Sunil Janah, *Photographing India* (OUP, 2013), 8–9, 15–16.

famine. Janah's photographs as the 'picture-story' complemented the passionate reports of Joshi and the strong linocuts of Chittaprasad that were published in the Party's newspaper *People's War*.[34] Sunil Janah provided a critical lens to his amateur interest in photography, during times when textual information derived from journalists and writers appeared more credible and news worthy. Other technicians of photography often referred to Janah's works as contributions of the 'photokwalla' (a photo vendor or outsider) in the hierarchical art world, who furnished a realistic snapshot of misery that technically fed into the Communist propaganda against hunger.[35] In the eyes of the urban literati, amateur and professional informants and Party volunteers, the city was conceptualised not as a spatial entity, but as a life form that was changing and metamorphosing as a result of the unusual times.

The urban space of Calcutta was transformed into a land of anguish, with a prevailing sense of insecurity, confusion and chaos characterising what was often called the *aporadhpuri* or the territory of crime. The war blackouts over the city intensified the panic over food shortage, robbery, beggary and suspicion towards neighbours. Suspicion and fear among the privileged city dwellers, spilled into other areas of social anxiety. The behavioural difference between the upper class *bhadralok* (urban literate elite) and the migrant *chotolok* (streetwise displaced non-elite) became a recurrent marker of upper class anxiety. For them, it was a normal urban scene to watch the beggars or the *bhikaris* (dispossessed agrarian community mostly landless agricultural labourers or fishermen), representing the *chotolok* to litter the city streets. They usually died a wretched death and were disposable like heaps of garbage along the side streets. The privileged followed the state command, when they abandoned the dead body of a stranger, a destitute lying un-demarcated on the streets. In his memoir, Ian Stephens wrote: 'Death of suffering if on a vast enough scale sounds almost meaningless, like the stars or waves of the sea ... And death by famine anyway in a big Indian city, may from casual glance be scarcely noticed at first.'[36]

[34]Ibid., 10.
[35]Ibid., 16.
[36]Stephens, *Monsoon Morning*, 169.

Contemporary literature reflected on the contrasting image of the indifferent and smug office-goer or the clerical *bhadralok* with the half-naked or ill-clad numerous *bhikaris* of the city, whose plight and hunger were normalised amidst the ever-flowing stream of rural migrants and the general crowd of the city. These distinctions were apparent in the eyes of the migrant Rampal Mistry in Manik Bandopadhyay's *Darpan* ('Mirror') (1945). Subodh Ghosh in *Tilanjali* ('Ritual of Bereavement') (1944) describes the constant flow of migrants as if they were like field rats reaching out for the 'chars' (flood plain sediments) of Calcutta, in sheer desperation to survive. Nabendu Ghosh's *Dak Diye Jai* ('Calling Out') (1946), Gopal Halder's *Tero-sho-panchash* ('1350/1943') (1945) and Sarojkumar Roychaudhury's *Kalo Ghora* ('Black Horse') (1943) give a classic contrasting image of the city, where differences between poverty and opulence were normalised as part of a routine spectre of city life. While the starving millions searched for food in dustbins and desperate cries filled the city *langarkhanas* (gruel kitchens) on one hand, political rallies, food demonstrations and processions of skeletons co-existed with hoarding and black marketing of staples, opulence of rich weddings and temple glitters.[37]

Amidst the social imageries of sharp contrasts, intellectuals were keen to locate the growing urban discontent in different sites of wealth and poverty. The questions of who gained and how profit was acquired through black market in grain sale, remained central to the literary quests in Tarashankar Bandopadhyay's colloquial Bengali novel *Manwantar* ('Famine') (1944), *Jhod o Jharapata* ('Storm and Scattered Leaves') (1946); Krishan Chand's *Annadata* ('The Giver of Grain') (1944) and Bhabani Bhattacharya's *So Many Hungers* (1947), among other key contributions.

The portrayal of material differences between the rich and poor, inscribed in the writings and art were used to delineate

[37]The contrasting urban images in famine literature stem from a desire to expose the corrupt and the powerful, and their selfish motives to promote the Hindu festivities, despite the surrounding misery. See Gopal Halder, *Tero-sho-panchash* ('1350/1943') (Calcutta: Punthighar, 1945). This point is also raised in Srimanjari, 'War, Famine and Popular Perceptions in Bengali Literature, 1939–45', in Biswamoy Pati, *Issues in Modern History: for Sumit Sarkar*, (Mumbai: Popular Prakashan, 2000), 280.

social imageries of crime and other hunger-related behavioural apprehensions.[38] Issues such as garbage sifting, shop lifting, relentless cries for *phan*, petty crime, prostitution, looting and street-level conflict, were seen as part of the urban living experience. In *Saharbasher Itikatha* ('City Dweller's Tales') (1946), Manik Bandyopadhyay wrote about the impressions of a migrant Mohon, who was accompanied by two villagers Sripati and Pitambar towards Calcutta's opulent material possessions that appeared alluring but also contributed to a deepening identity crisis. The migrant's encounter with the manicured urban culture may have prompted him to mimic a social status by appropriating new values of consumerism, even at the height of hunger. The glitter of the city heightened the sense of displacement for the famine victim, leading to personal anguish. Intricate details of material objects of pleasure including elaborate descriptions of furniture, china cups, carpets, curtains, fan and light represented not just desirable wealth but necessary attributes of urban living that served as identity markers, distinct from filth or dirt associated in local renderings of the *udbastu*, destitute or displaced populations.

Among the various artist networks, Chittaprasad the self-taught artist-activist of the Communist Party of India in the 1940s explored images of hunger, genocide and popular resistance.[39] He made his linocuts, sketches, posters, cartoons and documented his memories of village journeys 'in pen and ink and brush' for the Party organs. Chittaprasad's visual vocabularies capturing his experiences of the famine trauma were masterly represented in the 22 drawings (originally) in black and white comprising the *Hungry Bengal: A Tour through Midnapore District, 1943,* in a milieu of an emergent critical Left art-practice in the 1940s. Chittaprasad's early works chronicle major trends from a satirical subaltern perspective that were meant for Communist propaganda. The propagandist nature of his art work and portrayal of lived experience earned wide public

[38]The significance of behavioural markers as identity in urban culture is brought out in Manik Bandyopadhyay's Chinha (The Sign) (1947); See *Manik Bandyopadhyay Racanasamagra* [Complete works of Manik Bandyopadhyay], (Calcutta: Paschimbanga Bangla Academy, 2007).

[39]Sanjukta Sunderason, 'As Agitator and Organiser: Chittaprosad and the Art for the Communist Party of India', *Object*,13 (2011).

recognition. But scornful attacks on the British government policy also meant that *Hungry Bengal* was burnt and banned.

Zainul Abedin born in 1914 in Mymensingh showed a milder disposition in his use of famine imaginaries but became a part of the establishment in East Pakistan, as the founding principal of what was then called the Government Institute of Arts and Crafts. Another artist called Somnath Hore, born in 1921, driven by the same passionate humanism had become a Communist activist early in life. In his works, the narrower socio-economic concerns of famine victims came to be distilled into a philosophic query about poverty.

Though the policy shifts and factional squabbles in the political party had already disillusioned some of the artists and writers, their works continued to showcase the social struggle of procuring food, often leading to more dynamic and varied contestations. In Bijan Bhattacharya's *Nabanna*, the famine as a watershed event cuts across familiar binaries of exploitation—coloniser-colonised dyad—and looks at the transformations, as a result of multidimensional exploitation, changes in social structures and individual consciousness.[40] The famine became emblematic in this literature much of which was generated by writers and artists associated with the influential groups Progressive Writers Association (PWA) later called the Anti Fascist Writers and Artist Association (1942) and IPTA (1943). The groups commented on the intersections of imperialist, capitalist, feudal, caste-based and patriarchal violence, and produced a pervasive climate of intense literary concern by those who witnessed, experienced and toured the famine districts.

Bhattacharya's *Nabanna* exemplified a specific kind of critical realist engagement with urban history where the relationship between fact and language was taken seriously to propagate *lived experience*. *Nabanna* is a classic example of how Calcutta literary groups were engaged in a productive space for a discussion and dissemination of how food/rice and its varied meanings entangled in shaping both human suffering and emancipation from misery. In order to uncover the exploitative circuits of power, the enemies unmasked in the literary genres were not only the Japanese army

[40]Bijana, Bhattacarya, *Nabanna* (Calcutta: Prama, 1984).

who waited outside the borders, but also the administrators, the hoarders and the profiteers against whom no control was exercised.

In Bhabani Bhattacharya's novel *He who Rides a Tiger* (1954), Kalo the blacksmith migrant faced a similar range of obstacles that usually awaited the fate of the large number of landless and hungry rural population moving to the city of Calcutta. The protagonist (Kalo) after 'foraging' relentlessly for food and selling his tools, joined the hungry masses in the city to 'fetch' rice or gruel. Kalo arrived in the city to commence a new moral and political journey. The migrant's journey began with the interrogations of an impassive government magistrate who fitted the description of a 'man of justice in his sombre English clothes'. He asked for Kalo's identity: 'why did you have to leave?' Typically upon interrogation, the survivor exclaimed: 'I was hungry, Sir. Madness came upon me. It was because I thought I had to live or I would die. Madness came upon me. I had to live'.[41]

Kalo in *Tiger* and Pradhan in *Nabanna*, both as exemplary and direct victims of famine observed 'in silence' or passively the unfolding human tragedy in the city. Silence on their faces, but hiding the madness within, their actions culminated in a final phase of self-introspection and political subversion. In the case of Kalo, the typical queries of a magistrate haunted the victim's own ideological and moral concerns. Kalo discusses the implications of the trade in women's bodies with his young cellmate, wondering why a woman needed to die for the sake of honour. Kalo's interrogations were based on a real fear about his daughter Chandralekha who was duped into migrating to the city, by virtue of false information about his illness. Women like Chandralekha in the novel had to wind up in a brothel in order to procure food or save their relatives (such as in the case of Kalo) from illnesses. Presumably, Bhattacharya aims to represent bodily annihilation leading to search of food in the city, as the climax of a deep-seated conflict that structured the relationship between food, hungry bodies and morality/corruption in the narrative.

Survival was not only a physical strategy but reflected an ideological compulsion too. The woman migrating to the city for

[41]Bhabani Bhattacharya, *He Who Rides a Tiger* (Bankhall, Liverpool: Lucas Publications, 1988), 31.

example, begged for a bowl of rice to save her child, but she was also prepared to fight a dog or scavenge through the dust bins as a last resort for her survival. Women were usually illustrated as clinging onto the *aanchal* of their saree (the bit of cloth that covers breasts to overcome *lajja* or shame in front of a male intruder), to collect some rice that is intimately precious to feed a dying child. But food may have been exchanged for her own body, an act of rebellion against the norms of household morality in order to survive the famine. Rice from her *aanchal* symbolised the last resort of survival, exhausting the seed-stock in the household *macha* or roof-top storage that was kept for family subsistence. The last morsel of grain from the woman's *aanchal* became a last blow to her chastity as well. The grain was then designated as impure and filthy in content like the woman's saleable body in form. Queuing up for the gruel kitchen for some rice in the city's relief camp was viewed in similar immoral terms, as it would be to stand in the queues for prostitution or surreptitiously visit the city's rice contractors.[42] In other words, rice denoted as the intimate household commodity of subsistence became a remote commodity that had to be 'fetched' through manipulations in different urban circumstances, dissociated from its moral and emotional underpinnings.

Manik Bandopadhyay in *Darpan* (The Mirror) (1945), depicted the degradations in urban morality by deploying literary strategies to feminise famine suffering. Gruesome details of female emaciated bodies exchanged in lieu of grain were equated with local expressions of urban filth and dirt.[43] Representations of environmental filth were mingled with nude or half-clad female bodies with moral overtones. Literary descriptions of the city's streets comprised of various objects such as *nalah* or drain pipes carrying dirty water and filth, abandoned dead cats, torn rugs, sleeping mats, broken pots, wastes of vegetables, fish scales with hovering flies, materially symbolised aspects of deprivation, immorality and crime. Filth and nudity became the rhetorical devices of city life that represented not

[42]This imagery of famine feminization, signifying the exchange of food with *lajja* is found in Mrinal Sen's film *Akaler Sandhane*, 1980.

[43]For other examples see Margaret Kelleher, *The Feminisation of Famine: Expressions of the Inexpressible?* (Cork: Cork University Press, 1997).

only the sufferings of the women victims,[44] but also characterised the *bustee* or urban slum life that needed to be revived.

Given the scope of public charity, the most contested urban site between local governance and the famine victims was the city's *langarkhanas* (charitable rice dispensaries/gruel kitchens) that served as food distribution mechanisms that were different from the city's controlled shops (opened in August 1942) that sold food grains at a reasonable price. While the middle class in the city managed to get their rice through the 'priority classes' scheme or the controlled price shops, the destitute migrants had to procure food from the gruel kitchen. The *langarkhana* served cooked food free to the destitute. These gruel kitchen relief centres attracted thousands of migrants, who took up residence on the streets and in air-raid shelters. There were about 6,625 gruel kitchens opened in the whole of Bengal, of which 551 were manned by non-government relief societies.[45]

In the *langarkhanas*, poor villagers could get some food to survive, but these were mostly ill-organised official relief measures, where food took the form of a watery, unhealthy gruel of grains other than rice, their habitual food.[46] A strange concoction described as *khichudi* was served that neither filled the stomach nor saved life. The gruel offered not only failed to meet the relief regulations laid out for a basic nutritious recipe, but the unpalatable combination of cheap rough grains such as bajra, brought on disease and death. Yet the *langarkhanas* became a site of struggle to acquire relief from starvation, where the destitute would attack the kitchen-workers and loot, if gruel was in short supply. Although they would patiently queue up for the gruel, eye witnesses reported that they would 'grab and scream and push' and did not hesitate to use a brick.[47]

The *langarkhanas* were not only a site where the famine victims fought for survival. Many of the non-government enterprises were

[44]Jyotiprasad Basu, *Tero Number Basati* (Calcutta: 1946).

[45]Greenough, *Prosperity and Misery*, 130, fn.122.

[46]A low estimate of 82,000 destitute immigrants in Calcutta is given by Gopal Chandra Niyogi, *Banglar Durbhikhsa, 1350* (Calcutta: Silpa-Sampad Prakasani, 1351 B.S./1944), 67; a high estimate of 150,000 was reported by T.G. Narayan, *Famine over Bengal* (Calcutta: Book Company Ltd., 1944), 116.

[47]*Nanavati Papers*, 107, quoted in Greenough, *Prosperity and Misery*, 131 in fn.124.

manned by an amorphous urban group, whose interests often clashed, turning kitchen relief to factional ends. P.C. Joshi pointed out that Shyama Prasad Mookerji's relief kitchens were run by hired employees and Fifth Column youngsters from the Forward Bloc and Anushilan Samiti volunteers.[48] The Fifth Column was getting into the kitchens to build mass contact and secure support for the organisation of food riot and sabotage. Joshi wrote: 'The lay-out inside the opposition is this: Dr. Shyamaprosad gives the lead, the Hindu hoarders pay the cash and call the tune, the Fifth Column gives the cadres. It is a strange combination of the factionalist, the profiteer and the traitor.'[49]

The city epitomised the layered nature of social and political accountability in the novels. There were different sites of contestation that resulted from ill-advised government policy, fluctuations of food supplies on the market and indigenous profiteers taking advantage of crisis conditions. The mechanisms of food relief coped with the panic and uncertainty about future hoarders, when competition thrived among consumers as well as sellers.[50]

As an example of panic over access to food, it may be pointed out that the city was the site of selective relief, based on distinctions of caste and class. These distinctions brought out the sharp tensions between different groups over available material resources that impacted upon their modes of protest. Tensions in the city's *langarkhana* demonstrated the material status and/or related behavioural markers of the famine victims that either facilitated or obstructed their access to food. The urban food relief system showed that special efforts were in place to aid certain communities and castes like Brahmins in distress. The most elaborate arrangements were directed towards the 'loosely bounded middle class', while

[48]In July 1943, Shyamaprosad Mookerji's Bengal Provincial Hindu Mahasabha Relief Committee aimed to save the high caste and the respectable, and the Bengal Relief Commitee appeared more general in its purpose. See Ibid.,134–135.

[49]P.C. Joshi, *Who Lives,* excerpt from *Khudartha Bangla,* ed. Madhumoy Pal, 41.

[50]For a detailed account of how the Communist Party organized the People's Relief Committee and provided aid in the city as well as in rural areas see Suranjan Das and Premansukumar Bandyopadhyay, *Food Movement of 1959* (Calcutta: K.P. Bagchi, 2004), 495–506.

the selective process was applicable to the Muslims and the lower castes.[51]

In Bhabani Bhattacharya's *He Who Rides the Tiger*, Kalo disguised himself as a Brahmin, accompanied by his daughter Chandralekha, in order to protest against caste-based identity markers. By performing a miracle, both the father and the daughter were transformed into a priest and a priestess. In mimicking an upper-caste ritual process, Kalo and Chandralekha not only 'defile' their god and religion but also take revenge on the victimisers. They were worshipped by the urban elite showing utmost respect. But over time, Chandralekha felt suffocated, as she could not come to terms morally with the situation. This tension between food, body and identity of the protagonist, becomes clear in the way the author critically engaged with the selective supply of relief among the rich and privileged upper echelons of the city. Bhattacharya's rendering of the blacksmith-turned-holyman Kalo, capable of posing as a high-caste man provides a certain twist to the plot. Kalo and Chandralekha's resistance and revenge against the perpetrators of injustice takes a broader form of urban struggle that stems from their experience of famine, which itself has intense religious significance. Kalo's contravention of the caste code for the sake of survival during famine was an attempt to be *born again* into a privileged society.[52]

The dynamism of the emergence of distinct forms of caste protest and community mobilisation in the first half of twentieth century Bengal, points to the escalating significance of appropriating religious and culturally symbolic resources to produce formations that were anti-hegemonic, subversive, and could shift radically, along with changing configurations of class and power relations. Kalo in *Tiger* and Pradhan in *Nabanna*, both endorse a dissident performative project with great ability. Their attempts to transcend the material circumstances of poverty have more than one equation of 'suffering

[51]See the priorities of the Marwari merchants' relief organization—Marwari Relief Society in Greenough, *Prosperity and Misery,* 133–136.

[52]David Arnold attributes to religious rituals and associated cultural practices, distinctive areas where strategies of resistance may have developed that are not always obvious to the elitist scholar. See David Arnold, *Famine, Social Change and Historical crisis* (New York: OUP, 1988).

in silence'. While Kalo weds to a higher caste through purification of the bodily form, Pradhan resorts to a mental rendition contemplating the vacuous human existence in the disease and hunger-ridden city. Though deified, Chandralekha remains 'sensitive, introspective and intriguing',[53] as she chooses to be an honest human being in lieu of material interests. Pradhan similarly appeals to the basic instincts of human kindness and fairness, as he struggles to sift through the city's filthy dustbins for rice. This participation of the body and mind in the appropriation of either ideological or material symbolic resources was not only a means of upward mobility,[54] but a strong message against social inequalities that was intensified in the opulent surroundings of a city.

The works of artists and authors as vehicles of urban propaganda showed how the famine experience itself called for a responsible and complex engagement with different aspects of starvation and relief that were subject to shifting meanings in ethical, political, and social perspectives. In this context, it is worthwhile to take into account the scholarly criticism that exists against the fragmented nature of the urban artistic enterprise in this period. Although there was no unity in action in terms of both political and intellectual agendas, the authors in turn drew upon the historical context of the urban chaos, exacerbated by the famine experience, in far more profound ways than simply foregrounding the events, in a fictional narrative of personal vengeance or survival. Bijan Bhattacharya was one of the first authors of his time to weave a social drama exposing the multiple vectors of exploitation, rather than focus on the fate of an individual village household. Similarly, Bhabani Bhattacharya played out a drama of intense divided allegiances with multiple characters to map the ways in which different ideological and political systems compete to evolve the famine survival strategies in the city. A famine victim's narrative exemplified how a multitude of

[53]Bhabani Bhattacharya, *He Who Rides*, 103.

[54]Sekhar Bandopadhyay in *Caste Politics and the Raj: Bengal 1812–1937* (Calcutta: K.P. Bagchi, 1991), shows that lower caste leaders had appropriated symbols of authority not only as a means of upward mobility, but an attempt to divest them of their formal significance as a mark of protest against inequalities of political and economic power.

differences coalesced around the immigrant's identity that was partly constructed and/or reconstructed by encountering the urban culture.

The literary and artistic representational strategies[55] evoked a sense of complex entanglement between empowered urban groups (elite, high caste, businesses) and disenfranchised immigrants over access to food. Other than the corrupt mechanisms of food distribution and resource management, the famine victim's narrative exemplified a breakdown of entitlement, loss of women's chastity and tensions arising from the emerging cleavages of Hindu-Muslim, rural-urban and among caste divisions. The chapter looks at some aspects of these intersections in the complex urban arena, where allegiances were fluid and symbols were appropriated along various lines. It argues for an intimate relationship between physical survival strategies and socio-cultural semantics that became forceful in the complex urban surroundings and networks. These queries point to Greenough's reflection that 'famine is not only starvation but concerns the meaning of starvation and how a society chooses to distribute the social costs'.[56] In the process of surviving the famine, various networks redefined the spatial configurations of Calcutta's relief units, garbage sites, brothels, temples, pavements, dwellings, camps, shelters, kitchens, control shops, among others, in terms of human rights and justice.

CONCLUSION

It is generally perceived that the sheer scale of human tragedy as a result of famine had collectively brutalised the Bengali moral consciousness to an extent that there was no point of return. Famine images left an indelible mark of the famished human body in social memory. The onset of the Calcutta killings in 1946 manifested this psychological numbness in a highly divisive political environment. While communal explanations abound, the riots stemmed from

[55]The difference between art works as representative of famine as an event, and a representational strategy of an experiential artist bound by an event and its afterlife, is briefed in Sanjoy Mallik, 'Responses in the Art of Bengal to the 1943 Famine and the Tebhaga Movement', *Culture and Democracy* (1999), 65.

[56]Greenough, *Prosperity and Misery*, 275.

a diverse range of emotions and a complex convergence of contestations.[57] This chapter has shown how Calcutta succumbed to a divisive survival strategy with the elite divided over their moral commitments to famine victims on one hand, and on the other, remained compromised to state administered relief measures. Amidst such polarisation and partisan politics, the city was embedded in the cultural production of famine victimisation, survival and relief that outlived its temporal and spatial significance. Various networks, social alliances and individuals initiated a process of propaganda that contributed to building up a stock of new vocabularies, ideals and ethics of food consumption. In the aftermath of Partition, political and cultural action against poverty and hunger entered the domain of a rights discourse, based on these diverse resources of popular politics.

[57]For more details see Janam Mukherjee, *Hungry Bengal.*

PART three

Communal Relations: Solidarities and Violence

Direct Action Day, August 16, 1946. (Calcutta riots)
(*Courtesy:* Anandabazar Patrika)

Direct Action Day, August 16, 1946. (Calcutta riots)
(*Courtesy:* Anandabazar Patrika)

Mahatma Gandhi leaving Sodepur Ashram, Panihati, Bengal, on his way to Madras, January 19, 1946.
(*Courtesy:* Anandabazar Patrika)

Silent procession in Calcutta in memory of Mahatma Gandhi, January 31, 1948.
(*Courtesy:* Anandabazar Patrika)

CHAPTER eleven

On a Birthday (1946)

Samar Sen

Translated by Sumit Sarkar

Take me back to the city where I was at ease
Where after a ten—to—five office day
Men come home—tired but not in terror:
Where a crimson sunset flames in the western sky
Where housewives take their evening bath
And where some Babus, spurning their home
Use the cloak of evening darkness
To slip quickly into disreputable alleys.

Old times never return.
I look at the sky
Where a ball of fire blazes;
Dust flies, a bare tree stands erect
Leafless, tired.
Trees regain their youth every year

We drown in the mire dug by ourselves.
Death after a normal life—
Why, that is but moonlight on a tree
Or mist on a bare mountain.
That classical peace is not for us;
Along our voyage from sleeplessness to nightmare
Crows scream,
Dark sounds from anxious faces burnt out by the sun.
In Bengal, in Bihar, at Garmukteshwar

People carry mauled bodies to the graveyard
Or to the cremation ground.

Maybe Death reunites:
After life's games are over
All are the same—
Hindus of Bihar, Muslims of Noakhali
Hindus of Noakhali, Muslims of Bihar.

2
I do not hear any more how the ocean sings
Discordant beats of trams and buses
No longer pound in my blood.
I remember no more the red earth of the Santhal Parganas,
The soaring hills I once saw on the horizon
The music of Basantabahar heard at a courtesan's soiree.
I have forgotten the delectable gatherings at Baghbazar balconies.
The effeminate elegance of Ballygunge,
The sharp diamond glitter of Clive Street and Dalhousie,
The call to foreign parts from ships at the Dock.
That romantic malady no longer translates into poetry.

Passions of youth have become lusts of ageing men.
In ten year's time, I will trot off to Holy Kashi.

CHAPTER twelve

A Different Calcutta
INA Trials and Hindu-Muslim Solidarity in 1945 and 1946

Sohini Majumdar

The years 1945 and 1946 are commonly viewed as the most decisive period of conflict among religious communities in our history. They are characterised as entirely a time of communalisation of Hindu-Muslim relations in the city, a point of no return, which made Partition, as well as a permanent mutual bitterness, inevitable. By studying two localised mass movements in Calcutta in the winter of 1945–46, this paper, however, explores an alternative pattern of politics. In November 1945 and February 1946, Hindus and Muslims in the city reconciled their political differences and united on a common political podium against British imperialism. The context was provided by the trial of Indian National Army (INA) prisoners. Anti-trial agitations galvanised hundreds of people belonging to different religious communities against the colonial authorities. The political sentiment in the city was essentially anti-colonial and non-communal.

THE FIRST SERIES OF TRIALS OF THE INDIAN NATIONAL ARMY

The Japanese surrender to the Allied powers in 1945 had a profound impact on the Indian political situation. The INA, which was formed under the leadership of Subhas Chandra Bose with prisoners of war from captured Japanese camps, was fighting against the Allies from abroad with Japanese assistance. Japan's defeat dramatically affected the fate of the INA. Eventually, it was forced to surrender to British troops in 1945. The British government arrested most INA members and put them in Indian jails. They were accused of treason and put on trial.

The first major trial opened at Red Fort in Delhi on 5 November 1945.[1] On trial for their lives were Major General Shah Nawaz, Colonel Prem Kumar Sehgal and Colonel Gurbaksh Singh Dhillion:[2] a Muslim, a Hindu and a Sikh. Ten charges, including 'waging war against the King and murder or abetment thereof', were brought against them and to each of these they pleaded not guilty.[3] The Congress decision to defend the INA convicts was followed by the formation of the INA Defence Committee. An array of lawyers comprising Tej Bahadur Sapru, Dr M.R. Jayakar and Bhulabhai Desai stood for the defence of the accused and 'urged clemency' for the INA members.[4]

In his address to the first INA court martial, Bhulabhai Desai argued that the 'very charge of waging war brought against the three accused, Major General Shah Nawaz, Colonel Prem Kumar Sehgal and Colonel Gurbaksh Singh Dhillion, carried with it recognition of the insurgent Government of Free India'.[5] Quoting from authorities on international law, he asked the court to accept the proposition that 'if it was recognized that a war was being carried on, then the recognition of the insurgent Government followed as a necessary consequence'.[6] He argued that such a recognition would mean the grant of belligerent rights to the INA, 'that, in turn, implied the grant of immunities and privileges to members of the INA for acts done in the due prosecution of war.'[7] Therefore, the INA members were not guilty.

[1]N.N. Mitra (ed.), *The Annual Register, 1919–1947*, Vol. 55 (New Delhi: Gyan Publishing House, 2000), 197.

[2]Ibid.

[3]Ibid., 198.

[4]Ibid.

[5]Ibid., 277.

[6]Ibid.

[7]Ibid.

The Congress Defence Committee also argued that the INA was 'not a tool of the Japanese'.[8] Desai said that the accused followed the 'Rules for prisoners of war' and did not allow themselves to be the tools or instruments of the enemy.[9] He declared, 'I wish to make the point that there is no obligation whatever which prevents a person who was a prisoner of war from fighting on his own account for the liberty of his own country.'[10] The Defence Committee maintained that the objective of the members of the INA was to secure freedom for their own country.[11] And in their struggle, they were ready to fight with anyone who came in the way of the independence of India, including the Japanese.[12] It took its stand on the right of a subject race to wage war for its liberation.[13] Desai stated that the question of allegiance of Indians to the British, in this regard, was irrelevant. But at this time, when it is said that big mistakes are impending in India, it would be a very grave mistake, leading to far-reaching consequences, if they were treated just as ordinary rebels. The punishment inflicted on them will, in effect, be a punishment for the whole of India, and a deep wound would remain in millions of hearts. In this matter, fortunately, there is no communal question, for these officers and men are Hindus, Muslims and Sikhs.[14]

'THE EDGE OF A VOLCANO'[15]

The political situation in Calcutta was changing rapidly in the winter of 1945, as a growing number of popular political activities unfurled. In November 1945, the trial of Shah Nawaz Khan, Prem Kumar Sehgal and Gurbaksh Singh Dhillion inaugurated a country-wide agitation and Lord Wavell feared that there would be serious rioting in Calcutta over this.[16]

[8]Ibid., 285.

[9]Ibid.

[10]Ibid.

[11]Ibid.

[12]Ibid.

[13]Ibid., 277.

[14]S. Gopal, *Selected Works of Jawaharlal Nehru* (New Delhi: Orient Longman, 1972), 332–33.

[15]Penderel Moon (ed.), *Wavell: The Viceroy's Journal* (Delhi: Oxford University Press, 1973), 173.

[16]Ibid., 87.

From the first half of October, increasing demands were made for the abandonment of action against the INA men. Secret Provincial Fortnightly Reports mention that towards the end of November and the beginning of December widespread demonstrations, meetings and processions were held, mostly by students.[17] There was sympathy for political bodies that helped the INA and a growing bitterness against the government.[18] In many cases, officers of the INA compelled great local interest, especially as they belonged to influential and elite social backgrounds.[19] Many ex-judges of high courts and gentlemen with official titles, therefore, openly defended the INA convicts out of class solidarity. The Intelligence Bureau (IB) reported that there had seldom been a matter which attracted so much public interest and sympathy.[20]

Propaganda became closely intertwined with election campaigns. Given the popularity of the anti-trial campaigns, politicians contesting elections were advised by their parties to include the issue in their election agenda.[21] Intense anti-government feelings were attributed partly to a wave of postwar resentment against a government which had so spectacularly mismanaged the war effort, especially in Bengal, and partly to a genuine sympathy for the INA men.[22] IB reports found that public feelings were increasingly inflamed by speeches made by political leaders, and by press campaigns.[23] As a result, on the one hand, election campaigns helped to expand popular support for the INA, while on the other hand, the INA issue provided the political space to different parties to mobilise public feeling in their favour. This made the INA something like an arena for competitive

[17]Fortnightly Secret Report on the political situation in Bengal for the second half of December 1945, Home Political, File No 37/45, West Bengal State Archives (WBSA).

[18]Government of India, Home Department to the Secretary, Political Department, India office, 20 November 1945, in *Transfer of Power,* ed. Nicholas Mansergh, Vol. IV (London: HMSO, 1970–83), 514.

[19]Ibid.

[20]Government of India, Home Department to the Secretary, Political Department, India office, 20 November 1945, in *Transfer of Power,* Vol. IV, 512.

[21]Ibid., 513.

[22]Ibid.

[23]Ibid.

mobilisation. Wavell wrote in his diary that the trial of the INA officers afforded Congress leaders a splendid opportunity for arousing popular feelings against the government which they were not slow to exploit.[24] Not to be outdone in patriotism, the Muslim League also associated itself with the defence of the accused.[25] The IB alleged that the League was entirely moved by considerations of expediency.[26] The trial of Muslim INA members, however, had aggravated all Muslims.[27]

The British were not slow to recognise the danger. From the middle of November, they apprehended that 'dangerous possibilities' existed in the country.[28] Penderel Moon described these months as 'The Edge Of A Volcano'.[29] Colonial authorities now reasoned that it would be unwise to ignore the threat to the security of the Indian Army. They argued that 'the possibility of the development of the agitation in a dangerous direction exists in a degree which demands constant watchfulness'.[30]

PATTERNS OF THE NOVEMBER RIOTS

The *Amrita Bazar Patrika,* a nationalist newspaper, wrote in November 1945 that students of Calcutta went through their first post-war bloodbath on the INA Day.[31] Over thirty people were killed, several hundred injured, and a large number of cars and police vehicles were destroyed.[32]

The November riots occurred in two phases.[33] The first was the procession of students, which was stopped by the police; Casey

[24]Moon, *Wavell*, 187.

[25]Ibid.

[26]Government of India, Home Department to the Secretary, Political Department, India office, 20 November 1945, in *Transfer of Power,* Vol. IV, 513.

[27]Ibid.

[28]Ibid., 515.

[29]Moon, *Wavell,* 173.

[30]Government of India, Home Department to the Secretary, Political Department, India office, 20 November 1945, in *Transfer of Power,* Vol. IV, 515.

[31]*Amrita Bazar Patrika*, 23 November 1945.

[32]Moon, *Wavell,* 187.

[33]Field Marshall Viscount Wavell to Lord Pethick-Lawrence, 27 November 1945, in *Transfer of Power*, Vol. VI, 553.

described it as 'a collection of quite hysterical young men, with whom it was impossible to reason, but who were not violent'.[34] They eventually dispersed, probably from sheer exhaustion, after some fifteen hours of shouting and demonstrating. In the next phase came attacks on all forms of transport. Large numbers of lorries and private cars were stopped and burnt.[35] Road blocks were formed across many streets and some of the railway lines were blocked by the crowds.

On 21 November, student organisations like the Bengal Provincial Students' Congress and the Bengal Provincial Students' Federation combined to stage a demonstration against the resumption of the trial.[36] The first of these student organisations was controlled mainly by the Jugantar Party, a revolutionary organisation.[37] At this time, it had announced its intention of merging with the Congress.[38] The second organisation was controlled by the Revolutionary Socialist Party of India, the Forward Bloc, and the Communist League of Soumyendra Tagore, otherwise known as the Revolutionary Communist Party of India (CPI).[39] Students played a prominent part in the demonstrations. Muslim students also joined the protest and increasing efforts were made by Hindu and Muslim students to enlist the support of the entire Muslim community. The Central Intelligence officer reported that the CPI, too, supported the movement, which

[34]Ibid.

[35]Ibid.

[36]Inquiry from provinces about causes of disturbances from November 1945 to February 1946, Home Political, File No 5/8/46, NAI.

[37]The Jugantar Party was one of the revolutionary groups in Bengal. In 1906 the Dacca Anushilan Samiti was founded by Pulin Behari Das; subsequently, an all-Bengal conference of revolutionaries was held in December. In the same year, a distinct group within the Calcutta Anushilan Samiti, under Barindra Kumar Ghosh and Bhupendra Nath Datta, started a periodical called Jugantar on the suggestion of Aurobindo Ghosh. Bengali revolutionaries like Hemchandra Qanungo and Prafulla Chaki were associated with revolutionary terrorism. In the Gandhian period many Jugantar members became associated with the Bengal Provincial Congress Committee. See: Sekhar Bandyopadhyay, *From Plassey to Partition, A History of Modern India* (New Delhi: Orient Longman, 2004), 260.

[38]Inquiry from provinces about causes of disturbances from November 1945 to February 1946, Home Political, File No 5/8/46, NAI.

[39]Ibid.

was evident from the participation of large sections of labourers in it.[40]

Throughout the morning and early afternoon of 21 November, students and workers—the latter organised by the CPI—assembled at Wellington Square for a mammoth meeting.[41] After the meeting, which consisted of about a thousand persons, a procession began from Dharamtolla and proceeded towards Dalhousie Square. The president, Dilip Kumar Biswas, announced that the intention of the processionists was to parade through the 'official' areas; i.e. Dalhousie Square, which contained the Government Secretariat, along Strand Road, up Harrison Road, finally to disperse at College Square. Secret reports mention that although no deliberate disobedience of the government was intended, the situation worsened when the procession was stopped from going to Dalhousie Square.[42] The Calcutta Police tried to stop the procession at the junction of Madan Street and Dharamtolla and attempts were made to turn it towards Central Avenue. Leaders of the procession, however, refused to follow the instructions of the police and squatted on the road. Trouble started as the main body of students began to put pressure on the police walls. The police began to charge the front-rankers with *lathi* blows.[43] The students responded by throwing brickbats and stones. The police opened fire on the protestors, which considerably worsened the situation.

The clash between the armed forces and frenzied crowds became savage and cruel. It inaugurated a chain of violence in the city. On Thursday, 22 November 1945, about two hundred to three hundred processionists squatted on the spot till 5.00 am from where they moved to various parts in the northern half of the city, following an inflammatory address by Mrs Bimal Prativa Devi of

[40]Situation on the morning of 23 November 1945, Intelligence Report, Home Political, File No 21/16/45, NAI in *Towards Freedom: Documents on the Movement for Independence in India 1945*, ed. Bimal Prasad (New Delhi: Indian Council for Historical Research/Oxford University Press, 2008), 802.

[41]Report on Calcutta Disturbances 21–24 November 1945 by HQ Eastern Command, Home Political, File No 21/16/45, NAI, in Prasad, *Towards Freedom*, 814,816.

[42]Ibid., 815.

[43]*Amrita Bazar Patrika*, 23 November 1945.

the Congress Socialist Party (CSP).[44] According to a Special Branch report, when the processionists halted for some time she again addressed them and advised them to divide into groups and enforce a *hartal*. By this time, the numbers had swelled to thousands.[45] All Corporation workers came out on strike and public transport ran till 10.30 am in the morning.[46]

The first signs of trouble appeared in the early hours of the day when crowds in Bhowanipore began to stop British military vehicles.[47] In the afternoon, the police opened fire several times on the crowds and by evening, trouble spread to Lansdowne Road in the east, Kalighat Bridge on Tolly Nala in the west and Lower Circular Road in the north.[48] The *Amrita Bazar Patrika* reported that neither the Deputy Commissioner of Police Headquarters, nor the Deputy Commissioner of South Division gave orders to open fire.[49] Nevertheless, the reaction to the firing was unprecedented. Frenzied crowds set police trucks on fire. Fire brigades were called to put out fires on police and military lorries, mostly in south Calcutta.[50]

Numerous processions paraded through the city. In the meantime, the people in the procession held a rally at noon, much bigger and more representative than that of the previous day. About two lakh people from all communities—Hindus, Muslims, Sikhs—and representing all shades of opinion—Congress, Muslim League, Communists, Hindu Mahasabha, and Khaksars[51]—

[44]Report on Calcutta Disturbances 21–24 November 1945, by HQ Eastern Command, Home Political, File No 21/16/45, NAI, in Prasad, *Towards Freedom*, 815.

[45]Ibid.

[46]Situation on the morning of 23 November 1945: Intelligence Report, Home Political, File No 21/16/45, NAI in Prasad, *Towards Freedom,* 802.

[47]Report on Calcutta Disturbances 21–24 November 1945, by HQ Eastern Command, Home Political, File No 21/16/45, NAI

[48]Ibid.

[49]*Amrita Bazar Patrika*, 23 November 1945.

[50]Ibid.

[51]The Anjuman-in-Khaksaran was founded in 1931 by M. Inayatullah Khan Mashriqi. Its ostensible objects were to organise the Muslims for social service, to obtain *swaraj* by quicker methods than those of the Congress and by promoting unity, so as to become the dominating political power in the country. Although theoretically open to all communities, in practice there were very few non-Muslim Khaksars and a 1940 report estimated that they had never exceeded 50 in number.

attended.[52] By midday, all the processions had congregated at Wellington Square and an all-parties' platform was spontaneously formed.[53] Communal cooperation was explicitly visible in the meeting. The tricolour of the Congress, the shimmering green of the Muslim League, the red of the Communists and the swastika-bearing Hindu Mahasabha flag began to flutter together in the mid November sky.[54] *The Amrita Bazar Patrika* wrote that a batch of Muslim students from Islamia College received a rousing ovation and their presence at the protest meeting elicited many emotional scenes.[55] Many Muslim students approached the leaders of the Muslim League to join the CPI and the Congress to prolong the agitation. However, the League leaders gave them non-committal answers. It was only Md. Osman, secretary of the Calcutta Muslim League and one of the leaders of the Provincial Muslim Students League, who openly spoke against Muslim participation in the disturbances.[56] A clear disjunction between popular action and institutional leadership became discernible as numerous Muslims from various ranks of society, joined the protest demonstrations.

Protestors again formed a procession and renewed their march to Dalhousie Square, which they were not allowed to reach on Wednesday. The police made three rounds of *lathi* charges and

---

The secret object of the organisation was to provide Mashriqi with a large, disciplined pan-Islamic body ready to undertake, at a moment's notice, any activity initiated by him. Interest in the organisation was kept alive by the announcement, from time to time, by Mashriqi, of grandiloquent schemes for the advancement of Muslim interests. The Khaksars were organized along military lines with officers (*Salars*) of various grades and other ranks known as *Pakbazes, Janbazes* and *Khaksars*. In the early stages of communal disturbances in 1945, in Bengal, Khaksars were instructed to intervene and prevent strife between communities. But soon communal feeling began to develop among the Khaksars. See Sumit Sarkar (ed.),*Towards Freedom: Documents on the Movement for Independence in India 1946,* Part 1 (New Delhi: Indian Council of Historical Research/Oxford University Press, 2007)182–184.

[52]*Amrita Bazar Patrika*, 24 November 1945.

[53]Ibid.

[54]Ibid.

[55]Ibid.

[56]Report on Calcutta Disturbances 21–24 November 1945, by HQ Eastern Command, Home Political, File No 21/16/45, NAI, in Prasad, *Towards Freedom,* 818.

opened fire twice but the procession did not disperse.[57] Thereafter, the police withdrew and did not interfere anymore. The procession paraded through Dalhousie Square and afterwards took the body of Rameshwar Banerjee, the victim of Wednesday's firing, on a two-mile-long procession to the Keoratola burning *ghat* for cremation.[58] Both Sarat Bose sympathetic to the Forward Bloc and Shyama Prasad Mookherjee from the Hindu Mahasabha claimed that it was at their insistence that permission was obtained, on the second day, for the procession to pass through Dalhousie Square.[59] However, the government said that no such permission was given.[60] It is quite reasonable to surmise that all parties were trying to make political capital out of the disturbances.

There was a complete *hartal* throughout the Indian parts of the city, and all communities joined it.[61] By late afternoon, main roads in and out of Calcutta from the north, south and southwest were blocked by barricades and other obstructions. Military, service vehicles and other forms of government transport were severely affected. The IB admitted that the *hartal* was practically complete.[62]

On Friday, 23 November, the police reported that more hooliganism had occurred in north and south Calcutta.[63] There were many isolated instances of assault upon Europeans and also on Indians wearing ties and hats. These were taken off and burnt or destroyed because they were symbols of European influence. Violence soon became quite indiscriminate and brutal. An American was burnt alive in an ambulance.[64] Students and protestors often held up motorists and cyclists and only allowed them to pass after they had uttered 'Jai Hind'. Groups of such protestors were most visible

[57] *Amrita Bazar Patrika*, 24 November 1945.

[58] Ibid.

[59] Inquiry from provinces about causes of disturbances from November 1945 to February 1946, Home Political, File No 5/8/46, NAI.

[60] Ibid.

[61] *Amrita Bazar Patrika*, 24 November 1945.

[62] Report on Calcutta Disturbances 21–24 November 1945, by HQ Eastern Command, Home Political, File No 21/16/45, NAI, in Prasad, *Towards Freedom,* 816.

[63] Ibid.

[64] Field Marshall Wavell to Lord Pethick-Lawrence, 27 November 1945, in *Transfer of Power*, Vol. VI, 553.

in areas like Alipore, Ballugunge, Entally, Sealdah, Beliaghatta and in the area near the Lake.

The Dock area, hitherto unaffected, grew restive and crowds began to congregate there.[65] The EIR trains in and out of Howrah station were eventually stopped. Protestors squatted at the Lillooah platform.[66] There was a complete absence of ordinary Thana and Traffic Police. The entire responsibility for maintaining law and order was left to sergeants and the Armed Police. In the opinion of the Central Intelligence officer, the situation was the worst the city had experienced in the past twenty years.[67]

DEFINING THE UPSURGE: ANTI-COLONIAL, NON-COMMUNAL, REVOLUTIONARY?

Francis Tuker wrote: 'In November there had been riots, the worst that Calcutta had as yet experienced; they had been mainly anti-British in complexion but their violence, though short—lived, had shocked all decent people.'[68] Despite excesses, they were marked by inimitable communal solidarity. On the whole, the disturbances and the violence that accompanied it were clearly anti-police, anti-European, and anti-government.[69] On 27 November 1945, Lord Wavell wrote to Lord Pethick-Lawrence that Casey was overwhelmed by the very strong anti-British feeling displayed during the agitation.[70] The Intelligence Branch reported that the main victims of the riots were the British services in the order of the army, RAF, and the navy.[71]

The November disturbances had certain striking features. Outbursts were mainly sporadic and unplanned but, at the same

[65]Report on Calcutta Disturbances 21–24 November 1945, by HQ Eastern Command, Home Political, File No 21/16/45, NAI, in Prasad, *Towards Freedom,* 812.

[66]Ibid., 816.

[67]Situation on the morning of 23 November 1945: Intelligence Report, Home Political, File No 21/16/45, NAI in Prasad, *Towards Freedom,* 802.

[68]Francis Tuker, *While Memory Serves* (London: Cassell, 1950), 99.

[69]Report on Calcutta Disturbances 21–24 November 1945, by HQ Eastern Command, Home Political, File No 21/16/45, NAI, in Prasad, *Towards Freedom,* 818.

[70]Field Marshall Viscount Wavell to Lord Pethick-Lawrence, 27 November 1945, in *Transfer of Power*, Vol. VI, 553.

[71]Ibid., 812.

time, they were extremely united and militant. There was complete agreement among the British officials that in the initial phase, there was no deliberate organisation by any particular political party.[72] Casey thought that the root cause of the trouble was the inflammatory speeches made by most political leaders which inflamed the unstable Bengali youth.[73] The procession was a deliberate act of defiance, primarily by students who were associated with the Forward Bloc, loyal to Subhas Chandra Bose, the leader of the INA.[74] Once rioting started, students took full charge. In his report to Lord Wavell, Casey wrote that there was certainly some amount of organisation behind the second phase of disturbances, which was marked by attacks on transport, road blocks and even squatting on railway lines.[75] The Intelligence Branch also concluded from the summary of the whole episode that an organisation had now come into being. [76] But disturbances did develop a momentum of their own.[77]

Tramway workers and other transport unions declared strikes in sympathy with students. These were mainly controlled by the CPI. But it was predominantly bands of students who were responsible for the stoppage of transport. Strikes in some industries were organised in accordance with CPI orders but on many occasions they were spontaneous.[78] The CPI actively supported the disturbances in the hope of regaining popularity, which it had lost due to its opposition to the Quit India movement in 1942.[79] Enquiry reports documented:

[72]Inquiry from provinces about causes of disturbances from November 1945 to February 1946, Home Political, File No 5/8/46, NAI.

[73]Mr Casey (Bengal) to Field Marshall Viscount Wavell, 2 January 1946, *Transfer of Power*, Vol. VI, 724.

[74]Ibid.

[75]Field Marshall Viscount Wavell to Lord Pethick-Lawrence, 27 November 1945, in *Transfer of Power*, Vol. VI, 553.

[76]Report on Calcutta Disturbances 21–24 November 1945, by HQ Eastern Command, Home Political, File No 21/16/45, NAI.

[77]Sir J Colville (Bombay) to Field Marshall Viscount Wavell (Extract), 14 December 1945, *Transfer of Power*, Vol. VI, 642.

[78]Inquiry from provinces about causes of disturbances from November 1945 to February 1946, Home Political, File No 5/8/46, NAI.

[79]In 1942, the Communists adopted an anti-imperialist tone and emphasised that India is a multi-national state. Such a stance arose from their defence of the Soviet

> When students and a large mass of public had achieved their 'victory' by marching in procession round Dalhousie Square the Congress and the majority of students would probably have considered the demonstration at an end. But a group of students represented by the extremist groups controlling the B.P.S.F and C.P.I were reluctant to stop especially as the demonstration was developing into a type of 'mass action' which communists have looked as a preliminary to revolution.[80]

However, the withdrawal of Congress support and the threat of the governor to call in the military stopped further disturbances.

Interestingly, popular militancy became a matter of concern not only to the British but also to the nationalist leadership. Various Congress and Mahasabha leaders took an active part in restoring peace. Kiran Shankar Roy, Dr Shyamaprasad Mookherjee, Dr Radha Benode Pal and Dr Sunil Bose tried to tone down the pitch.[81] Some Congress vans carrying loudspeakers went round the affected areas and broadcasted that Jawaharlal Nehru had requested all students and other elements to desist from hooliganism.[82] But political leaders were unable to control militant protestors. This became evident when, about ten minutes later, students moved into the same areas shouting slogans and asking protestors to continue the agitation.

The British maintained that this outburst was a 'trial run' by the Congress to revive their organisation and to discover the reactions of

---

Union and the adoption of the 'peoples' war line'. The latter called for unity of the 'national government'. To implement this in India, the Communists called for unity among the divisive forces in the country. This was followed by their acceptance of the Muslim League as the true representative of Muslims in the country and they also came very close to accepting the League's demand for Pakistan. The Congress severely criticised the Communists and they became considerably unpopular. However, post–1942, especially during the famine of 1943, they regained some of their popularity by pursuing efficient relief work. For further details see, Sumit Sarkar, *Modern India, 1885–1947* (London: Macmillan 1983), 389 and 412. The November riots provided them with another opportunity to increase their mass base.

[80]Inquiry from provinces about causes of disturbances from November 1945 to February 1946, Home Political, File No 5/8/46, NAI.

[81]*Amrita Bazar Patrika*, 23 November 1945.

[82]Ibid.

the civil authorities and the army to such action.[83] But the Congress at no point was prepared for a violent outbreak. The Congress leadership became fearful of the revolutionary zeal exhibited by the masses. They feared that the movement would soon reach a point where leaders would lose all control over the masses. Moreover, business interests close to the Congress opposed violent methods. The fear of popular militancy, even when of an anti-British cast, could, they feared, spill over into a larger movement for radical social change. So, in haste, business groups pressed for restraint.[84] As a result, Congress leaders condemned the movement.[85]

On 9 December, Nehru, in a speech in Calcutta, said:

> But mere enthusiasm is not enough. Even self-sacrifices are not enough. We must have disciplined and organized effort at the right time. Otherwise, our enthusiasm will be frittered away in small individual acts. Therefore, our young men must learn this great lesson of curbing and directing our enthusiasm in right channels and at the right time.[86]

He concluded with: 'But today we have to adopt organised and peaceful methods which the Congress has so far followed, and brought much success and strength to us'.[87]

On 3 December 1945, Nehru was reported in the *Hindustan Times* as having said that no major political development was expected until after the elections ended.[88] In a public statement

[83]Report on Calcutta Disturbances 21–24 November 1945, by HQ Eastern Command' Home Political, File No 21/16/45, NAI, in Prasad, *Towards Freedom,* 813.

[84]Sarkar, *Towards Freedom,* XVII.

[85]Tanika Sarkar also focuses on the interaction between the Congress leadership and subordinate groups from 1928 to 1934. She argues that the Congress acted as both the organiser of and the brake on mass radicalism during that period. Tanika Sarkar, *Bengal 1928–1934: The Politics of Protest* (Delhi: Oxford University Press, 1987).

[86]S. Gopal, *Selected Works,* 343.

[87]Ibid.

[88]Field Marshall Viscount Wavell to Lord Pethick-Lawrence, 5 December 1945, in *Transfer of Power*, Vol. VI, 602.

on the November disturbances, Sarat Bose put the blame on the Communists instead of claiming credit for anti-colonial action on behalf of the Congress.[89] When disturbances became violent, he too condemned the demonstrations and declared that it was prompted by 'agents provocateurs'.[90] Gandhi said that such instances were a 'bad and unbecoming example for India ... a combination for Hindus and Muslims and others for the purpose for violent action is unholy.'[91] He declared, 'Conserve all your energy by maintaining peace and order in a disciplined manner for the impending non-violent struggle for independence which is ahead.'[92] On 1 December, Abul Kalam Azad said that the present policy of the Congress was to maintain peaceful, undisturbed conditions in the country and to contest the elections. [93] It was only Aruna Asaf Ali who recognised the fact that it was far easier 'to unite Hindus and Muslims at the barricade than on the constitutional front'.[94]

The November riots made the Congress leaders realise that violent rhetoric used for electioneering was likely to provoke undesirable violent action.[95] The British stated that a mass movement as a weapon to be used at the right moment and according to a plan was being prejudiced by the creation of an atmosphere in which disturbances might occur anytime and anywhere.[96] They argued that the Congress leaders were also aware of the fact that they might lose control over a popular upheaval. This, in all likelihood, would misrepresent the Congress in the eyes of the world. Hence, it was almost certain that Congress leaders did not want trouble

[89]Ibid., 603.

[90]Inquiry from provinces about causes of disturbances from November 1945 to February 1946, Home Political, File No 5/8/46, NAI.

[91]News Report, ' Peace can come only when military retire', *Free Press Journal*, 25 February 1946, in Sarkar, *Towards Freedom*, 60.

[92]Field Marshall Viscount Wavell to Lord Pethick-Lawrence, 5 December 1945, in *Transfer of Power*, Vol. VI, 602.

[93]Ibid., 602.

[94]News Report, 'Peace can come only when military retire', *Free Press Journal*, 25 February 1946, in Sarkar, *Towards Freedom*, 60.

[95]Field Marshall Viscount Wavell to Lord Pethick-Lawrence, 5 December 1945, *Tansfer of Power*, Vol. VI, 602–603.

[96]Ibid.

till the elections to the central and provincial assemblies were over[97] as anti-government outbreaks of disorder—anti-British or communal—on a large scale were now inimical to a Congress which was about to step into state power.[98] Wavell also wrote that it was unlikely that the Congress leaders would try to stir up trouble before the elections ended.[99] However, the Congress still wanted to be in a position to launch a mass movement, as soon as possible, thereafter.

Some months later, Wavell acknowledged that 'it was undoubtedly a serious blunder to place on trial men against whom no brutality could be proved.'[100] He confessed in his diary that 'we must at all costs avoid becoming embroiled with both Hindus and Muslims at once.'[101] Towards the end of December, he wrote that the November riots served to form a temporary detente and constituted a 'turning point' when the Indian nationalist leaders advocated a policy of restraint.[102]

BACKGROUND TO THE FEBRUARY RIOTS

Political emotions in Calcutta, however, continued to rise to a would be breaking point. Widespread campaigns of sedition continued.[103] The government reasoned that dealing firmly with every sign of sedition and incitement to violence, in the politically unstable situation, 'might' nip the trouble in the bud.[104] But a more likely result of such preventive action might result in an upheaval, which

[97]Sir H. Dow (Sind) to Field Marshall Viscount Wavell, 3 November 1945, in *Transfer of Power*, Vol. VI, 438.

[98]Chief of Staff Committee, Papers C.O.S. Internal Situation in India, Appreciation by Commander-In-Chief, 24 November 1945, 1 December 1945, in *Transfer of Power*, Vol. VI, 576–577.

[99]Moon, *Wavell,* 182.

[100]Ibid., 191.

[101]Sarkar, *Towards Freedom,* XVI.

[102]Wavell to George VI, 31 December 1945, in *Transfer of Power*, Vol. VI, 713.

[103]Inquiry from provinces about causes of disturbances from November 1945 to February 1946, Home Political, File No 5/8/46, NAI.

[104]Government of India, Home Department to Provincial Chief Secretaries and Chief Commissioners, 5 December 1945, in *Transfer of Power*, Vol. VI, 600.

would make any settlement impossible. Hence, the British advocated a policy of 'patience and restraint'. They chose to tread the middle path, even while recognising the risks. Moderate Congressmen also supported this.[105]

The government feared that the next few months were going to be difficult and dangerous in certain parts of India. G. D. Birla in his letter to Mr Henderson wrote that 'we are sitting on a heap of dynamite.'[106] The INA trials continued to add tension to the already edgy political situation. Pethick-Lawrence advised Lord Wavell that governors should be more in touch with the political feelings rather than with the military in their respective areas of jurisdiction.[107]

A few months later, violence again erupted on the streets of Calcutta. This time the issue was the trial of Captain Abdul Rashid Ali of the INA who had declared his loyalty to the Muslim League. In February 1945, it was a Muslim League demonstration which caused trouble in the city. The agitation that ensued, once again, brought Hindu and Muslim masses on the streets together. The pattern of violence was similar to the November riots.

TRIAL OF ABDUL RASHID ALI AND MUSLIM PUBLIC OPINION

In February 1946, the Muslim League decided to stage a forceful protest against the sentence of seven years' rigorous imprisonment passed by the commander in chief on Captain Abdul Rashid.[108] Seven charges including waging war against the king and committing offences of a cruel kind were levelled against him and he pleaded not guilty.[109] He was defended by Mian Abdul Aziz of Lahore, Qazi Mohd, Isa Nawab Qadir-ud-Din Ahmed and Mr Abdul Aziz Khan

[105]Ibid.,

[106]Mr G. D. Birla to Mr Henderson, 6 December 1945, in *Transfer of Power*, Vol. VI, 612–615

[107]Lord Pethick-Lawrence to Field Marshall Viscount Wavell, 20 December 1945, in *Transfer of Power*, Vol. VI, 665–669

[108]Field Marshall Viscount Wavell to Lord Pethick-Lawrence, 13 February 1945, *Transfer of Power*, Vol. VI, 969–970.

[109]*Dawn*, 10 January 1946.

of the Muslim League's INA Defence Committee.[110] Lord Wavell wrote to Pethick-Lawrence that

> the argument apparently was that the leniency shown in the first INA trial was due to Congress pressure and that the Muslim League must show in the case of Abdul Rashid that they are equally good at agitation.[111]

The All-India Muslim League Working Committee passed a resolution which stated that the members 'strongly disapprove of the policy adopted by the Government in not taking immediate steps to release Captain Abdul Rashid and other INA men.'[112] It further stated that the reviewing authority had committed a great error in discriminating between their cases and that of Mr Shah Nawaz, who was convicted of a graver offence, was acquitted while Captain Abdul Rashid was indicted on the plea of the degree of brutality in the Captain's case. Such a judgment, the League declared, was neither legally not morally tenable. The Working Committee, hence, called upon the Viceroy to intervene and, if no other course was open, to grant pardons to them and remit their sentences.

The verdict on Abdul Rashid evoked strong reactions from different quarters of the Muslim public. Secretary to the UP Muslim League, Hasan Mian, stated that the sentence was a challenge to the entire Muslim Nation. *Dawn* in its issue of 10 February 1946, published his words:

> The British Government is hastening her days in India by putting to list patience of Muslim Nation. The discrimination shown by the C-in-C in awarding a sentence of 7 years to Capt. Rashid is not only provocative and indirect but an open challenge to us.[113]

Muslims often suspected a conspiracy between the British and the Congress against the League. Hence, Hasan Mian went on to say:

[110]Ibid.

[111]Field Marshall Viscount Wavell to Lord Pethick-Lawrence, 13 February 1945, *Transfer of Power*, Vol. VI, 967–969.

[112]Syed Sharifuddin Pirzada (ed.), *Foundations of Pakistan: All-India Muslim League Documents: 1906–1947* (Karachi: National Publishing House, 1970), 504.

[113]*Dawn*, 10 February 1946.

> The action of a highly placed representative of the British Government is suggestive of a deep conspiracy and sinister collaboration between British bureaucracy and capitalist Hindu Congress to crush Muslim once for all.
>
> The unconditional release on the eve of general election of the three I.N.A. prisoners namely Dhillion, Sehgal and Shah Nawaz apparently meant to influence the election since the prisoners served to champion the cause of Akhand Hindustan as a reward for the defence by the Congress Defence Committee.[114]

Fortnightly Reports of February 1945, mentioned that many Muslims felt that the government had discriminated against the Muslim League.[115] League leaders regarded the sentence as a deliberate blow against the League.[116] League leaders in Calcutta firmly believed that the Viceroy was about to form a Congress Central Government as a preliminary to the convening of a single constitution-making body.[117] As this implied that the League was to be bypassed and the demand for Pakistan completely ignored, they decided to create a turbulent political atmosphere; only by such means could Pakistan be gained.[118]

Muslim public opinion strongly advocated the release of Abdul Rashid. *Dawn* reported that there were strong protests throughout India against the discriminatory treatment of Captain Rashid.[119] Slogans like 'Down with the British Imperialism', 'Long Live Muslim League', 'Release Captain Rashid' and 'Quid-e-Azam Zindabad' were widely published in the Muslim press. The propaganda for the release of Captain Rashid often had communal connotations and an anti-Congress stance. The Congress was not very active in the campaign and their support for Captain Rashid was lukewarm. Nehru issued a statement in the press, which reflected the official Congress position in this matter:

[114]Ibid.

[115]Fortnightly report for the month of February 1946, Home Political, File No 18/2/46, NAI.

[116]INA trials, Disturbances in Calcutta protesting against the conviction of Abdul Rashid, Home Political, File No 5/22/46, NAI.

[117]Ibid.

[118]Ibid.

[119]*Dawn*, 11 February 1946.

> But I must say that the sentence passed on Capt. Rashid of the I.N.A. seems to be very unjust and wrong. I do not admire or appreciate in the least the stand taken or the statement made by Capt. Rashid in the course of his trial. That was something not in keeping with the dignity of an individual or group or the I.N.A. or the nation. Nor can we have any sympathy with any acts of cruelty indulged in by anyone against officers and soldiers of the Indian army.
>
> I do not know the facts of individual cases and am unable to judge. But it must be borne in mind that the circumstances were very special and extraordinary and normal standards cannot be applied to these cases.[120]

Protest meetings and demonstrations were held in different regions of India that demanded the termination of the INA trials. But the political agitation put the Muslim League in a precarious position.

TEXTURES OF THE FEBRUARY RIOTS

> Blood and destruction shall be so in use,
> That mothers shall but smile when they behold
> Their infants quartered with the hands of war.[121]

These words seemed too familiar, real, and ghastly to Francis Tuker when he recalled the February riots of Calcutta in 1946. Referring to the mass violence that engulfed Calcutta, Tuker stated that once people get a taste for violence they tend on the one hand to look readily to it as a quick means of settling affairs rather than to accept the delay and doubtful issue of long-drawn negotiations and discussions, and on the other to become so habituated to the use and sight of violence as to regard it as a natural condition.[122]

On 11 February, protest demonstrations against the conviction of Abdul Rashid of the INA led to serious rioting in Calcutta.[123] The participants were mainly students of the Bengal Provincial Student's Federation (RSPI), which was the Calcutta branch of the All India

[120]Gopal, *Selected Works*, 379.

[121]Tuker, *While Memory Serves*, 99.

[122]Ibid.

[123]Field Marshall Viscount Wavell to Lord Pethick-Lawrence, 13 February 1946, *Transfer of Power*, Vol. VI, pp. 969–970.

Students' Federation and the Muslim Students' Federation.[124] Secret information stated that the Muslim League was sympathetic to the agitation though they did not, openly, back it in the initial stages.[125] However, the Muslim League expressed its intention of organising a procession, demonstration, and *hartal* on 12 February 1945, regardless of the consequences.

The agitation that resulted, however, united Hindus and Muslims on the streets. On 11 February 1945, Hindu and Muslim students gathered in Wellington Square for a meeting where it was decided to march to Dalhousie Square, which was a restricted area.[126] League leader H. S. Suhrawardy who attended the meeting said, 'Today the great desire of my life is fulfilled, that Hindu and Muslim students have stood united under the banners of Congress and the Muslim League'.[127] He concluded by urging the protestors to rouse the whole of Calcutta against police brutalities. The Intelligence Branch reported that the Muslim League was sponsoring the agitation and that students of all political denominations came together under the auspices of their parent political organisations. All parties were united.[128]

Students paraded through different streets in the city. Congress and League flags once again fluttered together. Students passed the Lal Bazar police station where the police broke up the parade with *lathi* charges. They tried to reach the Square by another route. As the procession was again stopped by the armed Gurkha Police, Ananda Bhattacharya, general secretary of the Bengal Provincial Student's Federation, demanded the right of passage peacefully.[129]

[124]INA trials, Disturbances in Calcutta protesting against the conviction of Abdul Rashid, Home Political, File No 5/22/46, NAI.

[125]Ibid.

[126]N.N. Mitra (ed.), *The Indian Annual Register, 1919–1947*, Vol. 56 (New Delhi: Gyan Publishing House, 2000), 269.

[127]Extracts from news report, 'Calcutta students' demonstration grows into big tide of Hindu–Muslim, anti-imperialist unity'. By wire from Nikhil Chakrabarti, *People's Age*, February 1946, in Sarkar, *Towards Freedom*, 34.

[128]INA trials, Disturbances in Calcutta protesting against the conviction of Abdul Rashid, Home Political, File No 5/22/46, NAI.

[129]Extracts from news report, 'Calcutta students' demonstration grows into big tide of Hindu-Muslim, anti-imperialist unity.' By wire from Nikhil Chakrabarti, *People's Age*, February 1946, in Sarkar, *Towards Freedom*, 35.

In the meantime, Mr Mohammed Osman, secretary of the Calcutta City League reached the place and greeted the gathering with slogans of Hindu–Muslim unity.[130] The deputy commissioner of police, Shamsud-Doha, arrested him and shouted at the crowd, 'Either you go away or I will smash you'.[131] Ananda Bhattacharya responded by saying, 'You can beat us, you can shoot us, but you cannot smash us'.[132] Thereafter, about 200 policemen attacked the students.[133] Nearly a hundred students were wounded including all the leaders of the Bengal Provincial Students' Federation and the All-Bengal Muslim Students' League (ABMSL).[134]

The situation gradually worsened and lorries were burnt in north Calcutta. The police opened fire on three occasions in different parts of the city. [135] Five military vehicles were set on fire near the crossing of Central Avenue and Vivekananda Road.[136] In Bhowanipore, at Jogu Babu's Bazar, a crowd erected barricades on Russa Road.[137] The police opened fire on a crowd near the crossing of Beadon Street and Chittaranjan Avenue.[138] Most shops in north and south Calcutta were closed.[139] Following another day of disturbances, the army was called in and armoured cars patrolled the city.[140]

On 12 February, Mr Azizur Rahman, secretary of the ABMSL presided over a students' meeting at Wellington Square. A Muslim student, Zahiruddin said:

> The British Government by making discrimination against Abdul Rashid who was defended by the League, schemed to keep Hindus and Muslims apart. We here stand united today to confound the British calculations. By settling the question of Hindustan and

[130]Ibid.

[131]Ibid.

[132]Ibid.

[133]Ibid., 5.

[134]Ibid., 5.

[135]Mitra, *The Indian Annual Register,* 269.

[136]Ibid.

[137]Ibid.

[138]Ibid.

[139]Ibid.

[140]Extracts from a news report, 'Military called out in Calcutta' *The Statesman,* 13 February 1946, in Sarkar, *Towards Freedom,* 28.

> Pakistan ourselves, we will drive the British out by our united movement. By our blood we will wipe off this shame.[141]

Another meeting was convened to condemn the police *lathi* charges and the firing on the protesters the previous day. Suhrawardy presided and the gathering was addressed by some Congress and Communist leaders.[142] According to a press estimate, 50,000 people attended the meeting.[143] Suhrawardy demanded the release of the arrested, and advocated the continuation of the joint campaign till all the INA men were set free. Maulana Akram Khan, president of the Bengal League spoke, 'I might be old in age, but today I shall not only not lag behind, but will lead you.'[144] Abdul Hashim, secretary of Bengal Provincial League said:

> I can clearly visualize the day, which is not far distant, when British Imperialism will crumble like a house of cards in a new Plassey or Panipat. Yesterday's tragedy has been turned from a curse to a blessing since it has brought Hindus and Muslims together. Through greater unity in the whole country we shall build our Azad Hind Fauz. Don't bother about arms. If we unite, weapons will fall from the sky.[145]

Suhrawardy also hoped for cooperation between the League and Congress and wrote in *Dawn* on 14 February:

> The reason for our success is the sincerity of purpose, behind all this agitation and if all the parties concerned could come together on one common platform with the same sincerity the problem of India would be solved.[146]

[141]Extracts from news report, 'Calcutta students' demonstration grows into big tide of Hindu-Muslim, anti-imperialist unity.' By wire from Nikhil Chakrabarti, *People's Age* February 1946 in Sarkar, *Towards Freedom*, 36.

[142]INA trials, Disturbances in Calcutta protesting against the conviction of Abdul Rashid, Home Political, File No 5/22/46, NAI.

[143]Extracts from a telegram by the Governor of Bengal, to the Viceroy, dated 13 February 1946, File No 5/22/46, Home Political, NAI, in Sarkar, *Towards Freedom*, 29.

[144]Ibid., 36.

[145]Ibid., 36.

[146]*Dawn*, 14 February 1945.

In the afternoon, the same day, a mile-long procession, in which over 1,00,000 people—Hindus and Muslims, Congressmen, Leaguers, Communists, students, and women—participated; they paraded through the Dalhousie Square area as a mark of protest against the sentence passed on Captain Rashid.[147] The processionists carried Congress, League, Communists, and Khaksar flags and shouted slogans demanding the release of Rashid and other INA prisoners, and urged Hindu—Muslim unity.

After the mammoth public meeting, the procession, which started at Wellington Square, was led by Suhrawardy and the Gandhian leader, Satish Chandra Dasgupta of the Khadi Pratishthan, the two leaders moving arm in arm under Congress and League flags, which were tied together and held aloft by volunteers.[148] Deafening cries of 'Congress–League ek ho', 'Down with the British Raj', 'Stop Police *zoolum*', galvanised people of various localities into joining the procession.[149] Emerging from Wellington Square, the procession passed through Ganesh Chandra Avenue and Mission Row extension and finally went round Dalhousie Square, where a similar procession organised under the joint auspices of the Congress and the League had been disallowed and dispersed twice by *lathis* charges the previous day, on the grounds that the area was a prohibited one.[150] The procession was allowed to pass on the assurance of Suhrawardy and Nazimuddin that peace would be restored.[151] But it was read as a victory for Muslims. Suhrawardy boasted that Muslims could achieve what they wanted.[152]

A police constable was injured by the procession. As it went past the Central Police Headquarters, a police lorry returning to the Headquarters with the injured constable forced its way through the procession. This was followed by large-scale throwing of brickbats

[147]Mitra, *The Indian Annual Register,* 271.

[148]Ibid.

[149]Extracts from news report, 'Calcutta students' demonstration grows into big tide of Hindu–Muslim, anti-imperialist unity.' By wire from Nikhil Chakrabarti, *People's Age*, February 1946, in Sarkar, *Towards Freedom,* 37.

[150]Mitra, *The Indian Annual Register,* 71.

[151]Fortnightly report for the month of February, Home Political, File No 18/2/46, NAI.

[152]Ibid.

by people in the procession. Tear gas smoke was used to disperse the crowd. Soon violence spread rapidly to different parts of the city. The Congress, the Muslim League, and other political parties joined in the disturbances.[153]

From a small beginning, an orgy of lawlessness developed in the city, similar to the November riots.[154] The police observed that the same trouble areas and the same modus operandi were involved.[155] Worst affected were the predominantly Muslim areas of Calcutta.[156] Crowds split into small groups of hooligans who looted and set fire to houses and private buildings mostly in the European residential areas.

On 13 February, the commissioner of police reported that the situation continued to deteriorate until 3.30 pm in the afternoon.[157] Two battalions of British infantry and one battalion of Gurkhas were called in as serious rioting continued for three consecutive days.[158] A post office at Manshatola in Kidderpore in south Calcutta and the University post office in Coloootola in north Calcutta were set on fire. Similarly, the Kalabagan post office was looted and burnt down. Most of the disturbances were reported from the area around Chittaranjan Avenue, which was the biggest thoroughfare in north Calcutta running from the northern extremity to Esplanade.[159] After several military trucks were burnt, the police dispersed large crowds at the crossing of Bow Bazar Street and Central Avenue by firing tear gas cartridges.[160] They opened fire at the Esplanade junction.[161] There were also incidents of stray assaults on passersby and the police in the Dalhousie Square area. A Gurkha officer was also assaulted.[162]

[153]INA trials, Disturbances in Calcutta protesting against the conviction of Abdul Rashid, Home Political, File No 5/22/46, NAI.

[154]Fortnightly report for the month of February, Home Political, File No 18/2/46, NAI.

[155]INA trials, Disturbances in Calcutta protesting against the conviction of Abdul Rashid, Home Political, File No 5/22/46, NAI.

[156]Ibid.

[157]Ibid.

[158]Ibid.

[159]Mitra, *The Indian Annual Register*, 272.

[160]Ibid.

[161]Ibid.

[162]Ibid.

Jagu Babu's Bazar in Bhowanipore became a major trouble spot.[163] In south Calcutta, the Kalighat Tram Depot was set on fire and the Kalighat post office was damaged.[164] A lorry belonging to the Khadi Pratisthan at Sodepore was attacked and set on fire at Ashutosh Mukherjee Road in south Calcutta.[165] Serious rioting continued on Harrison Road, College Street, and Lower Circular Road and four vehicles were burnt at the Dhokinandan Road junction.[166] An Associated Press representative who toured Chowringhee found that the glass windows of shops and restaurants were smashed.[167] Metro Cinema, a landmark in Chowringhee, presented a sorry picture with all its glass broken.[168] Bodies were lying at Dharamtolla while buildings on Park Street were seriously damaged. British troops patrolled different areas of the city.

There was some improvement in south Calcutta though trouble spread to the outskirts of the city. Muslim League students sent instructions to district organisations in Bengal to stage demonstrations with Communist students. Dock areas caused trouble and all the Jute Mills in Barrackpore and Kankinara were closed.[169] In Kankinara, 22 miles from Calcutta, several hundred mill hands, who had abstained from work to protest against police firing in Calcutta, held up 99 Santipore local trains.[170] According to secret information, this had been engineered in accordance with a pre-arranged plan by the Bengal Provincial Muslim Students' League and some Communist students who were led by Communist leaders.[171]

Attempts were made to boycott everything that was European, to instigate servants of Europeans and to prevent the sale of food

[163]INA trials, Disturbances in Calcutta protesting against the conviction of Abdul Rashid, Home Political, File No 5/22/46, NAI.

[164]Mitra, *The Indian Annual Register,* 272.

[165]Ibid., 273.

[166]INA trials, Disturbances in Calcutta protesting against the conviction of Abdul Rashid, Home Political, File No 5/22/46, NAI.

[167]Mitra, *The Indian Annual Register*, 273.

[168]Ibid.

[169]INA trials, Disturbances in Calcutta protesting against the conviction of Abdul Rashid, Home Political, File No 5/22/46, NAI.

[170]Ibid.

[171]Ibid.

to Europeans.[172] European shops were damaged, persons wearing European clothes were molested and the YMCA was burnt and looted.[173] All vehicles, British and American, were attacked.[174] As in November, symbols of colonial power were the primary targets of attack. The Thoburn Methodist Church on Dharamtolla Street was set on fire.[175] Several European establishments and flats in the Park Street area were looted and set on fire. Around half a dozen Anglo–Indians residing at Creek Row were attacked. However, Indian residents of the locality persuaded the crowds to disperse.[176]

Disturbances finally came to an end on 19 February, when troops were withdrawn from Calcutta and the industrial areas.[177] On 14 February, it was reported that the total number of deaths was 3190.[178] Even after normalcy was restored, people across the political spectrum—with Suhrawardy at one end and the Central Intelligence officer at the other—confirmed that anti-British hostility still simmered.[179]

SPONTANEOUS OR PRE-MEDITATED: ROLE OF THE ORGANISED POLITICAL LEADERSHIP

Sir Francis Tuker, then General Officer Commanding-in-Chief (GOC), Eastern Command, said that it was now obvious that the people were extremely angry with the government.[180] The most important question at this time was whether the riot was planned or spontaneous.

[172]Mitra, *The Indian Annual Register,* 280.

[173]Fortnightly report for the month of February, Home Political, File No 18/2/46, NAI.

[174]Mitra, *The Indian Annual Register,* 280.

[175]INA trials, Disturbances in Calcutta protesting against the conviction of Abdul Rashid, Home Political, File No 5/22/46, NAI.

[176]Mitra, *The Indian Annual Register,* 273.

[177]INA trials, Disturbances in Calcutta protesting against the conviction of Abdul Rashid, Home Political, File No 5/22/46, NAI.

[178]INA trials, Disturbances in Calcutta protesting against the conviction of Abdul Rashid, Home Political, File No 5/22/46, NAI.

[179]Fortnightly report for the month of February, Home Political, File No 18/2/46, NAI.

[180]Tuker, *While Memory Serves*, 99–110.

The Intelligence Branch reported that the situation was worse than in November 1945.[181] All political parties—Congress, the Muslim League, Communists, and Khaksars—had come together in the disturbances. Muslim League students and the CPI were responsible for the first procession but they were joined by other student organisations including the Bengal Provincial Students' Federation and the Bengal Provincial Students' Congress.[182] The Calcutta Police confirmed that the ultimate objective of the protesters was to cause civil disorder.[183] No clear link was discernible between the second procession that was dispersed at Clive Street and the first instance of mob violence at Chittaranjan Avenue. The IB reports mentioned that conclusive proof was lacking as to whether the students had engaged or abetted acts of violence or whether hooligans were behind them.[184] But once trouble started, all students participated in the disturbance. In defining the central motive behind their participation, the commissioner concluded that the November disturbances had created a model and that students had defied the authorities, knowing that this would start a chain reaction leading to civil disorder.[185]

Rakesh Batabyal argues that Rashid Ali Day had a perceptible communal character.[186] This was because attempts were made by League leaders to present Captain Rashid as a crusader for the Muslim cause. He says that a section of the Muslim leadership, which was preparing the ground for the agitation, quoted Rashid Ali who had said that he had joined the INA predominantly to serve his community. However, Batabyal misreads the nature and pattern of the disturbances since he sees the motives of the political leadership as representative of the feelings of the crowds. The agitation that developed on the ground had a clearly non-communal character. In fact, it was Hindu–Muslim unity on the

[181]INA trials, Disturbances in Calcutta protesting against the conviction of Abdul Rashid, Home Political, File No 5/22/46, NAI.

[182]Ibid.

[183]Ibid.

[184]Ibid.

[185]Ibid.

[186]Rakesh Batabyal, *Communalism in Bengal: From Famine to Noakhali* (New Delhi: Sage Publications, 2005), 204–211.

streets that actually decided the attitude of the League leaders towards the agitation. With the onset of mob fury, the League leaders fully realised that they had launched something which they were unable to control. Intelligence Branch reports confirmed that the Muslim League leaders' support for the agitation was largely driven by popular pressure.[187] Actually, the League was forced into an awkward situation by the militant action of the Muslim students. With elections round the corner, Suhrawardy could not afford to lose popular support. Like all other party leaders, his control over the rank and file was weak.[188] He knew that he had to agitate for the conviction of Abdul Rashid even if the agitation led to violence. Being a member of the cabinet, he was fully aware that the procession through prohibited areas would be dispersed by force and would lead to serious trouble. Yet his effort to prevent it was only feeble. The commissioner of police concluded that this was because his control over the students was weak.[189] At the same time, he knew that the procession would be allowed to pass through the prohibited areas on 12 February, and by joining the agitation, he could then pose as a militant hero and a protagonist of Hindu–Muslim unity.

Muslim leaders who had not initially encouraged the demonstration made a virtue out of necessity and came out in support of the students.[190] They, thereby, avoided the mistake that Sarat Bose had made. Bose became unpopular as he did not appear in the strife-ridden Dharamtolla area during the November disturbances. The commissioner of police reasoned that 'had votes not been necessary the Muslim League might have adopted a much stronger line in relation to the students.'[191] But given the prevalence of mass militancy, he concluded that such a measure would, in all probability, have ended in a failure.

[187]INA trials, Disturbances in Calcutta protesting against the conviction of Abdul Rashid, Home Political, File No 5/22/46, NAI.

[188]Ibid.

[189]Ibid.

[190]Fortnightly report for the month of February, Home Political, File No 18/2/46, NAI.

[191]INA trials, Disturbances in Calcutta protesting against the conviction of Abdul Rashid, Home Political, File No 5/22/46, NAI.

The position of the Congress was more ambivalent. As Congress president, Sarat Bose at first denounced these acts of lawlessness as sheer hooliganism but, later, tried to retrieve his position.[192] He strongly criticised the government for using troops against the protesters.[193] So, there was Congress vacillation, depending on the strength of the agitation. On the whole, the Congress remained an unwilling supporter at best.

The Bengal Provincial Government stated that there was no evidence of deliberate organisation of the disturbances.[194] It was a Muslim League demonstration that started the trouble and in every instance, the IB reported, trouble once started was exploited by the Communists[195] and they were the most disruptive elements.[196] Communist leaders instigated workers to go on strike and caused a stoppage of the transport services. They were strongly represented in all political demonstrations that took place during those days. They issued objectionable posters and leaflets. Gautam Chattopadhyay argued that the CPI was the only party which had remained with the masses throughout the agitation.[197] They were inspired by the directive sent by P. C. Joshi, general secretary of the CPI, to the Calcutta students' faction on the second day of the uprising.[198] The directive read: 'Get all war-time understanding out of your heads. Post-war revolutionary situation developing fast. New tactical line needed. Be with the people.'[199] However, they were restrained somewhat by the Congress and the Muslim League. The commissioner of police argued that even after matters

[192]Fortnightly report for the month of February, Home Political, File No 18/2/46, NAI.

[193]Ibid.

[194]Inquiry from provinces about causes of disturbances from November 1945 to February 1946, Home Political, File No 5/8/46, NAI.

[195]Ibid.

[196]INA trials, Disturbances in Calcutta protesting against the conviction of Abdul Rashid, Home Political, File No 5/22/46, NAI.

[197]Gautam Chattopadhyay, 'The Almost Revolution: A Case Study of India in February 1946' in *Essays in Honour of Prof S.C. Sarkar*, ed. Barun De (Calcutta: People's Publishing House, 1976), 444–445

[198]Ibid.

[199]Ibid.

had been brought under control by the police and the military, the leaders of the CPI were considering ways of prolonging the agitation.[200] The government concluded that this party may always be expected to be a danger during troubled times. Its aim is violent revolution. If it remained quiet and constitutional its following would rapidly melt away and go over to the Congress or other organisations with great popular appeal. To retain a hold on its supporters, it has to be continually attracting attention by using agitation against the Government. As it has so many low class supporters the step from agitation to mob violence is but a short one.[201]

CONCLUSION

The November and February riots were organised neither by the Muslim League nor by the Congress. Rather, they were examples of popular insurgency that produced a remarkable Hindu–Muslim unity on the streets of the city. It showed a way of transcending communal barriers. What defeated this potential was the attitude of the organised political leadership. Leaders knew that given the new electoral situation, and the strength of popular militancy, they had to appear supportive of the general mood. In doing so, they were riding a tiger that they could not fully tame and which they tried to control as much as they could. The Congress and the Muslim League made an earnest effort to discontinue the agitations when these developed into violent mass movements of a revolutionary kind. They wanted to get back to the question of impending independence and the political shape of the nation state. As soon as they left the agitated streets and returned to the negotiating table, animosities about spoils of power returned and communal antagonism was stoked yet again.

Gautam Chattopadhyay argues that the revolutionary possibility, inherent in the agitation, was cruelly wasted by the national

[200]INA trials, Disturbances in Calcutta protesting against the conviction of Abdul Rashid, Home Political, File No 5/22/46, NAI.

[201]Ibid.

leadership.[202] The mass involvement of workers revealed that agitations could develop into radical movements under popular initiative. The prospect intimidated Congress and League leaders. Hence, they opted for a path of bargaining and let go of the unity brought about by popular agitations. The militant unity could have prevailed against Hindu–Muslim enmity and the towering violence that their negotiations soon produced.[203]

[202]Gautam Chattopadhyay, *The Almost Revolution: A Case Study of India in February 1946* in *Essays in Honour of Prof. S.C. Sarkar*, ed. Barun De (People's Publishing House, 1976), 428.

[203]Sarkar, *Modern India,* 414.

CHAPTER thirteen

The Role of Colonial Administration, 'Riot Systems' and Local Networks during the Calcutta Disturbances of August 1946*

Nariaki Nakazato

INTRODUCTION

The Calcutta Disturbances of August 1946 are counted among the most serious communal riots the Indian subcontinent has ever experienced.[1] They began in the early morning of 16 August 1946, and continued for five days until 20 August.[2] The rioting erupted as a violent confrontation between Muslims and Hindus, mobilized by the All-India Muslim League and the Indian National Congress, respectively; but, before long, a broad variety of social groups inhabiting the large colonial metropolis came to be involved in collective violence in one form or another. The police proved lethargic and unreliable. The British authorities and the Muslim League's

*I am thankful to Gyanendra Pandey for his comments on the draft of this essay.

[1]The general description of the riot in the two paragraphs that follow is based largely on Nariaki Nakazato, 'The Politics of a Partition Riot: Calcutta in August 1946', in *Muslim Societies: Historical and Comparative Aspects,* ed. Tsugitaka Sato (London: Routledge Curzon, 2004).

[2]As regards the date of the termination of the Disturbances, the official view has been adopted here. Some scholars hold the view that they ended on 19 August.

provincial government managed to quell the disturbances only after resorting to emergency measures in the forms of the imposition of a curfew and, after much vacillation, deployment of British troops to regain control of the city. Even the conservative official estimate claims that 4,000 people were killed, 10,000 injured,[3] and 30,000 evacuated to safety.[4] Due to this alarming number of casualties and unprecedented intensity of violence, the Calcutta Disturbances are often referred to as the 'Great Calcutta Killing'.

The Disturbances are also considered to have been acts of collective violence which were heavily political in character. It had become obvious by the winter of 1945–46 that the British had no choice but to grant India independence. The Cabinet Mission arrived in India in late March 1946 to negotiate with Indian leaders over the steps to be taken towards India's independence. As the two major nationalist parties, the Congress and the Muslim League, carried on a hard fought political struggle over framing the future of the independent state(s) under conditions of progressively diminishing British influence, a singularly fluid political situation, which may be termed a 'power vacuum', came to prevail.[5] It was in the midst of this political crisis that the Muslim League resolved at a meeting held in Bombay on 29 July to withdraw its acceptance of

[3]These figures were given by the British government in a 'Written Answer to a Parliamentary Question', Nicholas Mansergh and Penderel Moon, eds., *The Transfer of Power 1942–7*, Volume VIII (London: Her Majesty's Stationery Office, 1977 [hereafter *TP*, vol. viii]), 303. Wavell, the then viceroy, gave Pethick-Lawrence, secretary of state for India, another set of figures: 4,400 dead, 16,000 injured, and over 100,000 homeless (ibid., 323). Outside Calcutta proper, total casualties were reported to be 160 killed and 296 injured in the 24-Parganas, 150 and 381 in Howrah, 22 and 75 in Dacca, and 4 and 70 in Chittagong ('Secret Report on the Political Situation in Bengal' [hereafter 'SR for Bengal'], 2nd half of Aug. 1946, India Office Records, The British Library, London [hereafter IOR]: L/PJ/5/154).

[4]'Report of the Officer-in-Charge, Rescue Organisation', Government of Bengal [hereafter GB], Home Department, Political Branch, Confidential Files [hereafter Home (Poll) Confidential] File No. 351/46 Part B II, West Bengal State Archives, 10 [hereafter WBSA].

[5]Lambert's pioneering work on the history of communal riots in South Asia first drew this writer's attention to this unique situation. Calling the Raj 'a sort of 'lame duck power', he opined that 'the critical change during this period [1946–8] was the shift in power, and the pattern of communal rioting in 1946–8 reflected this basic fact'. See Richard D. Lambert, 'Hindu-Muslim Riots' (PhD diss., University of Pennsylvania, 1951), 162, 180.

the Cabinet Mission's plan to transfer power and take 'Direct Action' on 16 August. The objective of the 'Direct Action' was to push the League's demand for the founding of Pakistan, as well as to voice strong protest against the way in which the setting up of an interim government had been negotiated, by organising across India both mass rallies and *hartal* (shut down of transportation facilities and stoppage of all work at offices, mills, shops, etc.). The political offensive launched by the Muslim League met with a deeply hostile reaction from the Congress and its supporters. Preparations for the political showdown that occurred on 16 August had been made well in advance by both parties; and the violent Hindu-Muslim clash, which took place in the prime city of British India exploded almost immediately into communal rioting unprecedented both in scale and ferocity. The Calcutta Disturbances had tremendous repercussions. Not only did they trigger a series of partition riots in East Bengal, Bihar, and other provinces, but they also made it almost impossible for both sides to come to a political compromise for the sake of preserving the unity of India. As to Calcutta itself, the quelling of the Disturbances by no means meant a return to normalcy for the city. Despite such stern measures as the continued enforcement of curfew up to 13 December (reimposed in certain parts of the city from the following April onward), the constant presence of troops in the streets until late December (called in three times the following March, May, and July), the prohibition of the assemblage of five or more persons under Section 144 of the Criminal Procedure Code until mid-February 1947 (reintroduced from the following mid-March onward), the exercise of authority granted under the Special Powers Ordinance to search anyone on the street, and stringent control of the press under the Defence of India Rules, periodic waves of murderous violence persisted in the city, with the exception of a general lull during January and February 1947.[6] Furthermore, there were still 14,000 persons in government refugee

[6]'SR for Bengal' from 1st half of Aug. 1946 to 2nd half of July 1947, IOR: L/PJ/5/154. The casualties in Calcutta were reported to be 45 killed and 181 injured in September 1946, 117 and 618 in October, 15 and 43 in the second half of November, 14 and 35 in December, nil in January and February 1947, 97 and 320 in March, 63 and 517 in April, 49 and 367 in May, 56 and 214 in June, and 83 and 426 in July ('SR for Bengal'; 'Casualties in Communal Disturbances, etc.', GB, Home (Poll) Confidential, 1947 (the file number cannot be mentioned), WBSA.

camps in Calcutta as late as July 1947, comprised of 8000 refugees from Bihar and 1400 from Noakhali, together with 4700 Calcutta riot victims.[7] All in all, one could feel justified in saying that the Calcutta Disturbances marked a shift in the Indian political situation from a simple 'power vacuum' to 'civil war', a form of the 'state of exception'.[8]

Historians have studied communal riots mainly from the viewpoint of identity politics;[9] and there is good reason to do so, since bitter antagonism over issues of religious identity is a chief cause of communal violence. However, communal riots, particularly those of the largest scale, are multi-faceted complex events which are embedded

[7]'SR for Bengal', 1st half of July 1947, IOR: L/PJ/5/154.

[8]The massive waves of communal violence that continued from August 1946 to the end of 1947 have often been referred to as 'civil war'. For example, Governor-General Wavell and his staff expected the grave situation in Calcutta to develop into civil war across India. Wavell wrote in his diary on 20 August 1946: 'Both he [Ian Scott] and George seem to be convinced that our only course is to get out of India as soon as possible and leave her to her fate, which will be civil war'. Penderel Moon, ed., *Wavell: The Viceroy's Journal* (Delhi: Oxford University Press, 1977), 336.

In this paper, the term 'civil war' is used in a more specific way than Wavell's, following Carl Schmitt who gave a penetrating elucidation of 'civil war' in internal politics and 'war' between organised nations from an existential point of view (Carl Schmitt, *The Concept of the Political*, trans. George Schwab (Chicago: The University of Chicago Press, 1996) (originally published as *Der Begriff des Politischen* in 1932), 32 passim). Applying his friend/enemy theory, he holds that the '(civil) war' is 'necessarily unusually intense and inhuman because ... it simultaneously degrades the enemy into moral and other categories and is forced to make of him a monster that must not only be defeated but also utterly destroyed' (ibid., 36). A 'state of exception', *Ausnahmezustand* in German, means any kind of severe economic or political disturbance that requires the application of extraordinary measures, but not mere anarchy or chaos. Apparently, this is an ambiguous concept and both civil war and revolutionary violence come under it. For a full discussion of this concept, see Carl Schmitt, *Political Theology: Four Chapters on the Concept of Sovereignty*, trans. George Schwab (Chicago: The University of Chicago Press, 2005) (originally published as *Politische Theologie: Vier Kapitel zur Lehre von der Souveränität* in 1922; revised ed. 1934), 5, 14 passim. An important recent contribution to the question of the 'state of exception' is Giorgio Agamben, *State of Exception*, trans. Kevin Attell (Chicago: The University of Chicago Press, 2005). The significant debate between Walter Benjamin and Schmitt over the problems of the 'state of exception' is subjected to a close examination by Agamben in *State*, chap. 4.

[9]For example, see Gyanendra Pandey's exemplary work. Gyanendra Pandey, *Remembering Partition: Violence, Nationalism and History in India* (Cambridge: Cambridge University Press, 2001).

in thick layers of social reality and upon which diverse social forces converge. It is therefore only natural that when perusing the rapidly growing literature in this field of research, one notices social scientists trying to address the problem from a very wide range of angles. To give a few conspicuous examples, Veena Das takes up the suffering and pain of female victims of violence basically from the perspective of gender and peace studies.[10] Stanley Tambiah by and large draws upon the crowd theory developed by Gustave Le Bon, Elias Canetti, and George Rudé,[11] while Beth Roy bases her study of a forgotten riot in Bangladesh upon a insightful narrative analysis.[12] Charles Tilly and his group attempt to apply their general theory of 'contentious politics' to the specific case of communal violence in South Asia.[13] Martha Nussbaum draws our attention to, among other things, the aspect of social psychology, arguing that the psychological origins of violence perpetrated by the Hindu far right can, in the final analysis, be assigned to its attempt to compensate and heal the deep wounds of humiliation which the Indian people endured under British colonial rule. She sees the growth of Hindu nationalism in India as a phenomenon comparable to the rise of fascism in Germany after suffering the devastating humiliation of defeat in the First World War.[14]

Theoretical pursuits in these directions appear to have reached a peak in the 2000s when the three political scientists, Paul R. Brass, Ashutosh Varshney, and Steven Wilkinson, engaged in a debate which

[10]Veena Das, 'Our Work to Cry: Your Work to Listen', in *Mirrors of Violence: Communities, Riots and Survivors in South Asia*, ed. Veena Das (Delhi: Oxford University Press, 1990); idem, *Critical Events: An Anthropological Perspective on Contemporary India* (Delhi: Oxford University Press, 1995) chaps. 3, 7.

[11]Stanley J. Tambiah, *Levelling Crowds: Ethnonationalist Conflicts and Postcolonial Histories* (Princeton, NJ: Princeton University Press, 1996) chap. 10.

[12]Beth Roy, *Some Trouble with Cows: Making Sense of Social Conflict* (Berkeley: University of California Press, 1994).

[13]Doug McAdam, Sidney Tarrow, and Charles Tilly, *Dynamics of Contention* (Cambridge: Cambridge University Press, 2001), 124–30 passim; Sidney G. Tarrow, *Power in Movement: Social Movements and Contentious Politics*, 3rd ed. (Cambridge: Cambridge University Press, 2011), 140–45 passim. For a critical comment on this theory from the South Asian perspective, see Paul R. Brass, *Theft of an Idol: Text and Context in the Study of Collective Violence* (Princeton: Princeton University Press, 1997), 9–11.

[14]Martha C. Nussbaum, *The Clash Within: Democracy, Religious Violence, and India's Future* (Cambridge, Mass.: Belknap, 2007), 333, 336.

attracted the active interest of many scholars working on communal problems,[15] mainly because their views had important implications for the down-to-earth question of the control and prevention of communal violence. Brass emphasises the significance of 'institutionalised riot systems', which can be deployed when the need arises as a mechanism triggering and sustaining a violent incident,[16] whereas Varshney maintains that 'the pre-existing local networks of civic engagement' between the two religious communities, namely, 'everyday' as well as 'associational' forms of engagement, have the capacity to withstand communal violence.[17] For Brass, the dismantling of 'institutionalised riot systems' is essential in preventing and controlling communal violence, while for Varshney, cultivation of 'everyday' and 'associational' ties among citizens is vital. Taking a position closer to Brass's, Wilkinson attaches a particular significance to what he calls 'the electoral incentives for ethnic violence', believing that 'ethnic riots, far from being relatively spontaneous eruptions of anger, are often planned by politicians for clear electoral purposes'. He goes on to argue that 'town-level electoral incentives account for where Hindu-Muslim violence breaks out and that state-level electoral incentives

[15]Ashutosh Varshney, 'Aligarh is not India', *India Today* Nov. 10, 2003; Paul R. Brass, 'Response to Ashutosh Varshney', 30 Nov. 2003 (http://www.mail-archive.com/sapac@www. residentlounge.com/msg00137.html); Steven I. Wilkinson, *Votes and Violence: Electoral Competition and Ethnic Riots in India* (Cambridge: Cambridge University Press, 2004), 52–57.

[16]Paul R. Brass, 'Introduction: Discourse of Ethnicity, Communalism, and Violence', in *Riots and Pogroms*, ed. Paul Brass (Houndmills: Macmillan, 1996), 12–16; idem, *Theft of an Idol*, 9, 15–18; idem, *The Production of Hindu-Muslim Violence in Contemporary India* (Seattle: The University of Washington Press, 2003), 12–16, 30–34, 377–79; idem, *Forms of Collective Violence: Riots, Pogroms, and Genocide in Modern India* (Gurgaon (Haryana): Three Essays Collective, 2006) chap. 3. Brass's 'system' consists of networks of known actors, such as criminal elements, members of youth gangs, local militant group leaders, politicians, businessmen, religious leaders, college and university professors, pamphleteers, and journalists. In this system these 'known actors specialise in the conversion of incidents between members of different communities into ethnic riots'. See Brass, 'Introduction', 12–13.

[17]Ashutosh Varshney, *Ethnic Conflict and Civic Life: Hindus and Muslims in India*, 2nd ed. (New Haven: Yale University Press, 2002), 3, 9. By the term 'associational forms of civic engagement', Varshney means business associations, professional organisations, reading clubs, film clubs, sports clubs, festival organisations, trade unions, and cadre-based political parties.

account for where and when state governments use their police forces to prevent riots'. So, from this point of view, the government's decisive action is crucial.[18] Ian Copland's recent comparative study of the communal riots of 1871 and 1970 is one response to this debate by a historian of modern India. Broadly corroborating with historical evidence Wilkinson's view about the pivotal role played by state-level politics, Copland concludes that '"strong" states are likely [to] have lower levels of mass violence than "weak" ones, strong states here meaning those that possess both the capacity and the desire to rein it in', adding an important stipulation that such strong states must be democratic ones, because only those endowed with moral authority can discharge their responsibility to keep the peace effectively without risking a massive popular backlash.[19]

If the Calcutta Disturbances are to be located in the historical context of a shift from a simple 'power vacuum' to a 'civil-war' situation or 'state of exception', it need hardly be said that historians should pay more attention to the political aspects *per se* than they have done so far from their rather limited viewpoint of identity politics. Indeed, as Carl Schmitt argues, in the last analysis, the political, which can be reduced to the friend and enemy distinction, pushes aside and subordinates all non-political antitheses, whether moral, aesthetic, economic, religious or national (in the ethnic or cultural sense).[20] The present paper seeks to shed new light on the Calcutta Disturbances, drawing upon the theoretical awareness increased mainly by the work of political scientists, particularly upon the Brass-Varshney-Wilkinson debate and Copland's response to it. It attempts to probe more deeply into the political aspects of the Disturbances by introducing a three-dimensional model comprising the three reference points of the colonial government, riot systems, and local networks of civic engagement. The first of the three dimensions—namely, problems concerning the administration of the state—has already been discussed elsewhere.[21] Here, these

[18]Wilkinson, *Votes and Violence*,1, 4–5.

[19]Ian Copland, 'The Production and Containment of Communal Violence: Scenarios from Modern India', *South Asia*, 33, no. 1 (2010), 147, 150.

[20]Schmitt, *Concept*, 38.

[21]Nakazato, 'Politics'.

same problems will be examined from a different angle; that is, in terms of the contradictions inherent in the colonial state structure. Regarding the remaining two dimensions, despite the animated debate between Brass and Varshney, their approaches do not appear to be contradictory to or incompatible with one another, at least when they are viewed as theoretical frameworks for studying the politics of communal riots, rather than as policy options for riot control. 'Systems' and 'local networks' may be regarded rather as two of the major moments that constitute communal rioting; the former a modern monster created out of the religious component of Indian society, the latter representing an important aspect of the natural communitarian relations nurtured by the dwellers of urban India. The crucial point seems to lie not in making a sharp and rigid distinction between 'systems' and 'local networks', but in, first, investigating to what extent both of them have grown and what shape they have come to take within the given confines of the state-level politics and administration, then considering in what manner they function under the high pressure of intense violence, and finally, looking at the way in which they intersect to render political structure to a seemingly chaotic, violent event.

A GOVERNMENT ADRIFT—THE GOVERNOR'S 'SPECIAL RESPONSIBILITIES'

In April 1946, Huseyn Shaheed Suhrawardy of the Muslim League formed a ministry and became premier of Bengal. Although in independent India, a chief minister is mainly held responsible for law and order in his/her state, under colonial rule after 1937, the provincial governors shared that responsibility with the premiers, and the relationship between the two offices was not always clear. Available archival evidence seems to suggest that it is this ambiguity built into the colonial system that goes a long way in explaining the confusion and disarray in state administration during the Calcutta Disturbances.

The Suhrawardy government was established after the 1946 provincial elections held under the provisions of the Government of India Act, 1935. Regarding the actual functioning of this Act,

Reginald Coupland, a specialist in the study of India's constitutional problems, remarked in 1944 that 'in Bengal, Assam and Sind the Governments have normally depended from day to day on the support of the majorities in their legislatures', meaning that what was called 'responsible government' had come into being in those three provinces. However, even according to Coupland's semi-official explanation, this 'responsible government' meant no more than Indian self-government on the Westminster model over *most* provincial matters, subject to the 'safeguards' provided by the Act.[22] Under the 1935 Act, 'the executive authority' lies with the governor who is to be appointed by the British king, whereas 'a council of ministers' headed by the premier is merely to 'aid and advise the Governor in the exercise of his functions'. This strong governor is to discharge seven 'special responsibilities', among which top priority is placed on 'the prevention of any grave menace to the peace or tranquillity of the Province'. Moreover, he enjoys special powers to select the advocate-general, to alter police rules, and so forth. He is to 'exercise his individual judgment' on these two sets of matters, which were bundled together under the category of 'safeguards'.[23] What is more, he can take over and run indefinitely the administration of his province under Section 93 of the Act, which was put into practice in Bengal in March 1945.

It is true that the Congress made a political issue of the 'safeguards' when it chose to take office after the elections in 1937; and Governor-General Linlithgow issued a carefully worded statement to work out a compromise with the nationalist party. However, Coupland affirms that 'in fact no constitutional ground had been surrendered' to the Congress by Linlithgow.[24] While this should be accepted as a straightforward interpretation of the law, in point of fact, it is well known that Syama Prasad Mookerjee,

[22]Reginald Coupland, *The Constitutional Problem in India* (London: Oxford University Press, 1944) pt. 1, 134–36; pt. 3, 64. See also Sumit Sarkar, *Modern India* (Delhi: Macmillan, 1983), 336–38.

[23]*The Government of India Act 1935*, sections 50, 52, 55–58; Coupland, *Constitutional Problem*, pt. 1, 134–36; Arthur Berriedale Keith, *A Constitutional History of India, 1600–1935* (London: Methuen, 1936), 348–52.

[24]Coupland, *Constitutional Problem*, pt. 2, 20.

a senior minister of the Fazlul Huq administration, submitted his resignation in November 1942, releasing an open letter bitterly criticising the then Bengal governor for his intervention in the state's administration, which had resulted in the 'establishment of a government within a government'.[25]

THE POLICE CONTROL ROOM

There is no direct evidence showing that 'a government within a government' led by the governor was still in operation in parallel with the premier's administration in 1946. However, in view of the top priority being given to the law and tranquillity question in the list of safeguards, it would not be off the mark to assume that the governor and British high officials maintained and asserted strong control over the public security machinery. A glimpse into the actual state of affairs can be gained from the detailed notes kept by P.D. Martyn, who was additional secretary to the Home Department at the time of the Calcutta Disturbances.[26]

Martyn had already worked in the department for the past ten years in the capacities of deputy, joint, and additional secretaries in charge of police administration, military liaison, the build-up of civil defence organisations, and so on. In other words, he was a specialist in home security matters. For four days beginning on 16 August, this senior officer spent most of his time in the Control Room of the Calcutta Police, making one important decision after another to deal with the fierce rioting in consultation with the chief secretary, the top brass of the military and police, and district magistrates. At the same time, he was busy making arrangements for keeping vital services like railways, telephone lines, electricity and food supplies operating, drafting government orders, releasing press briefings, providing for the removal of victims' bodies, and organising peace committees. The following is a typical example of Martyn's routine during the Disturbances:

[25]Syama Prasad Mookerjee, *A Phase of the Indian Struggle* (Kushtia: Monojendra N. Bhowmik, 1942), 57.

[26]'Diary prepared from Rough Notes kept during the Disturbances ...' and 'Memoirs of P.D. Martyn', Indian Civil Service (District Officers) Collection/P.D. Martyn, IOR: MSS Eur F180/13.

> 3.55 p.m.—4.10 p.m. [17 August]. Phone call from Acting Area Commander to the effect that he had been discussing with D.M. [district magistrate], 24-Parganas the question of mily. [military] assistance in the Matiabruj area. Discussion with I.G. [inspector-general of police, Bengal] who confirmed that the situation was serious there—2 mills being involved but he could not give any assistance as police were already fully occupied—100 men from Rajshahi not yet arrived. Ascertained from the D.M. that there had been a number of dead and 100 were injured and that trouble was still going on in that area. Arrests had been made but force available was small and a long area was involved.... D.M. wanted military patrols that evening which in his view would be the critical time. Discussed with the Acting Area Commander (Brig. Sixsmith) and explained the situation to him as ascertained from the D.M. and requested that mily. patrols should be provided during the evening in the Garden Reach area ... Ascertained that the Officiating Area Commander would be able to provide and that he would contact the D.M.[27]

It is noteworthy that Suhrawardy also spent a lot of time in that same Control Room, being entitled to do so by virtue of concurrently acting as home minister. Nevertheless, later on he was to be severely criticised for gross misconduct by British high officials, who asserted that he had caused unnecessary confusion by at times bombarding them with questions and impractical suggestions, and at others trying to compel them to treat his party and friends with special favour. There is plenty of evidence in support of such accusations.[28] For example, D. R. Hardwick, Calcutta commissioner of police, testified before the Enquiry Commission as follows:

> ... I had very little time to study the situation, because the Chief Minister was there and at once would enter into a discussion with me as to why I cannot rescue people or put down pickets—the two chief things on which I usually had a lot of argument and then a certain

[27]P.D. Martyn's 'Diary', p. 7, IOR: MSS Eur F180/13.

[28]*Minutes of Evidence of the Calcutta Disturbances Commission of Enquiry*, 11 vols. (Alipore: Superintendent of West Bengal Government Printing, n.d.) [hereafter *CDCE*], vol. ii, 70–71, 115–19; vol. iii, 127–28; vol. iv, 261–62; Tyson to Folk, No. 365, 23 Aug. 1946, Tyson Collection, IOR: MSS Eur E341/46.

> number of other officials of the Muslim League or Parliamentary Secretaries always came with the Chief Minister and also there would be noise in the Control Room because they were frequently arguing among themselves.... That is why I asked the Chief Minister to remove his friends. I ordered most of the people out, but I could not order out the Chief Minister as I had no right to do so.[29]

Although Hardwick probably failed to withstand the temptation to exaggerate, on the whole, his story is corroborated by other evidence.

The crucial point of the above two inside accounts is that there seems to have been little contact, to say nothing of consultation, between the home minister and a senior official of his department, despite the fact that they were in the same room together for many hours at the height of the rioting. In his detailed notes, which come to about 20 pages in length, Martyn refers to Suhrawardy only in connection with four or five minor matters, one exception being when Suhrawardy confronted the British chief secretary and insisted upon calling out the military at midnight of the 16/17th. It could have been that Martyn decided to ignore this grandstanding politician in the belief that he could do so with virtual impunity, and most probably with the governor's support.[30] By contrast, Suhrawardy appears to have tried to play the role of a strong political leader by incessantly raising trivial points with the commissioner of police, but refrained from such theatrical performance when dealing with the senior ICS officer decorated with CIE and CBE, who was actually in charge. Perhaps this was the way in which the 'safeguards' were expected to function with respect to law and tranquillity by the framers of the 1935 Act. Official records show that it was only at 11.30 am on 18 August, fifty hours after the outbreak of the Disturbances, and it was only through the intervention of General Francis Robert Roy Bucher, officiating general officer commanding

[29] *CDCE*, vol. ii, 119.

[30] Martyn later recalled: 'Suhrawardy was a subdued man during the crucial days of the Great Killing. I remember very well at the meeting to examine the general situation on the 19th August that he uncharacteristically refused to meet the Press and left it to officials to undertake the task' ('Memoirs of P.D. Martyn', IOR: MSS Eur F180/13).

in chief of the Eastern Command at that time, that Indian cabinet ministers, including Suhrawardy, and British high officials finally came together to deliberate on how to quell the rioting.[31]

VACILLATION AND DELAY

The contrast that existed between the actions taken by Martyn and by Suhrawardy during the Disturbances may be taken as an indication that the 'safeguards' worked after all to the benefit of the Indian people, since they enabled British high officials to deal with the violence firmly and efficiently, keeping partisan interference on the part of Indian politicians to a minimum. However, the actual state of affairs was not that simple.

First of all, one has to take into account the fact that as the reports about large numbers of Muslim casualties poured in, Suhrawardy, who had been advocating his own version of 'Direct Action', retracted his hard-line stance and began to make a belated attempt to cope with the chaotic situation. Apparently, communal violence was not unfolding in the way that he and his followers had expected, causing the pragmatic politician misgivings that his political future was in danger. Secondly, the British were not neutral arbitrators between the two contending nationalist parties, but should rather be thought of as a third player in a dangerous political game. They were also biased, but in a manner different from their Indian counterparts.[32] For example, at the end of July, the military had already deployed troops into the suburban areas and called in an additional battalion as a precautionary measure, enabling it to boast after the Disturbances that 'there is little doubt that the initial distribution of troops before the 16th ... largely prevented the trouble from spreading to the industrial area outside the city'.[33] Setting aside for the time being an assessment of the real situation,

[31]Nakazato, 'Politics', 125.

[32]Ibid., 111, 129.

[33][Eastern Command], 'Report on the Muslim-Hindu Conflict in Calcutta following "Direct Action Day" the 16th August 1946' [hereafter 'RMHC'], p. 15, GB, Home (Poll) Confidential, No File No./46, WBSA. See also *CDCE*, vol. ii, 14; vol. iii, 2–3.

which will be attempted shortly, preparedness in the industrial belt stood in stark contrast to the chaos in Calcutta proper, and it was in connection with the deployment of the military inside the city that the British Raj displayed great vacillation, which hardly measures up to its reputation for 'steel-framework' administration. The hesitancy may be summed up in time series as follows.[34]

16 AUGUST

7.00 am	Reports of the first clash arrive.
8.00 am	Police forces are withdrawn from the streets in accordance with the 'Emergency Action Scheme' introduced in early 1946.[35]
2.30 pm	Commissioner of Police Hardwick decides to apply for military assistance.
2.40 pm	Governor Burrows gives his approval to deploy troops.
2.45 pm	Premier Suhrawardy gives his consent to deployment.
3.00 pm	Burrows, Hardwick, and Area Commander Sixsmith make a tour of the city to appreciate the situation.
4.15 pm	Burrows et al. decide that the situation does not justify military intervention and that the troops should be brought into the Sealdah camp as a precautionary measure.
5.30 pm	Suhrawardy meets with Sixsmith, demanding that the military pickets be posted in the city. Sixsmith refuses.
7.00 pm	An Indian senior police officer sent out to assess the situation and decide if the military action is called for reports to Hardwick that the military should be called in. However, Fortress Commander MacKinlay intervenes, telling Hardwick that he wishes the military not to be deployed immediately.

[34]A full account of the sequence of regrettable incidents may be found in Nakazato, 'Politics', 120–28.

[35]Under this 'Scheme', armed, traffic, and mounted police were gathered at police headquarters in Lalbazar to form a strike force. Local constables were also ordered to remain in the police station compound. The central control room was to despatch these concentrated forces to trouble spots when needed. This means that no police forces were present in the streets of Calcutta on the morning of 16 August. See ibid., 120.

9.00 pm	A curfew is imposed.
10.30 pm	Chief Secretary Walker prepares to leave the Police Control Room, but Suhrawardy protests. A serious assessment of the situation ensues.
11.30 pm	Suhrawardy, Walker, MacKinlay, and Hardwick agree that the military will 'patrol' north Calcutta.

17 AUGUST

1.45 am	The first military 'patrol' is despatched from the Sealdah camp with express orders not to open fire on the crowds.
11.00 am	Burrows, Walker, Sixsmith, MacKinlay, and Hardwick leave on a second tour to assess the situation. They find conditions in north Calcutta so bad that they give up their inspection halfway out and hasten back to order troops to 'dominate' the area.
3.30 pm	Three British battalions enter the worst zone in north Calcutta.
5.30 pm	The military gain control of the zone, as the rioting spreads to other areas.

18 AUGUST

2.00 am	Troops are despatched to the Dock area. Later in the early morning, Army Commander Bucher arrives from Ranchi.
10.00 am	Troops are despatched to Barrackpore and Naihati.
11.30 am	At a meeting between Bucher, Indian cabinet ministers, and British high officials, it is decided that military pickets be posted at strategic points throughout Calcutta.
Noon	Bucher, Burrows, Suhrawardy, and Walker embark on a third tour of inspection and find the situation still out of control.
4.30 pm	A British reserve battalion with fifteen to twenty tanks in the lead enters Upper Chitpore Road.

In sum, it took no less than twenty-one hours (from 2.30 pm on 16 August to 11.30 am on 17 August) for the Raj's 'steel framework' to make up its mind to take the initial effective measure. Being plunged into total confusion on the first day, all-out efforts only began after the arrival of Army Commander Bucher on the morning of 18 August. In particular, a fatal error in judgment was made in the choice to adopt such lukewarm half-measures as the military 'patrol' during the critical night of 16/17 August, when murder and mayhem were engulfing the city.[36]

Why so much delay and vacillation? Assuming no malicious intent on the part of the Raj, there is only one convincing reason, deep hidden fear. It is pertinent here to mention the interesting fact that F.J. Burrows, governor of Bengal, concluded his telegram to London reporting the outbreak of serious rioting in Calcutta with the assurance that 'Disturbances so far have been markedly communal and not, repeat not, in any way anti-British, anti-[omission] or anti-Government'.[37] The Raj was extremely vigilant concerning any outbreak of anti-British civil disturbance that threatened to upset the delicate and complicated process of its withdrawal from India, which had already been set in motion in March with the visit of the Cabinet Mission. As a matter of fact, army generals of the Eastern Command feared the possibility that communal rioting could evolve into an anti-British uprising, as Sixsmith, a brigadier in charge of the Calcutta area, disclosed in his notes written a few years after the Disturbances: 'Although the first incident [on 16 August] might well be communal, I considered, and it was my impression that others considered, the most likely turn would be Anti-Government and Anti-British'.[38]

Even for a legitimate, popular government, ordering the military to take actions against civilians is always a highly sensitive matter requiring careful consideration. It must have been all the more so for a foreign colonial administration, especially for the Raj, which in August 1946 was already an ailing body which had reached the final stage of life, whose legitimacy to rule India had been relentlessly on the wane. There was a sufficient reason to fear that military actions

[36]As regards the questionable behaviour of British high officials, see also Sandip Bandyopadhyay, *Itihaser dike Phire: Chhechollisher Danga* (Kolkata: Utsa Manush, 1992), 47–48. Bandyopadhyay lays the responsibility for the rapid spread of the rioting on Governor Burrows.

[37]Governor of Bengal to Secy. of State for India, 16 Aug. 1946, IOR: L/PJ/8/577 (reproduced in *TP*, vol. viii, 239–40). Burrows repeated this view in his report to Wavell (Burrows to Wavell, 22 Aug. 1946, *TP*, vol. viii, 298, 302).

[38]E.K.G. Sixsmith, 'Note on the Calcutta Riots', p. 1, Tuker Papers, 71/21/3/12, Imperial War Museum, London.

against Indian civilians would set an anti-British sentiment ablaze, creating a worst scenario for the British.

In fine, in August 1946, the power centre of the Bengal government was virtually divided into two branches, the one headed by the Indian premier and the other by the British governor, which were involved in a tug of war. The former had political legitimacy in that his party had won the recent provincial election, although by limited suffrage, but was now pursuing narrow political gains via cynical populist techniques. The latter was in control of some strategic points within the reputed administrative machinery, but seriously lacked legitimacy. It is very likely that it was this legitimacy convolution that underlay the strange drift of the provincial administration amidst the intense violence that broke out in its capital.

INSTITUTIONALISED RIOT SYSTEMS?

In anticipation of a political showdown on Direct Action Day, the leaders of the two nationalist parties, the Muslim League and the Congress, utilised a whole repertoire of available techniques for mass mobilisation. They launched blatant propaganda campaigns in the newspapers, printed inflammatory leaflets, held a large number of small gatherings locally, and organised a few mass rallies at the city centre.[39] The novel thing about this sort of political mobilisation during the 1940s was that nationalist politicians had under them paramilitary party organisations called 'volunteers', which included even *goondas*, as an apparatus to translate their propaganda of words into practice, and actually put them into operation. In the following two sections, from Brass's 'institutionalised riots systems', the element of 'specialists' will be chosen for discussion, although it is by no means this writer's intention to argue that *all* the 'volunteers' should be considered to be 'specialists' in violent or criminal activity, nor that the Calcutta Disturbances can be reduced to infighting between the two cliques of the Calcutta underworld.

[39]Suranjan Das, *Communal Riots in Bengal 1905–1947* (Delhi: Oxford University Press, 1991), 167–70; GB, Home Deptt., Political Branch, *Note on the Causes of the Calcutta Disturbances, August, 1946* (Alipore: Bengal Government Press, 1946), 7–8 passim.

VOLUNTEERS

A phenomenal growth in all sorts of 'volunteer' organisations was one of the most salient features of Indian society during the Second World War and its aftermath. Originally, the term 'volunteers' referred to political party workers, who, in principle unremunerated, engaged in the logistics of political rallies and conferences, social work, famine or flood victim relief efforts, general vigilance, and so on. They came to form a stable component of political party organisation in the early 1920s;[40] and by the end of the 1930s, a part of them had developed into paramilitary forces. Some non-political bodies also followed this tendency. With names like the All-India Muslim National Guards, Rashtriya Swayam Sewak Sangh, Khaksars, Congress Volunteer Corps, Hindusthan National Guards, Azad Hind Volunteer Corps, 'volunteer' organisations usually supplied their members with unofficial uniforms resembling military dress, regularly drilled with or without arms (usually with *lathis*), staged paramilitary parades to display their strength and discipline, and set up youth training camps. Members were mainly recruited from local youth, while the leadership came from various social backgrounds, such as ranking party member, lawyer, doctor, teacher, religious leader, ex-terrorist, shop owner, college upperclassman, and so forth.[41] Due to this paramilitary character, 'volunteers' were often referred to as 'private armies' by the colonial government.

Looking back upon the history of 'volunteer' organisations, the government of India remarked in 1947:

> By 1938 it was becoming apparent that the volunteer movement in India was gaining both in point of members and in intensity, even though organisation and control were lacking in full efficiency.

[40]In the Congress the volunteer organisation got under way in 1921, when the 'Volunteer Pledge' was stipulated for all members of the 'National Volunteer Corps'. For more details, see 'R.S. Pandit's Interim Report on the Provincial Volunteer Organisation', All-India Congress Committee Papers, Non-Category File No. 70 (Pt. 1)/1946–47, Manuscript Section, Nehru Memorial Museum and Library, New Delhi [hereafter NMML].

[41]See half-yearly reports on volunteer organisations collected in GB, Intelligence Branch Records [hereafter IB Records], Serial No. 111/1941, File No. 324/41, WBSA.

> With the outbreak of war in September 1939, the pace began to further quicken and in the first half of 1940 there was hitherto unparalleled activity throughout the country. This was primarily due to the *panic* caused by unfavourable developments in the war situation in Europe, which gave rise to *a feverish anxiety* on the part of the great communities and political parties to establish strong and disciplined volunteer forces for use in *an emergency*. At the same time, increasing communal mistrust, combined with a general apprehension of internal disorder or external aggression gave a strong impetus to volunteer activity in several Provinces.[42]

The 'several Provinces' apparently include Bengal, while 'internal disorder' refers to the Quit India Movement and the Bengal Famine, and 'external aggression' to the Japanese invasion of Burma. This report indicates that the social psychological tension that occurs in wartime was heightened by a series of unexpected military defeats by the colonial ruler, which activated a dialectical interaction between the two poles of valour and 'panic' ('a feverish anxiety'), or between manliness and effeminacy, in the colonised people's mind. War was a source of great anxiety, but at the same time provided them with a long-awaited chance of overcoming what Nussbaum calls a sense of humiliation. Moreover, to be the target of the newly acquired manliness, an enemy did not necessarily have to be an alien aggressor, but could also be found within Indian society itself. It was this sort of psychological mechanism that appears to have formed the emotional basis of the proliferation of 'private armies'.[43]

Keeping 'volunteers' under careful surveillance as 'the danger to public order and communal relations', the Indian government announced a ban on regimental drilling in August 1940, and on

[42]Government of India [hereafter GI], Home Deptt., Intelligence Bureau, 'Volunteer Organisations in India', GI, Home Deptt. Political (Internal) Branch [hereafter Home (Poll-I)], File No. 28/5/46, National Archives of India, New Delhi [hereafter NAI]; 'Volunteer Organization/Private Armies in India', Mountbatten Papers, IOR: MSS Eur F200/117. Emphasis added.

[43]See also Joya Chatterji, *Bengal Divided: Hindu Communalism and Partition 1932–1947* (Cambridge: Cambridge University Press, 1995), 233–39. There is room for further study on the reliability of intelligence reports and on the actual strength of 'private armies'; but there is little doubt that these organisations exercised a deep symbolic and psychological influence on the populace.

uniforms and training camps in August 1944, but to little avail.[44] In point of fact, these measures were bound to be futile, because the government itself had begun to set up similar organisations, namely, 'Civic Guards', 'Home Guards', and 'A.R.P.' (Air Raid Precaution), among the civilian population for the purpose of bolstering morale and preparing for aerial bombardment and the possible landing of Japanese troops.[45] The government admitted as early as February 1942 that their policy had produced an unanticipated side effect; to wit: 'The organisation of civil defence has been followed by proposals to revive the formation of volunteer bodies of political parties, particularly the Congress'.[46] In other words, official policy was serving as a model for non-official bodies to follow.

Although geographical distribution of volunteer organisations was highly skewed and their strength considerably fluctuated over time, the growth of 'private armies' appear to have reached a peak in 1946.

> During 1946, however, the renewed political activity in the country—elections were held in the early part of the year and political governments were in power in the Provinces by the end of April—and the negotiations with the Cabinet Mission, whose plan was rejected in July by the Muslim League, occasioned a deterioration in communal feeling, which led to a marked revival of the communal volunteer organizations, particularly the Rashtriya Swayam Sewak Sangh, the Muslim League National Guards, and the Shiromani Akali Dal.[47]

In sum, rather than being a creation of short-sighted unscrupulous politicians, 'volunteers', or 'private armies', were deeply embedded in the critical realities of Indian society during the turbulent decade marked by total war and decolonisation.

[44]R. Tottenham, 'Summary', 28 Aug. 1944, GI, Home (Poll-I), File No. 28/3/44, NAI; Intelligence Bureau, 'Volunteer Organisations in India', GI, Home (Poll-I), File No. 28/5/46, NAI.

[45]'Report of War Activities for the Quarter ending 31 Mar. 1942', GB, Home (Poll) Confidential, File No. W-77/42, WBSA.

[46]Secy., Civil Defence Deptt., GI to All Provincial Govts., 24 Feb. 1942, GB, Home (Poll) Confidential, File No. W-145/42, WBSA.

[47]C.P. Scott, 'Volunteer Organizations', 12 Apr. 1947, Mountbatten Papers, IOR: F200/117.

Returning to the Calcutta Disturbances, among the various volunteer organisations involved, the most prominent were the Muslim League National Guards. However, the Congress and the Hindu Mahasabha do not appear to have lagged far behind in mobilising their 'volunteers' in anticipation of violent clashes. According to an interview given by Surendra Mohan Ghose, president of the Bengal Provincial Congress and a senior leader of the Jugantar, a secret terrorist organisation, the party already had a group of disciplined 'volunteers' in place in each locality of Calcutta when the rioting broke out. The city was divided into '36 or 37 blocks'; and Ghose boasts about having been familiar with 'the volatile elements in all these areas'. Those 'volatile elements' knew, he asserts, how to use a knife or a bomb.[48] The Hindu Mahasabha also had a network of Mahasabha volunteers and Hindusthan National Guard commanders throughout the city.[49]

'Volunteer' organisations made their presence felt from the early morning of the first day (16 August) of rioting. In Taltalla in central Calcutta, for example, loud-speakers and 'a number of vehicles of different types containing various groups of Muslim volunteers' were seen around 7 o'clock in the morning, and it was most probably this group that played a major role in violent clashes with Hindu youth and in the extensive looting of jewellery shops on Surendra Nath Banarji Road between 9.00 am and noon. Wearing khaki uniforms, they shouted slogans from lorries.[50] Meanwhile,

[48]Oral History Transcript No. 301: Shri Surendra Mohan Ghose, 288, 291, 295, NMML.

[49]Lambert, 'Hindu-Muslim Riots', 239. Lambert says that he saw an original confidential record showing the distribution of the Mahasabha volunteer forces in Calcutta. The 'Hindusthan National Guards' are one of the volunteer organisations under the Mahasabha's wing.

Ghose also relates a rather bizarre story about how he was approached by 'two European military officers' in the midst of the Disturbances, and told: 'We two will give you whatever help is possible, any time during the day or night'. When he tried the telephone number for Fort William that they had given him, he found to his surprise that the necessary 'help' was indeed available. There is no reason to doubt that the military officers approached the leaders of other political parties as well (Oral History Transcript: S. M. Ghose, 292, NMML).

[50]GB, *Report of the Commissioner of Police on the Disturbances and the Action Taken by the Calcutta Police between the 16th and 20th August Inclusive*, Alipore, 1946 [hereafter *RCPD*], p. 55, GB, Home (Poll) Confidential, No File No./46, WBSA.

the Congress instructed their 'volunteers' to 'organise themselves for resistance'.[51]

On the other hand, it is worth noting that this type of organised violence ceased to be reported by the police after the morning of 17 August, as street violence came to take on a more amorphous and fragmented character, despite gaining extraordinary momentum. This suggests that when put under the pressure of intense violence, Brass's networks of 'specialists', which might have existed at the onset of the rioting, were then broken up into smaller and less coherent groups. In fact, a marked change in the nature of the actual violence is observable in terms of organisational coherence. Up until 16 August, the Muslim League National Guards appear to have been trying to achieve a more or less clearly defined political goal. Its core members, if not the entire body, donned uniforms, carried flags, and shouted slogans from lorries provided by the League. To be sure, there were many cases of violence perpetrated by them; but, on the whole, their cause was the political struggle for the legitimate establishment of Pakistan; thus, there seems to have been no reason for them to hide anything from public view. However, from the night of 16/17 August onward, such core 'volunteers' virtually disappeared from the streets of Calcutta.[52] It is characteristic of the fighting on and after 17 August that flags ceased to be carried and that the police virtually stopped using the word 'volunteers'.[53] There is no doubt that certain members of volunteer organisations continued to be active in the streets, but the police, unable to recognise them as organised forces, could no longer distinguish 'volunteers' from 'mobs'.

[51]Oral History Transcript: S.M. Ghose, 291, NMML.

[52]Incidentally, Lambert writes without citing evidence that on 17 August Jinnah telephoned Suhrawardy, instructing him to stop the rioting (Lambert, 'Hindu-Muslim Riots', 171).

[53]It is known from an account of events compiled by the Calcutta Police and testimony before the Enquiry Commission that the Muslim League flag was no longer seen by the police after 9.00 am on 17 August, when a group of Muslim League volunteers carrying flags posted pickets near the Electric Power House in Garden Reach, probably marking the last incident described by the Calcutta Police using the term 'volunteers' (*RCPD*, p. 111, GB, Home (Poll) Confidential, No File No./46, WBSA).

In this connection it is also interesting to note that the middle-class participants, including students, withdrew from the streets on the evening of the first day, almost simultaneously with the 'volunteers'. According to the testimony of one senior police officer before the Enquiry Commission:

> I always gathered the impression myself from all reports I received that the educated class or persons withdrew from the field some time towards the evening of the 16th, and thereafter the killings on both sides were done by the lower classes of their communities.[54]

It may safely be said that arriving with the dawn of 17 August, was a new stage of the Calcutta Disturbances, for as 'volunteers' melted into amorphous 'mobs' and the middle-class participants retreated from the 'hot' streets to their homes, the character of the collective violence would have had to undergo a considerable transformation. It was in this context that the *goondas*, who had previously been engaged in violent action under the umbrella of 'volunteer' organisations and shoulder to shoulder with educated respectable middle-class people, emerged as a formidable force now largely unfettered by party discipline and free of social inhibitions.[55]

Goondas

There is no doubt that *goondas* played a prominent role in the Calcutta Disturbances. However, this does not mean that Governor Burrows was right in saying that the riots were 'a pogrom between two rival armies of the Calcutta underworld'.[56] The violent disorder was not a cut and dry incident that can be reduced merely to rivalries among outlaws and criminals; rather, it was a historical event far more complex than the British high officials appear to have wanted everyone to believe at the time.

Goonda was a rather new term, apparently used by the police authorities around 1920 to refer to a special category of

[54]*CDCE*, vol. iv, 303.

[55]This is the pattern suggested by the available data. The real state of affairs may have been more complex.

[56]Burrows to Wavell, 22 Aug. 1946, in *TP*, vol. viii, 302.

criminal.[57] Usually operating in organised groups, often in the guise of clubs and local gymnasia, this type of criminal gained his livelihood from multifarious illegal or quasi-illegal activities, like smuggling, gang robbery, gambling, prostitution, labour negotiations, and delinquent violence, while rendering various services to politicians and the police in exchange for their protection.

Connections of politicians to *goondas* began drawing special attention during the 1930s, a period when various political forces vied with one another to broaden their power base, allowing shady elements to sneak into the body politic. For example, Surendra Mohan Ghose of the old generation of Bengal terrorists became alarmed in 1937 to find the house of Subhas Chandra Bose full of 'riff-raffs [*sic*] and street urchins'.[58] Suhrawardy, as a powerful trade union leader with a large following among seamen, dock workers, and factory workers, came to be called 'the leader of the Calcutta *goondas*' by his political opponents.[59] What complicated the problem further was that these criminal elements were not confined to the lower classes of society. The inspector-general of police, who studied the stabbing cases in the Dacca communal riot of 1944, reached the conclusion that 'these assaults are always started as a provocative measure by the newly created type of semi-*bhadralog* Hindu blackguard, which has sprung up in the last dozen years or so'.[60] Thus, those who were broadly called *goondas* had not only become a factor built into the Bengal political system by the late 1930s, but also had come to hail from a fairly wide spectrum of society.

In the opinion of the Intelligence Branch of the Bengal Police, *goondas* were being 'enrolled' to show up in the mammoth rally

[57]Debraj Bhattacharya, 'Kolkata "Underworld" in the Early Twentieth Century', *Economic and Political Weekly* (18 Sept. 2004), 4276. The Goondas Act was enacted in 1923.

[58]Chatterji, *Bengal Divided*, 134. See also Leonard A. Gordon, *Brothers against the Raj: A Biography of Sarat & Subhas Chandra Bose* (New Delhi: Penguin Books, 1990), 88.

[59]Begum Shaista Suhrawardy Ikramullah, *Huseyn Shaheed Suhrawardy: A Biography* (Karachi: Oxford University Press, 1991), 27.

[60]G.H. Mannooch, inspector-general of police, Bengal to U. Mukherjee, superintendent of police, Dacca, 24 May 1944, GB, Home (Poll) Confidential, File No. 239/44 K.W., WBSA.

held by the Muslim League in the Maidan on 16 August.[61] Whether 'enrolled' or not, it is a fact that a large number of them were observed among the crowd on that day:

> The crowds at the OCHTERLONY Monument included large numbers of Muslim goondas. These slipped away from the meeting and swelled by other [*sic*] after the meeting had finished, looted and burnt Hindu shops and houses in the North CHOWRINGHEE, DHARAMTOLA, WELLESLEY and CORPORATION STREET Area, including the gun shop of KC BISWAS in CHOWRINGHEE.[62]

The dispersion of this mass rally marked the beginning of *goonda* violence in central Calcutta; and from that time on they were found engaged in all sorts of violence, including street fighting, looting, arson, and killing. For example, *goondas* were observed looting large shops like Coondu's Gun Shop and Shaw's Radio and Gramophone Stores on Dharamtolla Street,[63] attacking the Marwari Union,[64] menacing Carmichael Medical College,[65] and setting fires in *bustees* (slums) and killing their inhabitants.

A number of sources describing the Disturbances provide sufficiently detailed information about one well-known *goonda* at that time, one Habibur Rahman of north Calcutta, enabling us to trace his life in the context of the social changes taking place during the 1930s and 40s.[66] Interestingly, his actions during the Disturbances became in their aftermath the objects of both praise and derision.

[61] *CDCE*, vol. iii, 105. Furthermore, Das, quoting a press report of *Amritabazar Patrika*, suggests that the Muslim League introduced a large number of *goondas* from outside Bengal a few days before the riot (Das, *Communal Riots*, 184).

[62] 'RMHC', p. 5, GB, Home (Poll) Confidential, No File No./46, WBSA.

[63] *RCPD*, p. 52, GB, Home (Poll) Confidential, No File No./46, WBSA.

[64] Ibid., p. 6.

[65] Ibid., p. 80.

[66] On the *goondas*'s role in the Calcutta riots, see Das, *Communal Riots*, 184–85. Das gives a colourful description of a well-known Hindu *goonda*, Gopal Mukharji, who led a group of *goondas* called the Bharat Jatiya Bahini. Regarding Mukharji, see Suranjan Das, 'The "Goondas": Towards a Reconstruction of the Calcutta Underworld through Police Records', *Economic and Political Weekly* (29 Oct. 1994), 2879; Suranjan Das and Jayanta K. Ray, *The Goondas: Towards a Reconstruction of the Calcutta Underworld* (Calcutta: Firma KLM, 1996), 10, 14, 31; Annwesta

Habibur Rahman, alias Habu, Habu Goonda, or Sheik Habu, is probably the best known of the big *goondas* active during the Disturbances.[67] First, we find him among the leaders of a well-organised procession that tried to march through Cornwallis Street on Direct Action Day:

> At this time [around 2.00 pm] we saw a Muslim procession coming from North on Cornwallis Street near about Shambazar Tram Depot headed by a big Military type lorry with a band and Muslim flags on it and loaded with men all shouting slogans. They advanced nearer to us when I [a British senior sergeant] noticed that some of [the] men on the lorry had naked swords and others *lathis*. There were about 1,000 people in the procession including those on the lorry and walking.... They proceeded on and when they got near Town School they became very disorderly and I saw them running on to the footpaths and then I noticed a Hindu crowd coming out from adjoining streets and brickbats being exchanged. The lorry suddenly turned round and the Muslim crowd retreated with it followed by the Hindus.... The lorry No. CH584 I noticed, was driven by Sk. Habu of Lalbagan Bustee. He was known as a bad character to this Police Station.[68]

However, Habibur Rahman was to die a grisly death on the street within a few days:

> Corpses became more frequent, and on the Grey Street-Chitpur Road crossing the leading tanks had to stop so that troops ... could clear some of the bodies to one side to give room for vehicles to pass.... Over one hundred and fifty bodies were cleared from the cross-road the next day and it was here that one of the chief *goondas* of Calcutta died fighting with a knife in each hand. His green three-ton truck

Roy, 'Anatomy of a Riot: The Great Calcutta Killing, August 1946', *Bengal Past and Present*, no. 128 (2009), 99–100; Bandyopadhyay, *Chhechallisher Danga*, 41.

[67]My account of Habibur Rahman is based on *CDCE*, vol. iii, 45; vol. v, 195; vol. vii, 190–1, 250, 309–10; vol. viii, 24–26; vol. ix, 13–14, 22–24, 33.

[68]*CDCE*, vol. ix, 13–14 (Supplementary Statement by C.R. Smith). In the case of the Calcutta Disturbances, the 'swords' brandished by Muslim processionists were mostly mock swords used on festive occasions like Moharram. Nakazato, 'Politics', 117.

was standing in Grey Street and proved of great use in the street clearing which was soon to follow.[69]

This chief *goonda* of Calcutta lived with his family, consisting of his wife, son, and son's wife, in his own house in the Lalbagan *bustee* in Sovabazar, which was cleared by the Calcutta Improvement Trust after the Disturbances. He was known as 'the terror' of the *bustee*. He often got drunk and the police had to rush there to put down 'disturbance[s] that he created when he was drunk'. At the same time, he was 'a prominent figure in the locality'. He was a successful small businessman, owning not only the green lorry but also a taxi and a private car. He engaged in illicit trafficking in petrol, which was being rationed since the time of the Second World War. When the Calcutta Improvement Trust tore down then ploughed under Lalbagan *bustee*, it was said that 'one drum of petrol was found every ten yards'; and at the time of his death, there were two outstanding cases against him for contravening petrol rationing orders. After his death the police found that his house had been broken into and looted. The three members of his family had fortunately survived the attack and sought and received shelter at a police station. He was also an active Muslim League worker and seemed to be regarded as the author of a leaflet entitled 'Muslim League Direct Action Plan'. Probably due to the prominent position he occupied in the League hierarchy, *Dawn*, the League's organ, reported his death as soon as the critical situation had calmed down:

> In the Sham Bazar the handful of Muslims were all killed to a man. The women and children were also killed. There was one Habib who was the Head of the Muslims of this locality. Habib was surrounded on all sides. Single-handed he fought against the Hindus and killed several Hindus before he was overpowered. Habib's head was cut away from his body. The body was then hung on a tree with a label on his body 'Habib got Pakistan'.[70]

Despite the lurid, stereotyped style of the item and the fact that the beheading cannot be established among any of the other

[69]Francis Tuker, *While Memory Serves* (London: Cassell, 1950), 162–63.
[70]*Dawn*, 10 September 1946.

documentation, it is clear that the Muslim League tried to project him as a local hero who had bravely fought a desperate battle and sacrificed his life for the cause of Pakistan.

Although Habibur Rahman was a heavy drinker and brawler, he was no mere hooligan. He was probably educated and had built a modest fortune in the transport business, in all likelihood under the patronage of the Muslim League government, as well as through black marketing, which had begun to pervade Indian society from the introduction of the elaborate wartime economic control system. Moreover, he was able to successfully build strong ties with the party in power. It may not be an exaggeration to conclude that he was indeed the child of a turbulent age.

From the viewpoint of the present enquiry, one cannot help pondering why such a powerful *goonda* had to die in the streets. Several alternative interpretations come to mind, but this incident at least seems to indicate that a full-blown 'institutionalised riot system' had not yet *fully* materialised in the Calcutta of the 1940s, although its main components were already present in the form of unscrupulous politicians, corrupt police, volunteers, *goondas,* and members of the press spreading sensation and attempting to justify the violence in retrospect. Had Habibur Rahman operated within the 'institutionalised riot system' that has developed in contemporary India, it should not have been very difficult for him to extricate himself from danger with both ease and confidence. It is interesting that police protection was provided only after his death.

CONTROLLING THE RIOTING

From the viewpoint of what we know about 'institutionalised riot systems', one may safely state that the Calcutta Disturbances fell far short of being perfect, despite being one of the largest in scale and most well-known communal riots in India's history. Certainly, something like Brass's 'systems' was already present; however, political control over the law and order machinery was deeply divided, while 'specialists' such as 'volunteers' and *goondas* were not sufficiently organised to endure a great wave of intense violence for extended periods of time. Such imperfections also mean that the nationalist politicians of the time had to deal with such bitter communal strife with only imperfect 'systems' in hand. It was therefore little wonder that when the rioting began to gain unexpected momentum of its own, they lost control of a situation which they themselves had created. The 'riot systems' at their disposal did not seem to have yet matched the magnitude and intensity of the Disturbances.

To illustrate this point, one can cite the interesting sequence of events on the morning of the first day, in which the attitudes of politicians towards collective violence underwent a marked change. In the beginning the nationalist leaders seem to have been confident that they could intervene to bring any disorder under control whenever the situation threatened to get out of control. However, it was not long before they came to the realisation that they had opened up a Pandora's box. For example, Congress leader Surendra Mohan Ghose kept watch on the movements of the crowds with great confidence on the morning of 16 August, but then around noon he came to the conclusion that the situation was so bad that the whole of Calcutta would be ablaze in no time. Consequently, he rang up Khwaja Nazimuddin and Suhrawardy, the Muslim League's top leaders, to seek their co-operation in preventing further violence. Suhrawardy rushed to one trouble spot accompanied by leaders of the Congress and the Communist Party of India (CPI); but it was too late. He was stoned by the angry crowd, forcing the three leaders to beat a hurried retreat.[71] This ignominious story continues with a second attempt by the representatives of the three parties to pacify the violent crowd on the morning of 17 August, during which Kiran Shankar Roy of the Congress, Shamsuddin Ahmed of the Muslim League, and Mohammad Ismail of the CPI addressed a crowd near European Asylum Lane in central Calcutta. However, their concerted efforts were completely ignored and registered no effect at all on the course of events.[72]

LOCAL NETWORKS

Nirmal Kumar Bose reported in 1968 that Calcutta had 'a little less than two thousand institutions which cater to the educational,

[71]Nakazato, 'Politics', 118–19.

[72]*CDCE*, vol. v, 40.

religious, professional and recreational needs of the communities', excluding government and commercial institutions, as well as those established by the Municipal Corporation of Calcutta.[73] In other words, the city was dotted with innumerable voluntary associations, which match 'associational forms of civic engagement' in Varshney's terminology. It is also well known that the residential areas of Calcutta were divided into small localities (called *para* in Bengali), where residents were integrated into a well-knit territorial social group with common ties cutting across the differences in religion, caste, occupation, etc.[74] The *para* no doubt corresponds to what Varshney calls 'everyday' forms of civic engagement. The next question to ask is in what manner those voluntary associations and *paras* responded to the unprecedented outbursts of communal violence, when the nationalist political leaders fell into their own traps.

TRADE UNIONS

Actually, not much factual data is available on the reactions of various voluntary associations to the Calcutta Disturbances, except for trade unions. There were two local libraries—one in Beniapukur, the other in Watgunge—that became targets of vandalism and arson, which might suggest that reading circles were drawn into the violence in some way or another, but the data is too scanty to come to any firm conclusion.[75] Therefore, this section will be confined to describing a few salient features of how organised labour responded to the Disturbances. It appears that contrary to Varshney's assumption, even Calcutta's powerful leftist trade unions failed to both resist and effectively counter communalism.

[73]Nirmal Kumar Bose, *Calcutta: 1964, A Social Survey* (Bombay: Lalvani Publishing House, 1968), 41. For the definition of Varshney's civic or associational engagements, see note 17.

[74]From the viewpoint of Muslims, it was the *muhalla*.

[75]*CDCE*, vol. x, 169–72; *RCPD*, p. 110, GB, Home (Poll) Confidential, No File No./46, WBSA. Bose and his group counted 163 libraries in Calcutta, a few of which were run by political parties for political education of youths. Libraries often served as 'clubs for children or citizens who wish to have associations of their own'. See Bose, *Calcutta*, 49–50.

Let us begin by looking at the situation in the industrial zones in suburban Calcutta, 24-Parganas, Howrah, Hooghly, and Asansol. On the morning of 16 August, these areas were enshrouded in an extremely tense atmosphere. Very large-scale disturbances took place in the Howrah Maidan,[76] while sporadic incidents, mostly minor but occasionally very serious, occurred in the other places throughout the five days between 16 and 20 August.

The first news of trouble came in from an important public utility in the suburbs of Calcutta. Although 16 August had been declared a holiday by the government,[77] essential services such as electricity and water had to be maintained, and workers reported for duty at such facilities. Minor trouble was reported near the entrance to the Cossipore Electric Power House of the Calcutta Electric Supply Corporation. At that very moment a communal clash also occurred in Champdany, a mill area in the Hooghly district, where two Muslims were killed.[78] Champdany was a town where relations between Hindu and Muslim workers had been strained in November 1945.[79] Then towards evening 'a Muslim procession' appeared in Asansol, blocking the Grand Trunk Road and refusing to move.[80]

When workshops resumed operations on the morning of 17 August, a report of communal troubles came in from the Presidency Jute Mill in Serampore and in Shahaganj, Hooghly.[81] In Garden Reach serious riots broke out in the Kesoram Cotton Mills and

[76]R. Banarji (Superintendent of Police, Howrah), 'Direct Action Day', GB, IB Records, Serial No. 276/46, File No. 717/46 (Howrah), WBSA; Memo No. 825C Howrah, by District Magistrate Howrah, dated 25/26 Sept. 1946, GB, Home (Poll) Confidential, File No. 398/46, WBSA.

[77]This action, which aroused vehement protest on the part of the Congress, was first suggested by R. L. Walker, the then chief secretary of Bengal. Suhrawardy agreed with the action after some discussion. See Nakazato, 'Politics', 116.

[78]Burrows to Secy. of State for India, 16 Aug. 1946, IOR: L/PJ/8/577; 'Brief Note of Action taken by Dy. Inspector-General of Police, Burdwan Range' [hereafter 'Brief Note: Burdwan Range'], p. 1, GB, Home (Poll) Confidential, File No. 393/46, WBSA.

[79]'Report on the Most Discussed Topics of Public Opinion for the Week ending the 4th November, 1945', GB, Home (Poll) Confidential, File No. 163/45, WBSA.

[80]'Brief Note: Burdwan Range', p. 1, GB, Home (Poll) Confidential, File No. 393/46, WBSA.

[81]Ibid., 2.

the Clive Jute Mill, where more than fifty Oriya workers were killed by fellow workers,[82] while a riot squad was despatched to disperse a 'mob assembled at the gates of Messrs. Lever Brothers Soap Factory' in the same area.[83] The broad gauge services of the Bengal Assam Railway had to be suspended because of a strike by its locomotive personnel, who refused to work, 'leaving their families unprotected'.[84] However, Barrackpore was quiet, with the exception of Naihati, an important jute mill area.[85]

On 18 August, the situation in Burnpore, where workers of the Iron and Steel Works had been on strike, was reported to be so tense as to 'require extra force to be kept there', while Raniganj was struck by the first wave of communal troubles which were to persist there at least for a week until 24 August.[86] The mills in the Baranagar area 'worked most of the time' during the day, but were engulfed in communal rioting after sunset.[87]

The situation seemed to be improving on 19 August, as the railway workshop in Kanchrapara and all the jute mills in Budge Budge were operating, although three mills remained shut down in Naihati.[88]

However, early on the morning of 20 August, rioting broke out at the Hukumchand Jute Mill in Chinsurah;[89] and several hours later the police fired ten rounds to disperse a crowd at the Cossipore Gun and Shell Factory.[90] There was also 'slight trouble between Hindu and Muslim workmen at the ESD [Engineering Stores Depot]

[82]*RCPD*, p. 116, GB, Home (Poll) Confl., No File No./46, WBSA.

[83]Ibid., 111.

[84]'RMHC', p. 7, GB, Home (Poll) Confl., No File No./46, WBSA; 'Diary of Events of Eastern Command Intelligence Centre from the 16th August 1946 to the 20th August 1946 (both dates inclusive)' [hereafter 'DE'], 1215 hrs., 17 Aug. 1946, GB, Home (Poll) Confidential, No File No./46, WBSA.

[85]'DE', 1215 hrs, 17 Aug. 1946, GB, Home (Poll) Confl., No File No./46, WBSA.

[86]'Brief Note: Burdwan Range', p. 3; *The Statesman*, 22 & 24 Aug. 1946.

[87]'Report in connection with the Recent Disturbances in 24-Parganas' [hereafter 'Rep. from 24-Parganas'], p. 3, GB, Home (Poll) Confidential, File No. 392/46, WBSA; Burrows to Secy. of State for India, 18 Aug. 1946, IOR: L/PJ/8/577.

[88]'DE', 1400 hrs. & 1615 hrs., 19 Aug. 1946, GB, Home (Poll) Confidential, No File No./46, WBSA.

[89]Ibid., 0800 hrs., 20 Aug.

[90]*CDCE*, vol. v, 129 (Statement by S.N. Mukherji).

Kankinara', which had to be closed down.[91] Furthermore, trams were still not running on the streets of Calcutta even on 20 August, for 'the leaders of the tramway workers' union declined to allow their members to work except on certain conditions, one of which was that the leaders of political parties would give them an assurance that there would be no more rioting'.[92]

It should be clear even from the above brief account that the situation prevailing among the industrial workers was highly complex, fluid, and polarised. Among the workers of a few well-organised sectors like railways and tramways, trade unionism appears to have avoided turmoil to some extent and managed to carry out its minimum mission to ensure the security of workers and their families, although it could not play any political role except at the final stage. At the opposite pole was the nightmare of killing, looting, and burning. In between, there lay the world of normal work attendance. However, as the case of Baranagar shows, this semblance of normalcy could degenerate into violent chaos at any moment. It is also noteworthy that a few incidents which the police reported as 'communal' were closely connected to the preexisting labour disputes.

Now, let us focus on two significant cases: one at Cossipore Power House, the other at Kesoram Cotton Mills. Small as it was, the incident at the Cossipore Power House clearly points to the complexity of the situation surrounding the industrial workers in August 1946. The Calcutta Electric Supply Corporation (CESC) was a purely British-owned company established in London, while its workers' major union, the CESC Mazdur Union, was under the control of the CPI.[93] On 1 and 4 August 1946, the union, which had already organised an agitation in 1945,[94] adopted resolutions

[91]'DE', 1350 hrs., 20 Aug. 1946, GB, Home (Poll) Confidential, No File No./46, WBSA.

[92]P. D. Martyn's 'Diary', p. 20, IOR: MSS Eur F180/3. See also *CDCE*, vol. iii, 45–46.

[93]'Calcutta Electric Supply Corporation Employees, D.N. [Daily Notes] dated 16 Apr. 1946', GB, Calcutta Police, Special Branch Records [hereafter SB Records], File No. KPM/SB/01012/05 (SW 972/43), Kolkata Police Museum, Kolkata [hereafter KPM].

[94]'SR for Bengal', 2nd half of July 1945 and 2nd half of Sept. 1945, IOR: L/PJ/5/152.

demanding the re-instatement of the externed workers, recognition of the union, a 45-hour work week, profit bonus, etc. and to serve a strike notice if their demands were not met by 1 September, declaring that 'the workers and the employees of the Calcutta Electric Supply Corporation are determined not to submit to the tyranny of this foreign British Company which has not considered their appeal but is carrying on exploitation, profiteering and tyranny'.[95] In this respect, the workers in the Coal Department at the Cossipore Power House actually did go out on strike on 10 August.[96] Military personnel had to be drafted into the power station to maintain the supply of electricity.[97] Work was resumed only on 12 August, after the troops left. As to the Muslim League's 'Direct Action' plan, Indrajit Gupta, a well-known CPI leader, reportedly told his colleagues and supporters on that same day that his party would see to it that no coercion of any section of the labourers would take place on 16 August and would endeavour their utmost to keep peace.[98] At the same time, we know that the CESC workers were divided along at least two party lines: the CPI's CESC Mazdur Union and Congress's Calcutta Electric Supply Workers Union.

It is therefore not surprising that the officer-in-charge of the Cossipore police station was very apprehensive on the morning of 16 August. Moreover, he had received 'some information' in advance that 'the Muslim League followers will bring pressure on Hindu shopkeepers and labourers to join the demonstration in observance of the 16th'.[99] He visited the Power House that morning 'to verify whether the attendance was normal and whether there was any trouble'.[100]

[95]'CESC Workers' Union/CESC Mazdur Union, D.N. dated 7 & 14 Aug. 1946', GB, SB Records, File No. KPM/01012/05 (SW 972/43), KPM.

[96]Ibid.

[97]'SR for Bengal', 1st half of Aug. 1946, IOR: L/PJ/5/153.

[98]'CESC Workers' Union/CESC Mazdur Union, D.N. dated 7 & 14 Aug. 1946', GB, SB Records, File No. KPM/01012/05 (SW 972/43), KPM. This information seems to have been supplied by a Special Branch agent planted in the CPI's organisation.

[99]*CDCE*, vol. viii, 250–51. In view of the fact that 'a number of volunteers [of the Muslim League]' were found 'picketing near the Electric Power House' at Fatehpur-Metiabruz in Garden Reach on the morning of the 17th (*RCPD*, p. 111, GB, Home (Poll) Confidential, No File No./1946, WBSA), it is probable that the Muslim League had selected power houses as targets of their 'Direct Action'.

[100]*CDCE*, vol. viii, 202–3.

It was around 8 o'clock on the morning of 16 August that both Hindu and Muslim workers were seen assembling near the entrance to the Power House. Flag waving Muslim workers were preventing Hindu workers from entering the plant. An armed picket had to be despatched from police headquarters in Lalbazar to protect this important essential service facility. Moreover, the incident formed part of the larger disturbances which rocked the Cossipore area on the same day. On nearby Dum Dum Road, 'Muslims were creating disturbance ... and soda water bottles were being used'. This trouble was to develop later in the afternoon into fighting between Hindus and Muslims, each estimated at about 500 strong. The day after next the Power House was again caught up in trouble, as the police were informed early in the morning that the facility was being attacked by a mob. A squad was despatched and found a serious riot erupting in the vicinity. It fired ten rounds of ammunition to disperse the mob.[101]

Three months after the Disturbances, the Special Branch of the Calcutta Police reported that 'the communal riots in Calcutta have resulted in communal bitterness and division between the Hindu and Muslim workers of the Calcutta Electric Supply Corporation Ltd'. The report alleged that certain leading Muslim workers had been fanning anti-Hindu hatred amongst the Muslim workers in the workshop since August.[102] It also made the important observation that:

> The majority of the Hindu workers of the Electric Supply and Tramways is losing confidence in the C.P.I. because the Party not only failed to give protection to the Hindu workers slaughtered in Matiabruz during the first phase of the Calcutta riots, but was instrument in considerable measure for causing their deaths as the C.P.I. organisers gave them false hopes of safety and security by saying that they were not in danger and asked them to continue to remain in that locality and in the Union office, instead of evacuating to safe areas.[103]

[101] *RCPD*, pp. 79, 92, GB, Home (Poll) Confidential, No File No./46, WBSA; *CDCE*, vol. viii, 192 (Statement by B. B. Bose); vol. v, 144, 146–47.

[102] 'Calcutta Electric Supply Corporation Mazdur Union, D.N. dated 12 Nov. 1946', GB, SB Records, KPM/01012/05 (SW 972/43), KPM.

[103] Ibid.

While the researcher must be extremely cautious when interpreting the police reports about public security matters, the overall evidence does seem to suggest that the CPI's anti-imperialism and militant trade unionism collided head-on with the Muslim League's Pakistan demand at one of the most important British-owned industrial plants in Calcutta and in the end was overpowered.

Our second case is the slaughter in Metiabruz, which took place early on the morning of 17 August within the jurisdiction of the Garden Reach Police Station. Involved were two workshops, the Kesoram Cotton Mills and the Clive Jute Mill, and a nearby large *bustee* called Lichubagan. In the violence that ensued fifty Hindu mill workers from Orissa were killed and 250 injured.[104]

According to the police, a little after two o'clock on the afternoon of 16 August a group of twenty Muslim League volunteers made their appearance at Metiabruz. They seemed to have come from Calcutta and 'urged the public to equip themselves with weapons, disseminating startling news that the police had fired on Muslim mobs in Chitpore'.[105] At the same time, rumours began to circulate that Muslims had been assaulted in Bhowanipore in south Calcutta.[106] That evening, residents returning from Calcutta began to give graphic accounts of violent incidents that had happened in the city.[107] It was around this time that the police received a report that 'Muslims in the Metiabruz area were preparing to attack the Hindus of the Kesoram Cotton Mills'.[108] The next morning, the officer-in-charge of the Garden Reach Police Station was informed of a clash between the 'coolies' of the Kesoram Cotton Mills and the

[104]'Rep. from 24-Parganas', pp. 2–4, GB, Home (Poll) Confidential, File No. 392/46, WBSA; *RCPD*, pp. 99, 105, 111, 116, GB, Home (Poll) Confidential, No File No./46, WBSA

[105]Ibid., 105.

[106]This account is based on the personal memoir of Madhab Munshi. Munshi was a full-time Communist worker, who ran a CPI office in Metiabruz with his fellow workers, Krishna Ghosh and Farooqui. The memoir first appeared in *Swadhinata* on 3 September 1946 and has been reproduced in Amalendu Sengupta, *Uttal Challish: Asamapta Biplab* (Calcutta: Pearl Publishers, 1989), 200–1.

[107]'DE', 1945 hrs., 16 Aug. 1946, GB, Home (Poll) Confidential, No File No./46, WBSA.

[108]*RCPD*, p. 105, GB, Home (Poll) Confidential, No File No./46, WBSA.

Clive Jute Mill that had occurred around 7.00 am. He rushed to the spot and 'dispersed this assembly without resorting to force'.[109] At 8.30 am he dispersed 'another mob assembled at the gates of Messrs. Lever Brothers Soap Factory'.[110] These incidents were followed by the massacre of Oriya Hindu workers, which took place in Lichubagan *bustee* between 10.30 and 11.30 am.

Kesoram Cotton Mills was a large concern managed by Birla Brothers, employing 8000 workers, who were organised into a trade union controlled by the CPI.[111] The workers had gone out on 'a sudden strike without any previous notice' in November 1945, demanding for an increase in rates of pay, dearness allowances, etc.[112] Another wildcat strike ensued in April 1946.[113] The following month they struck again, demanding an increase in wages and protesting the dismissal of fellow workers.[114] In June 1946, they participated in the protest against the arrest of Jawaharlal Nehru by the Kashmir state government;[115] and on the morning of 30 July, '2000 workers of the Spinning Section ... staged a stay-in-strike', demanding a dearness allowance at a flat rate.[116] No doubt, this mill had been an important centre of the militant trade union movement prevalent in Bengal from the end of World War II.

The regular sirens were not sounded at 5.00 and 5.45 on the morning of 17 August, and when puzzled workers arrived in front of the main gate for work, they found it closed and Hindu gate-

[109] Ibid., 111.

[110] Ibid.

[111] 'Rep. from 24-Parganas', GB, Home (Poll) Confidential, File No. 392/46, WBSA; Sengupta, *Uttal Challish*, 201. See also Medha M. Kudaisya, *The Life and Times of G. D. Birla* (Delhi: Oxford University Press, 2003), 195, 331; Nirban Basu, *The Political Parties and the Labour Politics 1937–1947* (Calcutta: Minerva, 1992), 70.

[112] 'Weekly Review of Labour Situation for the Week ending on 1st December 1945', GB, Home (Poll) Confidential, File No. 20/45 Coll II, WBSA.

[113] 'Strike in Kesoram Cotton Mills, 25 Apr. 1946', BG, SB Records, File No. KPM/SB/03125/05 (SW 567/46), KPM.

[114] 'SR for Bengal', 2nd half of May 1946, IOR: L/P&J/5/153.

[115] 'Congress, 24 June 1946', GB, SB Records, File No. KPM/SB/03125/05 (SW 567/46), KPM.

[116] 'Strike at Kesoram Cotton Mills, 1 Aug. 1946', GB, SB Records, File No. KPM/SB/03125/05 (SW 567/46), KPM.

keepers standing around with *lathis* and guns in their hands.[117] Suddenly brickbats were thrown at the workers from the third floor of a building inside the plant. Frightened by the attack, Hindu operatives from Orissa, who resided in a Muslim-majority *bustee*, are said to have approached the gate-keepers and mill authorities to request shelter on the factory premises. However, their request was turned down on the grounds that they had participated in a previous strike. Meanwhile, CPI organisers, Madhab Munshi, Krishna Ghosh, and Farooqui, contacted Dr Ayyub, the secretary of the local Muslim League, and Sudhikar Palak, a local Congress leader, in an attempt to bring the explosive situation under control. Both the leaders readily promised to cooperate; yet, before they could set out in Ayyub's car, a group of people from the staff quarters and coolie lines at Kesoram Mills attacked adjoining Muslim-majority Lichubagan *bustee*, looting Muslim shops and killing some Muslims. The five leaders found people too frenzied to respond to any peace efforts. It is important to note that at this moment it was still possible for local political leaders to assist one another across communal and ideological lines; however, the chance of such mutual fortification was lost around 11 o'clock, when the bodies of murdered Muslims were carried through the streets. About fifty Oriya workers who had remained in Lichubagan were then mercilessly murdered and about sixty women molested. The entire *bustee* was looted, and many houses set ablaze. The efforts of the Kesoram Mills authorities to rescue the Hindu workers from Lichubagan turned the mill's premises into a 'refuge of some two or three thousand Hindu workers'.[118] The rioting then began to spread to areas beyond Lichubagan. Meanwhile, 11.00 am also marked the time of the torching of the Kesoram Tent Factory and death of fifteen more Hindus,[119] while, an hour before, Muslim League volunteers were found picketing near the Power House at Fatehpur-Metiabruz.[120]

[117]This paragraph is mainly based on Madhab Munshi's account (Sengupta, *Uttal Challish*, 201–3).

[118]'Rep. from 24-Parganas', p. 2, GB, Home (Poll) Confidential, File No. 392/46, WBSA.

[119]Ibid., 6.

[120]*RCPD*, p. 111, GB, Home (Poll) Confidential, No File No./46, WBSA.

The situation became so grave that the district magistrate of the 24-Parganas requested military assistance. The matter was taken up by the acting area commander, the inspector-general of police, and the additional home secretary (P. D. Martyn), who decided at about 4.00 pm to despatch a Gurkha company to patrol the entire Garden Reach area including the docks.[121] The troops arrived there at 5.30 pm, but the situation did not show a marked improvement, for the Gurkha patrols had not been very effective. Around 8.00 pm Kesoram Cotton Mills was besieged.[122] The following morning some stones were thrown at the officer-in-charge of the police station, ten constables, and a military patrol while they passed through 'the coolie lines' of the mill. Around 10.00 am a 'fight between Hindus and Muslims in the vicinity of Kesoram Cotton Mills' recurred, and 'the mob was fired upon resulting in six persons being injured'.[123]

On 19 August, Premier Suhrawardy, who wielded considerable influence among the Muslim workers, personally visited Metiabruz with Sarat Chandra Bose 'in an attempt to improve the situation'.[124] A peace meeting was arranged, but failed to reach any agreement, 'because K. C. Mills do not employ enough Muslims'.[125] It is similarly reported that at a meeting organised by the relief authorities on 22 August, 'most inflammatory speeches were made, chiefly by the Muslims present, in which they appeared to blame the Marwari Cotton Mill authorities for causing the riots by not employing a sufficient number of Muslims'.[126]

This complex incident, which occurred in the heart of Calcutta's industrial area, appears at first glance to defy any straightforward causal explanation. However, it might at least be said, first,

[121] P. D. Martyn's 'Diary', p. 7; 'Memoirs of P. D. Martyn', IOR: MSS Eur F180/3, IOL.

[122] 'DE', 1945 hrs., 17 Aug. 1946, GB, Home (Poll) Confidential, No File No./46, WBSA.

[123] *RCPD*, p. 116, GB, Home (Poll) Confidential, No File No./46, WBSA.

[124] 'Rep. from 24-Parganas', p. 4, GB, Home (Poll) Confidential, File No. 392/46, WBSA.

[125] 'DE', 1615 hrs., 19 Aug. 1946, GB, Home (Poll) Confidential, No File No./46, WBSA.

[126] 'Rep. from 24-Parganas', p. 3, GB, Home (Poll) Confidential, File No. 392/46, WBSA.

that previous labour disputes were closely intertwined with the 'communal' violence of August 1946; secondly, that the anger of Muslim workers was directed against the Marwari management, which had most probably employed Hindu Oriya operatives despite Muslim workers' opposition; next, that the local political leadership, which seems to have been organised into a loose personal network among the CPI, the Congress, and the Muslim League, found itself helpless once the violence began; and finally, that the workers not only hurled defiance at the police and the military, but also developed a deep distrust of their top leaders, Suhrawardy and Sarat Bose.

As the Bengal government claimed, in comparison with the really abominable situation in the city proper, the state of things in its industrial district seemed relatively stable. And this might be attributed to the existence of trade unionism as well as to the special precautionary measures taken by the government and the army to protect British economic interests there. However, the fact remains that communal violence managed to fracture fraternal ties among unionised workers in not a few instances.[127] The question to ask is why this sort of situation was created in Bengal, which had witnessed a sharp rise in militant trade unionism until the end of July 1946. We may find a clue in a press report concerning a debate on 'Direct Action' conducted among the tramway workers.

With a membership of more than 7000, the Calcutta Tramways Workers' Union (CTWU) was counted among the largest labour organisations in Calcutta belonging to the All-India Trade Union Congress, which was under the control of the CPI.[128] The CTWU held a conference on 14 August to deliberate over its plan of action for 'Direct Action Day'.[129] During the proceedings a fierce debate

[127]The All-India Trade Union Congress indirectly admitted in its annual report that some of its followers in Bengal had taken part in the rioting, remarking that '*On the whole*, the Bengal working class was able to keep itself aloof from the riots' (emphasis added. All India Trade Union Congress, 'Report of the General Secretary (January 1945 to December 1946)', p. 9, P.C. Joshi's Archives, T.U./Labour, 1946/18, Archives on Contemporary History, Jawaharlal Nehru University, New Delhi [hereafter P.C. Joshi's Archives].

[128]All-India Trade Union Congress, 'Report of the General Secretary, Twenty-second Session, Calcutta, 1947', p. 108, P.C. Joshi's Archives, T.U./Labour, 1947/25.

[129]*The Statesman*, 15 Aug. 1946. See also Sengupta, *Uttal Challish*, 177–78.

developed between Muslim and Hindu speakers, which lasted for four hours. 'While Muslim workers spoke', the *Statesman* reported, 'in favour of stopping work on "Direct Action Day," several Hindu speakers were opposed to the Union being used to advance the political interests of the League'.[130] It was only due to the intervention of union leaders like Mohammed Ismail, Somnath Lahiri, and Dhiren Mazumdar that the meeting managed to arrive at a decision to stage a one-day strike on 16 August. Toeing the official party line, the resolution stated that 'the Union, while not agreeing with the League viewpoint, had taken the decision for a one-day strike to maintain the solidarity of the workers in their fight against British imperialism'.[131] The fact that it took four hours for such a powerful trade union to come to an agreement that it would simply follow the prearranged party plan is indicative of how deeply the urban organised workers were divided along communal lines. At the same time, the resolution was tantamount to a tacit admission on the part of the union's leftist leaders that being unable to display leadership at a most critical moment, they chose to shun political contention so as to prevent the organisation from breaking up along those same lines.[132]

It was, one may recall, only on 29 July that workers and students of Calcutta had conducted a successful general strike in sympathy with striking postal employees.[133] However, the case of the CTWU clearly shows that communal consciousness had quietly penetrated even into leftist trade unions and politically disabled

[130] *The Statesman*, 15 Aug. 1946.

[131] Ibid.; Sengupta, *Uttal Challish*, 177–78.

[132] This is not to deny that many Communist workers stood against communal violence. For example, the workers at the Rajabazar tram depot put up brave resistance to violence (Sadhan Banerjee, *Asamanya Birgatha* (Kolkata: National Book Agency, 2003), 18–44. I am grateful to a postgraduate student of Visva Bharati University for giving me this Bengali pamphlet). They also actively engaged in relief work during and after the Disturbances. Manikuntala Sen, *Sediner Katha* (Calcutta: Nabapatra Prakashan, 1982) chap. 17; idem, *In Search of Freedom: An Unfinished Journey*, trans. Anonymous [an English translation of *Sediner Katha*] (Calcutta: Stree, 2001) chap. 17.

[133] Sarkar, *Modern India*, 428; Nirban Basu, 'Urban Popular Movements in the Post-Second World War India (1945–47)', in *Recent Trends in Humanities and Social Sciences: Prof. A.P. Mathur Felicitation Volume* (Agra, 1995), 457–59.

them. A strong tendency towards communal antagonism had already manifested itself among unionised workers even before the Calcutta Disturbances brought about a cataclysmic change in the overall situation.

Such disarray among CPI followers might well have been a reflection of a vacillation in the party line on the Pakistan question. In pursuance of the so-called 'Adhikari thesis' on 'Pakistan and National Unity' adopted in August-September 1942, the CPI had considered the founding of the Pakistan state as the exercise of a legitimate right of self-determination by a minority community, and therefore expressed sympathy towards the Muslim League's demand.[134] However, in the wake of the rapid changes that had occurred in the political climate since the end of World War II, the relevance of the CPI's wartime policy began to be increasingly questioned; and in 1946, the Party leadership was considering shifting the main thrust of its Pakistan policy from the support of minority rights to securing the unity of India.[135] The lukewarm stand

[134]Sarkar, *Modern India*, 411–12; Sengupta, *Uttal Challish*, 176–78; Mushirul Hasan, *Legacy of a Divided Nation: India's Muslims since Independence* (Boulder: Westview Press, 1997), 113–14; Sunanda Sanyal and Soumya Basu, *The Sickle and the Crescent: Communists, Muslim League and India's Partition* (Kolkata: Frontpage, 2011), chaps. 6, 8, 9. There is also a report by the DIB, Government of India, stating: 'At the end of the war, when the expectation of early constitutional changes first began to make the Pakistan question a live issue, the Communist Party of India was definitely in favour of the Muslim League's demand for partition as being in accordance with the generally accepted principle of self-determination' ('Communist Party of India: A Change in Policy', dated 27 Nov. 1947, IOR: L/PJ/12/432).

[135]Amalendu Sengupta says that the official Pakistan policy came into question when Rajani Palme Dutt visited India in April-May 1946. Labelling the demand for Pakistan reactionary, Dutt resolutely opposed the partition of India. See Sengupta, *Uttal Challish*, 176. As regards Dutt's visit to India, see also 'C.P.I.—Great Britain', GB, SB Records, File No. KPM/SB/02209/05 (S 541/46/47 Part), KPM. An SB agent planted in the CPI organisation reported on 11 May 1946 that 'British Communist party leaders in recent times did not always agree with the political policy of Indian Communist Party and its analysis on Pakistan demand' and that 'Dutt came down to India to help the CPI to take a pro-Nationalist stand in these critical days'. The director of the Intelligence Bureau, Government of India, was aware of Dutt's standpoint, but placed the actual change in the party line at the later date, some time between December 1946 and May 1947 ('Communist Survey, No. 7, Dec. 15th, 1946 to May 15th, 1947', IOR: L/PJ/12/432).

on the part of the CPI with regard to the Muslim League's call for 'Direct Action' seems to have been caused by that very vacillation and hesitation which accompanied the contemplated reversal of its fundamental policy.

This kind of indecision suggests that the great waves of militant mass movements among workers and students from late 1945, which are described by some leftist historians as constituting a 'revolutionary situation',[136] were in reality lacking clear political direction with regard to the most fundamental and urgent issue of the time, the unity or division of India. It may be worthwhile to consider whether these waves of activity were not part of the social upheaval attributable to the 'power vacuum' created by the gradual withdrawal of the British Raj, rather than phenomena resembling a 'revolutionary situation'.[137]

PARA: NEIGHBOURHOOD SOLIDARITY

The word '*para*' in Bengali literally means 'locality', but in common parlance in Calcutta, it denotes a small territorial community, or neighbourhood, which is formed by inhabitants of the same narrow lane, or '*gully*' in Bengali, off the main streets. '*Para*' is an essential social unit through which citizens create and cement close, face-to-face social bonds in the midst of the sprawling megalopolis, where anonymity and indifference ordinarily reign.

When the unprecedented rioting broke out in Calcutta, many citizens appear to have fallen back upon the familiar social ties of *para* to render mutual help of various kinds to one another. It is said that in some places local inhabitants organised impromptu

[136]Gautam Chattopadhyay, 'The Almost Revolution: A Case Study of India in February 1946', in *Essays in Honour of Prof. S.C. Sarkar*, ed. Barun De (New Delhi: People's Publishing House, 1976), 427. For a more cautious description of the popular movements during this period, see Sumit Sarkar, 'Popular Movements and Nationalist Leadership 1945–47', in *A Critique of Colonial India* (Calcutta: Papyrus, 1985), 116–44.

[137]Here, only the CPI's confusion over the Pakistan issue has been taken up for discussion. For a more comprehensive analysis of the lack of clear-cut political leadership on the part of the left as a whole throughout this crucial period, see Basu, 'Urban Popular Movements', 461–65.

'defence parties'. For example, the railway workers who lived in Narkeldanga *bustee* set up 'a united Hindu volunteer corps to prevent outsiders from entering [the neighbourhood]'.[138] In other places local people constructed barricades to defend their '*para*'. Barricading was particularly conspicuous in the Park Circus area, where 'a good number of *gullies* had been barricaded with iron gates and hand carts' by their Muslim inhabitants. On Ripon Street to the west of Park Circus, which was inhabited by a mixed population, Muslims built 'barricades with [the] help of Anglo-Indians on information of impending attacks by Sikhs' on the evening of 17 August.[139]

In north Calcutta, where a minority of Muslims lived in isolated small pockets, neighbourhood solidarity occasionally worked as an effective safeguard to protect them against attacks from Hindu intruders. On Masjidbari Street, for example, there was a small *bustee* consisting of 6 *pucca* (brick-built) buildings and huts, where about 100 Muslims lived. When a Hindu mob attempted to attack this *para* on 16 August, its Hindu residents stood fast. The Hindu outsiders could not attack the Muslims 'because all the Hindus of the locality dispersed them'. 'Not a single Muslim was killed, because the Hindus protected them'. Upon another attempt the following day, prompt action on the part of the police resulted in the rescue of the Muslims and their evacuation to a safer place.[140]

One more remarkable thing about the Calcutta Disturbances is the large number of people who put the spirit of compassion into practice by giving shelter to threatened neighbours of a different religion, or even a different race. Thus, 'a number of Hindus found temporary shelter in the houses of Chinese in the Chinatown area'.[141] Anglo-Indians on Marquis Street gave shelter to 'approximately a hundred Hindu refugees'.[142] One Muslim citizen

[138]*CDCE*, vol. vi, 69. See also ibid., vol. viii, 34.

[139]Ibid., vol. iv, 64, 66–67; vol. v, 63; 'DE', p. 17, GB, Home (Poll) Confidential, No File No./46, WBSA. As regards barricading, see also *CDCE*, vol. iii, 24–25; vol. xi, 11, 54; *RCPD*, p. 96, GB, Home (Poll) Confidential, No File No./1946, WBSA; 'DE', p. 18, GB, Home (Poll) Confidential, No File No./46, WBSA.

[140]*CDCE*, vol. vii, 20–22, 73, 106.

[141]*RCPD*, p. 70, GB, Home (Poll) Confidential, No File No./46, WBSA.

[142]Ibid., p. 71.

sheltered 'many Hindu refugees in his house on Ripon Street'.[143] A group of Sikhs came to the police station to report that 'they had hidden a number of threatened Muslims in their quarters on Ashutosh Mukharji Road'.[144]

In north Calcutta, where Muslim residents were under threat of massacre, quite a number of Hindus played an active role in providing them with shelter and protection. To cite a few cases, after the looting of Nikaripara *bustee* in the Baghbazar area, the police were informed that '150 to 200 Muslim females, males and children had been given shelter in the house[s] of different Hindu local people'. Of them about 30 men and women were found in the house of one J.B. Dutta.[145] In Kumartoli, two Hindu *bhadralok*, Bankim Bose and Sudhir Kumar Ghose, came to the police station and reported that 'Muslim males and females have been sheltered by the local gentlemen'. Some 80 to 90 Muslims were removed to the house of Kalimuddin Chowdhury at Murali Bagan.[146] In Sham Square one Dhirendra Nath Sen protected some Muslims, who had been 'his servants for the last 15 years'. They were taken to the house of Kalimuddin Chowdhury through the mediation of one Dr Jallani.[147] Those who did not have the courage to offer their own homes as places of safety appear to have shown compassion to troubled neighbours in more low-key ways, as shown in the following case:

> There a gentleman came and told me [i.e. the officer-in-charge of the police station] that a Muslim elderly lady got some injuries. He said: 'I had given her milk and some bandage. Please come and take her to hospital.' So I went there, entered the house, and as she was a heavy lady it took some time to pick her up in the lorry.[148]

[143]Ibid., 68.

[144]Ibid., 114.

[145]*CDCE*, vol. vii, 240–241; vol. viii, 132. About J.B. Dutta of Ram Krishna Lane, see also ibid., vol. ix, 15.

[146]Ibid., vol. viii, 35–36, 133. Apart from Kalimuddin Chowdhury of Murali Bagan, there were a few more Muslim gentlemen who voluntarily placed their houses at the disposal of rescue operations.

[147]Ibid., vol. ix, 16.

[148]Ibid., vol. vii, 292.

In spite of such cases of mutual protection and aid, it is difficult to conclude that solidarity and fraternity based on *para* social relations had much real effect as a countervailing force against the communal violence. As a matter of fact, the *para* can by no means be characterised as some idyllic community in which all kinds of social tensions could be reconciled and healed. In this connection it is important to note that those who sheltered Muslims in north Calcutta did this at considerable personal risk. They were often threatened by people in their own localities for their actions. A case in point is the experiences of Debendranath Kundu of Jorasanko, who offered his home as shelter to three or four Muslims only to be threatened by 'all the Hindus' in the neighbourhood that 'they would set fire to his house if he does not turn them out'.[149] The strong propaganda for religious solidarity seems to have already penetrated the social fabric of the *para*, turning it into an arena where territorial solidarity and religious loyalty did battle with one another. And it seems that the latter came out as the victor on the night of 16/17 August, which marked the turning point in the evolvement of the Calcutta Disturbances. On the other hand, it should be noted that territorial solidarity could at times serve as a social base from which to perpetrate violence against the members of other religious groups.[150] In short, *para* solidarity bore the clear stamp of ambiguity as far as the events of August 1946 are concerned.

It is difficult to answer why that was so, but there is an interesting case illustrating how *para* politics actually operated. As background to the problem, let us first consider evidence regarding 'fratricide', which seems to be widely believed to have taken place on a very large scale at the *gully* or *para* level. There are actually two opposing testimonies. On the one hand, a military intelligence officer testified before the Enquiry Commission that 'there was fighting in every *gully*' and that 'I found a lot of corpses in the *gully* off Sovabazar Street and off Chitpore Road; there was a lot of corpses in the *gully*'.[151] By contrast, an army officer who actually went through narrow lanes and alleys in north Calcutta with his men to carry

[149]Ibid., vol. xi, 212.

[150]Lambert, 'Hindu-Muslim Riots', 174; *Dawn*, 24 Aug. 1946.

[151]*CDCE*, vol. iv, 66–67. See also ibid., vol. vi, 258.

out mop-up operations on the afternoon of 17 August, told the Commission that he saw no bodies in the bye-ways.[152] The *gullies* of north Calcutta that he saw with his own eyes were singularly quiet:

> They [the inhabitants] were in their houses before we got there so far I could see. I encountered no trouble all the way from Lower Circular Road to the Central Avenue. I do not think I encountered any persons myself outside their houses. They were looking from the windows, but they were not outside. But there were persons at a distance from me who were dispersed by my troops.[153]

This view was corroborated by another army officer, who patrolled *gullies* between Upper Circular Road and College Street on the evening of 17 August. He wrote: 'The back streets were particularly quiet. I do not remember seeing any corpses; neither do I remember seeing fires of any description'.[154] He added that 'everyone thought that the back streets were quiet'.[155] The police were so frightened that very few of them dared step foot into a *gully*, but one courageous British inspector, who did step out, got a similar impression: 'Going through these lanes I saw no sign of any looting or arson'.[156]

It is probable that the riotous crowds had already dispersed before the military patrol party reached the spot of trouble; yet, the fact that not a single corpse was encountered by patrols in large parts of north Calcutta immediately after the 'wild night' of 16/17 August does indicate that killing in the *gullies* was not so widespread a phenomenon as is generally believed.

An incident that occurred in the Dhulipara locality on Ram Chand Ghose Lane off Beadon Street in north Calcutta on 16 and 17 August gives us a glimpse of how a neighbourhood community could function under immense emotional pressure. There was a small Muslim *bustee* in this *para*. It was about 6.50 pm on 16 August that the officer-in-charge of the Burtolla police station received a

[152]Ibid., vol. v, 123.

[153]Ibid.

[154]Ibid., vol. v, 320.

[155]Ibid., vol. v, 325. See also ibid., vol. viii, 112.

[156]Ibid., vol. vi, 187.

letter from one Satyendranath Bose, a Hindu lawyer residing in Dhulipara, reading:

> Dhulipara locality is in great danger. The Mohammedan inhabitants of our locality, who are quite innocent and non-interfering are being unnecessarily attacked by the pimps, ex-convicts, and the ruffians of the Sonagachi and Rambagan area. These rough elements are now being swelled up by those of Natun Bazar area. These people about 200 in number are in a hopeless condition. Whoever of our Hindu neighbours go to help them are also being attacked. Sometimes these ruffians are coming in hundreds and making attacks. Their sole objective being to loot the people of the locality and nothing else. Most of the *para* people will help the police if some of them are posted here and give patrols. This is very urgent and important and I hope you will lend your helping hand at once. I am making this appeal on behalf of the people of the Dhulipara area and specially for the innocent Mohammedan people of the locality, who have been temporarily sheltered in the mosque at 15, Ram Chand Ghose Lane.[157]

The officer-in-charge rushed to Dhulipara and 'had a sort of conference for about half an hour' with the local people. This resulted in the Hindu and Muslim residents concluding an agreement, in which the Hindus promised that they would protect their Muslim neighbours at the cost of their lives, while the Muslims avowed the belief that the Hindus would keep their word.[158]

The mosque where the Muslims had taken shelter was attacked at least three times after this 'conference'. During the second attack, which was attempted at night, 'two or three Hindus of that locality stood side by side with the Muslim defenders and some of them were injured'. However, on the occasion of the third attack, solidarity in Dhulipara collapsed, for 'on the morning of the 17th when the third attack began many of the local Hindus were found joining those ruffians in looting the houses of these Muslims and killing the Muslims'.[159] Upon arriving at Dhulipara on the evening

[157]Ibid., vol. vii, 23.
[158]Ibid., vol. vii, 23–24.
[159]Ibid., vol. vii, 24.

of the same day, the officer-in-charge found 12 to 13 dead bodies in the mosque.[160]

It appears that local leadership in Dhulipara was in the hands of a group of Hindu *bhadralok*, who believed it their moral obligation to extend protection to 'innocent and non-interfering' Muslim members of their *para*. That is to say, they had assumed a typical attitude of paternalism towards their minority Muslim neighbours. True to their word in their agreement with the local *bustee* dwellers, a few of them actually 'stood side by side with the Muslim defenders', leading us to believe that this paternalism was not mere talk, but fairly deeply rooted in the social fabric of the *para*. Nonetheless, it is also clear that solidarity based on such paternalistic leadership was not strong enough to withstand repeated violent attacks by 'the pimps, ex-convicts, and the ruffians'. The fact that 'many of the local Hindus were found joining those ruffians' when solidarity dissipated is interesting in that the normally accepted social boundaries separating insiders and outsiders, disreputable persons and respectable Hindu householders, disappeared under the pressure of repeated violence; and in its stead, another dividing line, marking religious difference, rose to the surface.

This small incident in north Calcutta clearly shows how the multilayered structure of connections and solidarities among the residents of *para* was reduced to a single-dimension by the perpetration of pure violence. One would reasonably assume that the local people of this neighbourhood had been living their lives not only as adherents of a religious community but also as citizens of a territorial community, a *para*, participants in a particular occupational group, members of respectable families, and so forth. In contrast, after experiencing one violent attack after another in their community, they found themselves reduced simply to Hindus or Muslims, the sense of communal identity completely overpowering the forms of social existence that bound them in the process of everyday life. This might be termed the 'levelling effects' of violence.[161] The case of Dhulipara seems to suggest that strong and decisive actions should be taken at the initial stage of rioting in

[160]Ibid., vol. vii, 25.

[161]Tambiah, *Levelling Crowds*, 279.

order to give full support to the maintenance of local social relations before the 'levelling effects' can be activated.

Thus informal social bonds such as the *para*, which had cultivated face-to-face relations that could morally restrain senseless violence against one's neighbours, broke down, while at the same time, as shown above, established voluntary associations like trade unions became disabled. It was in this manner that the citizens of Calcutta were practically stripped of the social ties which constituted the foundation of civic life in this colonial metropolis. Moreover, this kind of social vacuum was enveloped in another far more extensive vacuum, the 'power vacuum' created during the transitional period of transferring power from the Raj to the nationalist elite. From the night of 16/17 August onward, it may be argued, the people of Calcutta had become engulfed in this twofold vacuum, drawing them into an intensely unstable and insecure situation, which, in this writer's opinion, aroused an acute bottomless 'fear' in their minds, resulting in the transformation of their religious opponents into monsters. It appears that it was such a 'state of exception' at the individual, existential level of the people of Calcutta that set the psychological stage for a wild explosion of communal violence that can be rightfully termed 'civil war'.

CONCLUSION

I have tried in this essay to situate the Calcutta Disturbances within the context of a shift in the fundamental political environments from a simple 'power vacuum' to a 'civil war' situation, or a 'state of exception'. The evidence presented suggests that we need to reconsider the common view that the Indian political situation changed all of a sudden in August 1946 from a 'revolutionary situation' to a frenzy of communal passion. Such conventional views underrate the extent of the ideological disorientation existing within the revolutionary party (CPI) and among some militant trade unions controlled by it over the Pakistan issue, and perhaps overestimate the radicalism embraced by popular movements. The crucial months from the end of 1945 down to August 1947 may more usefully be looked upon and studied as a historical period in which a less spectacular and less discontinuous shifting of gears occurred from the simple 'power vacuum' to a 'civil war' situation than as an enigmatic era during which Indian society was suddenly torn apart.

As to the 1946 violence called the Calcutta Disturbances, this study has sought to bring its political aspects into relief, focusing on the political interactions at three levels.

With regard to the role of the first of these levels, that of state administration, recent research has stressed the need for the decisive use of either or both police and military force at the initial stage of rioting. In the case of Calcutta in August 1946, the Bengal administrative authorities were so slow and hesitant in taking action that they let communal violence grow into an almost incontrollable disaster within a short space of time. No doubt, both the Suhrawardy administration and the British Raj were biased, each in its own way. However, in order to explain administrative failure on this scale, more attention should be paid to the structural problems that fettered the provincial administration under the Government of India Act, 1935.

As regards the remaining two levels, our findings give full support to neither of the two theoretical generalisations proposed by Brass and Varshney. The frameworks of 'institutionalised riot systems' and 'associational' and 'everyday' forms of civic engagement need to be modified when applied to particular cases. These two generalisations only provide the two extreme reference points between which actual events may be located.

So far as the Calcutta Disturbances are concerned, 'institutionalised riot systems' *as such* are not observable, since such 'systems' were still in the initial stage of development. Admittedly, there was a 'system' of a sort consisting of 'volunteer' organisations and so forth; and most probably the physical clashes which occurred during the early hours of 'Direct Action Day' were pre-planned. But the rioting thus created began to accumulate enormous momentum at an astonishing speed which surpassed every politician's calculations. The situation rapidly grew into a monster that could not be controlled by the 'systems' available in the 1940s. On the other hand, we all know that fully 'institutionalised riot systems' were at work in the Gujarat carnage and that the Babri-Masjid incident was orchestrated like a dramatic performance. How and why the embryonic form of 'riot systems' evident in the 1940s has in the course of half a century matured and been integrated into the body politic of South Asia is one of the basic questions before the historians of communalism in South Asia.

Concerning 'associational' ties, our study of trade unions seems to suggest that large 'associations' were rather susceptible to political propaganda along communal lines, given the fact that one of the most powerful leftist trade unions in Calcutta was easily disabled even before 'Direct Action Day'. This observation contradicts Varshney's contention that 'associational' forms are stronger than 'everyday' forms of civic engagement. The actual state of things is probably more complex and fluid.

In contrast, it is notable that many people in the city of Calcutta showed their civic spirit in 'everyday' forms in their *para*. In Calcutta during August 1946, such forms appear to have been more important and active than 'associational' forms of engagement as social bases to resist the pressure of embryonic 'riot systems'. However, in the absence of administrative support, neighbourhood solidarity was short-lived. 'Levelling effects' were activated and *para* inhabitants began to be drawn into communal violence. When the *para* collapsed in this way, the citizens of Calcutta found themselves stripped of all three layers of social bonds, the state, voluntary associations and, finally, their own neighbourhoods, all of which had protected them against an anomic chaos. This marked the beginning of a 'state of exception' at the individual level of the citizens. Furthermore, it should be emphasised that *para* solidarity was based on traditional paternalistic social relations developed between a Hindu majority and Muslim minority in some neighbourhoods and vice versa in others. It need hardly be said that such a traditional relationship was hard hit not only by the rapid growth of urban population after independence, but also by the mass migration that took place at the time of partition and thereafter and radically changed patterns of social segregation within the city.

Finally, the results of the present study seem to suggest that political attempts at reforming the state administration and dismantling 'institutionalised riot systems' should be combined with efforts to create new social relations which go beyond the limits of the old established 'associations' and the traditional *para* elysium. This may be one of the more positive and constructive messages to the present day people of Calcutta from beyond the graves of the over 4000 victims of the Disturbances.

CHAPTER fourteen

A City Feeding on Itself

Riots, Testimonies and Literatures of the 1940s in Calcutta

Debjani Sengupta

This article looks at the Great Calcutta Killings (August 1946) and the subsequent unrest in the city not just as events but as long shadows on the lives of its people. As communal conflagration enveloped the city streets, it brought in its wake many other kinds of upheavals within the middle-class Hindu family. Richly captured in two novels set in the backdrop of the rioting city, Ashapurna Devi's *Mittirbari* (1947) and Manik Bandopadhyay's *Swadhinatar Swad* (1951) explore public violence through fictional private lives. Both the texts go beyond the experience of chaos and disorder to investigate issues of freedom within the 'modern' family and of citizenship in the new nation. In them, the centrality of gendered voices, shifts in language, open-ended and fragmented narratives raise questions regarding the homogeneity of identity that the communal riots tried to create. They also complicate the template of macabre violence and destruction by positing another view of the city where men and women live, love and labour. The persistence of the human subject within the narrative, at a time when humanity is most terribly debased, makes these texts profoundly *moral* in tone.[1] The novels enunciate various issues about the secular liberal nation and its

[1]See Frank B. Farrell, *Why Does Literature Matter?* (Ithaca: Cornell University Press, 2004), 11. He postulates that literature 'can make visible significant patterns

citizenship that is reflective of some of the earliest articulations of these debates in the Bangla literary canon.

It is well-documented that Hindu and Muslim identities in Indian institutional politics had hardened from the 1920s onwards. In a Public and Judicial Department report covering the first half of 1940, the British Government noted the alarming rise of Volunteer Corps or 'private armies' of the political parties, a sure indicator of the increased communal tensions.[2] With this political army as standby, the Direct Action Day riots in Calcutta also saw, for the first time, a large-scale participation of the upper and middle classes in violence. The conjunction of 'elite' and 'popular' communalism had never before been manifest to such a vivid extent.

In 1946, Gopal Pantha, a notorious goon of north Calcutta, was thirty-three years old. Everybody called him by the nickname Pantha, a 'goat', because he ran a meat shop in College Street. Although he was the leader of a gang of neighbourhood thugs, Gopal did not belong to any criminal underclass of the city. His Brahmin upper caste family (his patrilineal name was Mukherjee) had links to the Congress Party and had contributed their share to the militant nationalist movements of the 1930s. On the morning of 16 August 1946, he left for his shop as usual but when he heard about the trouble he came back to his locality. 'Muslim League volunteers were marching with long sticks in their hands. From Boubazar More to Harrison Road you could hear their slogans, 'Larke lenge Pakistan'. Then I heard that two *goalas* (dairymen) had been killed in Beliaghata and riots have started in Boubazar'.[3]

He organized his 'boys' because he thought: 'It was a very critical time for the country; the country had to be saved. If we become a part of Pakistan we will be oppressed ... so I called all my boys and

---

of how the world is arranged that cannot be had by any other means' and thus literature is 'truth revealing'.

[2]Secret communications from the Secretariat of the Governor General to the Under Secretary for India, prepared by the Intelligence Bureau, *Public and Judicial Department Reports covering the first half of 1940,* L/PJ/8/678, India Office Library and Records.

[3]The oral testimony of Gopal Pantha and others used in the essay are from interviews conducted by Andrew Whitehead and Anuradha Awasthi for a BBC programme on 50 years of India's independence. The tapes are available in the SOAS Archives, London. Subsequently, they will be referred to as Partition Tapes, with the relevant number—the Gopal Pantha interviews, Partition Tapes (1997), 74.

said this is the time we have to retaliate, and you have to answer brutality with brutality'.[4]

They armed themselves with small knives, swords, meat-choppers, sticks and rods, while Gopal had two American pistols tucked at his waist. He had procured these as well as some grenades from the American soldiers quartered in Calcutta in 1945. 'If you paid two hundred and fifty rupees or bought them a bottle of whiskey the soldiers would give you a .45 and a hundred cartridges.' As soon as the news of rioting spread, his group of vigilantes swelled. They were joined by the Hindustani *goalas* or cowherds from the Janbajar area who came armed with *lathis*.

> We were fighting those who attacked us ... we fought and killed them ... So if we heard one murder has taken place we committed ten more ... the ratio should be one to ten, that was the order to my boys.[5]

Like Gopal Pantha, Jugal Chandra Ghosh also had some men at his disposal and belonged to the city's middle classes. He ran a wrestling club at Beliaghata, and his followers carried out retaliatory attacks in Beliaghata area and the Miabagan *busti* (slum). Jugal Chandra raised money from the neighbour-hood sawmills, factories and *khatals* (dairy-sheds) and distributed it among the attackers. 'One murder would fetch ten rupees and a wounding would bring five.'[6] He had links to certain political leaders of the city and knew the Hindu Mahasabha Secretary Bidhubhusan Sarkar as well as the Congress affiliated trade union (INTUC) leader Suresh Chandra Bannerjee. Ghosh's anger against the Muslim League flared when he saw the dead bodies from the first days of rioting. 'I saw four trucks standing, all with dead bodies, piled at least three feet high; like molasses in a sack ... that sight had a tremendous effect on me.'[7] The riot that erupted on 16 August, came to an end on 19 August, but sporadic outbursts continued throughout 1946 and in the months leading to the Independence. A statement made by Baidyanath Mullick as late as October 1946, showed that the city was still in the grip of fear: 'In

[4]Partition Tapes, 74.
[5]Partition Tapes, 74.
[6]Partition Tapes, 72.
[7]Ibid.

Benia Pukur Sub area there were disturbances last night (on 28.10.46) in the following lanes: Gobra Gorasthan Lane, Rai Charan Pal Lane, Mahendra Rai Lane, Hingaon Jamadar Lane. The most disturbed area was Rai Charan Pal Lane. The Muslim mob set a number of houses on fire. The police came but could not help'.[8]

The long, unending days of rioting made certain that Calcutta was never to be the same again.

The picture that emerges from the interviews of these men, active during those days, also underlines the character of the mob that had gone on rampage in the by-lanes and streets of Calcutta. Along with the city's upper and middle classes, it, every so often, comprised men working in a city not their own—the *goalas* (the dairy-men) the *darwans* (doormen), the coachmen, the *garoyans* (drivers) from the coal-depots, the tailors, boatmen and petty traders who were 'up-countrymen', migrants who lived in the city for their livelihood.[9] The city, with its bustling bazaars, sprawling garden houses of the rich merchants, and clusters of slums standing cheek by jowl to them provided job opportunities and residence to a large labour force drawn from the neighbouring districts of Bihar, Orissa and the United Provinces. Although Calcutta, as British India's largest metropolis, had started on its downward slump when the capital was transferred to Delhi in 1911, the number of migrant labourers also started to slowly decline after 1918. In the middle of the twentieth century, only three-tenths of the city's population was born there and the working class of the city continued to come from outside.

In 1931, the total percentage of people living in Calcutta but born in other states of India was 31.7 per cent while those who were born in other districts of the state numbered 0.3 per cent.[10] A large percentage of this workforce was employed as unskilled labour in jute and cotton mills as well as in railway workshops, glass and pottery works and leather tanning industries. It constituted a highly volatile social group. Living in close contact with other immigrant workers, with strong ties of language and religion, they lived in an alien city in extreme squalor and poverty. The new immigrants tried to find accommodation

[8]S.P. Mookerjee, *Papers and Correspondences*, II–IV Installment, Subject File 148, 1946, 35, Nehru Memorial Museum and Library, Delhi.

[9]Suranjan Das, *Communal Riots*, 182.

[10]M. Ghosh et al., *A Study in Urban Growth Dynamics* (Calcutta: Firma, 1972), 103.

close to people they already knew and the bonds of kinship helped in the process of accretion. They had no family near them, and in their daily struggle against poverty and insecurity, they depended to a large extent on the *sardar* or foreman of the mill they worked in who often belonged to their own religious and village community. This group of 'labouring poor' thus came to assume a strong notion of communal identity based on religion and language and habitat. 'Calcutta developed as a city of lone men, and it was the single upcountrymen, Hindus and Muslims alike, who were most active in the Calcutta riots' before 1946 and after.[11] A large number of Muslim rioters were *kasais* or butchers from north and central Calcutta, as well as *khalasis* or dockworkers, masons and hackney carriage drivers. Some Muslim millhands who came to join the Direct Action Day rally called by the ruling Muslim League government in Bengal also took part in the looting and arson. The rioters were armed with bricks, crackers, burning cloth soaked in petrol, acid bulbs, bombs, soda water bottles and petrol filled bottles. The *bustis* with a large number of working poor became easy targets and many perpetrators came from there as well. Among the Hindus, contemporary accounts mention the large presence of up-countrymen as rioters. The *goalas*, sweepers, *darwans* took part in the riots as did the local thugs. An editorial in a city newspaper reports on a 'battle royal between the League hooligans and the *Doshads* (low class Hindus trading in pigs) at the south-eastern corner of Tirettabazar'.[12] The dwellers of Kasai and Kalabagan *bustis*, as well as the slums in Belgachia, Ultadanga, Raja Bazar, Entally, Narkeldanga, Bakulbagan formed armed gangs to set upon each other. Apart from north Calcutta, the roads and areas severely affected by rioting were mostly in the western dock areas and parts of north and south Calcutta: Mechuabazar and College Street, Bowbazar and Chittaranjan Avenue, Chitpur Road, Canning Street, Amratolla Street, Ekbalpur Lane, Khidderpore and Garden Reach, Park Circus and Watgunj. The region most affected by violence was the densely populated areas of the metropolis: the sector bound on the south by Boubazar Street, on the east by Upper Circular Road and on the west by Strand Road. The industrial belt of Howrah that had a

[11]Suranjan Das, *Communal Riots,* 20.

[12]Editorial, *Amrita Bazar Patrika*, 26 August 1946.

number of factories and go-downs with a large population of labourers and workers also witnessed widespread murder and mayhem.[13]

The rioters were, however, not confined only to the lower social strata. Prominent Muslim League leaders spent a great deal of time in police control rooms directing operations and the role of Suhrawardy in obstructing police duties is documented.[14] The notorious criminal Bombaiya, living in the New Market area, had links with the League and participated in riots as did other goons like Mina Punjabi of Cornwallis *busti* and Munna Chowdhuri in the Harrison Road area. Their direct links with institutional politics naturally made the outbreaks highly organized in nature. Hindu businessmen, prominent merchants as well as politicians of the Hindu Mahasabha and some sections of the Congress provided leadership to the mob.[15] A number of Indian National Army men who came to the city to celebrate INA Day on 18 August, were involved in rioting.[16] Even the minority sections of the population like the Anglo-Indians took part in the conflagration.[17] Rumours doing the rounds in the city a few days

[13]Suranjan Das, *Communal Riots,* 172.

[14]Suranjan Das, *Communal Riots*, 178. For an opposite view, see Shaista Suhrawardy Ikramullah's account of Premier Suhrawardy's role, *From Purdah to Parliament*, Karachi: OUP, 1998, 153–55.

[15]In the diary of one Haricharan Ghosh, (who seemed to be a closed associate of S.P. Mookerjee) an entry as late as 31. 10. 46 notes: 'i) Funds for Defence (about Rs 2000), ii) Sikhs to be stationed at 33 Paikpara Road, iii) Search in certain areas referred to in the map, iv) Presence of leaders—that will improve morale'. This surely refers to the Hindu Mahasabha leaders and not leaders of the Muslim League. See Tapan Raychaudhuri, *Bangalnama* (Calcutta: Ananda Publishers, 2009) 155–56, for an eyewitness account of Hindu involvement in the riots, especially of *bhadralok* students from his Beadon Street hostel who had actively participated in attacking the Muslim *busti* in Upper Circular Road. Also by the same author, *Romonthon Othoba Bhimrotipraptor Porochoritchorcha* (Calcutta: Ananda Publishers, 1993), 94–96.

[16]The military ingredient of communal violence was also a feature of the Punjab where ex-INA men were seen as leaders of the mob. See Indivar Kamtekar, 'The Military Ingredient of Communal Violence in Punjab, 1947' in *Partition and Post-Colonial South Asia: A Reader,* ed.T ai Yong Tan and Gyanesh Kudaisya, vol. 2. (London: Routledge, 2008), 197.

[17]Syed Nazimuddin Hashim, a student at Presidency College in August 1946, bore testimony to the unrestrained rioting in Calcutta as well as the fatalities of the massacre. 'The first victim I saw was a poor Oriya porter ... he hadn't a clue what was happening ... he had a basket and had just come into the side street ... a Muslim in a *lungi* broke away

before Direct Action Day added to the anxiety and tension in the city streets but the rumours were just that, no Hindu or Muslim families had tried to remove themselves to safer areas and if the Muslim League government was involved then government officials had no inkling of that.[18] As the riots raged on, at the end of the first forty-eight hours, the hot, muggy and rainy days were marked by an air of death and desolation that hung over Calcutta.

II

Fictional representations of the riots, written in the months that followed, stress that communities are not undifferentiated or homogenous blocks and they restore

> the subjecthood of subaltern social groups, including women, in the making of history, while noting that even their active agency cannot always prevent them from becoming tragic, though not passive, victims of the games of power played by claimants, makers and managers of colonial and postcolonial states.[19]

---

from the procession and hit him on the head with an iron rod. The fellow was absolutely startled, the blow broke open his ear.... All the food shops had closed, New Market had closed, three days of unrestrained rioting and looting, in which the Anglo Indians took full part; pick-up trucks were used to loot a music and radio shop; departmental shops were looted in Wellington Square and Chowringhee Road, all the liquor shops were looted as well'. The Partition Tapes, number 71. This is corroborated by the following interview: 'Anglo Indian Sergeants and Pathan soldiers raided the above-mentioned houses (4, Jugipara Bylane and 232, 234A A and B Vivekananda Road) at 2.30 PM. Assaulted not only the male members of those houses but the female members were also assaulted and molested'. Entry (probably 2.4.47) in the meticulously kept news diary of Haricharan Ghosh, *S.P. Mookerjee Miscellaneous Papers*, 24.

[18]Tapan Raychaudhuri, *Bangalnama,* (Kolkata: Ananda Publishers, 2009), 150–51 states: 'If the Muslim League had planned to start widespread rioting, then it was unknown to even people who were politically important. Kiranshankar Roy's elder daughter and her husband lived in a house in Christofer Lane. All around lived poor Muslims, mostly non-Bengali. My uncle went to look up his daughter after the riot started and found that the assailants had entered the house. His son-in-law had been stabbed and his little son was being abducted. If he had the slightest inkling that there was a possibility of such an event, he would not have left his daughter in the midst of such danger.' [Translation mine]

[19]Sugata Bose and Ayesha Jalal, *Modern South Asia: History, Culture, Political Economy,* (Delhi: OUP, 2004), 165.

The eyewitness accounts are set off, as if in a cameo, by the literary narratives with the Calcutta riots as their backdrop. Some of this 'fictive testimony' often self-consciously indicates its own limits even as it recreates the riots. At other times, it gives an ironic, subtle and self-reflexive account of the carnage that is allegorical. Written between 1947 and 1951, they are in some ways trying to interrogate the nature of violence. The brutality on the streets was of such horrifying magnitude that human vocabulary was incapable of representing it; yet it had to be talked about or else, how would we learn about the past that we all share? It is this dilemma of representation that is at the heart of Manik Bandopadhyay's novel *Swadhinatar Swad*. As a Marxist, Bandopadhyay sees the Calcutta riots as a culmination of the low-grade communal conflict that had accompanied British electoral politics. Yet, the riots also enable the characters in his novel to ask fundamental questions not only of themselves but also of each other.

The narrative of *Swadhinatar Swad* (The Taste of Freedom)[20] is set in Calcutta, immediately after the August riots, and ends after the Noakhali riots and the Independence in 1947. Bandopadhyay's hitherto unpublished diaries testify to the ways the Direct Action had been an instructive moment in his life as an active member of the Communist Party of India and as a writer: 'Today is *hartal*—direct action day. When I heard the news of rioting, I felt depressed. We had known riots will happen, still I thought—what a pity! What a pity! Rumours were rife everywhere—there was a sense of anxiety all around. Heard there has been a big clash between Sikhs and Muslims in the Kalighat area. [...]Went out and saw a big crowd in front of the mosque. [...] At around ten, two young men from the Party came. They were trying to form a peace committee. [...] After talking to them the state of my mind changed. However bad the situation may be, there was no need to give up'.[21]

[20]Manik Bandopadhyay, *Swadhinatar Swad'*, in *Rochonashomogro*, Vol. 7 (Calcutta: Paschimbongo Bangla Academy, 2000), 265–392. [All subsequent translations from the text are mine.]

[21]Jugantar Chakraborty (ed.), *Aprokashito Manik Bandopadhyay*, (Calcutta: Dey's Publishing, 1976, rpt, 1990, 88–89. [Translation mine] Another brilliant example of Manik Bandopadhyay's transformation of a historical event into art is his short story 'Choto Bakulpurer Jatri' that he wrote on police repression during the Tebhaga Andolan in Hoogly's Bora-Kamlapur area.

Manik Bandopadhyay's ideological dedication to Marxism permits him to be optimistic about the ways in which people resist communal stereotypes and continue to co-exist. In his novel too, he creates a multi-layered text of many dimensions, articulating disparate even conflicting arguments. Along with the impending political transition, the text marks the originary moment of the country's independence, through intense polemical debates. The progression of discussion and argument includes gender and the autonomous subjectivity of women to mark this novel as encompassing yet resisting the ideology of what Aamir Mufti calls 'national realism' of the 1940s that showcases the secular citizen's relationship to the newly emergent nation.[22] Manik Bandopadhyay refigures the riots as that moment of great historical crisis when his novel (and we) can focus on the riot's effect both on the human psyche and on the political life of the city. The writer's Marxist aesthetic praxis involves the exposure and revelation of historical situations and the human agency involved in shaping and influencing them. Therefore, this work is an exploration of the transitory phase between colonialism and liberation as it is also a compendium of responses and adjustments of different characters to the newly acquired freedom, both political and social. Along with the experiences and perceptions of political independence, the novel explores the changing dialectics of the relationship of the sexes, all seen in the context of the riots in Calcutta.

The narrative opens with an unusual description of the city under the grip of arson, loot and stabbing. Fear has choked the quotidian life of the city, transforming the recognizable space into the inexplicably menacing:

> It was a stifling monsoon afternoon; the lowering sky was like a force bearing down on the breast of the city and the wind, deathlike, did not stir. Like a cremation ground, the city streets were silent, empty, lifeless and quiet. Sometimes a few cars went past, like moveable bursts of anxiety, in a rush of sound. On the footpaths, there were a few pedestrians, looking around with fear and walking quickly. Everywhere there was a palpable, artificial terror. From afar, the

[22]Aamir R. Mufti, 'A Greater Story-writer than God: Genre, Gender and Minority in Late Colonial India', in eds. Partha Chatterjee and Pradeep Jeganathan, *Subaltern Studies* XI (Delhi: Permanent Black, 2000), 11.

> sound of many voices came to the ear. Even in that indistinct sound, one could make out a sharp sliver of disgusting animosity.[23]

The heightened perception of fear and anxiety threatens the ordered urban structural space of the city so that even the familiar objects of urbanity like the car and the meandering streets become symbols of the uncanny. Bandopadhyay's language, spare and controlled, tries to understand the transformation of the familiar city into a site of fratricidal violence. In this city, Promotho comes looking for his niece Monimala to north Calcutta where riots have broken out. As he gets off a taxi, he is attacked and killed.

> Armed with iron rods and daggers, two men came upon them, quietly, without uttering a single sound of either animosity or recognition, simply to kill. [...] They had not seen the other two men ever, except their clothes that proclaimed them as enemies. [...] In the recent life of the city, incidents like this happened daily, a saga of day and night—the clash of the two men with two others was an insignificant part of the larger happenings all around.[24]

Deeply aware of the forces of history, Bandopadhyay tries to give shape in his art to the clash of the contradictory processes of an anti-colonial liberation that will bring in freedom—in politics, economics and society but is accompanied by untold brutality. By opening his narrative with the riots on the eve of Independence, he seems to set out an ominous sign of impending doom. His political and aesthetic ambivalence about the freedom that lay just round the corner is expressed through this juxtaposition.

Monimala, Promotho's niece, has taken shelter in her husband's ancestral home. The house is crammed with terrified relatives and friends and the rooms are partitioned off to hold couples and their children. This temporary shelter is a microcosm of the world outside where the psychopathology of violence has robbed people of their humanity. Yet the quotidian life lived within, with its hardships and collusions and strange alliances also makes it possible to contain and minimize the effects of violence on the human psyche. Pranab, Monimala's brother-

[23]Manik Bandopadhyay, *Swadhinatar Swad*, 265.

[24]*Swadhinatar Swad*, 267.

in-law, tries to bring a semblance of order in their chaotic lives. Lack of rations and black-marketeering has ensured that there is always a sense of precariousness to their existence: yet the occupants, brought together by a common concern for safety, work together to survive. An abundance of fear and despair make their daily lives seem on the verge of disintegration, yet they gather every night to discuss the situation in the city or help each other out in distress. The rioting city is a physical presence in the novel and works as a metonymy for the partisan disorder unleashed by political expediencies. The novelist's omnipresent voice paints a bleak portrayal of the riot's aftermath:

> Tram-cars roll on, buses too ply infrequently. In some sections of the city, they stop after some trouble, maybe for half a day, sometimes for a day or two, but then again the drivers take out the trams, the conductors give tickets. In some terribly sensitive areas, a uniformed guard is also seen next to the driver, much to the amusement of the city-dwellers. On the roundabouts, uniformed police armed with rifles can be seen, sometimes even in military uniforms; the armoured trucks pass through the streets in sombre reverberations, yet in other parts of the city the festival of knives, daggers, acid bombs, murder-mutilation, looting, and arson increase. Security lessens, anxiety increases, there is no end to lawlessness. [...] This is the playfulness of the creators of rioting and murder, their servants are now employed to patrol the city to quell the flames. What a farce![25]

In an atmosphere of anger and hatred, the daily lives of the poor go on because they have to survive, like the old woman of the area who sells dung cakes for a living:

> She is like a slap on the face of the English, the League, the Congress, the black-marketeer, the *goonda*: a symbol of eternal humanity, with her wrinkled skin, her bent back, her white fleecy hair set like a crown. [...] What does it matter who is Hindu and who Muslim![26]

Manik Bandopadhyay's political ideology perceives human history as made up of opposing forces, like the riots that necessarily give rise to its opposite:

[25] *Swadhinatar Swad,* 288.
[26] *Swadhinatar Swad,* 291.

> When there is a riot there is also an attempt to stop it. We can't have one without the other [because] in spite of savagery, man is not so, he is civilized. But these definite and clear words like civilization and humanity have become such playthings of those inhuman men that their meanings have become unclear to common people.[27]

Pranab, the author's spokesman, believes that the working class does not contribute to riots; they are victims of the political machinations of the middle and upper classes. The novel is an attempt on Manik Bandopadhyay's part not only to understand why things happen the way they do, but to see how human will and effort can change the course of events. So the efforts of a few men like Pranab and Girin who try to stop the madness of riots is right and natural.

> All the people who are workers are one, their unity is their biggest strength—still riots happen. Why do riots happen? Why do riots take place that make victims of the poor who are both Hindus and Muslims? [...] We have lots of examples of the unity of the working-men and women. The trams and buses you ride in the city are plying with the help of Hindu and Muslim workers. But on this side we have Noakhali, on the other side we have Bihar, who knows when the conflagration will stop! We have to remember this riot is imposed from the top, for the benefit of those who rule over us. [...] Keep your belief intact on the downtrodden [because] revolution happens within the rules and parameters of human happiness and human sorrow.[28]

Manik Bandopadhyay believes that even when the riots stop, 'the Hindu–Muslim problem will remain unsolved; the problem of Independence will remain. We will have to strive against both these problems'.[29] The aspects of social and economic revolution that national liberation promises is a constant preoccupation of writers of Bandopadhyay's generation, even when they are aware of the existing contradictions in social relations. Therefore, the novel makes clear that the postcolonial moment of freedom is self-contradictory: it is also a time of growing capitalism and opportunism. The riots

[27] *Swadhinatar Swad*, 300–301.
[28] *Swadhinatar Swad*, 304.
[29] *Swadhinatar Swad*, 310.

are the results of 'compromises and barters' between politicians and the government, 'a homely compromise with the English Emperor to get as much as possible'.[30] In this political climate, the domestic and the private spheres undergo massive transformations too. When Sushil laments that his family life is ruined because his children, under Monimala's guidance, want to join a political demonstration, the poet Gokul tells him:

> Why do you think it is only your family? Everyone's family is breaking up: the old kind of family. They are making way for a new kind of family. Don't lament the change.

Monimala too realizes that the world is expanding at an enormous pace:

> She is concerned about things that had never bothered her before—the Congress, the League, the Communist Party, freedom, the rich, the worker, the peasant and revolution. She is now so carried away by these that she sometimes forgets the children, whether they are alive or dead. She has no time to worry about them.[31]

Monimala's change parallels the changes in a nation that undergoes great social and political upheavals. Within the family, as well as in society, she has, like a thousand other women, 'studied till second class, after marriage ... surrendered to her husband's caresses, cooked and eaten, given birth, raised children' and whose entry to the 'world of light' is not at all easy.[32] Yet, the busy city, trying to recover after the War and the devastating famine, sets new paradigms for labour as women come out to work in factories and shops, unthinkable even a decade back. The partition of the country brings in unprecedented changes in the polity; not least are the changes that are fashioned in gender relations, in the questions of economics and politics. Bandopadhyay's critique of the national liberation/nationhood paradigm is made through the concept of freedom, *swadhinata*. Freedom on the personal level is qualified

[30]*Swadhinatar Swad,* 348.
[31]*Swadhinatar Swad,* 366.
[32]*Swadhinatar Swad,* 324.

by the meaning of freedom in the political and public levels. In this debate the Hindu Muslim question is explicitly implicated. Gokul says,

> The Congress and the League coming together is not the same as the unity of Hindus and Muslims [....] Even if the two unite it will be a union of upper class interests. Real unity is only possible amongst the poor and the downtrodden, amongst the ordinary people.

So the independence we are getting is 'adulterated' because it comes through compromises while keeping intact the status quo: the possibilities of power for the powerful remains unchallenged: 'The objective is to give us explicit freedom so that indirectly we can still be slaves.'[33] Therefore, the question remains 'if the foreign powers leave the country have we truly achieved freedom? Even when thousands of problems beset us through an artificial partition?'[34]

The narrative flow of *Swadhinatar Swad* is often impeded by discussions among the characters; so does the obligatory belief that the system can be changed (and secular idealism established) that is a part of the writer's commitment to Marxism. Yet, this is not just an ideological gesture on the writer's part. This difference between the artist's political optimism and the novel that is a site for the articulation of the anxieties of the age underlies a desire to understand the contours and meaning of freedom. This impulse creates a fragmented, uneven narrative different from the temporally linear structure of Bangla realist fiction. The novel focuses on the emergence of a socially attuned subjective consciousness in a way that is a part of the Progressive Writers Association (PWA) vision that endorsed realism in the arts to promote social change.[35] Yet Bandopadhyay's text brings in the

[33]*Swadhinatar Swad*, 364.

[34]*Swadhinatar Swad*, 383.

[35]Manik Bandopadhyay was closely associated with both the Progressive Writers Association (PWA) and the Indian People's Theatre Association (IPTA), with links to the Communist Party of India. Artists affiliated to them believed that the objective representation of reality would expose the underlying contradictions in social relations and pave the way for revolutionary change. Within the two organizations, there were broad differences regarding the nature of realism in the arts. Ritwik Ghatak, for example, used an epic and melodramatic mode of narration to portray the terrible ravages of the Partition in his three films namely *Meghe Dhaka Tara,*

public polemical debates in a way that underlines the novel's critical relationship to the new nation's secular credentials. The Marxist progressive ideology among Indian writers has seen the various manifestations of communal disturbances as economic conflicts. Manik Bandopadhyay's aesthetic-political praxis is more complicated with a larger range, as he tries to understand the sustained presence of religion within the progressive secular ethics of liberal modernity, whose manifestation is the sectarian politics of the Calcutta riots.[36] The country is divided into two: into *sthan* (place) and *stan* (as in Pakistan) that hide within it the appalling question: 'The terrible self-destruction through which the two sections are born, will this separation be the end or a beginning?'[37] To this last and dreadful question the answer seems to lie in the subcontinent's postcolonial reality.

III

One notable exception to the common accusation that Bangla writers of the 1940s were mute about the impending independence is Ashapurna Devi's novel *Mittirbari* (The House of the Mitras, 1947).[38] The novel is set in north Calcutta within a joint family that lives in a huge, sprawling building, driven by petty quarrels and heartaches. A symbol of the decadent middle-class life in undivided Bengal, the house is situated in a small street:

> that has quite a modern name. It had an older name, but recently, in anticipation of the independence of the country, some eager neighbourhood boys have rejected that old-fashioned name and renamed it after a certain popular leader to make sure that the India's freedom struggle was helped a few steps of the way.[39]

Komolgandhar and *Subarnarekha*. Manik Bandopadhyay's use of psychological and gendered realism is another mode.

[36] Sekhar Bandyopadhyay, *Decolonization in South Asia: Meanings of Freedom in post-independence West Bengal* (London: Routledge, 2009).

[37] *Swadhinatar Swad*, 387.

[38] Ashapurna Devi, *Mittirbari* reprinted in *Ashapurna Devir Rachona Shombhar* (Calcutta: G. Bharadwaj & Co., 1977), 229–364. [All translations from the novel are mine.]

[39] *Mittirbari*, 233.

The family home is spacious, yet its inmates do not live comfortably, and do not have space even to feel a sense of comfort. This house was once more than adequate for a family—but now after two generations, the space is insufficient for the requirements of so many members.

In the novel, the gradually emerging clash of old and new values is symptomatic of the new and changing times. The lives of the many inhabitants of Mittirbari revolve around an endless cycle of eating, sleeping, and quarrelling. In such a family, widowed Umashoshi drinks tea during her ritually mandated day of fasting. It is seen as a monstrous crime. But the novel represents much more than the clash of tradition and modernity. Set in 1946, when the Cabinet Mission is making headlines, the narrative revolves around how the Hindu joint family structure suffers an onslaught from historical forces that are sometimes incomprehensible to its members. Yet, that assault is an indication of a creative longing, for it sweeps away old superstitions, meaningless rituals and brings freshness and light to ruined selves. In so many ways, Ashapurna Devi's novel is a look at the times when momentous changes take place in the social, economic, and political life of West Bengal. All these changes reverberate in the private lives of the characters, caught up in the agonizing forces of history.

In the novel, both men and women encounter these changing times with bewilderment but sometimes also with strength. The joint family system clashes with a new individualistic sensibility: when the newly married Surekha decides to attend a political meeting with her husband Manoj, her transgression creates a family uproar and she is termed 'shameless'. Yet, the changes of the new age are too powerful to be ignored. In a violently rioting city, the very house of the Mitras, symbolic of an older tenor of life, is under attack by a mob. This brings unexpected saviours to do battle, people who show a reserve of strength and fortitude that nobody knew they possessed. Shudho, the wastrel of the family, who has all along spent his time flying kites and pigeons takes up bamboo staffs to guard the main door:

> Who knew he had so much in him? He took up two staffs in his hands and stood guard at the door. The long rods flew about like

> saucers, Borda and Mejda became busy trying to remove all the women to safety but Shudho said angrily, Nobody will go away. Why should women be different? God has given them arms and legs [...] bring out your knives and scissors, your *boti* and your pestle, and stand here.[40]

The belief that both men and women are equally to be the new citizens, marked by new responsibilities, makes the novel an exploration of the possibilities of freedom in the new nation state. Yet, this allegory of freedom is both incomplete and unfinished as far as the women of the novel are concerned. Ashapurna Devi's ironic depiction of domestic life in *Mittirbari* is not based on the large political upheavals of the 1940s but on their subtle effects on the lives of the characters: the riots are the outward manifestations of far deeper changes taking place in society. Postcolonial modernity blows away the cobwebs of tradition-bound lives and profoundly changes gender relations. Apart from Surekha, who is the new woman, other characters like the schoolteachers, Meena and Tatini, Aloka, the distressed housewife, and Hemlata, the matriarch, realize the churnings of their times. The new age is acknowledged in the way the women respond to some of its pressures: to the new sexual, political, and familial norms that seek to bind or enable them. The widowed daughter of the house, Umashoshi, who works in the household for food and shelter, also searches for the meaning of freedom.

> Did Umashoshi know the meaning of freedom? Yes, she knew it with certainty. It was the availability of food and clothes; when you spent money, that is, a reasonable sum of money, you would be able to buy things at the market. [...] Sugar would become easy to procure so she would be able to have a few stolen cups of tea without receiving humiliating insults from her elderly aunt.[41]

The advent of the coming independence of the country creates ripples in the social and economic fabric of society. Prices rise, rules change, as do the norms that govern relationships. Meena's love affair with the married Arunendu is a case in point. She is abandoned

[40]*Mittirbari*, 362.
[41]*Mittirbari*, 257.

by her lover and as she wanders through the burning city she thinks it has, over a few nights, 'changed into a dense jungle where no other living things exist but tigers and lions [...] Man existed though, he always would. Otherwise, who was capable of taking away the hungry fang marks from the body of the world?'[42]

Meena's quest brings her to Sagar who loves her and she requests him to give her some task that will bring succour to the riot victims. Her desire not to be a part of the idealized domestic role that society imposes on women however meets with failure and her fate in the novel remains ambiguous. This encounter, in the midst of the burning city, is symbolic of a failure to form closure and goes against the grain of the larger message in the novel. In the narrative rupture created by Meena's probing self-explorations, the novel brings about a new aesthetic of experience and affect. By foregrounding the individual female body, Ashapurna Devi examines how the traumas of the times are re-inscribed into their selves, both physical and psychic. Although the text looks at the momentous years of the Partition as a time of a new beginning and tries to give a final definition to what that may be, the novel is ultimately not prescriptive. Ashapurna's text recasts political reverberations as seismic changes in the social and familial life of the city; the times may be out of joint but they will bring in a new order, both in the world outside and within the family. Yet, this hope is also constantly negated and fragmented by the failure of the characters to achieve any kind of stability within or without, nor achieve any closure to their quest for self-independence.

The riots bring life in the city to a standstill; Calcutta is no longer recognizable. Hemlata, the matriarch of *Mittirbari*, while travelling back to the city, realizes the implications of what she sees:

> What is that on the main thoroughfares? Have thousand bolts of lightening struck the city? No, not from the sky—from the caverns of hell have come thousands of monsters! Mad, hungry from ages and aeons ago! It seemed a thousand-headed serpent was walking about, biting, spewing venom, and splitting the dry earth into pieces. Its poisoned breath was evident everywhere! In its black fumes,

[42]*Mittirbari*, 358.

> hungry monsters are taking birth, ready to devour everything. They will not be satisfied only with flesh and blood offerings but want much, much more. Their sharp claws and teeth will tear asunder all—civilization, beauty, self-control, society, family as well as tradition, family name, and culture. They will shake the very roots of human life to send us back to prehistoric times.
>
> There is another name for that—a communal riot. Did human hearts ever know love and trust? Or will these words disappear forever from the human dictionary? Will humans have different definitions, like the word 'mob'? The strange contorted dead bodies, piled here and there like fallen leaves, will soon disappear into dust or like flotsam and jetsam swirl away in a stream. The curious reader in the faraway future may glance back at this dark, primitive moment in time in silent wonder, speechless.[43]

The violence on the city streets has an important casualty: language and human discourse through which we know the world. The relationship of the dead 'like leaves' on the streets is reminiscent of the writings of another contemporary author, Sa'adat Hasan Manto who is constantly troubled by the limitations of language to memorialize the dead. But the spectre of death is not the final resting point. Surekha's father tells her after she has left her conservative in-laws that human society is marked by creative effort: 'Nothing is impossible to man. Men who built the pyramid were the same who destroyed Hiroshima and Nagasaki. The question is how are we to use force [...] you have to go back Surekha, to those who have hurt you, who constantly hurt themselves.... Because destruction has taken place, it has also opened the way for creation. We must realize the truth of that one day.'[44]

It is interesting to recollect that Ashapurna Devi once stated that her writings depict the small, private world of middle-class domesticity, and that she does not take cognizance of the turmoil outside the domestic sphere:

> I could not write (political/nationalistic novels) because I had little real experience. In our times we had to stay indoors. There was

[43]*Mittirbari,* 351.
[44]*Mittirbari,* 358.

little opportunity to go out, so with what little I heard, it was not possible (to write such novels).[45]

But in *Mittirbari,* she makes the personal enmesh with the political. In her short story *Mahagodyo* (The Prose Epic, 1951) the protagonist jokingly suggests to a young writer that the subject of his epic can be the great famine, food scarcity, and the independence struggle of the country, for 'where else would you find such a huge subject' for an epic?[46] The story, however, is an ironic one. The epic is never written and the young writer is unable to compose his magnum opus. This short story draws our attention to the problem that writers of Ashapurna's generation faced. How can one write of riots, death, and destitution of millions: in what language and using what form and style? Ashapurna Devi's irony and black humour, a relentless and clinical analysis of men and women's deepest fantasies, and a refusal to give clichéd formulations of our relation to the world outside make her an exceptional writer of her generation. She knew how World War II, the 1943 famine, and the approaching independence of the country had changed the Bengali middle-class family and its values irrevocably; the foundations of the joint family system had become vulnerable in those turbulent times.

The rise of the modern nuclear family in both novels sets the connection between the individual and society but with different novelistic functions. Bandopadhyay's novel creates a dialogic space where the riots are centre stage: to be discussed, dissected, understood, and repudiated for a vision of a new working-class unity in the postcolonial nation state. Ashapurna Devi's novel has a more circuitous scheme: the riots are evoked in as an aberration yet their effects are far-reaching. The violence of the riots is anticipated by another violence that lives at the heart of the Hindu joint family: a gendered violence that is the result of a deep-seated psychopathological patriarchy drunk on power. The riots are a

[45]Ashapurna Devi's interview in *Dainik Bosumoti*, 25 January 1983 quoted in Upasana Ghosh, *Ashapurna Devi* (Calcutta: Paschimbongo Bangla Academy, 2004), 24. [Translation mine]

[46]Ashapurna Devi, 'Mahagodyo' in *Golpo Shongroho*, vol. 3. (Calcutta: Mitra O Ghosh, 1995), 284–295. [Translation mine]

manifestation of this desire for power over the other: once this is recognized, the violence can be sublimated and channelized to constructive purposes. In *Mittirbari* there is a palpable absence: the riot is not present in its horrifying immediacy; rather it is an aporia, an absence that provokes us to ask questions about the world we live in and the ways we can represent it. This may be because the novel was written close on the heels of the last months of colonial rule and the trauma was too fresh to dwell on. *Swadhinatar Swad* was written after a few years and therefore, the necessary time had elapsed before the memory of the riots confronted and its teleology understood. However, both the texts launch important aesthetic mediations through the form of the novel to understand the aftermath of a traumatic cataclysm on our secret and public selves.

CHAPTER fifteen

Calcutta and its Struggle for Peace

Anti-Communal Resistance, 1946–47

Anwesha Roy

Starting with August 1946, India was introduced to something like a civil war, particularly in Bihar, Punjab and Bengal, the three worst affected provinces in this phase of violence. The year extending between 1946 and 1947 witnessed one of the most terrible communal holocausts in Calcutta. The Great Calcutta Killing, as it came to be known in both official and non-official circles, was the first in a chain of riots that shook the city and which peaked during the post-Partition riots in September 1947. Although the Great Calcutta Killing subsided in September 1946, for almost a year after that, communal passions smoldered in the city.

16 August 1946, had been chosen by the Muslim League as 'Direct Action Day'. It proposed to organize a citywide *hartal* to escalate the demand for Pakistan. For five days, till 20 August, the city reeled under the most horrific violence; gruesome murders, rapes, widespread arson and loot. It was not a spontaneous outburst but had been carefully planned by Hindu and Muslim politicians[1]. Communities started

[1]Both the Hindus and Muslims, with active support from the Bengal Muslim League, the Bengal Provincial Hindu Mahasabha and some sections of the Bengal Provincial Congress had made active preparations in stocking up arms like swords, daggers and *lathis*. Leaders of both the communities had made fiery speeches in different parts of Calcutta to ensure that the communal barometer remained high in the city.

migrating to 'safe zones' leading to a partition of the city; in a way, it was a precursor to the migrations post Partition. By 28 August, about 2322 Hindus and 1832 Muslims had been admitted to different hospitals all over the city. Hospital reports placed the death toll at about 151 Hindus and 138 Muslims; 11 Hindus and 12 Muslims were reported to have been brought in dead. In addition to this, there was an 'unclassified' category in the hospital reports, which stated that the number of 'brought in dead' was 174.[2] But this did not include the countless people who lay dead on the streets. *The Statesman* reported the death toll to be between 2000–3000. A memorandum by the Secretary of State for India on 11 November 1946, wrote: 'Riots of an unprecedented gravity occurred in Calcutta between 16 and 19 August. The proximate cause of the outbreak was the decision by the Muslim League Council to celebrate 16 August as Direct Action Day. The most recent estimate of casualties during the four days is given as roughly 4,000 dead and 10,000 injured'.[3]

While communal violence has been widely studied by historians,[4] one aspect that has been completely ignored is anti-communal resistance and peace processes that accompany violence. I am primarily concerned about peace initiatives in the city, both from common people and from popular organizations and political parties. I wish to see how the people of Calcutta responded to such peace efforts. Studying anti-communal resistance becomes extremely important when we try to analyse the extent of communalization in a particular place. Any attempt to understand communalism through the prism of violence alone leads to an incomplete understanding of its complex nature. Studying peace, on the other hand, enables us to understand the limits of communal politics. The relationship

[2]Government of Bengal, Home Department (Political), *Miscellaneous Reports on the Calcutta Disturbances*, August 1946, 6.

[3]Nicholas Mansergh and Penderel Moon (eds.) *The Transfer of Power 1942–47*, Volume IX: *The Fixing of a Time Limit, 4 November 1946–22 March 1947* (London: HMSO, 1980), 46.

[4]Among others, see, Joya Chatterji, *Bengal Divided: Hindu Communalism and Partition 1932–47* (Cambridge: Cambridge University Press, 1995), Rakesh Batabyal, *Communalism in Bengal: From Famine to Noakhali* (New Delhi: Sage Publications, 2005) and Suranjan Das, *Communal Riots In Bengal, 1905–1947* (New Delhi: Oxford University Press, 1991).

between communal violence and anti-communal resistance was very intricately wrought by the conflicting responses of the people of Calcutta to the peace measures during this phase.

I have divided the article into two sections. The first section explores the peace initiatives during and after the Great Calcutta Killing, August 1946. In the second section, I look at the work of Gandhi in Calcutta, when riots broke out soon after the partition of the province in September 1947. Gandhi also undertook his last but one fast in Calcutta at this time. I shall focus on the impact of his fast upon the people of Calcutta and see how the riot quickly waned as a result of the collective reaction of the city. Through the politics of the fast and the effect that it had on the communally charged people of Calcutta, I shall try to understand how the frail figure of an old man evoked the emotional response that it did amongst an intensely communalized city. I shall also comment on the limits of emotionalism.

I

The gruesome tale of violence and terror during the riot of August 1946, can be told in multiple ways, but amidst this darkness, there emerged instances of solidarity and friendship that transcended communal boundaries. Rescue and relief operations were carried on, with both government and non-government machineries working hard to restore peace and rescue victims. On 16 August, itself, local leaders of both communities met at Upper Circular Road in an attempt to form peace parties. On 20 August, a procession went out consisting of Hindus and Muslims with Congress and League flags fluttering together and shouting the slogan, '*Hindu-Muslim Ek Hauk*' (Let Hindus and Muslims be one). It started from Moulali and went towards Taltola in the morning and this had a reassuring effect on the people of the locality. Moulali and Taltola had been among the worst affected areas in central Calcutta.

Reports from the working-class belt indicated that hysterical frenzy had not invaded it; the jute belt from Hajinagar to Kakinara was quiet. Examples of people from both the communities who risked their own lives to save people from the other community were to be found in plenty. Manikuntala Sen recalls:

> Tobu sei ondhokarer dine kichu alor roshni jaliye rekhechilen communist Party'r kormira ebon besh kichu shonkhyak subuddhi sampanna Hindu Musalman parivar. (Still, in those dark times, some ray of hope came from the workers of the Communist Party and some Hindu and Muslim families who had retained their sense of sanity).[5]

She cites examples of such inter-communal friendship during the days of the riot; how several Communist Party of India (CPI) members and Muslim workers had been stranded in 'danger zones' in the city and Hindus in those areas, risking their own lives had moved them to safety: how it was impossible to travel in broad daylight, so several Muslim 'comrades' had helped Jolly Kaul and other CPI members to escape at night.

> There was no way in which we could have traveled through the usual roads. Therefore, with their help, we came back using a lot of by-lanes which ran through Muslim *bustees*.[6]

There were other examples of courageous fraternisation. The *Hindustan Standard* reported on 27 August 1946: In the dark clouds of Calcutta riots there is a silver lining of noble efforts made by members of both communities to bring order in the midst of chaos and assuage the feeling of infuriated mobs.[7]

The newspaper cites the example of Mr Durgadas Khanna, secretary of the Calcutta Bullion Association,

> who did yeoman's service in organizing peace moves in central Calcutta and received gun-shot wound s in trying to pacify an unruly mob on Friday night 16 August in Ripon college area.[8]

Mr Manick Mullick, the honorary magistrate of the city, who lived in Grey Street, gave shelter to six Muslims at the cost of

[5]Manikuntata Sen, *Sediner Katha* (Calcutta: Nabapatra Publication, 1982), 170–71. [Translation mine.]

[6]Ibid., 171.

[7]*Hindustan Standard*, 27 August 1946.

[8]Ibid., 4.

incurring the wrath of a Hindu mob.[9] A Gujarati Muslim leather businessman gave shelter to some Hindu CPI members, like Ajit Ray, Gita Mukherjee, and Annada Shankar Bhattacharya. He hid them in his house for three days, although, as Sen recalls, he was not a party member. Then there was also the case of Abdul Momin, a CPI activist, who had also given shelter to CPI members when they had to run away from their earlier hiding place. Abdul Momin and his wife risked their own lives to save Hindus and eventually had to leave their own home because local Muslims had begun to harass them.[10] Dr Ghani transported Hindus to safety in Ballygunge. His efforts served as an example to other Muslims in the Park Circus area, and they too began to shelter local Hindu families during the riot.[11] Manikuntala Sen writes in her memoir: 'It's easy to imagine the plight of the victims who were stranded. But, the way the rescuers suffered and risked their lives, is very difficult to understand.'

On 18 August, a Hindu gentleman at Dinabandhu Lane gave shelter to twenty of his Muslim employees, from where they were later moved by the police to the safety of Muslim majority localities like Zakaria Street.[12] At Garcha Road in Ballygunge, Hindus, Muslims, and Sikhs held a joint meeting and decided to guard the entire area to prevent the riotous mobs from entering it. On the 18 August when they realized that the Muslims in the locality could not be safely kept there anymore, they jointly evacuated the Muslims to 'safety zones'.[13] In Goabagan, in north Calcutta, an old Brahmin stood blocking the entrance to the lane that led to a small Muslim *bustee* in a predominantly Hindu locality. In the Baithak Khana area, about 300 Muslim *mochis* (cobblers) saved the lives

[9]Report of the Commissioner of Police on the Disturbances and the Action taken by the Calcutta Police between 16 and 20 August 1946 inclusive. M.K. Gandhi Papers, File No: 148 (Pyarelal Collection), Government of Bengal, Home Department, Political, Part 2, 2.

[10]Sen, *Sediner Katha*, 171.

[11]Ibid., 172–73.

[12]Report of the Commissioner of Police on the Disturbances and the Action taken by the Calcutta Police between 16 and 20 August 1946 inclusive, M.K. Gandhi Papers, File No: 148, Pyarelal Collection, Government of Bengal, Home Departmentt Political, Part 2, 34.

[13]*People's Age*, 1 September 1946.

of a group of Hindu tram workers from a riotous mob.[14] Professor Niren Roy openly sheltered a number of Muslim workers and himself stood guard until they were escorted to safety. Another professor, Dr Tarak Das of Calcutta University, heroically barred the way of a Hindu mob that was trying to loot the house of his colleague Dr Ahmed.[15] Surendra Mohan Ghose, president of the Bengal Provincial Congress Committee, when attacked by a Muslim mob on the 16th, was rescued by a Muslim, who not only drove away the miscreants but also escorted Mr Ghose to a place of safety.[16] There was another instance where a Hindu man had given shelter to his Muslim servant, and would not surrender him to the bloodthirsty Hindus who were threatening to take his life along with the servant's. Ultimately Mrs Lavanya Prabha Dutt, erstwhile Congress president, had to intervene and prevent the mob from killing the Hindu family and their Muslim servant.[17]

Rescue and relief operations were carried on by those undaunted by the riots and this included both governmental and non-governmental people and organizations. The number of relief centres that operated in the city once the riots began, shows that there was a substantial section of the population that had not yet given in to the madness, and still believed in the possibility of ordinary neighbourliness. Relief work often proved to be a daunting task, considering the steady increase in the number of victims and refugees, who had to be housed, fed, clothed, and then moved to safety. The *Hindustan Standard* claims that on 17 August, the Bengal Provincial Congress Committee, along with some Congress and Sikh workers took out an ambulance squad and visited affected areas in Machuabazar, Rajabazar and Harrison Road.[18] On 16 August, the secretary of the BPCC, along with the Muslim League High Command in Bengal and the Muslim mayor of Calcutta, proposed to take out a peace squad, which would move about in the disturbed areas and try to restore peace and

[14]Ibid.

[15]Ibid.

[16]Oral History Transcript, NMML, Surendra Mohan Ghose, 288–89.

[17]Ibid., 293.

[18]*Hindustan Standard*, 23 August 1946, 4.

order. The same afternoon, a peace squad comprising Mr Kalipada Mukherjee (secretary, Bengal Provincial Congress Committee), Syed Md. Usman (the mayor of Calcutta) and other Congress and League workers took out an improvised ambulance van, fitted with a microphone, and moved about in the disturbed areas trying to appeal to the local people to keep peace. On 20 and 21 August, even Mr Suhrawardy joined the peace convoy that toured some of the worst affected areas of the city.

The president of the All-India Trade Union Congress, Mr M.K. Bose, issued an appeal to the working class on 21 August, to try their utmost to stop the civil war that had broken out in Calcutta and applauded the workers for not participating in the riots.[19] The CPI campaigned extensively in the industrial belt around Calcutta and stressed the importance of maintaining peace, and of fighting against British imperialism which, they said, was the real enemy.[20] Jyoti Basu, Communist Labour MLA, announced that this would be done either with or without strikes depending on what the workers themselves democratically decided. The *People's Age* cites numerous examples of the heroism of workers and common men against the rioters. In certain areas of Ultadanga, which was an area otherwise very badly affected by the riot, festoons had been put up by workers, which read, 'Peaceful areas for Hindus and Muslims'. In Tittaghur, Hindu and Muslim workers brought out a joint peace procession and in Budge Budge, Hindu and Muslim workers held a public meeting and pledged to stand firm against riots.[21]

Several rescue centres came up in different parts of the city. The Bengal government reported 307 individual establishments in different parts of the city, and the total number of refugees cared for in these centres, according to government figures, was 189,015.[22] The Government of Bengal reported that the main problem was

[19]*Amrita Bazar Patrika*, 21 August 1946.

[20]*People's Age*, 25 August 1946.

[21]*People's Age*, 1 September 1946.

[22]Report of the Commissioner of Police on the Disturbances and the Action taken by the Calcutta Police between 16 and 20 August 1946 inclusive, M.K. Gandhi Papers, File No: 148, Pyarelal Collection, Government of Bengal, Home Department, Political, Part 2, 21.

the feeding and housing of the large numbers of refugees, that kept increasing at a steady pace, because of the large exchanges of population that took place within forty eight hours of the riot, as persons of one community left their homes for the safety of those zones where there was a preponderance of their own people. Amongst the earliest to function were the relief centres at St. Xavier's College, providing accommodation for 600, and Lady Brabourne College, which housed 2,500 refugees.[23] Another very important relief centre was opened at Ashutosh College which provided food and medical aid to the injured victims of the riot. Most of these centres did not distinguish between Hindu and Muslim victims and provided aid to both. Another First Aid Home was opened in Canning Hostel on 17 August, which admitted nearly 50 injured people, both Hindus and Muslims. The hostel later opened a shelter home, which accommodated women and children of both communities who had been brought over from Sealdah Station.

The Calcutta Emergency Relief Organization was set up by the Government of Bengal on 17 August, to deal with the problem of refugees who had accumulated in different parts of the city, particularly at the compound of the Calcutta police headquarters at Lalbazar.[24] The main government camp was the Destitutes' Home which had been operating since the Great Bengal Famine in 1943, at Bahir Sura Road. It had the capacity to house more than 2,000 refugees. Another had been opened at Hastings, and the accommodation was offered by the Turf Club. About 400 refugees from Lalbazar and Bhawanipur *thana* were moved to the Destitutes' Home on 17 August itself. The *Amrita Bazar Patrika* reported on 20 August 1946, that under instructions from the Government of Bengal, a rescue station was opened on the 19 August, by the military at the foot of the Ochterlony Monument at Maidan and that the main work of the station was to send relief parties where necessary to move Hindus from Muslim populated areas and vice versa.

[23]*People's Age*, 25 August 1946

[24]Report of the Commissioner of Police on the Disturbances and the Action taken by the Calcutta Police between 16 and 20 August 1946 inclusive' M.K. Gandhi Papers, file no: 148, Pyarelal Collection, Government of Bengal, Home Dept, Political-Part 2, 21.

The Indian National Ambulance Corps (INAC) also took in stranded people from different localities. A relief committee was opened by the *Sabuj Chakra* (a voluntary relief organization) from 20 August onwards, doing yeoman's work in rescuing people from affected areas. The Puddapukur Relief Centre operated in the Bhawanipur area, housing refugees and evacuees. The number of refugees admitted to this centre was between 3000–4000. In north Calcutta, a refugee camp was opened in Rani-Bhawani school near the junction of Vivekananda Road and Cornwallis Street, providing shelter to stranded refugees.[25] The Bharat Sevashram Sangha opened three relief centres at Rashbehari Avenue in south Calcutta, feeding and housing refugees (albeit only Hindu ones); arrangements were also made for rescuing people from affected areas. Two large relief centres accommodating Muslim refugees were opened at the League Headquarters in Zakaria Street and at the Islamia College Muslim Institute. The Indian Red Cross Society did valuable work in providing milk to the different relief organizations in the city. The National Red Cross Brigade of the Central Calcutta Seva Samiti, rendered first aid to victims, transported some to hospitals and also rescued stranded families from the various 'danger zones'.

The hospital situation began to worsen from the 17 August itself as the number of victims piled up at an alarming rate. Initially, the victims were taken to the Military College Hospitals and to the Presidency General Hospital, but soon these hospitals faced the need for more beds. Soon other hospitals like the Lake Hospital and the Indian Military Hospital began to function and the Civil Supply Department despatched rice, *atta*, *dal*, etc. to the hospitals to feed the inmates. Food supplies to hospitals were also maintained by the Red Cross; and it also opened two temporary hospitals to cope with the ever-increasing number of casualties. Emergency ambulance services were provided by the Red Cross, the Friend's Ambulance Service though some were also provided by the People's Relief Committee that had been opened by the CPI. The St John Ambulance Nursing Division supplied voluntary nurses to all the

[25]Ibid., Report of the Commissioner, 22.

hospitals. The London Missionary Society also supplied nurses on the first day of the disturbances.[26]

II

Vicious riots broke out in several parts of Bengal, especially in Calcutta and Noakhali from May onward and, according to some sources, this time the provocation came from the Hindus.[27] The Hindus felt that with the power of the League Ministry now broken, the police could no longer encourage Muslim *goondas*. The general feeling that prevailed was that the time had come for the Hindus to strike back and avenge the wrongs of Direct Action Day and Noakhali. Gandhi deferred his desire to go to Noakhali again following his earlier sojourn there in November 1946, because the deteriorating communal situation in Calcutta prompted him to spend some time in the city torn by communal strife. He toured Calcutta for nearly two hours and visited the worst areas. When he returned from his tour, Suhrawardy requested him not to leave for Noakhali but to stay in Calcutta and bring back peace to the city. Gandhi agreed but he laid down a condition: I would remain if you and I are prepared to live together [...] We shall have to work as long as every Hindu and Mussulman in Calcutta does not safely return to the place where he was before....[28]

This was a message that he had constantly harped upon when he was in Noakhali; he believed that true peace between Hindus and Muslims could not come about unless they lost their mutual fear and regained mutual trust. The ghettoisation of the city would only worsen the communal divide. He would personally set up a counter example of living with a Muslim who, only recently, had been a political opponent.

Suhrawardy finally agreed to this. The place that was selected for this new enterprise was a vacant Muslim residence at 150 Beliaghata Main Road, in a mixed locality. This and the surrounding areas of

[26]'Miscellaneous Reports on the Calcutta Disturbances, August 1946' M.K. Gandhi Papers (Pyarelal Collection), file number 148–Government of Bengal, Home Dept, Political-Part 4, 2

[27]Nirmal Kumar Bose, *My Days With Gandhi* (Calcutta: Nishana, 1953), 255.

[28]Ibid., 259.

Maniktala, Kankurgachi and Ultadanga had been most viciously affected by the riots. However, when Gandhi arrived here for his new 'enterprise', he met with immediate resistance. At the gate, a number of young men had gathered with black flags and some posters which said that Gandhi should go back and 'rather settle in a quarter like Kankurgachi or Ultadanga from where Hindus had been driven away, instead of coming here to look after Muslim interests'.[29] The angry crowd asked Gandhi why he had come; 'You did not come when we were in trouble. Now that the Muslims have complained, all this fuss is being made over it'.[30] Because of this resentment, Gandhi did not hold a prayer meeting that day. This allegation, that Gandhi had come to look after Muslim interests, was one that he had to encounter for some time during his stay in Calcutta. Cries of 'Gandhi Go Back' resounded in the air. Immediately after Gandhi went inside the house, stones were thrown through the window panes.

Day after day he met protestors, reasoning with them, giving them stern warnings. However, it was no easy task to placate the hate-ridden people. At another prayer meeting on 14 August, the crowd that had gathered there became unruly and demanded to meet Suhrawardy. They began to shout for his blood and stone throwing began again. It stopped only when Gandhi appeared in person in front of the violent crowd. Pyarelal recalls that 'Rapidly the tumult subsided. There was total silence'.[31] In Gandhi's presence, Suhrawardy confessed in front of the crowd that the Great Calcutta Killing had been his responsibility after all.[32] This was a momentous confession:

> This unequivocal, straight and candid confession of his guilt by one who had made arrogance and haughtiness his badge and never known humility, had a profound effect on the crowd.[33]

As at Noakhali, so with Suhrawardy, Gandhi could indeed, sometimes, change the hearts of men and women to produce

[29]Bose, *My Days*, 262.

[30]Pyarelal, *Mahatma Gandhi—The Last Phase Volume 2* (Navjivan Publishing House, 1958 365.

[31]Pyarelal, *Mahatma Gandhi*, 369.

[32]Ibid.

[33]Ibid.

repentance in place of hatred. Communal tension began to die down gradually; news began to arrive of a mixed gathering of Hindus and Muslims numbering about 5,000 that had come out on the streets crying for unity. Suhrawardy remarked that it was Gandhiji's presence in their midst that had worked this 'miracle' in a single day.[34]

On Independence Day 1947, men, women, and children gathered in front of Gandhi's house to seek his *darshan*. Members of the West Bengal Cabinet also came to seek his blessings. There were scenes of Hindu–Muslim fraternization throughout the city, 'It was as if after the black clouds of a year of madness, the sunshine of sanity and goodwill had suddenly broken through'.[35] On the same day, (it was also the day of Id) a number of Muslims gathered in front of the house to seek Gandhi's *darshan* and break their *Roza* (fast) only after that. A local newspaper reported: 'From early morning people began to pour in to Gandhiji's residence and as the day advanced their number swelled into a big crowd'.[36] Such constant emphasis on *darshan* highlights that he had attained a semi-divine status for the people of Calcutta. Gandhi came out of his residence, thanked the Muslims and later distributed fruits among his Muslim friends in celebration of the festival. Muslims also sent him many presents.[37] The prayer meeting that evening consisted of more than 30,000 people, all of whom had gathered for the *darshan*. However, Gandhi watched all this with some reservations. He had his doubts about this sudden wave of friendship and feared that this could be a short-lived phenomenon. He did not make any attempt to hide his apprehension and his face betrayed no signs of exuberance. In a letter to Rajkumari Amrit Kaur, Gandhi wrote: For the moment I am no enemy. Who knows how long this will last! Hindus and Muslims have become friends practically in a day. Suhrawardy has become transformed, *so it looks*.[38] (Emphasis mine)

On 18 August, Gandhi held a prayer meeting at the Maidan, ironically in the same area where the Muslim League meeting was

[34]Ibid.

[35]Ibid., 371.

[36]*Hindustan Standard*, 19 August 1947.

[37]Ibid.

[38]Pyarelal, *Mahatma Gandhi*, 372.

held on 16 August 1946. This meeting too was attended by lakhs of people from both communities. Long before the scheduled hour of the prayer meeting, thousands of people made their way to the Maidan, shouting slogans like '*Jai Hind*' and '*Hindu-Muslim ek ho*'.[39] In prayer meetings he congratulated the citizens of Calcutta for restoring peace. Calling the sudden example of friendship a 'delirious fraternization', Gandhi said that if this was permanent, then this 'noble example' of Calcutta would affect Punjab and other parts of India as well. Suhrawardy once again noted that 'by God's will and Mahatmaji's *kripa* (grace) what only three or four days before was considered an impossibility has miraculously turned into a fact'.[40] At night, when Gandhi and Suhrawardy toured the city, there were deafening cries of 'Mahatma Gandhi *Zindabad*' everywhere. Some sprinkled rose water (a sign of auspiciousness) on Gandhi. Even Suhrawardy, who only about a week ago, was considered to be an arch enemy of the Hindus, could now move about freely sitting next to Gandhi in a car. The festival of Id saw an unprecedented fraternization between members of the two communities. On their way back home from the mosque, Muslims exchanged greetings with the Hindus, sprinkled rose water on them and offered them *atar*. Sweets were sent to mosques by Hindus. Later, numerous processions composed of large numbers of Hindus and Muslims paraded the streets raising 'deafening shouts' of 'Hindus and Muslims unite'.[41] There were a number of such peace marches on subsequent days. On 26 August, there was a three-mile-long peace procession comprising members of both communities. Suhrawardy himself led the procession. When it crossed Gandhi's residence, he came out and acknowledged the cheers of the crowd. In this procession, members of the Muslim National Guard and the Hindustan National Guard marched side by side, proclaiming slogans of unity.[42] However, this victory was short-lived, as Gandhi himself had anticipated.

The situation in Calcutta suddenly took a turn for the worse when Gandhi was attacked at his Beliaghata residence. On 31

[39]*Hindustan Standard*, 19 August 1947.

[40]Pyarelal, *Mahatma Gandhi*, 371.

[41]*Hindustan Standard*, 19 August 1947.

[42]*Hindustan Standard*, 27 August 1947.

August, the night before Gandhi and Suhrawardy were to leave for Noakhali, at around 10:00 pm, a mob started demonstrating outside his residence. Window panes were smashed, some of them even entered the house and began destroying pieces of furniture and picture frames. The mob was well armed with hockey sticks, stones, and brickbats. Gandhi appeared at one of the doors and demanded the reason for such madness and even clasped his hands in a plea before the crowd. But it was of no use, the crowd wanted Suhrawardy. A brickbat, aimed at a Muslim in Gandhi's entourage, missed Gandhi only by inches. It was only when the police came in and used tear gas that the rowdy crowd dispersed, still chanting slogans. Gandhi's fears came true after all the scenes of fraternization that Calcutta had been witnessing.

Nirmal Kumar Bose recalls that 1 September, brought in more ominous portents. A report came to Gandhi that there had been an incident at Kanchrapara, 26 miles to the north of Calcutta, where there had been clashes over music in front of mosques and the police had been forced to open fire, killing several people. More news of anti-Muslim riots in central Calcutta began to reach Gandhi at Beliaghata. The *Hindustan Standard* reported on 2 September 1947: Calcutta's peace was disturbed by a regrettable flare up of communal trouble on Monday. Trouble suddenly broke out shortly after mid-day in the central part of the city. In course of the afternoon and evening, sporadic incidents occurred in different parts of the city.[43]

Night curfew, starting at 6:00 pm and ending at 6:00 am, was imposed in certain areas of the city, like, Barabazar, Jorasanko, Amherst Street, Beliaghata, Maniktala Bow Bazar and Taltola. These were some of the badly affected areas and potential tension zones during the riot. Once again the panic and the ghettoization that the city had witnessed during the Great Calcutta Killings resumed as people began migrating from one part of the city to another. Nirmal Kumar Bose recalls that, as the news of the fresh riots poured in, they felt nervous and one batch of them boarded a truck belonging

[43]*Hindustan Standard*, 2 September 1947.

to a Hindu merchant for being escorted to Rajabazar which is the nearest Muslim neighborhood'.[44]

An open truck with about thirty passengers went past Gandhi's residence and as soon as the truck crossed a nearby graveyard, hand grenades were hurled at it from the roof of a building which lay within the gate of the graveyard and two Muslims were instantly killed. Gandhi rushed to the spot as soon as possible. Nirmal Bose remarks, 'His face hardened'.[45] That was when Gandhi decided to go in for a fast unto death 'for the return of the sanity among the people of Calcutta'.[46]

Rajagopalachari argued with Gandhi against his decision to fast but Gandhi was adamant. He said that it was the responsibility of the government of both the countries to pursue their own course of action for the restoration of peace, but he had to fulfil his own sense of duty. He said that he had received urgent messages calling him to Punjab, and lamented,

> But now that the Calcutta bubble seems to have burst, with what face can I go to Punjab? The weapon which has hitherto proved infallible for me, is fasting ... it may touch the hearts of all the warring elements even in Punjab, if it does in Calcutta.[47]

He argued further that his duty lay in reaching out to each and every Hindu in Calcutta and make them realize that the attacks on their fellow Muslims were wrong. Given that it would not be physically possible for him to do so, Gandhi chose the other alternative, that of fasting. He started the fast on 1 September, and it lasted for three days. He called it off on the evening of 4 September, only when he felt that he had enough assurance from the residents of Calcutta that they would lay down their lives, if necessary, for the restoration of peace. Before breaking his fast, he laid down certain strict conditions in a document which was then signed by the leaders of different communities. He also, almost threateningly, added that

[44]Bose, *My Days*, 272.

[45]Ibid., 273.

[46]Ibid.

[47]*Hindustan Standard,* 2 September 1947.

if communal frenzy broke out in Calcutta again, he would go on an 'irrevocable' fast.[48]

Gandhi's fast soon had its desired effect upon the people of Calcutta. The government as well as the public were able to report to Gandhiji that not one incident had taken place during the last twenty-four hours. Group after group came to Gandhiji either with reports or with promises.[49]

They came to see him with the promise that they would do everything to quell the violence in the city and that unless he ended his fast, they would go on a sympathetic fast with him. Joint processions of Hindus and Muslims started in Beliaghata and elsewhere in the city. The processionists would often rush inside to have a *darshan* of the Mahatma in the hours of his fast. On one such occasion, a Muslim processionists visited Gandhi, and, weeping, asked for his forgiveness and said, 'Please give up your fast. We were with you in the Khilafat fight. I take the responsibility of seeing that no Muslim in this locality creates any disturbance'.[50]

Hindus too gave such assurances. Manubehn Gandhi, witnessing the scenes reflects, 'it was thus on the eve of the second day of the fast that the foundation of the hope for peace was laid by Hindus and Muslims by pledging themselves to Bapu'.[51] Gandhi's fasts had a similar effect even upon the *goonda* elements of the city. On the afternoon of 4 September, the third day of the fast, a party of thirty-five *goondas* came to visit Gandhi. They believed that forgiveness from the Mahatma in the hour of his fast would purge them of the sins that they had committed. The surrender of arms in front of Gandhi was obviously a huge symbolic action. On 5 September as well, several young men came to him and surrendered some country-made arms, guns, swords and cartridges, promising that they would never use them again. Gandhi looked at these arms with great interest and with a smile said, 'I see some of these for the first time in my life'.[52]

[48]*Hindustan Standard,* 6 September 1947.

[49]Bose, *My Days*, 279.

[50]Manubehn Gandhi, *The Miracle of Calcutta* (Ahmedabad: Navjivan Publishing House), 88.

[51]Ibid.

[52]*Hindustan Standard,* 6 September 1947.

Nirmal Kumar Bose recalls that those people in Calcutta, who had earlier looked upon Gandhi's peace attempts with suspicion, were now electrified by the fast. The fast, therefore, changed the meaning that violence had acquired in the city. From being seen as a necessary and meritorious action in defence of the community, it now came to be perceived as sinful—and, this too, among people who lived off criminality.

Dr Dinshaw Mehta, Gandhi's personal physician, issued a statement to *The Statesman* that acidosis would soon set in for Gandhi and due to his high blood pressure and advanced age, that would complicate his health to a great extent.[53] The governor of West Bengal issued a similar statement saying that 'The hours are steadily, and not too slowly, wearing Mahatma Gandhi away'.[54] The Governor pointed out that this time the people of Calcutta 'can throw the blame on no outsider or foreign government if his precious life ebbs away in Calcutta'.[55] These statements, publicized in newspapers, were meant to induce a sense of guilt among the rioting masses of Calcutta, so the daily press and medical information were harnessed to enhance the effects of the fast.

At the same time, it was for him that they lay down their arms, for him that they made promises to lay down their lives for the cause of communal unity, and not for the cause of non-violence itself. Therefore, the possibility of any form of 'new political community',[56] if it existed at all, lasted for a very brief period, as long as the person of Gandhi and his impending martyrdom stayed amidst them. The riots that soon broke out in East Bengal in 1950 bear testimony to this fact.

The idea that Gandhi's life was ebbing away in Calcutta while the city engaged in communal strife did introduce a strong sense of guilt, a guilt that the city found too heavy to harbour. It was a complex, almost entirely emotional response. Sumit Sarkar argues

[53]*The Statesman*, 4 September 1947.

[54]*The Statesman*, 3 September 1947.

[55]Ibid.

[56]The term has been taken from Gyan Pandey who states that the kind of bodily sacrifice that Gandhi made through his fasts was responsible for creating a new political community.

that although the fast was 'intensely moving and heroic', the Gandhian way in 1946–47, 'was no more than an isolated personal effort with a local and often rather short-lived impact'.[57] Therefore, in the long run, it failed to reverse the intensity of communalism, as his own assassination and the continuous rioting in Bengal and Delhi in the 50s proved.

It was therefore an ambivalent situation. There was an urge to interrupt violence so that Gandhi could live. Even those who did not subscribe to the politics of non-violence or secularism, found the idea that they would be held responsible for his death, unbearable. It was therefore a transient miracle. On the other hand, the steady trickle of local efforts at peace and friendship, of neighbourly gestures among ordinary people as well as a defined secular politics of anti-communal solidarity, especially among leftists and Gandhians, provided the really meaningful counterpoint and opened up the possibility of an alternative and enduring politics.

[57]Sumit Sarkar, *Modern India, 1885–1947* (London: Macmillan 2005), 438.

PART four

Postcolonial Transition

Calcutta people celebrating Independence Day, August 15, 1947. (*Courtesy:* Anandabazar Patrika)

Calcutta people celebrating Independence Day, August 15, 1947. (*Courtesy:* Anandabazar Patrika)

Refugees from East Pakistan crossing by railway tracks on foot on their way to West Bengal—1949 (*Courtesy:* Anandabazar Patrika)

CHAPTER sixteen

Calcutta, a City in Transition Expectations and Anxieties of Freedom, 1947–50[1]

Sekhar Bandyopadhyay

> Fred Burrows was in Government House, Calcutta, at the time of handing over British sovereignty. The parade to celebrate the taking over charge by the Indian Governor commenced in the grounds of Government House but the ceremonial was ruined by lorry loads of jute mill coolies who, quite peacefully, overran the parade ground and the grandstands and surged into Government House itself. Fred Burrows and his Lady left by a sweeper's staircase, a back door and a side gate. They got safely away to Dum Dum and were taken by air back to the place from which they had come.
>
> So ended the British Raj in Bengal....[2]
>
> [Sir Arthur Dash, Chairman of the Public Service Commission. September 1942 to August 1947]

INTRODUCTION

On 15 August 1947, Calcutta was in an extraordinary celebratory mood, which for obvious reasons looked like a conundrum to a colonial bureaucrat like Sir Arthur Dash. Over the last five years or so

[1]This essay discusses in a short space what I have discussed in greater details in my book, *Decolonization in South Asia: Meanings of Freedom in post-independence West Bengal, 1947–52* (London and New York: Routledge, 2009; Hyderabad: Orient BlackSwan, 2012).

[2]A.J.D. 'A Bengal Diary', 106. IOR: MSS.Eur/C188/6, British Library, London.

the city had gone through a series of calamities. It had withstood the devastating impacts of a famine, the worst of its kind in the history of British rule in India. It had weathered the unsettling psychological trauma of Japanese bombing. And finally, it was shocked by the unabashed blood-letting during the Great Calcutta Killings of August 1946—once again, the worst of its kind in the history of the metropolis. So August 15 came as a bit of good news, a ray of sunshine after long years of adversities and unheard of human tragedies. The exuberance of the new citizens of the city unsurprisingly knew no bounds.

In the early hours of the day the new governor, Chakrabarty Rajagopalachari, took oath of office, followed by Dr Prafulla Chandra Ghosh, the Congress prime minister,[3] and the other members of his first cabinet of the newly created province of West Bengal. This was followed by an official flag-hoisting ceremony at the Governor's House, where thousands of ordinary citizens congregated outside the locked gates. The locks soon gave in under peoples' pressure and the crowd rushed into the ground and then for the next two hours roamed inside the Governor's House, which was until previous day the most sacred space of the Raj. For the new citizens of Calcutta it was no longer the residence of the highest government official in the province. It was the relic of a past regime, which had now been relegated to history. So, as they often did while visiting historical monuments, when they finally left the building, they took away pieces of furniture and curtains as memorabilia. Elsewhere in the city throughout the day thousands of tricolour national flags and white cotton 'Gandhi caps' were sold on the pavements. In numerous functions people sang patriotic songs, gave inspiring speeches and celebrated the coming of freedom.[4]

Yet, amidst all these celebrations there were also touches of uncertainties and anxieties. There was a fear of the unknown, as the freedom that arrived was full of contradictions. Mahatma Gandhi was still camping in the city and did not participate in the celebrations. He spent the day in prayer and fasting as an act of penance for the recent communal violence and Partition. The Hindu Mahasabha on the right

[3]Heads of provincial governments were also called 'prime minister' until the promulgation of the new constitution on 26 January 1950. After that they were called 'chief minister'.

[4]*Anandabazar Patrika*, 17 August 1947; *The Statesman*, 18 August 1947.

and the Communist Party of India (CPI) on the left also boycotted the celebrations as a protest against Partition.[5] Its consequences were yet to unfold, but there was a sense of dissatisfaction as this freedom looked truncated. On the one hand, there was limitless optimism that everything that was wrong under British rule would be rectified in free India. But on the other there was the anxiety of responsibility; from now on there would be no foreign rule to blame if anything went wrong. And as days passed and the afterglow of celebrations faded, it became apparent that many things might indeed go wrong. For, the history of decolonization did not represent a sharp clinical break between the periods of unfreedom and freedom. It was, as Dipesh Chakrabarty has recently argued, 'a historical process that looks necessarily clumsy, complicated, and inherently incomplete (that is, fragmentary)'.[6] This essay will show some of these continuities, contradictions, and anxieties of the first few years of freedom, focusing closely on a metropolis that was no stranger to uncertainties. It will focus on the period between August 1947, when freedom arrived, and the early months of 1950, when the new constitution was promulgated, closely followed by the outbreak of communal riots in Calcutta for the first time since the days of Partition.

REALITIES OF FREEDOM

The first and foremost reality of the early days of freedom that hit the average citizens the hardest was the continuing food shortage, accompanied by spiralling general inflation. The food prices in Bengal had gone up since the outbreak of World War II, and the famine of 1943 showed that the British government had no credible food policy. The rationing system that was put in place in Calcutta in the wake of famine soon broke down because of lack of a proper procurement policy. The Congress government that took over power inherited this chaotic situation and did not have the time or

[5]For more on this see, T.Y. Tan and G. Kudaisya, *The Aftermath of Partition in South Asia (*London and New York: Routledge, 2000), 38–43.

[6]Dipesh Chakrabarty, 'Introduction', to *From the Colonial to the Postcolonial: India and Pakistan in Transition*, eds. D. Chakrabarty, R. Majumdar and A. Sartori (New Delhi: Oxford University Press, 2007), 3.

opportunity yet to evolve an alternative and workable food policy. The situation was further complicated by the anomalous geography of Partition. On 17 February 1948, in his first budget speech, Nalini Ranjan Sarkar, the West Bengal finance minister, reminded everyone that after the Partition, West Bengal had received most of the industries of the previous province, but much less of the arable land. This had adverse consequences for agricultural production in the province and the scarcity of food was partly caused by this imbalance. And the situation was made more precarious by a continuous influx of refugees.[7]

By September 1947, there was an unprecedented food crisis throughout India—it was particularly acute in West Bengal. In Calcutta and the surrounding industrial areas there was an almost complete breakdown of the rationing system, because procurement fell sharply due to the high black market price of rice.[8] By the end of December, food prices in Calcutta rose by 32 per cent in one year and were about 283 per cent higher than the 1941 prices.[9] As for general inflation, according to one report, there was an 86.8 per cent rise in average prices between June 1947 and June 1948.[10] An inquiry by the provincial labour department in 1948 revealed that the cost of living for the working classes in Calcutta and Howrah had risen three times over the 1938 prices, and food prices particularly rose four times and claimed 52.5 per cent of the working class family budget.[11] A central government report in August 1949 showed that 75 per cent of its employees in Calcutta with an income under Rs 500, were in debt, as against 40 per cent in Delhi, and were spending more than half of their family budget on food. If we remember that they were 'the most advantageously situated segment

[7]WBLAP, Vol. II, No. 1, 17 February 1948, 18–19.

[8]*Anandabazar Patrika*, 28 September 1947; 'Deputy High Commissioner [hereafter Dy HC] to High Commissioner [hereafter HC] for UK in India, Calcutta', 17 February 1948, India Office Records, British Library [hereafter IOR]: L/P&J/5/316.

[9]*The Statesman*, 31 December 1947.

[10]Acting Dy HC to HC for UK in India, Calcutta, 3 August 1948, IOR: L/P&J/5/317.

[11]Acting Dy HC to HC for UK in India, Calcutta, 15 June 1948, IOR: L/P&J/5/316.

of the middle class', having a stable source of income,[12] it will not be difficult to imagine the desperate conditions in which the less fortunate working classes lived in this beleaguered city. A Reserve Bank of India report showed that the price index further rose from 378.3 in June 1949 to a record 395.6 in June 1950.[13]

What everyone knew and no one did anything about, was that this scarcity and the high prices were to a large extent also due to rampant corruption. Charu Bhandari, the Food and Civil Supplies Minister made a fervent appeal to businessmen in December 1947, to refrain from corrupt practices and hoarding, as these things could not be tolerated after 15 August.[14] But this appeal for self-correction went largely unheeded. There was an artificial cloth scarcity in 1948, caused by black marketing and smuggling, but the city police commissioner expressed his inability to deal with the black marketeers and profiteers because of the lack of an appropriate law.[15] In 1949–50 adulterated mustard oil flooded the city, causing a widespread outbreak of the disease called dropsy, popularly known as beriberi; but the Calcutta Corporation health officer could not or did not do anything, because of the absence of an adequate legal tool.[16] The government tried to control the retail trade in sugar, and sugar disappeared from the market; so did salt in 1949. People stood in long queues, and in the end, in exasperation, looted shops. Some demonstrated in front of the chief minister's residence and received only volleys of teargas shells. Sometimes their anger was vented against Marwari families and their houses were attacked by irate crowds. But these sporadic incidents of violence were quickly and sternly handled by a police force and army[17] which the new state had inherited from its colonial predecessor.

[12]*Amrita Bazar Patrika,* 4 August 1949.

[13]*The Statesman*, 7 September 1950.

[14]West Bengal Legislative Assembly Proceedings [hereafter WBLAP], Vol. I, no. 1, 10 December 1947, 118.

[15]*Anandabazar Patrika*, 21 July, 27 August 1948.

[16]*Amrita Bazar Patrika, 3* July, 18 August 1949, 21 January 1950.

[17]*Amrita Bazar Patrika*, 7 October 1949; Dy HC to HC for UK in India, Calcutta, 21 October 1949; Fortnightly Report No. 2 for period ending 3 November 1949, IOR: L/P&J/5/320.

If this was not all, soon after Independence the city was visited by a cholera epidemic, while smallpox had already created a major public health scare. By the end of March 1948, Calcutta recorded a 68 per cent rise in the incidence of cholera. Between 3 January and 8 May 1948, 1,326 people died of cholera and 4,861 died of smallpox. Smallpox was contained, but did not disappear, while cholera continued for a much longer period.[18] It was only in August 1950, that cholera and smallpox were declared to be 'non-epidemic'.[19] But smallpox reappeared again in November 1950, affecting areas like Maniktolla and Kasipur, and the health officials once again considered declaring it an 'epidemic'.[20] To make matters worse, in April 1948, after an interval of nearly fifty years, an outbreak of plague was reported from parts of central and north Calcutta and five people died. [21] While it was contained temporarily, it reappeared again in the summer of 1949, and this time it was of a much more virulent pneumonic variety.[22] While plague in the end did not cause many casualties, and was finally contained, it certainly added to the psychological stress of the city residents, already reeling under various other kinds of social and physical pressures.

This disconcerting public health situation was not unexpected in a city where urban infrastructural facilities were bursting at the seams since the early 1940s. At the end of the decade, in West Bengal, 22 per cent of the population lived in towns, while for East Bengal the corresponding figure was only 4 per cent.[23] This urban crowding obviously put pressure on health, and the worst effects could be seen in Calcutta. According to available information, the supply of filtered water in the city had increased only by 10 per cent in ten

[18]*The Statesman*, 31 March 1948, 13 April 1948; *Amrita Bazar Patrika*, 5 January, 9 February 1949; Dy HC to HC for UK in India, Calcutta, 10 February 1948, IOR: L/P&J/5/316.

[19]Fortnightly Report No. 9 for the period ending 9 May 1950, IOR: L/P&J/5/320; *The Statesman*, 11 January, 30 August 1950.

[20]*The Statesman*, 11 November 1950.

[21]*The Statesman*, 17, 18, 19, 23, 29 April 1948; 2, 4, 12 May 1948.

[22]*The Statesman*, 2 June 1949; *Amrita Bazar Patrika*, 6 July 1949; Dy HC to HC for UK in India, Calcutta, 22 April 1949, IOR: L/P&J/5/320.

[23]West Bengal Legislative Assembly Proceedings [hereafter WBLAP], Vol. 3, No. 1, 19 February 1951, 185.

years since 1939, while the population had increased by more than 300 per cent—from about 1.2 million in 1931 to more than 4 million in 1944–45.[24] And this situation was made far worse by the massive influx of refugees in the wake of Partition. According to the statistics of the Relief Department of the Government of West Bengal, more than 1.2 million people had migrated to West Bengal from East Pakistan between August 1947 and April 1948, and about 66 per cent of them settled in Calcutta.[25] Given the lack of accommodation in the city, hundreds of them began to squat on the Sealdah station platforms. While describing the squalid conditions in which they lived, the reporter of the *Amrita Bazar Patrika* gave a rather sickening picture:

> How do these refugees spend their days and nights on the station platform? [...] Imagine ... a healthy baby eating and playing by the side of cholera patient. Imagine again sleeping in a place a few feet away from a room which is used by thousands as a latrine and which remains unwashed for days together. Imagine, again, cooking your food on the bricks with rubbish as fuel on the street along which pass hundreds of motor cars, lorries and other kinds of vehicles. This is how they spend their days.[26]

It was not surprising that cholera refused to leave Calcutta. We will discuss the plight of these refugees later, but it is worthwhile to mention here that this influx was an unending flow, and the numbers increased manifold after the Khulna riots of January 1950.

This urban crowding did not just put pressure on health, housing, and food prices, but most obviously worsened the employment situation. This was a time when, as the *Amrita Bazar Patrika* reported, the 'avenues of employment ... [were] shrinking every day, the number of unemployed ... [was] also growing daily'.[27] Particularly problematic, as Finance Minister Nalini Ranjan Sarkar conceded in the Assembly, was 'the extent of unemployment among the middle class educated youth'.[28] But no less important was the

[24]Dy HC to HC for UK in India, Calcutta, 18 February 1949, IOR: L/P&J/5/320.

[25]*The Statesman*, 6 June 1948.

[26]*Amrita Bazar Patrika*, 8 October 1948.

[27]*Amrita Bazar Patrika*, 8 July 1949.

[28]WBLAP, Vol. 3, No. 1, 19 February 1951, 185.

continuous retrenchment and rationalisation in the manufacturing sector. For example, in July 1949, the Indian Jute Mills Association decided to close the mills for one week in four, to cope with the shortage of raw jute (primarily produced in East Bengal—another anomalous consequence of Partition), causing retrenchment of some 575 permanent staff and reduced wages for all others.[29] In 1946 the number of factory workers employed in Bengal was higher than in Bombay; but by 1951 Maharashtra overtook West Bengal in numbers, and the situation was further rapidly reversed between 1951 and 1956.[30] Sarkar warned his countrymen that the problem of unemployment had its solution, but it could 'never be found in a day as if by the magician's wand'.[31] But what was more disconcerting was the fact that there were no reliable unemployment figures for this period, as the government did not have the proper machinery to know the 'exact statistics' about unemployment.[32] Nehru's First Five Year Plan was presented in the Parliament on 15 October 1951; its employment generating effects were still years away. So it was not surprising that the joys of freedom would soon disappear for the new citizens facing the hard realities of free India. Jubilation would give way to agitation and insurgency.

URBAN UNREST

Indeed, freedom did not have a good beginning in Calcutta, as the euphoria evaporated in less than two months. In late September 1947, an angry procession of hungry villagers from Howrah marched on the city's streets, demanding food from the minister of Civil Supplies.[33] Then on 21 November, when the West Bengal Legislative Assembly met for the first time after Independence, several thousand peasants, mobilized by the Kisan Sabha, peacefully

[29]Dy HC to HC for UK in India, Calcutta, 8 July 1949, IOR: L/P&J/5/320; for more on the problems of jute industry, see *The Statesman*, 8 March 1948, 19 February 1949.

[30]See A.Bagchi, 'Studies on the Economy of West Bengal', *Economic and Political Weekly*, XXXIII, Nos 47–48 (November/December 1998): 2975.

[31]*Amrita Bazar Patrika*, 8 July 1949.

[32]WBLAP, Vol. III, no. 1, 19 February 1951, 185.

[33]*The Statesman*, September 30 1947; *Anandabazar Patrika*, 1 October 1947.

marched towards the Assembly House to express their grievances. They were stopped near Curzon Park by the police using the conventional colonial tools of discipline, like *lathi* charge and tear gas. The Gandhian Congress prime minister of West Bengal, Dr P.C. Ghosh, announced in the Assembly that 'It ... [was] always distasteful for any popular Government to use force ... [But] Government must prevent disorder at all costs.'[34] Thus, a political action that would have been acclaimed as *satyagraha* a few months ago, came to be branded as 'disorder' by a national government, which did not know how to handle the problems it had inherited. And therefore, continuities in the modes of governance were truly remarkable in the face of growing urban unrest.

Apart from an increasing rate of crimes against property—or more precisely, armed robberies—in the middle-class areas of Calcutta,[35] in the urban industrial regions the most immediate result of the high prices, complicated further by retrenchment and unemployment, was the increasing industrial strife, which continued well into 1949. Almost every group of workers went into industrial action during this period. In 1947 there were 376 industrial disputes involving 412,432 workers causing the loss of 5,884,742 man-days. This came down to 197 disputes involving 220,862 workers and a loss of 2,319,782 man-days in 1948. But this statistical decline was caused by the loss to East Pakistan of about 6 per cent of the employed labour force of undivided Bengal. So the industrial situation remained on the whole critical and the worst affected were the jute mills, followed by the engineering sector, tea plantations and the cotton industry.[36] And this situation continued well into 1949.

Particularly hard-hit by this industrial strife were the European owned concerns, like the Imperial Chemical Industry, Britannia Engineering, Jessop & Co., Martin Burn, Lipton, Jenson & Nicholson and others. Apart from that, teachers, bank employees, government employees struck work for better pay and working

[34]WBLAP, Vol. I, no. 1, 21 November 1947, 3; 25 November 1947, 14–17.

[35]Dy HC to HC for UK in India, Calcutta 13 January 1948, IOR: L/P&J/5/316

[36]Government of West Bengal, Labour Dept., *Report on the Activities of the Labour Department, Government of West Bengal,* Vol. II (May-December 1948), (Alipore: Superintendent of Bengal Government Press, 1950) 24, 26, 65.

conditions. Without going into details, we may highlight here some important features of the industrial unrest of this period. One new feature was that in a number of cases, European engineers and supervisors became targets of physical assault.[37] There was a widely shared expectation that after Independence these European officers would leave and their jobs would go to local Bengalis. But when that did not happen, these officers became targets of abuse and attacks,[38] the worst case being the attack organised by the Revolutionary Communist Party of India on Jessop & Co. in February 1949, where three foreign nationals were thrown into the blazing furnace.[39] The European body no longer seemed inviolable, a sentiment which could be seen in other spheres of life as well. As the British deputy high commissioner reported from Calcutta, for the first time in 1948 European and Anglo-Indian ladies became targets for throwing coloured water during *holi*, something that had never happened during the days of the Raj.[40]

The workers interpreted their newly acquired freedom in myriad ways. Often this involved a refusal to accept the employers' 'inherent right of retrenching workers',[41] even when there were claims of reasonable financial grounds for such action. For example, when the Grand Hotel in Calcutta fired some of its table serving staff because of it being 'off-season', there was an instant strike by the kitchen staff, which continued until their colleagues were reinstated.[42] But workers were not so lucky all the time, as some of the employers took

[37]Dy HC to HC for UK in India, Calcutta, 8 April 1949; Dy HC to HC for UK in India, Calcutta, 22 April 1949, IOR: L/P&J/5/320; also see from Commissioner, Burdwan division to District Magistrate, Burdwan, 8 June 1949, Government of Bengal [hereafter GB] IB Records, Serial No. 9/1926, File No. 35/26, Part XI, West Bengal State Archives [hereafter WBSA].

[38]Weekly Report No. 4 for week ending 27 January 1949, IOR: L/P&J/5/320.

[39]Saroj Chakrabarty, *With Dr. B.C. Roy and other Chief Ministers* (Calcutta: Benson's, 1974),115; for details of this incident see, *Amrita Bazar Patrika*, 27, 28 February 1949.

[40]Acting Dy HC to HC for UK in India, Calcutta, 30 March 1948, IOR: L/P&J/5/316.

[41]Government of West Bengal, Labour Dept., *Report on the Activities of the Labour Department, Government of West Bengal*, 2.

[42]Acting Dy HC to HC for UK in India, Calcutta, 25 May 1948, IOR: L/P&J/5/316.

draconian measures, with the support of the government and the protection of the police. For example, in November 1948, when the union failed to implement an agreement, the Lloyds Bank dismissed 550 of its total staff of 650 and recruited new ones, with the full protection of the police.[43] As a result of such overt official support for the employers, there was a lot of anger against the government as well, which now appeared to be the new enemy of the workers' rights. This became more than apparent when in April 1948, the central government employees went on strike in Calcutta against the advice of Nehru. One of the posters displayed during the strike said:

> We have had enough of bullying and threats from Imperialist rulers. It was from Panditji that we learnt how to react to it. Panditji may change but his lessons are still clear and inspiring. We will rise a thousand times stronger against your threats Panditji! Till you meet our legitimate demands and let us live honourably in free India.[44]

The workers, it seems, had extended the meaning of freedom from a nationalist preoccupation with sovereignty to a concern for subjective freedom—'to live honourably in free India'—and in a remarkable role reversal, the Congress appeared to be the main enemy of their freedom. The city of Calcutta became witness to numerous expressions of such ideas of liberation.

Within such an environment of disquiet, the CPI held its Second Congress in Calcutta between 28 February and 6 March 1948, where it adopted its 'Political Thesis', which argued that the establishment of a national government on 15 August 1947, did 'not mean that the Indian people have won either freedom or independence, nor does it ensure that they will be moving in the direction of democracy and freedom for the people'.[45] '*Ye azadi jhuthi hai*' ['This freedom is fake'] became their new slogan. And to ensure real freedom the party decided to follow what popularly came to be known as the B.T. Randive line (after the name of its main protagonist), or the path

[43]Dy HC to HC for UK in India, Calcutta, 5 November 1948, IOR: L/P&J/5/317.

[44]Acting Dy HC to HC for UK in India, Calcutta, 6 April 1948, IOR: L/P&J/5/316.

[45]*Documents of the Communist Movement in India,* Vol. V (Calcutta: National Book Agency Ltd., 1997), 600–601.

of promoting in India a 'People's Democratic Revolution'. Within the specific political context of India, its aim was

> to bring about those fundamental changes in our political and social structure without which there can be no freedom and no prosperity for our people. The present state ... [would] be replaced by a people's democratic republic—a republic of workers, peasants and oppressed middle classes.[46]

In real terms what it meant for Calcutta was the mobilization of students and industrial workers and regular organized attacks on various representations of the state, the major targets being the police and the public transport system, which seriously disrupted public life. For example, on 21 January 1949, the leading Calcutta daily *Amrita Bazar Patrika* described the situation in the central College Street area in the following words:

> Troops and armed police guarded the university area, the scene of last two days' trouble. Four truckloads of Gurkha troops under the command of a captain and two armoured cars with mounted machine guns patrolled the university area from 2 in the afternoon. Troops also were posted on the roofs of Presidency College and other high buildings commanding the view of every lane and by-lane to guard against any behind-the-scene attack.

This description matches the scene of a battleground that will remind many readers of College Street in the early 1970s. This particular series of events had started on 13 January 1949, when Prime Minister Nehru visited Calcutta and there were attempts to disrupt the visit. It finally stopped by 23 January, and in four days of trouble, bombs were thrown at 15 places and the Tramways Company lost 19 cars.[47] Such student unrest often converged with violent industrial actions, such as at Lipton and Bengal Potteries, refugee agitations and trade union demonstrations. The newspapers of this period are full of reports of such incidents occurring at regular intervals, and across the length and breadth of the city.

[46]Ibid., 643.

[47]*Amrita Bazar Patrika*, 22, 23 January 1949.

The Congress government having no experience in dealing with civil unrest continued with repressive measures borrowed from the late colonial masters. The worst incident of high-handedness was that of 27 April 1949, when the police opened fire on a Communist procession in Calcutta, killing seven people, including five women volunteers.[48] Calcutta hereafter burst into flames, recording 57 violent incidents—described in Police Intelligence Reports as 'C.P.I. outrages'—between 1 May and 31 December 1949—that is, on an average, more than six incidents every month or more than one every week.[49] The worst incidents of this type took place on 24 and 25 December 1949. On the 24 December, following a meeting at the foot of the Monument, a procession organized by the Bengal Provincial Trade Union Congress (BPTUC) and the Bengal Provincial Students Federation marched towards the western side of the Presidency Jail and began to shout slogans. They were joined in the shouting by the political prisoners inside the jail. As the police intervened and asked them to disperse, bombs were hurled at the police party. A *lathi* charge followed, tear gas was used, and this was countered by a state-owned bus being set on fire. The following day, volunteers of the same organizations, and also the Civil Liberties Committee, congregated at Park Circus. Following the meeting the attending police party was attacked with bombs and brickbats, street lights were switched off and barricades of dustbins were placed on roads. A state-owned bus and five tram cars were set on fire; several policemen were injured in the process. Again on 31 December, following a meeting of the BPTUC near the Monument, a procession was taken out, bombs were thrown at the police party, three buses were attacked, barricades were laid on the streets and crackers were thrown at a police picket injuring several policemen. One bus was burned and a police wireless van was damaged. A few days later on 7 January 1950, the BPTUC organized a meeting at the Maidan. Again, the police force on duty was attacked with brickbats and bombs; one state-owned bus and a tramcar were set on fire; the police had to use tear gas to disperse

[48] *Anandabazar Patrika*, 28 April 1949.

[49] Details in GB IB Records, Serial No. 206/1928, File No. 32/28 (1949) K.W.folder, WBSA.

the unruly mob.[50] And then, a few weeks later, the city and the adjoining industrial areas of Howrah were once again engulfed by the outbreak of a major communal riot.

RIOT AND REFUGEES

A major feature of the celebrations marking the arrival of freedom on 15 August 1947, was the disappearance of communal tension that had plagued the city of Calcutta, as well as adjacent industrial areas of Howrah, for the last few months, compelling Gandhi to come to Calcutta. On the first day of Independence, almost like magic, all tension disappeared. In the city suburbs where communal violence had been endemic over the past year, Muslims and Hindus with small national flags stuck on their clothes came out on the streets from midnight and began to embrace each other with slogans like *Bande mataram* ['Hail mother'] *Jai Hind, Hindu–Muslim ek ho'*['Hindus and Muslims unite'] and *Allah ho Akbar'* chanted in the same breath.[51] In a letter to the editor in *The Statesman*, a Muslim citizen of Calcutta wrote: 'That night in Calcutta we ceased to be Hindus and Muslims, we became Indians.'[52]

In Calcutta, there was not a single incident of communal violence during the whole period between 15 and 30 August, and there were scenes of celebrations where the Hindus and Muslims participated and hugged each other, with national flags in their hands. There was a massive peace procession on 26 August, in which thousands of Hindus and Muslims participated, shouting slogans like *Hindu–Muslim zindabad*.[53] The Muslims of Upper Chitpore Road donated Rs 1001 to Gandhi for the repairing of Hindu temples damaged in the riots of August 1946.[54] This new public mood of reconciliation pleased Gandhi and in his post-prayer speech on 15 August, he expressed his hope that the example of Calcutta would show the

[50]Details in GB, IB Records, S. No. 206/1928, F. No. 32/28 (1949) K.W. folder, WBSA.

[51]*The Statesman*, 15 August 1947; *Anandabazar Patrika*, August 1947.

[52]*The Statesman*, 28 August 1947.

[53]*The Statesman*, 27 August 1947.

[54]*The Statesman*, 1 September 1947.

way to the rest of India.[55] In another speech at a civic reception on 24 August, at Calcutta Maidan, attended by about 200,000 people, he described the situation as an act of God.[56]

But this outburst of goodwill was temporary, as troubles broke out again on the night of 31 August-1 September. Whether or not it was in response to the announcement of the decision of the Boundary Commission on 17 August, it is difficult to ascertain, as the Hindus had a lot of resentment against the award.[57] The outbreak of violence forced Gandhi to fast from 1 September, this time with H.S. Suhrawardy, the man widely believed to be the spirit behind the riots of 1946, by his side. The riots stopped soon, as there were all-out efforts to restore peace—including a two-mile-long students' peace procession in Calcutta on 3 September.[58] Gandhi broke his fast with a glass of fruit juice from the hands of Suhrawardy in an overt gesture of reconciliation.[59] Five leaders of Bengal—two Bengali Hindus, one Bengali Muslim, one Punjabi Hindu and a Sikh—in a ceremonial pledge assured the Mahatma that they 'shall never again allow communal strife in the city and shall strive unto death to prevent it'.[60] At a giant meeting of Hindus and Muslims of Calcutta on 7 September, Gandhi appealed for peace in Bengal and announced his decision to leave for Punjab. If Calcutta remained peaceful, the rest of the country would follow her example, so Gandhi expressed his optimism in his departing message.[61]

But this optimism was misplaced; freedom's magic touch was temporary and Partition had not resolved the issue of Hindu–Muslim

[55]*The Statesman,* 16 August 1947.

[56]*The Statesman*, 25 August 1947.

[57]For a discussion on the Boundary Commission Award, see, J.Chatterji, *The Spoils of Partition: Bengal and India, 1947–1967* (Cambridge: Cambridge University Press, 2007), Chapter 1. In this riot 291 people were killed and 292 were injured. See Chakrabarty, *With Dr. B.C. Roy*, 59–60.

[58]*The Statesman*, 4 September 1947.

[59]*Anandabazar Patrika*, 7 September 1947.

[60]These five leaders were, N.C.Chatterjee, the president of Bengal Provincial Hindu Mahasabha, Debendra Nath Mukherjee, secretary, Hindu Mahasabha, H.S. Suhrawardy, ex-premier of Bengal, R.K. Jaidka, a Punjabi businessman and Sardar Niranjan Singh Talib, the editor of *Desh Darpan*, a Sikh daily. See, *The Statesman*, 5 September 1947.

[61]*Anandabazar Patrika*, 8 September 1947; *The Statesman*, 7 September 1947.

relations in this province, nor could it define with any amount of certitude the place of the minorities within the new nation state. Indeed, the fates of the minorities in two Bengals—the Hindus in East Pakistan and the Muslims in West Bengal—remained closely intertwined, and their mutual vulnerabilities became apparent in the course of what happened in 1950. It all started from an anti-communist operation by Pakistani police in the village of Kalshira in the district of Khulna in East Bengal. On 20 December 1949, the police came to the village in search of Communist suspects and were actively resisted by the villagers. A policeman was beaten up and killed by Namasudra villagers, inviting a massive reprisal the following day by the police and the Ansars. As anti-Hindu violence began to spread, the Hindu villagers began to flee and came over to Bongaon across the border, and from there by train arrived at Sealdah station in Calcutta.[62] By 10 February, there were 13,000 refugees at the Sealdah station, recapitulating horror stories of their suffering and privation for an incensed Calcutta press and an irate Hindu public.[63]

The emotions soon boiled over, as full-scale anti-Muslim riots started from 8 February, engulfing large parts of north and central Calcutta after a gap of nearly two years. It soon spread to the industrial areas of Howrah. In all these areas, Muslims were attacked, their slums torched, shops looted, and the trains raided for Muslim passengers. In some instances, the violence that was perpetrated was reminiscent of the Partition violence in Punjab. This was despite the fact that the state had moved quickly, imposing curfew and bringing in the army for patrolling duties. This saved lives, but properties were rampantly destroyed as there was also allegation of complicity of the security forces in the riots. The news of the outbreak of riots in Calcutta soon led to even more serious attacks on the Hindu minorities in large parts of East Pakistan. Within a few days the violence spread to districts like Rajshahi, Noakhali, Chittagong, Faridpur, Khulna, Sylhet, Mymensingh, and then finally to Barisal where it was at

[62]*Amrita Bazar Patrika*, 5 February 1950.

[63]*Amrita Bazar Patrika*, 11 February 1950.

its worst.[64] So in March there was a second wave of violence in Calcutta and Howrah, and this time it also affected the border districts of Hooghly, Nadia and Murshidabad, initiating a large-scale Muslim exodus.

Unable to trust the state machinery, the Muslims first relied on their community for protection, and fled to what they considered to be safe Muslim majority areas in Calcutta, like Park Circus or Khidirpur.[65] And then, when even those enclaves seemed insecure, many of them fled to Pakistan—both by air and land routes. By the beginning of 1951 about 700,000 Muslims had fled to East Pakistan.[66] Of course, many of them were from the border districts, but for Calcutta too the effects of this exodus was significant. Many jute mills and other factories in and around the city, which employed predominantly Muslim workers, had to be closed down because of this exodus.[67] There were loud demands from many quarters in the city for an exchange of population,[68] for the Hindu migration from East Pakistan was of even more alarming proportions. By the beginning of 1951, following the disturbances in Khulna, about 1.5 million Hindu refugees had arrived in West Bengal.[69] And many of them, if not all, were arriving through Sealdah station, adding to a further straining of nerves of a city that was already overwhelmed with many adversities.

[64]Sukumar Biswas and Hiroshi Sato, *Religion and Politics in Bangladesh and West Bengal, A Study of Communal Relations*, Joint Research Programme Series No. 99 (Tokyo: Institute of Developing Economics, 1993), 34–41.

[65]Details in Bandyopadhyay, *Decolonization in South Asia*, Chapter 2.

[66]J. Chatterji, 'Of Graveyards and Ghettos: Muslims in Partitioned West Bengal 1947–67', in *Living Together Separately: Cultural India in History and Politics*, eds. Mushirul Hasan and Asim Roy (New Delhi: Oxford University Press, 2005), 228–229.

[67]Supplement to FR No. 4 for period ending 23 February 1950; FR No. 6 for period ending 23 March 1950, IOR: L/P&J/5/320

[68]The Hindu Mahasabha made this demand, while Prime Minister Nehru scornfully rejected it. See 'Statement made by the Hon'ble the Prime Minister in Parliament on February 23, 1950, regarding recent events in East and West Bengal', S.P. Mukherji Papers, II–IV Instalment, File No. 160, Nehru Memorial Museum and Library [hereafter NMML]. Also see, *Amrita Bazar Patrika*, 24 February 1950.

[69]Chatterji, *The Spoils of Partition*, 112, Table 3.1.

It has already been mentioned that the refugee influx was a continuous flow since August 1947. By September 1950, according to the figures provided by the government, about 4 million refugees had come to West Bengal, of whom the government claimed to have rehabilitated just over 1.1 million at the cost of 60 million rupees.[70] This meant that an overwhelming number of refugees were still waiting to be properly rehabilitated. The majority of those who came before the riots of 1950 were middle-class professionals, and they looked for jobs in the city, while the government, hard pressed for accommodation, wanted to relocate them to the districts. The government opened relief camps—389 of them—in various districts to relieve the pressure on Calcutta. There were attempts to rehabilitate some of them in the neighbouring provinces of Assam, Bihar and Orissa.[71] There was also a modest plan to ship them off to the Andaman Islands. But none of these plans really worked.[72] The refugees flocked to Calcutta, where they expected better job opportunities and prospects of rehabilitation, but faced an acute shortage of accommodation.[73] In such a situation, a desperate group of about 500 families in June 1948, 'took over' the vacant army huts in the Dhakuria Lake area in south Calcutta;[74] a few days later another 80 families took possession of the Ballygunge military camp area.[75] This establishment of 'squatter colonies' soon became an organized campaign in early 1948, conducted often with the tacit approval of the government; but it also contained the seeds of conflict with the wealthy land speculators who had a vested

[70]WBLAP, Vol. II, 25 September 1950, 3–4. However, the opposition called the government claim of rehabilitating 1.1 million refugees a 'bluff'. *The Statesman*, 27 September 1950.

[71]S. Das, 'State response to the refugee crisis: relief and rehabilitation in the east', in *Refugees and the state: practices of asylum and care in India, 1947–2000*, ed. R.Samaddar (New Delhi, Thousand Oaks and London: Sage Publications, 2003), 106–51, especially, 112–13. Also see G. Kudaisya, 'The Demographic Upheaval of Partition: Refugees and Agricultural Resettlement in India, 1947–67', *South Asia*, XVIII (1995): 89–91.

[72]*The Statesman*, 17 April 26 October 1948; also see Chatterji, *The Spoils of Partition*, 133.

[73]*The Statesman*, 6 March 1949.

[74]*The Statesman*, 22 June 1948.

[75]*The Statesman*, 29 July 1948.

interest in the development and expansion of the city. From early 1949 establishment of squatter colonies was actively sponsored by the newly founded Nikhil Vanga Bastuhara Karma Parishad [All Bengal Refugee Council of Action].[76]

There is no space here to discuss in detail the government refugee rehabilitation policy, which came under fire from many quarters. After the fresh influx of 1950 the central policy was not for their rehabilitation, but repatriation, as Nehru sincerely believed that these refugees would go back if the security situation improved in East Pakistan. For this purpose he signed with Liaquat Ali Khan the Delhi Pact on Minorities on 8 April 1950. Under the provisions of the Pact refugees were to be encouraged to go back to their respective homes, and on their return their properties were to be restored.[77] It was this idea of reverse migration which made the Delhi Pact hugely unpopular in West Bengal and the Hindu Mahasabha decided to start a campaign against it.[78] Agitations against these policies, henceforth, became regular features of Calcutta's embattled public life, complicated further by the announcement in the mid-1950s of the Dandakaranya plan to rehabilitate these refugees in central India; but that discussion remains outside the scope of this paper.

CALCUTTA'S POLITICS

The Congress government that took oath of office on 15 August 1947, now became the main target of public criticism for all that went wrong in the early days of freedom. And faced with civil unrest from almost day one of its rule, it chose to follow the familiar tools of coercion to discipline the uncomfortable dissenting voices. In November 1947, in a notification it banned all 'sit-in' strikes or *satyagraha*. And then in December it introduced what became notorious as the West Bengal Security Bill, proposing detention without trial for up to six months. It actually intended to legitimise an ordinance issued by the previous Muslim League government,

[76]Squatter colonies came up in various parts of south Calcutta, like Jadavpur, Bejoygarh, Jodhpur military barracks, unoccupied lands in Sahapur, Durgapur, and Dharmatala. See for details Chakrabarti, *The Marginal Men*, 33–37, 64–66.

[77]*The Statesman*, 2 August 1950.

[78]*Amrita Bazar Patrika*, 27 April 1950.

under which between June and December 1947, 1,486 people had already been arrested.[79] The Legislative Assembly proceedings of this period make for interesting reading, as the Gandhian chief minister, P.C. Ghosh, introduced and defended the bill and a Communist, Jyoti Basu, opposed it clause by clause. When Basu reminded the chief minister that the bill went against 'the proclaimed policy of the Congress for last 40 years', the latter's cryptic reply was that the point was 'irrelevant here'.[80] Congress's time to rule had arrived.

Outside the Assembly, the main opposition to the bill came from Sarat Bose, who had lately resigned from Congress and formed his own Socialist Republican Party. In a number of public meetings he promised to fight to end this threat to civil liberties, which he argued was a device to muffle all critical voices against the Congress government.[81] There were violent student protests against the bill in front of the Assembly on 8 December, and then again on the 10 December, when police opened fire, killing one person and injuring 30 others.[82] On 11 December, in view of the mounting public protest, the Assembly was adjourned till early January. In the meanwhile, the Congress launched a vigorous campaign to generate public support for the bill. Nehru in a press conference at the Governor House in Calcutta on 17 December, and Sardar Patel at a mass rally at Calcutta Maidan on 3 January, lent their support to the bill, arguing that this one was in fact much milder than the ones proposed in other provinces. Then on 17 December, Suresh Banerjee, the deputy leader of the Congress in West Bengal, claimed in a public meeting that Gandhi had given his blessings to the bill.[83] It is difficult to verify the truth of this claim; but if it was true, then Gandhi must have changed significantly since the days of the Rowlatt *satyagraha*! This is what Sarat Bose reminded his audience at a public meeting at Desbandhu Park on 20 December.[84] Yet, in spite of all this opposition, the bill was passed on 15 January 1948, with the only concession to the

[79]Dy HC to HC for UK in India, Calcutta, 30 December 1947, IOR: L/P&J/5/315.
[80]WBLAP, Vol. 1, 8 December 1947, 69.
[81]*Anandabazar Patrika,* 6, 9 December, 1947.
[82]*Anandabazar Patrika,* 12 December 1947.
[83]*Anandabazar Patrika,* 17, 19 December 1947, 5 January 1948.
[84]*Anandabazar Patrika,* 22 December 1947.

opposition being a reduction of the period of detention without trial from six to three months.[85] Significantly, on the same day P.C. Ghosh resigned from chief ministership, which was taken up, a few days later, by Bidhan Chandra Roy.

What emerges from the debate over the Security Bill is that the Congress leaders and the media that supported them had been seeking to initiate a new discourse of politics that stood on the conflation of party, nation, and the state. In other words, the Congress was the inheritor of the legacy of the nationalist movement, and therefore whoever opposed the party was an enemy of the nation and an enemy of the state. The way people treated the foreign government should not be the way they should treat their own national government, said one Congress speaker at a public meeting at Maddox Square in Calcutta in December 1947, as the interests of the people and the interests of the government were now the same.[86] Critiquing the government would therefore mean endangering the hard-earned freedom, argued an editorial in *Anandabazar Patrika*, which remained staunchly pro-Congress throughout the period.[87] So it was clear that the Security Bill was meant to deal with the enemies of the Congress Party, as by definition they had become the enemies of the newly born nation state.

This authoritarianism and the urgency to deal with the opposition with a heavy hand came at a time when the Congress was internally very weak because of bitter faction fighting. There were three main contending groups, the Khadi or the Gandhian group, the Jugantar group, and the Hooghly group, competing for power within the Congress.[88] There were charges of corruption and in-fighting, and the resignation of P.C. Ghosh remains testimony to that state of affairs. It was widely rumoured, testified to by his own personal secretary, that he became a victim of factional rivalry, corruption

[85]Government of West Bengal, Judicial and Legislative (Legislative) Department, *The West Bengal Security Act 1948* (Alipore: West Bengal Government Press, 1948).

[86]*Anandabazar Patrika*, 23 December 1947.

[87]*Anandabazar Patrika*, 28 November 1947.

[88]For details on Congress factionalism, see Prasanta Sen Gupta, *The Congress Party in West Bengal: A Study of Factionalism 1947–86* (Calcutta: Minerva Associates, 1988), Chapter 2.

and the pressure of black-marketeers and 'big business'.[89] Ghosh himself made the allegation that he was removed from office through a conspiracy because he refused to include Gajanan Khaitan, a Marwari businessman, in his cabinet, even though the latter had the backing of Delhi.[90] Referring to the change of government, in a private conversation with the British deputy high commissioner in Calcutta, Sir B.L. Mitter of the Calcutta High Court offered an apt summary of the situation: 'The relatively honest but inefficient group are being replaced by a relatively efficient but dishonest group.'[91] There could be no better description of the affairs of the Congress Party and its government in 1948!

But who was going to oppose the Congress, which was still being revered by many as the true inheritor of the legacy of the freedom struggle? By February 1948, it had become clear that it had no formidable organised opposition on the right. In March that year the Bengal Muslim League disbanded itself.[92] And following Gandhi's assassination, the Hindu Mahasabha faced public wrath. An irate crowd threw stones and brickbats at Shyama Prasad Mukherjee's Calcutta residence and in view of this public backlash the party decided to withdraw from all political activities and focus henceforth only on philanthropic programmes.[93] On the left, the Socialists had no footing in Bengal, while Sarat Bose's Socialist Republican Party was yet to take off properly. So within this context, the major opposition to the Congress could only come from the Communists, and the Security Bill was primarily aimed at them. Since 1946, they had been mobilising the peasantry in the Bengal countryside, and had, by now, made significant inroads into the trade union sector and also gained popularity among the students. Evidence of this was clear in the recent demonstrations and industrial actions in the city of Calcutta and the suburbs, and the reports of rural unrest from the districts. And then, in its

[89] *Amrita Bazar Patrika*, 5 July 1949; S. Chakrabarty, *With Dr. B.C. Roy*, 65.

[90] Sudeb Raychaudhury, *Banglar Rupakar Dr Bidhan Chandra Ray* (Calcutta: Samparka 1999), 93.

[91] Dy HC to HC for UK in India, Calcutta, 20 January 1948, IOR: L/P&J/5/316.

[92] WBLAP, Vol. 2, No. 2, 18 March 1948, 246.

[93] Dy HC to HC for UK in India, Calcutta, 10 February 1948; Dy HC to HC for UK in India, Calcutta, 17 February 1948, IOR: L/P&J/5/316.

Second Congress in February 1948, the CPI declared an open war against the Congress regime. So in a dramatic move on 25 March 1948, the West Bengal Government decided to ban the CPI in this province, against the express wishes of Prime Minister Nehru.[94] Immediately after that the police arrested all the major leaders and pre-censorship orders were passed against its organ *Swadhinata*. In a statement to justify the ban, the home minister, Kiran Shankar Ray, announced in the Assembly that the government had evidence that the CPI's 'object' was 'to create a state of chaos, and to take advantage of that situation in order ultimately to seize power by violent means.'[95] What started thereafter was a regime of repression and anti-Communist witch-hunting.

Initially, the media supported the anti-Communist counter-insurgency measures and there was also some amount of public approval, as civic life in the city was regularly disrupted by demonstrations and bomb throwing. But this public support gradually began to wear out, as there was very little activity in other spheres of life, and the active complicity of the Congress politicians in corruption and black marketing became the talk of the town. The Gandhian Congress backbenchers tried to remind their leaders that Congress had moved further away from its ideal of a *krishak-praja-mazdur raj*, and its economic policies did not reflect any concern for that goal any more. But such pleas had little effect on a government which had other priorities.[96]

The firing incident of April 1949, particularly the death of five women, however, brought in a stream of protests, and this time, not just from the left-wing politicians whom the chief minister could conveniently dismiss as parts of a Communist conspiracy. So, in early May, Roy had to announce the long overdue by-election in the South Calcutta constituency, which was to be held on 12 June 1949, and this election eventually would become an important benchmark in the political history of those early uncertain years of post-Independence Calcutta.

[94]Chakrabarty, *With Dr. B.C. Roy*, 92–94.

[95]WBLAP, Vol. 2, No. 2, 8–30 March 1948, 346.

[96]WBLAP, Vol. 2, No. 1, 10 February–5 March 1948, 130–63; Vol. 5, No. 1, 23 February–16 March 1949, 65–73.

This was the third by-election since Independence and it proved even tougher as Sarat Bose, a veteran Congress leader now turned its most bitter critic, announced his candidature and all the leftist parties, including the Communists, decided to support him. Letters intercepted by the Police Intelligence suggest that there was a groundswell of support for Sarat Bose to stand in this by-election, as a leader who could stem the rot that had been brought in by a corrupt and autocratic Congress.[97] The election campaign, which became a straight battle between a united leftist front and the Congress,[98] was heated from the start, with the press openly and unabashedly partisan and violence becoming a regular feature. More significantly, Bose was then ill and convalescing at a nursing home in Switzerland and in his absence all the leftist parties launched a united election campaign. On the day before the election, 356 Communist security prisoners in Calcutta jails started a hunger strike to draw public attention to the absence of civil liberties in the province under the present regime.[99] On the other hand, all the Congress stalwarts, including Nehru and Patel, issued statements invoking the past glory of the Congress, reminding the electorate how this party had contributed to the achievement of freedom for the country.[100] Yet, when the results came out, Bose—still in his sickbed in Switzerland—won a spectacular victory by a handsome margin, getting 19,030 votes as against 5,780 for his Congress rival.[101]

The South Calcutta by-election result was a wake-up call for the Congress high command, which sent circulars to all provincial committees to see that this was not repeated anywhere else in the country and the Working Committee decided to launch a mass contact drive to get back to the people.[102] However, the problems

[97]See GB IB Records, Serial No. 195/1930, File No. 451/30, WBSA.

[98]There was a third candidate who was nonentity.

[99]*The Statesman,* 16 June 1949.

[100]*Anandabazar Patrika* was openly partisan in South Calcutta bye-election in favour of the Congress candidate. It published all the various statements of Congress stalwarts in favour of Suresh Das's candidature and in the form of news items published reports overtly preaching why people should not vote for Sarat Bose. On and from 9 June, it carried everyday a frontpage notice—not paid advertisement—urging voters to vote for Congress in order to stop indiscipline and destruction.

[101]*Anandabazar Patrika,* 16 June 1949.

[102]*Amrita Bazar Patrika,* 8 July 1949.

of the West Bengal Provincial Congress were too deep-seated to be rooted out so easily. The electoral debacle indeed exacerbated faction-fighting within the Congress. Its executive committee was reconstituted on 14 June, at a meeting requisitioned by 107 'rebel' members, while the supporters of the contending groups got embroiled in violent clashes on the streets of Calcutta.[103] Nehru came to the city, so did Sardar Patel, to reconcile the warring factions. There was a challenge to the leadership of B.C. Roy,[104] and the rival faction, led by J.C. Gupta, submitted to Nehru a list of charges of corruption and misuse of power against Roy's cabinet. Nehru dismissed them as 'vague charges', but in a letter to Nalini Ranjan Sarkar expressed his concerns at the fact that there was 'great deal of resentment against the West Bengal Government for a variety of reasons'.[105] On his return from Europe, where he had gone for treatment for his failing eyesight, Roy denied all the charges levelled against him and his government. He was summoned to New Delhi along with other important leaders. There was a patchy compromise, as the Congress Assembly Party reiterated its confidence in Roy's leadership. But no permanent formula to reconcile the rival factions emerged.[106]

Engaged in internal squabbles, the Congress had very little time to give attention to the urgent grievances of the people. The market remained volatile and a paradise for black marketeers. In January 1950, large quantities of adulterated mustard oil were seized in Calcutta, but the authorities could not do anything about it, allegedly because of the absence of an appropriate law. A letter to the editor in *Amrita Bazar Patrika* raised the legitimate question as to why the West Bengal Security Act could not be used against the black marketeers and adulterators. Were they not even greater threats to the security and freedom of the nation than the odd bomb thrower?[107]

[103] *The Nation*, 15 June 1949.

[104] *Amrita Bazar Patrika,* 30 July 1949.

[105] From Jawaharlal Nehru to N.R. Sarkar, 1.7.49; also, 'Confidential—not for publication: Allegations against the West Bengal Ministry', Nalini Ranjan Sarkar Papers, Correspondence with Jawaharlal Nehru, NMML

[106] *Amrita Bazar Patrika,* 4, 8, 11, 12, 13 September 1949.

[107] *Amrita Bazar Patrika,* 29 January 1950.

To many in the beleaguered city of Calcutta the recent by-election had shown the way out of this frustrating situation. It showed a new possibility, that is, of left unity against Congress dominance and misrule. The city and the province were to have more of that potion in the coming years. But for the time being, there was a pervading sense of despondency and anger over the faltering promises of freedom, and also a yearning to expand its meaning from the narrow political connotation of sovereignty to the broader socio-economic implications of citizens' rights to equity and justice.

CONCLUSION

When Mahatma Gandhi wrote his *Hind Swaraj* in 1909 he had warned his countrymen that India had to develop her own modes of governance, as otherwise she might end up with 'English rule without the Englishmen'.[108] In decolonization he was thus looking for a complete epistemological and ontological break with the colonial past. This was the expectation of many other nationalists too. But it is doubtful whether any such complete reversal of the colonial past has ever occurred in any history of decolonisation. It certainly did not happen in India. For India, freedom was not a dramatic moment of rupture, but a symbolic process of transference and adaptation—a process of hybridisation through which the meanings of freedom would be expanded exponentially. This essay has tried to explore some of these aspects of this continuum of change and continuity within the urban space of Calcutta in the first four uncertain years of freedom.

The first and foremost change that took place in 1947 was of course the transfer of power—the attainment of sovereignty for the new nation state. The foreign rulers were gone; although a few ICS and police officers continued, they had to report to the Indian ministers, who remained answerable to the people of India. This brought in another major change—a change in peoples' expectations. All that was wrong under foreign rule was expected to be rectified by a national government. New policies were to be formulated, new

[108]M.K. Gandhi, *Hind Swaraj and Other Writings*, ed. A.J. Parel (Cambridge: Cambridge University Press, 1997), 28.

modes of governance to be initiated; in short, the colonial past was to be reversed. Yet this optimism of the early days was shattered by the stark continuities. All those bad things that happened in the city's life in the last few years of colonial rule—scarcity, inflation, corruption, hunger, disease, death, despair, violence—showed no signs of abatement in the early days of freedom.

The Congress government that had taken over power in West Bengal had no previous experience of governance. Even after the Government of India Act of 1935, which had provided for provincial autonomy and allowed the Congress to form a government in a number of provinces, they remained out of power in the Muslim majority province of Bengal. So they stumbled into the new role of a ruling party with no policies, no strategies, not even a political consensus that was necessary to deal with the problems they had inherited. On the other hand, the peoples' yearning for political freedom now expanded into a desire for social and economic freedom. When civil unrest grew as a result of this mismatch, the national government used the old colonial tools of disciplining the people, tools which the nationalist leaders hated so intensely only a few months ago in their previous role in opposition. Yet, these early days of transition were not just a barren period of uncertainties, unrest and authoritarianism, as new idioms of liberation and new forms of politics were also emerging. And these were to give an entirely new meaning and direction to the history of the city and the province in the coming decades.

CHAPTER seventeen

Visually Imagining the City
Urban Planning in 1950s Calcutta and *Surjyatoran*

Sukanya Mitra

Popular Bengali cinema of the 1950s provides us with a rich visual archive of Calcutta. In this essay I read a representative film of this period, *Surjyatoran* (1958) as a text, which throws light on diverse aspects of urban life and represents the city in myriad ways. Within the popular narrative structure of this film lies visual codes, which often lend themselves to interesting interpretations. This particular film along with several others of the same genre, address social issues such as the problem of housing, lack of space in the city, migration from the countryside, or unemployment. They do so in an elliptical manner, as a subtext, as the overt theme may be about romantic love or friendship. While the journey from the countryside to the city is an important theme in many of the films from the beginning of the decade to the mid-1950s, the films of the late 1950s show the protagonists as having come to terms with the city, and visual representations of Calcutta too enter a more self-assured phase. *Surjyatoran* belongs to this later period.

Reading popular cinema in order to write social history is not very common in India and it is here that I seek to make an intervention. While literature has been a widely accepted resource for historical interpretation, films are not always given due weight in academic scholarship. In the case of Bengali cinema, literature and films share an interesting relationship. Bengali films have relied on literature as their primary source material since their inception and even though filmmakers like Satyajit Ray spoke about the need to develop a cinematic language that would rely more on images and be free from literary texts and mere storytelling, he too used well-known literary works as his prime source material. However, the quality of visual representation of the literary material is what distinguished his cinema from that of ordinary filmmakers. Bengali popular cinema during the 1950s, too, often relied on standard literature but it developed new cinematic codes, which made the films visually rich, thus enabling a more convincing representation of the city and urban life among other things. It is this cinematic imagination of 1950s Calcutta that I seek to explore and which I see as an integral part of understanding any city historically.

Cinema is very often the most accessible and popular register through which a city is sought to be visualised by its own inhabitants as well as by outsiders. For instance, much of the imaginary about New York or Manhattan is constituted by how they are depicted in the films of Woody Allen.[1] Film is *the* urban cultural form par excellence since it is a highly capitalised and labour intensive product, whose origins (in Lyon in 1895) and destination (the multiplex) are inextricably tied in with the fortunes of the city. Thus the city is constituted as much by images and representations as by the built environment, demographic shifts, and patterns of capitalist flight and investment.

Cinema is also one of the most intensely spatial forms of culture because it operates and is best understood in terms of its organisation of space. This takes place both within the film texts as well as outside the films themselves. The first includes the extent of the shot, the space of the narrative setting or the mapping of a lived environment on film. At the same time, films as cultural practice exist in and are a part of a larger social space in terms of where and under what conditions they are seen. At another level, cinema is an industry and its participation and involvement at the levels of production,

[1]New York City forms the backdrop of most of Woody Allen's films such as Annie Hall (1977), Manhattan (1979), Hannah and her Sisters (1986), Bullets over Broadway (1994) among others, although he uses cities like Barcelona, Paris, and Rome in his latest productions namely Vicky, Christina, Barcelona (2009), Midnight in Paris (2011) and To Rome with Love (2012). Nevertheless, in all of them, the city is a major character.

distribution and exhibition means that it is part of a vast social and economic network. Hence cinema is primarily a spatial system, spatiality is what makes it different and gives the medium:

> a special potential to illuminate the lived spaces of the city and urban societies, allowing for a full synthetic understanding of cinematic theme, form, and industry in the context of global capitalism.[2]

Indian cities have been crucial in cinematic representation over a long period. In the 1950s the city and urban space became an increasingly important location in Indian films; it was the site where survival and change, exploration and seduction were to be played out. The city was the embodiment of the life-world of a new individual that cinema had to create in the context of post-Independence modernisation. However, even during the heyday of nationalist euphoria in the immediate aftermath of Independence, the city and urban space were critically negotiated in cinema. Ravi Vasudevan's study of Bombay cinema shows how in films like *Shri 420*, *Awara* and *Baazi*,[3] a modern sense of space and movement is negotiated even as the narratives yearn for the security of a lost world through uprootedness.[4] Moinak Biswas has read a popular Bengali melodrama of the 1950s, *Harano Sur* (1957) in the new millennium, showing how it successfully imbibed certain formal characteristics of 1930s Hollywood cinema, thereby reconfiguring several global characteristics of film melodrama in a local milieu.[5] Biswas interprets the film keeping in mind the distance of the modern-day spectator from the period when the film was actually produced. Following Fredric Jameson, he characterises it as a product of the process called 'mode-retro' i.e. a phenomenon whereby a valorisation of black and white images occurs in the new media space by their large scale use

[2]Mark Shiel and Tony Fitzmaurice (eds.) *Cinema and the City*: *Film and Urban Societies in a Global Context*, (Cambridge, Massachussettes: Blackwell, 2001), 6.

[3]Shri 420 (Raj Kapoor, 1955), Awara (Raj Kapoor, 1951), Baazi (Guru Dutt, 1951).

[4]Ravi S. Vasudevan, 'Dislocations: The Cinematic Imagining of a New Society in 1950s India', in *Oxford Literary Review*, 16 (1994): 93–124

[5]Moinak Biswas, 'The Couple and Their Spaces: Harano Sur as Melodrama Now', in *Making Meaning In Indian Cinema'*, ed. Ravi S. Vasudevan (New Delhi: Oxford University Press, 2000), 122–142.

in advertisements, music-video, book and poster designing as well as in certain modes of painting in India.[6] In other words, Biswas places the film within a contemporary temporal and cultural context in order to understand its cultural value for modern-day audiences. In this essay I adopt a different approach. I use a popular Bengali film of the 1950s, *Surjyatoran* (1958), in order to make certain points about the city of Calcutta of *that* period as well as reflect on certain discourses on urban planning that were prevalent then. Since I approach the film as a social scientist interested in urban issues rather than as a trained film expert, more than analyzing the formal attributes of the film, my objective is to try and understand the public discourses about socio-economic issues in the city of Calcutta which it addresses, and the salient features of urban life in 1950s Calcutta that the film portrays.

Surjyatoran (1958) directed by Agradoot is the twenty-second film starring the very successful star-pair of Uttam Kumar and Suchitra Sen who acted together in a total of thirty films beginning with the comedy *Sare Chuattor* in 1953 and ending with *Priyo Bandhabi* in 1975. Though commercially successful, it is not one of their most talked about ventures. The reason for choosing this particular film for the present discussion is the range of issues it brings up and certain very interesting insights, which it provides to those interested in 1950s Calcutta.

Films belonging to this genre have been referred to by critics as romantic melodrama. Among other things, they were successful in exploiting 'a literary liaison established since the inception of sound cinema to draw a sustained charm of words, to create characters anchored in speech-idioms and narrative conventions supported by tradition.'[7] This, I would argue, lends an authenticity to the characters and situations portrayed in the films, which were often disregarded by conventional critics championing the cause of art cinema.

Popular Bengali cinema of the 1950s, 60s and 70s has a very interesting history in terms of its reception and position within the Bengali cultural milieu. While they were very popular with a large

[6]Biswas, 'The Couple', 125.

[7]Ibid., 123.

section of the Bengali audience at the time of their release, these films were largely thought to be of inferior quality by the art cinema critics of Bengal who often compared them to the films of Satyajit Ray and to films made by the masters of European cinema. To Bengalis whose tastes were shaped by a high literary culture, popular Bengali films occupied a lowly place in the cultural hierarchy though they were certainly placed higher than Hindi films, which were a part of the even 'lesser' north Indian culture.

Even though the turn of the new millennium witnessed widespread scholarly interest being focused on popular cinema, it was largely Hindi cinema, which was the recipient of this attention with very little work on Bengali popular films. Social scientists could not even think of using them to illustrate their arguments or theories with stray exceptions. Sudipta Kaviraj interpreted a Hindi film song of the 1950s while speaking about the culture of democracy and his essay is an indication of the power of popular films to articulate an image of the city which was more complex and nuanced than what Bengali 'high' literature was often able to do.[8] As Preben Kaarsholm points out, cinema in this sense was 'not just "representation", but in itself part and parcel of modernity as such'.[9] Keeping this in mind, I attempt to use a film like *Surjyatoran* to bring out the complexities of urban life in 1950s Calcutta with particular reference to the theme of urban planning. The reasons for choosing to highlight this particular theme will be dealt with in the next section. However, at the outset I would like to mention that as in the case of fine arts or cinema, in the field of architecture too there had been a yearning for indigenous forms uncontaminated by western ideals of planning since the colonial times. However, since town planning was not taken as seriously as it should have been by the indigenous elite with a few exceptions, no clear ideal emerged as to what would be the constitutive elements of this Indian form. This tension between the desire of a section of the intelligentsia for an Indian art form suited to the post-independent nation and the

[8]Sudipta Kaviraj, 'Reading a Song of the City', in *City Flicks: Indian Cinema and the Urban Experience,* ed. Preben Kaarsholm (Calcutta and New Delhi: Seagull Books, 2004), 60–82.

[9]Kaarsholm, Introduction to *City Flicks*, 10.

inability to clearly define it is what makes it interesting to explore this theme in the context of 1950s Calcutta.

I

Urban planning or the lack of it forms a major part of a city's imaginary and of the discourses surrounding it. Since the 1950s, urban planning has been a primary area of concern for political leaders and administrators in India, and city building formed an important part of the making of the modern Indian state in the Nehruvian era. Planning is usually not a neutral process; it is value-laden and is representative of the ideas of the ruling class. Madhu Sarin has analyzed the impact of planning intervention as an external factor influencing the settlement process in Chandigarh.[10] According to her, urban planning has consisted of the imposition of a set of rules presented as being neutral and legitimised on the grounds of being in the 'public interest'. However, within the so-called Third World characterised by extreme social and economic inequalities, it is not difficult to show that the neutrality of planning is a myth.[11]

In the case of Calcutta, an oft-asked question, though not unique to it, is whether the city developed in a planned or unplanned manner. The question assumes significance since much of the ills plaguing the city in the years following Independence have been presumed to have resulted due to its haphazard nature of growth. Even as late as the 1990s, plans drafted to build the new township of Rajarhat on the eastern fringes of the city make repeated claims that it was to be a significant departure in the history of planning of the city since it was to be built in a planned, scientific manner as opposed to the unplanned way in which the rest of Calcutta has developed.[12] This sense of Calcutta developing in a chaotic way is a reminder of Rudyard Kipling's oft-repeated words, 'chance directed chance erected laid and built on the silt.'

[10]Madhu Sarin, *Urban Planning in the Third World: The Chandigarh Experience* (London: Mansell Publishing, 1982).

[11]Ibid., 1.

[12]New Town-Calcutta, Project Report, HIDCO, May 1999.

However, much of Calcutta had been a result of planned development and urban planning had been a recurrent theme in public discourses on the city since colonial times. The reason behind the growth of Calcutta without any systematic plan was often attributed to the fact that nobody could anticipate that the city, which had only twelve thousand people living in it in the year 1710, would grow into such a huge metropolis with a population of twelve lakhs in two centuries.[13] The Calcutta Improvement Trust (CIT), which came into existence in 1911, was the primary planning agency entrusted with the responsibility of town planning by the British. Partho Datta argues in a recent work that the archival documents of Calcutta help us to push back modern planning from the generally accepted period of the 1850s to well into the beginning of the nineteenth century.[14] He also observes that what makes the story of the CIT so fascinating is that this was the first time that a consciously planned intervention was being formulated for an Indian city that would encompass much more than conservancy and sanitation.[15] The CIT continued its activities during the period after 1947 and was the pre-eminent planning body in the city until the establishment of the Calcutta Metropolitan Development Authority (CMDA) in 1970.

Town planning ideas were elaborately discussed by planners and technocrats in the public domain throughout the 1920s. The Garden City movement, begun by Ebenezer Howard in late nineteenth-century England, and its feasibility in India was spoken about in great detail alongside the lament that nobody thought of town-planning seriously even though it was the only solution to the ills plaguing Calcutta and its environs.[16] The concept of Regional Town Planning was also discussed extensively, which propagated among other things, the need for developing the suburban areas around Calcutta and not just the core areas of the city. The principal efforts of the CIT between 1921 and 1926 were directed to reserving

[13]R.K. Ganguli, 'Regional Town Planning: Why It Is Necessary In Calcutta', in *The Calcutta Municipal Gazette* (February 1923), 629.

[14]Partho Datta, *Planning the City: Urbanization and Reform in Calcutta, c1800–c1940* (New Delhi: Tulika, 2012), 5.

[15]Ibid., 201.

[16]Raj Bahadur Gupta, 'Garden Cities and Industrial Suburbs–II', in *The Calcutta Municipal Gazette* (January 1927), 339.

ample open spaces when developing suburban areas and also to purchasing land on the outskirts of the town in anticipation of future expansion.[17]All of this goes to show that urban planning as a discipline occupied the minds of a section of educated Indians and began to gain popularity following the establishment of the CIT. Even so, most of the ideas were borrowed from the west and particularly Europe, where it had emerged as a professional and intellectual movement in the twentieth century as a response to the filth and squalor of nineteenth century Victorian cities.

Such borrowed ideas of planning continued to predominate in India even after Independence. The First World War had given an impetus to industrialisation and this led to the construction of a number of new industrial towns such as Jamshedpur, which was planned by a British sanitary engineer Fred Temple.[18] However, it was only after the Second World War and the attainment of Independence that urban improvement and planning were given serious thought by Indian policy makers and the problem was taken cognizance of at the national level.

Partha Chatterjee has argued that after Independence there were no new or original models of the Indian industrial metropolis. The available models of the industrial city were western ones such as Manchester. These had been copied by the British in India such as in the case of Calcutta with mixed results. They led to imperfect copies of the original and often there was a feeling that the cities had failed to develop into 'proper' metropolitan cities in comparison to their European counterparts.[19] Ravi Kalia's studies of the building of Chandigarh, Bhubaneswar and Gandhinagar[20] show the conflict

[17]C.H. Bompas, 'The Work of the Calcutta Improvement Trust 1921–1926', in *The Calcutta Municipal Gazette* (22 January 1927): 435.

[18]Madhu Sarin, *Urban Planning*, 24.

[19]Partha Chatterjee, 'Are Indian Cities Becoming Bourgeois At Last?', in *The Politics of the Governed: Reflections on Popular Politics in Most of the World* (Delhi: Permanent Black, 2004), 140–141.

[20]For Chandigarh see Ravi Kalia, *Chandigarh: The Making of an Indian City* (Delhi: Oxford University Press, 1987) For Bhubaneswar see Ravi Kalia, *Bhubaneswar: From A Temple Town to a Capital City* (Delhi: Oxford University Press, 1994) and for Gandhinagar see Ravi Kalia, *Gandhinagar: Building National Identity in Postcolonial India* (New Delhi: Oxford University Press, 2005).

between the 'modern' western vision of new townships as envisaged by the erstwhile prime minister of India, Jawaharlal Nehru and the traditional socio-cultural practices and everyday uses of space in India. Kalia shows the dichotomy between two competing visions of the nation in the process of the building of these cities. One was the Gandhian attachment to villages as a source of ideals for building a new India. The other was Nehru's inclination for cities based on a modernist, western ideal according to which a new town should be symbolic of the freedom of India, unfettered by the traditions of the past—an expression of the nation's faith in the future.[21]

James Holston, in his study of the planning of Brasilia, argues that the modernist aesthetic appeals to governments across the political spectrum in so-called third-world countries due to the affinities between modernism as an aesthetic of erasure of prevailing conditions and the inscription of modernisation as an ideology of development in which governments, regardless of persuasion, seek to rewrite national histories.[22] For instance, Brasilia built as a new township in the Central Plateau of Brazil during the 1950s, portrayed an imagined and desired future as well as a negation of the existing conditions in Brazil. Yet, at the same time, the government intended it as a means to achieve this future i.e. it was to be an instrument of change which would have to use the existing conditions it denied out of necessity. Holston's ethnographic study shows the ways in which the people of Brasilia engaged the utopian premises on which the city was built at their points of contradiction to reassert the social processes and cultural values the utopia tended to deny.[23] It may be argued that in the absence of an indigenous urban form to which one could aspire to, Nehru was similarly driven by an utopian modernist ideal which attempted to negate the existing social conditions of the country which were at odds with it and it was precisely the promise of such a negation that attracted Nehru and others like him to the modernist aesthetic of development.

[21]Kalia, *Chandigarh*, 21.

[22]James Holston, *The Modernist City: An Anthropological Critique of Brasilia* (Chicago and London: The University of Chicago Press, 1989), 5.

[23]Ibid.

This context of urban planning in India during the 1950s provides the necessary backdrop to understanding the film *Surjyatoran* (1958) which identifies the predominance of European ideas of planning among Indian specialists after Independence and the need for Indian architects to look for inspiration in their own past urban forms such as the Indus Valley civilisation in order to come up with indigenous ideas of planning. It is worth mentioning here that debates about the need to develop indigenous methods and plans in order to impart individuality and national character to Indian cities had begun during the colonial period itself.[24] However, the western bias in terms of institutional training and designs seems to have won the day in the years following Independence. The film begins with the expulsion of the male protagonist Somnath Mukherjee (Uttam Kumar), an architect, from the Indian College of Technology where he was a B.Tech student due to a disagreement with one of his professors regarding a theoretical point. The educational background of the hero is important since it must be remembered that higher technical institutions were being set up immediately after Independence for post-war industrial development and the first Indian Institute of Technology (IIT) was established in Kharagpur, situated around 128 kms from Calcutta in 1950. It was declared as an Institute of National Importance by the Parliament of India with the passage of the Indian Institute of Technology Act in 1956. In the first convocation address of IIT Kharagpur, the erstwhile prime minister of India, Jawaharlal Nehru said,

> Here in the place of the Hijli Detention Camp stands the fine monument of India, representing India's urges, India's future in the making. This picture seems to me symbolical of the changes coming to India.[25]

Therefore, the institutes of technology were not simply institutions of higher education. They were to be a part of the project

[24]For example, see the extensive discussion on this issue by Prof Raj Bahadur Gupta. Raj Bahadur Gupta, 'Garden Cities and Industrial Suburbs' in *The Calcutta Municipal Gazette* (December–January 1927).

[25]En.wikipedia.org/wiki/Indian_Institute_ of_ Technology.

of nation-building envisioned by Nehru and the planning ideas propagated through them were deeply influenced by the west due to the inadequacy of indigenous thinking about planning. After his expulsion from the institute, Somnath comes to Calcutta in search of Bipradas Choudhury (Kali Banerjee), an architect who has been marginalised by his peers in the academia due to his unconventional ideas about planning. According to him, Indian architects should be inspired by their own planning traditions, which went back to Mohenjo Daro and Harappa instead of copying from the west. In a telling scene, Bipradas Choudhury takes a dig at Somnath when he comes to know that the latter had graduated with a diploma from the Indian College of Technology. He says that Somnath had not learnt anything there except certain fixed theories. This, in a way, undermines the Nehruvian vision of what the IITs would stand for and brings to focus the ambiguity regarding the model of planning which Indian architects would follow. Bipradas, however, never spells out the exact nature of the indigenous form, which he so passionately envisages. This is a gap, which the film fails to address.

If Bipradas Choudhury represents the non-mainstream or alternative ideas of planning in the film, the heroine Anita (Suchitra Sen)'s father, U.N. Chatterjee (Kamal Mitra) is the architect who is shown to be successful precisely because he follows the norms and ideas of planning which were popular then. Incidentally, Bipradas pays the price for refusing to follow conventions and dies of a heart attack since he could not accept professional rejection. However, it is his ideas which are finally triumphant in the film since Somnath, his disciple, continues his legacy.

Apart from the discourse about town planning with its resonance at the national level, the other major theme of the film is the problem of housing, which is specifically related to the city. Lack of space, congestion, high land prices were perennial problems plaguing the city and the situation worsened in the immediate aftermath of Independence due to Partition and the influx of refugees. The lack of adequate housing was the most important socio-economic problem facing the inhabitants of the city at this time. This was tied up with the equally important issue of the presence of a large number of unhygienic and insanitary slums. According to a survey of the State

Statistical Bureau conducted in 1958–59, the total *bustee* (slum) population in Calcutta amounted to 6,85,116 spread over a total area of 1701 acres.[26] The foremost scheme undertaken by the CIT in the 1950s to tackle this problem was the Bustee Improvement Scheme, which included the simultaneous improvement of existing slums along with the prevention of their further growth.[27] As a part of this scheme, multi-storied buildings were constructed in many areas of the city in order to house the slum population. A random example of this is a four storied building completed in Singhee Bagan consisting of four three-room and twenty-four two-room flats.[28] The need for planning on a large scale was emphasised which would be constitutive of planning the future configuration of the land, controlling its use, and providing an adequate machinery for ensuring that the preparation of the plan and its implementation were effectively carried out.[29] According to S.K. Gupta, I.C.S. and Chairman of the CIT between 1950 and 1960,

> the provision of adequate housing for the people in the low income group in conformity with the general physical plan of the town is the only ultimate remedy for slums that are already there, for when people have better houses to live in and the rents are brought down to a level which is within their means, the slums will die out from attrition.[30]

Hence, town planning was seen as the solution to the problem of housing and the undesirable presence of slums and this is what connects the two major themes in the film.

The problem of housing has been a recurrent theme in the Bengali popular films of the 1950s where the major characters, mostly belonging to the lower middle classes or the middle classes, are often depicted as either staying in a 'mess' or boarding houses or in rented accommodation and the hero or heroine often come

[26]Sunil K Munshi (ed.), *Calcutta Metropolitan Explosion: Its Nature and Roots* (New Delhi: Peoples' Publishing House, 1975), 116.

[27]*Report on Operations of Calcutta Improvement Trust* (CIT) *for 1956–57*, 32.

[28]Ibid., 31.

[29]Ibid., 35.

[30]Ibid., 37.

across each other in such a milieu.[31] However, *Surjyatoran* stands out since the problem is directly addressed in the film and the debates surrounding the planning process form its backdrop.

Surjyatoran refers to the name of a book written by the heroine of the film, Anita Chatterjee. The book is named after the housing complex that Anita desires to build for people living in a slum, a portion of which is owned by her father, U.N. Chatterjee who receives a regular sum as rent from the slum dwellers. A considerable portion of the slum belongs to Rajshekhar Mitra (Bikash Roy) who is unwilling to part with it as a result of which Anita is unable to go ahead with her plan of trying to demolish the huts occupying the area in order to build *Surjyatoran*. According to the pattern of *bustee* holding in Calcutta, a single *bustee*, as a physically distinct area of continuous huts, might have had a single owner or could have been divided into many separate holdings. Therefore, in the film, parts of the same slum are depicted as being owned by Mr Chatterjee as well as by Rajshekhar Mitra. Rajshekhar has a past which continues to haunt him. He used to live with his mother in a slum when he was a child and his mother was harassed by the slum owner, U.N. Chatterjee's rent collector. This resulted in her untimely death. Rajshekhar had vowed to avenge her death. After building a huge fortune he purchased the slum land on which he used to live as a child from Mr Chatterjee. Rajshekhar's character depicts the plight of *bhadralok*[32] refugees who established themselves in the city in spite of the misfortune that had befallen them as a result of Partition.

The film makes a distinction between the middle-class *bhadralok*—whom Partition has unfairly forced into slums—and under-class plebians who are portrayed as the natural inhabitants of slums and who deserve to be there. For instance, when Somnath expresses his desire to stay with Bipradas Choudhury's servant[33]

[31]Examples of such films are *Sare Chuattor* (1953), *Jiban Trishna* (1957), *Prithibi Amare Chaye* (1958) among several others.

[32]The term *bhadralok* is used to denote middle class Bengalis characterised by the qualities of civility and gentility. It has a class connotation and is used to differentiate the gentry from the under-classes distinguished by manual labour.

[33]Addressed as 'Kashida' in the film by Somnath.

(Tulsi Chakraborty) in his slum quarters, the latter admonishes him saying that the son of a *bhadralok* (*bhadraloker chele*) should not voluntarily offer to stay in a *bustee* since it is not a place where human beings live. This trope of privileged middle-class Bengaliness—even when in dire straits—runs through most of the films of this decade and it continues roughly up to the middle of the 1970s. It is interesting to note that while the middle-class hero was willing to déclassé himself when compelled by circumstances, the representative of the underclass found it difficult to accommodate this desire, thus indicating how the members of the underclass often internalise and naturalise their position within the class hierarchy. In another scene, the heroine Anita expresses her desire to visit the slums and the rent collector working on behalf of her father expresses shock and surprise at her wish. When Anita visits the slum in order to supervise a school for slum children, which she had started in the slum premises, the rent collector entrusted with the responsibility of teaching the children, tells her that she was wasting her energy since the children had no desire to study. The film conveys that benevolence towards the poor was often an exercise in futility since, in many cases, the latter was undeserving of it. The rent collector also tells Anita that he earns a commission of 75 rupees for collecting rent from the slum dwellers and there has not been any increase or decrease in this amount for years even though the amount of rent may have changed. The rent collector's unchanging fortune thus illustrates the plight of middlemen who worked on behalf of the land owners. It shows that even though the earnings of the latter from the slums may have increased, the incomes of the middlemen remain the same.

The scenes depicting slum areas in the city, though shot indoors, display a comparative lack of artificiality often associated with indoor shots in other films of this genre. This lends it a quality of realism. The moral economy of the slum area is depicted as different from that of the middle and upper classes. For instance, Anita witnesses disturbing scenes of domestic violence against women during her first visit to the slums. She also narrowly escapes being molested by a slum dweller since Somnath, who was staying in the slum with Kashida, chances upon the situation and saves her, thereby underlining the predicament which women belonging to her class may have to face if they choose to visit areas outside the limits of their own world. All of this indicates the rottenness of both the moral world as well as the material conditions in the slums.

If the film is read as a valorisation of the *bhadralok*, then the discipline of urban planning and the debates surrounding it seamlessly merge with this worldview since planning is essentially a middle-class endeavour and the majority of planners and architects belong to this class. Therefore, it follows that we view the city through an upper middle class gaze and vision about how a city should be made or unmade.

II

The heroine of the film belongs to the upper classes and she clearly shows an awareness of consumer driven culture. In one of her radio speeches she talks about belonging to an age in which the presence of television had increased communication between people even though middle-class households in Calcutta would have access to television only from the late 1970s. This indicates her awareness of global consumer trends. The radio forms an important mode of communication in the film indicating its popularity in the 1950s. Anita shows her concern for the living conditions of the poor in the form of a radio talk, which is listened to by her father as well as by Somnath, who at that moment was living in a slum. The presence of the radio both in Anita's upper class home as well as at a roadside tea-stall is an indication of the ubiquity of certain consumer goods across classes. In a later scene we also witness a song being played in a radio inside a car, which Somnath drives with Anita sitting beside him.

The fact that Anita writes about people living in the slums and wishes to improve their living conditions marks her out from many other heroines portrayed in other Bengali films of the time. Her characterisation may have been influenced by the involvement of many upper-class women in public life since the 1940s and even earlier. She is in conflict with her father who does not approve of her work for the poor since it directly clashes with his interests as the owner of considerable slum-land for three generations. This is another unique feature in the film since generational conflict in most other Bengali films revolved around disagreements over choosing life partners and this kind of ideological clash between father and daughter is hard to come by. Unlike other Bengali films of the time, this one creates and dwells on characters and professions such as that of share market speculators, businessmen, technocrats and corporate firms. It focuses on the market economy within the urban matrix of the city. The class position of the heroine is symbolised by the presence of French windows in her house, use of cutlery during daily meals, her style of dressing, her ability to play the piano, to drive and to read English novels and magazines: a book by A.J. Cronin lies on the piano in one scene, while she reads TIME magazine in another. The fact that the heroine belongs to the upper class allows the director to portray the parallel existence of contrasting worlds—that of the upper-class gentry and of the slums—effectively in the film and the heroine is allowed to traverse a diverse range of spaces as a character trying to familiarise herself with life-worlds outside her immediate existence.

In the film, Somnath and Anita meet under unusual circumstances. After Bipradas's death Somnath is asked to leave his house by his uncle since he is unable to find any job. He leaves Calcutta to work as a labourer in an iron factory in a place called Rangamati. This decision once again meets with the disapproval of Kashida, who looks upon Somnath as his own son. He cannot fathom as to why an educated person like Somnath wished to work as a factory hand. He upholds the sharp hierarchy dividing manual from intellectual labour that Bengali *bhadralok* society took for granted. Anita comes to stay there since the factory is owned by her father. Although both of them had met earlier in the *bustee* in Calcutta, they did not know each other. Anita mistakes him as a factory hand and behaves arrogantly with him. It is revealing that even a heroine who so uncharacteristically of her class and gender is concerned about the poor, does not avoid the typical responses of her class when she actually confronts a man whom she takes to be her social inferior. However, soon after, Somnath's true identity is revealed to her when he returns to Calcutta and is felicitated as the best architect of the year. By this time Rajshekhar has already proposed marriage to Anita, which she is almost forced to accept since her father is indebted to him as a result of a plot hatched by the latter. Rajshekhar then hires Somnath to build *Surjyatoran* and turn Anita's dream into reality. In the meanwhile, Anita and Somnath are in love with one another even though Anita is officially betrothed to Rajshekhar and the latter is unaware of their feelings for each other.

The romance in the film is subtle and since Somnath is hesitant to acknowledge his love for Anita openly, his body language is restrained. This allows Anita to express her feelings for him and leads to a very strong female initiative, one that changes from an initial expression of hauteur to one that is soft and yielding in love. This again makes her a doubly unconventional character who defies social and gender codes in her intimate as well as in her ideological choices. The absence of parental authority in the film[34] gives autonomy to the lovers and the fact that both Rajshekhar and Somnath work towards fulfilling Anita's dream of building *Surjyatoran* brings together the larger theme of planning and the more intimate sphere of romance. In fact while accepting Rajshekhar's marriage proposal, Anita asks him whether as her future husband she could expect him to stand by her if she wishes to give concrete shape to her desire to build *Surjyatoran*. He agrees. Thus for Anita, the realisation of her dream remains her lasting passion and this prevents the planning discourse from getting overshadowed by the romantic angle in the film.

When Somnath comes to know that Rajshekhar will marry Anita the day *Surjyatoran* is completed, he entrusts Subrata Roy, U.N. Chatterjee's assistant with the responsibility of building it. However, Subrata messes it up completely, so much so that the building is criticised as a place not fit for humans. Somnath then destroys the building and is taken to court where he justifies his act. The latter half of the film deals with the court proceedings, which go in favour of Somnath. The film ends with the unexpected death of Rajshekhar who had chanced upon the fact that Anita loved Somnath and had

[34]Somnath's parents are dead while Anita's father hardly behaves like the typical patriarch except for initially expressing his wish to get Anita married to Subrata Roy, his assistant. However, he never directly interferes in Anita's love life or objects to her choices.

realised that he would never be able to win her heart. In a couple of scenes at the end of the film, the new building is thrown open to its inhabitants in the presence of Somnath and Anita who are now free to marry each other.

Rajshekhar is an admirer of Bipradas Choudhury's architectural style. He commissions him to build a house for him outside Calcutta where he goes to spend a weekend with Anita, her father and Somnath soon after his engagement to Anita. In fact this is what prompts him to hire Somnath to build *Surjyatoran* since the latter learnt his craft from Bipradas Choudhury. U.N. Chatterjee too admits that Bipradas was the most creative architect of his generation even though his professional rivalry with the latter prevented him from admitting this openly. Therefore, even though Bipradas's ideas are unacknowledged in his lifetime, they do receive support from people like Rajshekhar. This may be because the latter himself rose from the margins and is hence able to appreciate ideas outside the mainstream. Ironically however, indigenous forms of planning did not really take off in India in the 1950s and Calcutta was not an exception to this rule. The housing problem continued to persist well into the 1950s and a complete demolition of slum areas in order to make way for community buildings continued to be a highly debated issue.

III

I conclude this essay with some reflections on the way in which Calcutta has been represented in *Surjyatoran*. The plot is taken from Ayn Rand's novel *The Fountainhead*. However, the director has changed it to such an extent that a piece of writing considered to be a gospel of capitalism and individualism has almost been turned into a film obliquely propagating socialist values if not directly championing the cause. The city is seen through the eyes of the *bhadralok* or middle class yet there is an interesting encounter with the underclass through a process of becoming déclassé, whether voluntarily or due to compelling circumstances. It also shows the importance of planning discourses in making the city as well as a possible solution to many of the ills plaguing it and its inhabitants.

The city does not simply act as a backdrop in the film; rather it seamlessly merges with its subject matter.

In many ways the film is about the city and the possible ways in which life in it can be made more tolerable for the poor. There is no attempt to idealise the poor nor is there a nostalgia for the countryside as the romantic other of the big city. Both slum dwellers and the middle classes benefit from opportunities in city life. This is demonstrated aptly through the lives of Somnath and Rajshekhar. While the former makes a name for himself as an architect even when he has to leave his home and his college, the latter becomes one of the richest men in the city even after starting his life in a slum and losing his parents early. The physical as well as the social mobility of the three main characters in the film, Somnath, Anita and Rajshekhar, enable an interaction among different classes and spaces in the film. Finally, the film uses realist modes of narration such as location shooting, both indoor and outdoor in order to bring a life-like quality to the situations unlike many other contemporary films of the same genre. There is a nuanced portrayal of the city. A relatively limited use of close-up shots of the stars and soft-focus lighting, features of several other films starring the same duo, help to keep the focus on the planning theme and not on the actors. The film therefore stands out due to the major issues it addresses and provides an interesting insight into the urban visions in the 1950s.

CHAPTER eighteen

Building Bijaygarh

A Microhistory of Refugee Squatting in Calcutta[1]

Uditi Sen

Historians of the Partition of India broadly acknowledge that the demographic upheaval that followed in its wake permanently altered the faces of the capital cities of South Asia. Karachi and Dhaka were transformed overnight into national capitals; Delhi changed from a Mughal city to a Punjabi one, while Calcutta, which had always been a city of migrants, rapidly earned the dubious distinction of becoming a city of refugees.[2] This is not to suggest that the number of refugees from East Pakistan exceeded the numbers of those who considered themselves to be local to Calcutta or West Bengal. According to the Census of 1951, 33.2 per cent of Calcuttans were city-born while another 12.3 per cent came from elsewhere in West Bengal. However, migrants from East Bengal emerged as the single largest group of migrants, amounting to 26.9 per cent

[1]This article is a different version of a previous publication, 'The Myths Refugees Live By: Memory and history in the making of Bengali refugee identity', *Modern Asian Studies*, 48, 2014, pp. 37–76.

[2]The forced occupation of Hindu properties and land in Dhaka and Lahore, was matched by the 'cleansing' of Muslim neighbourhoods in Delhi. For a comparative study of the impact of Partition upon the demographic, cultural, and architectural aspects of seven key cities of South Asia see 'Capitol Landscapes' The imprint of Partition on South Asian capital cities' in *The Aftermath of Partition in South Asia*, ed. Tai Yong Tan and Gyanesh Kudaisya (London and New York: Routledge, 2000), 163–203.

of the city's population.[3] More importantly, their presence was a highly visible one, which was frequently framed as a 'problem' by contemporary observers and politicians. The squalor and destitution of hundreds of refugee families living on pavements and railway platforms, fear of disease, alarm over the rise of slum populations and a declining law and order situation became the hallmarks of refugee presence in Calcutta, during the late forties and fifties. This was also the time when frustrated refugees took matters into their own hands and launched a veritable movement of squatting in empty buildings and fallow land in and around Calcutta. By 1950, there were 149 illegal refugee settlements or *jabardakhal* colonies awaiting regularisation and by the late sixties, the list had grown to 604.[4] This massive influx of refugees into Calcutta in the decades after Partition altered the political landscape and social geography of Calcutta in profound ways. The string of refugee colonies in the southern and northern suburbs of Calcutta were instrumental in the rapid extension of Calcutta's urban sprawl, as the city outgrew its old boundaries to emerge as greater Calcutta. Refugees, unlike economic migrants from Bihar and Orissa, migrated with their entire families, thus effecting an absolute increase in the number of women in Calcutta's population. Another inevitable change, linked to the refugee influx, was the displacement and ghettoisation of Calcutta's Muslim population.[5] These transformations have become a part of everyday life in Calcutta, where a series of socio-cultural practices evoke and contain the difference and rivalry between the 'local' or West Bengali population of Calcutta, commonly known as *ghatis* and the East Bengali migrants, called *bangals*. These rituals

[3]See Republic of India, Census of 1951, Vol. VI, part III, *Calcutta City,* (Delhi, Office of the Registrar General) also cited in Nilanjana Chatterjee, 'The East Bengali Refugees: A Lesson in Survival', in *Calcutta the Living City: The Present and the Future,* ed. Sukanta Chaudhuri, Vol.II (Calcutta: Oxford University Press, 1990), 70–77.

[4]See Tushar Sinha, *Maranjayee Sangrame Bastuhar a* (Refugees in a death-defying battle) (Calcutta: United Central Refugee Council, 1999), also cited in Appendix D of Prafulla Kumar Chakrabarti, *The Marginal Men: The Refugees and the Left Political Syndrome in West Bengal* (Calcutta: Lumiere Books, 1990).

[5]See Joya Chatterji, 'Of Graveyards and Ghettos: Muslims in West Bengal, 1947–67', in *Living together separately: Cultural India in History and Politics*, eds. Mushirul Hasan and Asim Roy (Delhi: Oxford University Press, 2005).

of difference, such as the rivalry between East Bengal and Mohun Bagan on the football field, social introductions that evoke lost geographies of belonging with the question '*desh kothaye*?' (where is your home/country), and competitive cataloguing of meritocratic achievements that incessantly pit the *bangal* against the *ghati*, have received surprisingly little scholarly attention. Historians have mostly focused on two radical changes in the politics and social mores of West Bengal wrought by Partition refugees' struggle to survive: the rise of left political parties riding on the back of refugees,[6] and the 'coming out' of Bengali middle-class women into the workforce which, according to some scholars, challenged and fundamentally altered patriarchal social mores of *bhadralok* society.[7] This essay moves away from the analysis of broad social and political changes wrought by Partition and its aftermath to conduct a microhistorical analysis of the emergence of one refugee colony, Bijaygarh, in the southern suburbs of Calcutta. The goal of this essay is not so much to write a history of Bijaygarh colony per se, but to bring into sharp focus the web of social relationships, economic means and everyday politics that made the success of such a venture possible, despite widespread apathy and opposition from the government.

Numerous histories of specific refugee colonies of Calcutta, or of specific endeavours of place-making by refugees, such as establishing a market, a school, or initiating a community-run *Durga puja* already exist. These range from popular Bengali pamphlets, autobiographies and amateur histories to more organised scholarly endeavours relying on the collection and interpretation of interviews.[8] This essay, while drawing upon several such histories of Bijaygarh colony, is substantively different from this genre of history writing that functions within an additive logic of recovering marginal histories and recording for posterity people's experience of Partition 'from

[6]See Chakrabarti, *The Marginal Men*.

[7]See Jasodhara Bagchi and Subhoranjan Dasgupta, *The Trauma and the Triumph: Gender and Partition in Eastern India* (Calcutta: Stree, 2003) and Gargi Chakravartty, *Coming out of Partition: Refugee Women of Bengal* (New Delhi: Bluejay Books, 2005).

[8]See, for example, Pradip Kumar Bose (ed.), *Refugees in West Bengal: Institutional Practices and Contested Identities* (Calcutta: Calcutta Research Group, 2000) and Kaliprasad Mukhopadhyay, *Shikorer Sandhane (*Quest for Roots*)* (Calcutta: Bhasha O Sahitya, 2002).

below'. Though they focus on the small-scale and the intimate, these narratives are distinct from the concept of microhistory, as popularised by Carlo Ginzburg.[9] In microhistory, the focus on a single event or individual or any social phenomenon on a reduced scale is seen to be advantageous as it brings into stark relief the relationships between 'systems of belief, of values and representations on one side, and social affiliations on another'.[10] In this essay, the focus on Bijaygarh is an attempt to understand the social affiliations, economic realities and political negotiations that made squatting possible. In the spirit of microhistorical analysis, this study seeks to locate refugee politics of squatting within the larger socio-political milieu of post-Partition Calcutta. By doing so, it moves away from the present unfortunate tendency to uncritically celebrate the resolve, self-sufficiency and militancy of East Bengali refugees who built the squatters' colonies. It reveals unexpected affinities between the marginal figure of the refugee-squatter and dominant social values in post-Partition Calcutta, thus calling into question the representation of East Bengali refugees as a marginal and radical political force.

LOCATING BIJAYGARH: THE MEANINGS OF *JABARDAKHAL* IN POST-PARTITION CALCUTTA

The inadequacy of relief and rehabilitation offered and the resultant hardship faced by East Bengali refugees has not only been described in numerous historical accounts but also poignantly captured in popular Bengali culture. Representations range from Jogen Choudhury's realistic sketches of refugees living on the platform of Sealdah station, Ritwick Ghatak's complex portrayal of life in refugee colonies in *Meghe Dhaka Tara* and Salil Sen's play, *Natun Ihudi* (New Jews) that ran to packed houses in Calcutta in

[9]See Carlo Ginzburg, *The Cheese and the Worms: the Cosmos of a Sixteenth-Century Miller*, trans. John and Anne Tedeschi (Baltimore: John Hopkins University Press, 1980).

[10]Roger Chartier, 'Intellectual History or Sociocultural History ', in *Modern European Intellectual History: Reappraisals and New Perspectives*, eds. Dominick LaCapra and Steven L. Kaplan (Ithaca: Cornell University Press, 1981), 32, also cited in John Brewer, 'Microhistory and the Histories of Everyday Life' in *Cultural and Social History*, 7, No. 1 (March 2010): 87–109.

1953. The struggle for survival waged against stupendous odds by once prosperous refugee families from respectable or *bhadralok* backgrounds, now reduced to destitution by Partition's vicissitudes, forms the common core of these representations. In historical and fictional narratives, one particular group of East Bengali refugees are singled out for their ability to triumph over adverse circumstances. These are the architects of the hundreds of refugee colonies born of illegal squatting in and around Calcutta. This phenomenon of organised illegal occupation of empty land that became ubiquitous in post-Partition West Bengal was first narrativised by Prafulla Chakrabarti as the '*jabardakhal* (forced acquisition) movement'[11] and later retold, and often reframed, by numerous popular histories. Bijaygarh colony, founded in 1948, is included in the official list of squatters' colonies. Its status as a *jabardakhal* colony is however, disputed. Prafulla Chakrabarti dismisses it for not being a 'true' *jabardakhal* colony. In contrast, many of its residents claim to be the first successful squatters in the southern suburbs of Calcutta, and thus a role model and an inspiration for refugees. This dispute over the place of Bijaygarh in refugee histories is indicative of the density of meanings that accumulated around the concept of *jabardakhal* in post-Partition Calcutta, which is only inadequately translated as squatting. Beginning with a discussion of the meaning of *jabardakhal* in post-Partition Calcutta allows us to move beyond a dispute over bureaucratic definitions and understand the political and moral claims that were at stake in claiming the status of a *jabardakhal* colony. The dispute over Bijaygarh's status thus provides insights into how refugees negotiated their social presence and articulated their identity in post-Partition Calcutta.

Bijaygarh colony was born as the unauthorised occupation of a wireless centre and barracks built for Allied soldiers during World War II in Jadavpur region of 24 Parganas. The squat was initially called the Jadavpur Refugee camp. The families who moved into abandoned military huts organised themselves into a committee, called the Jadavpur Refugee Camp Association. Such unauthorised occupation of abandoned houses, military structures, warehouses or closed factories was standard practice amongst displaced persons in

[11]Chakrabarti, *The Marginal Men*, 33–66.

the large cities of India and Pakistan in the aftermath of Partition.[12] In this era of forced occupation and illegal squatting, the pattern that evolved in Calcutta was somewhat distinct. The refusal of the Government of India to implement an exchange of population in the East meant that there was no 'evacuee property' in Calcutta where refugees could be resettled. Calcutta received a steadily rising number of Partition refugees, while it had no concerted plan of rehabilitation.[13] This combination of circumstances led to the emergence of a veritable movement of unauthorised occupation of not only abandoned buildings, but also of all available fallow land in and around Calcutta. Groups of refugees got together to form *dals* or association. Familial ties, connections from a past life in East Bengal and political contacts formed the basis of these initiatives. After suitable fallow land was identified, its occupation followed a standard pattern. The land was measured, divided into plots and parcelled out amongst refugee families. The occupiers of each plot had to erect a thatched shelter overnight and move into it. By the time the landlords or the authorities arrived on the scene, they had to contend with a full-fledged illegal settlement. These overnight occupations of land more often than not managed to survive as refugee colonies. This particular form of illegal occupation of land came to be known as *jabardakhal*. Literally meaning acquisition by force, it parodied the current terminology for government requisition of properties, *hukumdakhal*, which meant acquisition by order.

The narrative of Bijaygarh's genesis that can be pieced together from various autobiographical accounts and refugee reminiscences is

[12]The 'evacuee property' of minority communities, who were forced out by a conjunction of refugee belligerence and state complicity, provided the 'shock absorbers' enabling the new states to house their refugees. For a detailed study of state complicity in the displacement of Muslim and Hindu minorities in India and Pakistan, respectively, see Vazira Fazila-Yacoobali Zamindar, *The Long Partition and the Making of Modern South Asia: Refugees, Boundaries, Histories* (New York: Columbia University Press, 2007).

[13]According to the Census of 1951, 433,000 of West Bengal's total refugee population of 2,099,000 went to Calcutta alone. Another 527,000 settled in the contiguous district of Calcutta, 24 Parganas. See Republic of India, Census of 1951, Vol. VI, part III, *Calcutta City* (Delhi, Office of the Registrar General), 305.

slightly different from this standardised pattern.[14] The colony grew out of a squat of twelve refugee families in an abandoned military camp at Jadavpur. In November 1947, they travelled ticketless from Sealdah to Jadavpur station under the leadership of a group of local residents who hailed from East Bengal but had either migrated earlier, or had managed to find jobs and housing in Calcutta. Shombhu Guha Thakurta, Kalu Sen, Ashish Debray and Shantiranjan Sen were a close-knit group of young East Bengali men who decided to help their less fortunate brethren. In this planned occupation of wooden huts abandoned by the army, the refugees transported their meagre belongings, such as utensils and sleeping mats, by a hand drawn cart from the nearest railway station. As news of the squat spread through word of mouth amongst the thousands of displaced families pouring into Calcutta, a steady stream of refugees started to arrive in the military camp. The founders and residents formed the *Jadavpur Vastuhara Samiti* or Jadavpur Refugee Camp Association to promote co-operation amongst the refugees and to work towards providing the basic amenities of life within the camp. As the military barracks got filled to capacity, the later arrivals started building thatched shelters on neighbouring fallow land. There seems to have been little organisation or coordination behind this first phase of squatting. Shanti Sen, the general secretary of the refugee association, stressed on its spontaneous nature. 'At that time, none heeded the other. People squatted wherever they could.'[15] Nevertheless, the

[14]Given the illegal nature of squatters' colonies, reconstruction of their histories has to rely entirely on unconventional archival sources, such as police records, the occasional mention in newspapers, but above all, on the archive of memory. This essay draws upon a range of Bengali autobiographical monographs, namely Indubaran Ganguly, *Colonysmriti: Udbastu colony pratishthar gorar katha, 1948–1954 (Memories of Colonies: An Account of The Early Period of the Establishment Of Refugee Colonies)* (Calcutta: Selg-Published, 1997), Debabrata Datta, *Bijaygarh: Ekti udbastu upanibesh* (Bijaygarh: A Refugee Colony), (Calcutta: Progressive Publishers, 2001), Hiranmoy Bandyopadhyay, *Udbastu* (Refugee) (Calcutta: Sahitya Sansad, 1970) and two compilations of interviews with residents, namely Mukhopadhyay, *Shikorer Sandhane* and Tridib Chakrabarti, Nirupama Ray Mandal and Paulami Ghoshal (comps and eds.) *Dhangsa-o-nirman: Bangiya udbastu samajer svakathita bibaran* (Destruction and Creation: Self-descriptive Accounts of Bengali Refugee Society) (Calcutta: Seriban, 2007).

[15]Interview with Shantiranjan Sen in Mukhopadhyay, *Shikorer Sandhane,* 48.

Association attempted to preserve a modicum of order, demarcating household plots measuring up to a maximum of 4 *kottahs*[16] for each family and registering them in lieu of a contribution of two rupees.

The squatters were acutely aware of the vulnerability of their position and resorted to various strategies to gain legitimacy and government aid. A common practice was to invite leading members of Calcutta society, who enjoyed close ties with the Congress in West Bengal, to be the president of their refugee association. Thus, Basanti Debi, the widow of the veteran Congress leader Chittaranjan Das was president of Jadavpur Refugee Association for a few months.[17] Following this pattern, leadership passed to freedom-fighter Santosh Datta in 1948. The residents of the growing refugee settlement had hoped to gain the favour of the Congress government of B.C. Roy through Santosh Datta's political connections. The period from late 1948 to late 1949 marked a crucial period in the history of this settlement. In the middle of 1949, the landlord, Layalka, hired goons to evict the refugees. This erupted into a pitched battle, which the refugees won. To commemorate this victory, what had till then been referred to as the Jadavpur Refugee camp was renamed Bijaygarh colony. The transformation from camp to colony indicated the determination of the refugees to build a permanent settlement in the area, while the name, literally meaning fort of victory, evoked a militant spirit as the driving force behind the establishment of the colony.

The subsequent history of the colony is an impressive litany of the rapid proliferation of institutions. By 1952, Bijaygarh could boast of four schools, one college, a market, a post-office, a temple, and even a hospital. Certain philanthropists, residents or groups of residents are credited with the foundation of specific institutions. For example, Nalinimohan Dasgupta is credited with establishing the first school in the colony, the *Jadavpur Vastuhara Bidyapith (Jadavpur Refugee School)*; while Dr Aparnacharan Dutta is remembered as the moving

[16]*Kottah* is a popular unit of measuring land in West Bengal. One *kottah* roughly equals 720 square feet.

[17]Despite retiring from active politics after the death of C.R. Das, Basanti Devi continued to be associated with Gandhian social reconstruction in East Bengal. She commanded great respect amongst politicians and social workers in Calcutta.

force behind the establishment of *Prasuti Sadan (Maternity Home)*, a maternity hospital.[18] Though the vicissitudes of memory coupled with differential political affiliations of respondents and authors often lead to contradictory accounts, this rudimentary outline of Bijaygarh's genesis holds water across party lines and perspectives. The consensus breaks down over the nature of the colony, with popular perceptions and contradictory perspectives beginning to inform its inclusion within or exclusion from the category of *jabardakhal* colony.

Hiranmoy Bandyopadhyay's autobiographical account of his involvement with refugee rehabilitation as the principal secretary and chief commissioner of the Rehabilitation Department, mentions Bijaygarh while speaking of the tendency amongst refugees to occupy abandoned Allied military barracks in the southern suburbs of Calcutta. According to him, the scale of the occupation, and the fact that a permanent refugee settlement emerged from it, set Bijaygarh colony apart from other contemporary occupations of army barracks.[19] Planned initiatives, such as the establishment of schools in the larger military halls and reserving open areas for parks and playgrounds, won Bandyopadhyay's respect despite their patent illegality. While praising the residents of Bijaygarh for their self-reliance and enterprise in establishing the first self-settled refugee colony within the Calcutta region, he nevertheless distinguished it from squatters' colonies, on the grounds that Bijaygarh enjoyed informal support from the government of West Bengal.

> Under the leadership of Santosh Datta these families proposed establishing a colony to the government. Evidence can be found suggesting that they received some indications of consent from the authorities. That is why this cannot be placed at the same level as an ordinary *jabardakhal* colony.[20]

[18]Datta, *Bijaygarh*, 28. Also see the interview of Shanti Ranjan Sen and Gouranga De Chowdhury in Mukhopadhyay *Shikorer Sandhane*, 46–66; and interview with Manindra Pal in Chakrabarti, Ray Mandal and Ghoshal, *Dhangsa-o-Nirman*, 123–124.

[19]Bandyopadhyay, *Udvastu*, 23.

[20]Ibid., 35.

Prafulla Chakrabarti seconds this characterisation of Bijaygarh as being in 'a class by itself'.[21] Like Bandyopadhyay, he mentions the existence of 'evidence' of verbal consent by the government, but provides the readers with no clue as to the nature of this evidence.[22] According to him, the real significance of Bijaygarh colony lay in the inspiration it provided to refugees.

> Very few people knew that Santosh Datta's lead ... had received prior approval of the Government. So when the colony which apparently sprang out of unauthorized occupation of land was allowed to exist, there were many amongst the refugees who believed that if only they could take an organized plunge, they could easily get away with the land.[23]

The refusal to describe Bijaygarh as a true *jabardakhal* colony is taken one step further by Indubaran Ganguly. He claims that far from being a squatters' colony, Bijaygarh actually approximated to a government-sponsored one. He claimed that Bijaygarh enjoyed covert and secret official support. Freedom fighter Santosh Datta provided a vital link between the residents of Bijaygarh and the chief minister of West Bengal, Dr B.C. Roy. Ganguly explains at some length the reasons compelling Dr Roy to keep his support secret.

> Dr Bidhan Chandra Roy had started trying to change official policy towards the East Bengali refugees. The land on which the Jadavpur military camp stood belonged to the Government of India. So, until and unless the central government changed its policy towards refugees, it was not possible for the state government to openly support an initiative of building a refugee colony on this land. Yet, he was unshaken in his belief that he would eventually be able to change the Nehru administration's policy towards refugees. That's why he remained in the background and provided patronage to Santoshbabu in his initiative to establish Bijaygarh. It's a matter of note that Santoshbabu too was careful to keep this matter of patronage from Dr Roy a secret.[24]

[21]Chakrabarti, *The Marginal Men*, 36.
[22]Ibid.
[23]Ibid., 37.
[24]Ganguly, *Colonysmriti*, 28.

It is unlikely that Indubaran Ganguly, a dissident member of the CPI who was also one of the leaders of the *jabardakhal andolan*, actually enjoyed the confidence of the chief minister of West Bengal. Tellingly, in an account based entirely on personal memory, while speaking about Bijaygarh he falls back on citing texts.[25] He had clearly not witnessed the establishment of Bijaygarh, and was not acquainted with the leaders, whose intentions he expounded on with such confidence. Nevertheless, his speculation on Santosh Datta's secret pact with Dr B.C. Roy is significant. It is indicative of the general belief amongst the residents of neighbouring refugee colonies regarding the special status of Bijaygarh.

This belief was born of the respect Santosh Datta commanded within the Bengal Congress in particular, and in political circles of West Bengal in general. He was famous for his exploits as the second-in-command of Faridpur district's Jugantar cell, one of colonial Bengal's famous revolutionary terrorist organisations.[26] On one hand, his celebrated status as a national hero gave him access to the contemporary luminaries of West Bengal. On the other hand, he was a refugee and a squatter. This no doubt enabled him to champion the cause of Bijaygarh amongst bureaucrats and politicians. However, his methods were not of open confrontation or political agitation against the government; but of negotiation and judicious exploitation of influence. It seems that these differences in method as well as in political allegiance lay at the core of Bijaygarh, under the leadership of Santosh Datta, falling foul of being a true squatters' colony.

The need for associative politics was urgently felt by the refugees of squatters' colonies. The early leaders had largely been supporters of the Congress or of various socialist parties, such as the Revolutionary

[25]Indubaran Ganguly quotes entire sections of Hiranmoy Bandyopadhyay's *Udvastu (Refugee)* and verbatim summarises Prafulla Chakrabarti's *The Marginal Men*.

[26]A scattered group of revolutionary terrorists who joined the Indo-German Conspiracy came to be known as the Jugantar group. For a history of Jugantar see Arun Chandra Guha, *Aurobindo and Jugantar* (Calcutta, n.d). Also see David M. Laushey, *Bengal Terrorism and the Marxist Left: Aspects of Regional Nationalism in India, 1905–42* (Calcutta: Firma K..L.M, 1975).

Socialist Party and the Praja Socialist Party. However, the obduracy of the authorities in upholding public order and property ownership in the face of an unprecedented crisis forced the squatters to take up a more radical anti-establishment stand. This radicalisation of refugee organisations was coupled by a shift in leadership to the Communists and other left parties. As a result, particular meaning accumulated around a typical squatters' colony of Calcutta. A typical squatters' colony in West Bengal was expected to be a hotbed of anti-establishment agitation and a fertile recruiting ground for the CPI. In this respect, Bijaygarh colony was indeed an exception. In the 1950s, when increasing militancy amongst the residents of squatters' colonies led to the emergence of 'refugee power' as a new player in the complex world of Calcutta politics, Bijaygarh, under Santosh Datta's guidance, held back from overt opposition to the Congress. Indubaran Ganguly has described this rift vividly.

DKSBS[27] was founded at a conference of refugee leaders from all the squatters' colonies in the southern suburbs of Calcutta, held in April 1950.[28] The representatives of Bijaygarh colony attended the conference but refused to be a part of the organisation. While supporting the cause of regularisation of the refugee colonies, Santosh voiced his inability to participate in the methods of agitation which were likely to be adopted by the DKSBS.[29] Bijaygarh colony thus occupied a contradictory position within the history of the *jabardakhal andolan*. On one hand, by virtue of being the first colony built by the independent initiative of refugees, it provided a model to be mimicked by refugee colonies subsequently set up in the area. These colonies not only looked to Bijaygarh for inspiration, but also benefitted from the institutional amenities developed by its residents, such as schools and markets. Nevertheless, Bijaygarh's leaders held aloof from contemporary refugee organisations and refused to participate in the growing movement for the regularisation of squatters' colonies. This soured its relations with other squatters' colonies and fed rumours of a 'secret pact'.

[27]*Dakshin Kalikata Sahartali Bastuhara Samhati* or the South Suburban Calcutta Refugee Association.

[28]Chakrabarti, *The marginal men,* 66; and Ganguly, *Colonysmriti* 28–29.

[29]Ganguly, *Colonysmrity,* 28–29.

The relevance of the contradictory position of Bijaygarh can only be understood within the context of contemporaneous refugee politics. The ill-devised 'Eviction of Persons in Unauthorised Occupation of Land Bill', drafted by the government of West Bengal in 1951 to 'reconcile the demands of the law with the needs of the refugees'[30] was viewed by the refugees as an elaborate scheme to demolish the squatters' colonies. It provided the catalyst for the heyday of belligerent refugee politics under the leadership of the United Central Refugee Council (UCRC). With meetings, processions and often violent demonstrations driving protesting refugees into a collision course with the government, it was no longer enough to merely be an illegal settlement of refugees. The typical squatters' colony in Congress-ruled West Bengal was re-configured as a settlement of militant underdogs. Its refugee inhabitants felt disenfranchised by the establishment. Guided by leaders inspired by the revolutionary ideology of the Left, the 'marginal men' of these colonies fought pitched battles with hired goons of landlords and the police to stall eviction.[31] Like all battles, these clashes too were mythologised in popular memory. They produced not only a fair share of martyrs and heroes, but also a standard narrative of battle between the refugees and the establishment. A combination of anti-establishment politics and direct clashes with the forces of the establishment emerged as the foundation myth of the squatters' colonies of Calcutta. They are repeatedly evoked in refugee narratives of their past, which use the tropes of struggle, martyrdom and sacrifice to legitimise the squatters' colonies. The residents of Bijaygarh, dismissed from the ranks of squatters on account of their proximity to the Congress government, rely on a similar myth of origin to express their cultural identity as refugees.

There is little doubt that many of the squatters' colonies were the repeated targets of police raids and private eviction operations of landlords using hired muscle. The target of these operations would often be the shanties built by the refugees rather than the refugees themselves. Nevertheless, refugees occasionally died defending their new homes. Those who fell to police bullets, such as a pregnant

[30]*Amrita Bazar Patrika*, 21 March 1951.

[31]For details, see Chakrabarti, *The Marginal Men,* 80–1.

woman named Binapani Mitra, were memorialised as martyrs of the refugee movement by the UCRC.[32] However, much more significant is the oft-repeated pattern of refugee resistance in these local battles which has gained the status of refugee folklore. This account envisions the entire refugee colony as a mobilised machine of war against the establishment. In uncertain times, all colony residents had the responsibility of keeping watch. At any sign of the police or suspicious outsiders, the women raised an alarm by blowing on conch shells and by beating steel utensils together. This was the signal for every able-bodied man present to rush out and join battle, armed, literally, with sticks and stones. Children also played a vital role in this idealised armed community. 'There was an informal information network at place which signalled their arrival (mostly done by young boys). Men resisted as women blew conch.'[33] Thus, within moments, a settlement of respectable middle-class refugees would be transformed into a militant army of resistance. At times embellishing these accounts would be accounts of the bravery of refugee women, who fought at the vanguard, or the strategic use of women and children as shields against the police.[34] The narratives of these battles inevitably ended in refugee victory, though the invaders did manage to destroy a few shanties before they left. With exemplary fortitude, the refugees rebuilt their shelters and continued their struggle for rehabilitation and for legitimacy within the socio-economic and political milieu of West Bengal.

The hold of this standardised origin myth of squatters' colonies upon popular imagination, and its impact upon the production of refugee histories is revealed in the text of an interview conducted by Kaliprasad Mukhopadhyay. The interviewer asks Shantiranjan Sen:

> So there had not been any clashes over the land? Then why did the people live in terror? The women were instructed to raise an alarm

[32]Ibid.

[33]Manas Ray, 'Growing Up Refugee: On Memory and Locality', in *Refugees in West Bengal: Institutional Practices and Contested identities*, Calcutta, ed. Pradip Kumar Bose, 166.

[34]The suburban squatters' colony at Mahesh evolved this strategy under the leadership of a local CPI student activist. For details see Chakrabarti, *The Marginal Men*, 81–2.

> blowing conch shells and beating upon tin, etc.—why had these precautionary measures been taken?[35]

The author, Kaliprasad, makes no secret of his empathy for the displaced from East Bengal. Born in Manikgunj in the Dacca district of East Bengal, he came to West Bengal as a young student seven years before Partition. According to Kaliprasad, he too could not escape 'the curse of partition'. He described the loss of his ancestral home in Pakistan and his subsequent battle against poverty as 'an unending quest for roots'.[36] He clearly identified with the refugees and had immersed himself in refugee folklore. Thus, once he set out to interview the residents of Bijaygarh, he aggressively sought confirmation of his pre-conceived notions from his respondents.

For Bijaygarh, this standardised folklore coalesced with an actual clash between the residents and hired goons sent by Layalka, the landlord, to produce the foundation myth of the colony. However, Manindra Pal,[37] Shantiranjan Sen, and Dhirendranath Ray Chowdhury's[38] memories of this clash do not fit the mythologised pattern of refugee warfare. The residents of Bijaygarh colony were largely taken by surprise by truckloads of hired musclemen who drove into the area. They strategically chose to attack in the afternoon, hoping that the men of the colony would be away at work. Their strategy paid off, as initially the refugees were outnumbered and several sustained injuries. According to Manindra Pal, a resident named Badal had been given the responsibility of keeping watch with a bugle at hand for raising the alarm.[39] Of the crowd which assembled in response, a fraction actually offered resistance. The students of Jadavpur Engineering College, who shared close ties with the founding members of Bijaygarh due to their common Socialist affiliations, came to the rescue of the colony. In 1950, when the residents commemorated this victory by renaming Jadavpur Refugee

35 Mukhopadhyay, *Shikorer Sandhane,* 54.

36 Ibid.

37 For the full text of Manindra Pal's interviews see Ibid., 112–5 and Chakrabarti, Ray Mandal and Ghoshal, *Dhangsa-o-Nirman,*. 117–34.

38 For the full text of Shantiranjan Sen and Dhirendranath Roy Chowdhury's interviews, see Mukhopadhyay, *Shikorer Sandhane,* 46–93.

39 Ibid., 114.

camp as Bijaygarh or fort of victory; few chose to credit the role played by 'outsiders'. By suggesting the new name, Shombhu Guha, who was a member of the Congress Socialist Party and played an active role in various constructive ventures within the colony, claimed this victory and its attendant self-image of victorious underdogs, for all the residents of the colony.[40] It fed into the squatters' self-image of self-settled, proud and independent East Bengalis, who relied on little other than a combination of wit and physical valour to wrest rehabilitation from an unsympathetic state. With the proliferation of popular and autobiographical accounts in Bengali from the mid-nineties, the tropes of physical courage, militant organisation and struggle against the establishment have found their way into refugee histories.

The stereotype of the militant refugee obscures more than it reveals of the micro-history of the squatters' colonies. As mentioned earlier, the community leaders of Bijaygarh colony had close ties with the Congress party. Their reminiscences are littered with numerous incidents of non-confrontational interaction with the authorities, such as memorandums, deputations, appeals and unofficial conversations leading to equally unofficial understandings with members of the police and the bureaucracy. Such negotiations were by no means unique to Bijaygarh. In other words, confrontation, especially violent confrontation with the authorities, was only one of the many modes in which the refugees dealt with the state. The significance of the mythic battle waged by refugees lay in its ability to produce a homogenised refugee identity in opposition to the external 'other', i.e., the state and the host society, as embodied in ruthless landlords. It papered over differences in caste, class and cultural capital, which divided East Bengali refugees into disparate groups.

INTERROGATING MARGINALITY: THE ROOTS OF 'REFUGEE POWER'

The history of Jadavpur Refugee camp and its eventual transformation into Bijaygarh colony is characterised by constant attempts by

[40]Interview with Manindra Pal, Chakrabarti, Ray Mandal and Ghoshal, *Dhangsa-o-Nirman,* 123.

the refugees to obtain government aid or legal recognition. The reminiscences of the residents suggest that far from being marginal to the political and bureaucratic order of West Bengal, it was their familiarity with the 'system' which enabled the founders of Bijaygarh to give permanence to an illegal settlement. The quest for new roots in an alien milieu was often aided by old ties of caste, class and locality. The affinity born of a shared past of living in the same district in East Bengal, of belonging to particular educational institutions, political parties or cultural movements, provided not only the building blocks of new communities or associations, but also markers for identifying potential sympathisers within the government and the bureaucracy.

Though illegal, the initial occupation of the Jadavpur military camp met with little opposition from the government. According to Ganguly, Kamalkrishna Ray, who was West Bengal's relief minister during Dr P.C. Ghosh's brief tenure as chief minister, opened all the abandoned military camps and barracks in and around Calcutta for the refugees. Ganguly suggests that since Kamalkrishna Ray came from Myemensingh in East Bengal, his actions were impelled by his empathy for fellow East Bengalis.[41] In his empathy towards East Bengali refugees born of notions of a shared home, and therefore, a shared displacement wrought by Partition, Mr Ray was not alone.

The elite amongst those displaced from East Pakistan were the 'optees.' They were the educated middle-class Hindus who had staffed the vast majority of the posts at various levels of administration in East Bengal. With Partition, they availed of special provisions made for government servants and 'opted' for India. These early migrants were the only ones encouraged, even welcomed, by the Indian state. Though government service solved their problems of livelihood, most were forced to abandon their ancestral homes and property in East Bengal. Not all were fortunate enough to secure official accommodation. Though they had to negotiate a sharp drop in their standard of life, few amongst this class claimed refugee status.[42] In the years after

[41]Ganguly, *Colonysmriti*, 25–6.

[42]It is only of late that the popularisation of the heroic trope of the self-settled Bengali refugee has made refugee identity a mantle worth wearing amongst the '*bhadralok*' of Calcutta.

Partition, the East Bengali optees maintained a conscious social distance from the squalor and desperation of the refugee colonies and camps.[43] Nevertheless, there was genuine empathy towards the refugees who hailed roughly from the same socio-cultural milieu. The more enterprising amongst the refugees specifically appealed to bureaucrats, administrators, and lawyers from East Bengal for help, hoping to exploit affective ties of a common homeland. It is possible that for the elite amongst the optees, who were also dealing with loss and dislocation, patronage of destitute East Bengalis offered a means of rebuilding social status and influence in West Bengal.

Several references to such interactions with authorities and appeals to individual bureaucrats or government officials can be found in the reminiscences of the leaders of Bijaygarh. One such incident which illustrates the role played by personal and social ties in Bijaygarh colony's struggle to gain recognition was the 'battle' with the hired goons of Layalka. Though in the skirmish the residents of Bijaygarh came out on top, it was, in fact, the beginning of their troubles. The police swiftly issued warrants for the arrest of all the refugees involved in the fight as well as for all the committee members. Moreover, Layalka, not to be so easily reconciled to the loss of his land, filed a case against the Jadavpur Refugee Camp Association. Desperate to avoid imprisonment and conviction for activities which were patently illegal, Santosh Datta and his cohort, Dhirendranath Ray Chowdhury alias Kalabhai, sought a meeting with Hiranmoy Bandyopadhyay. The latter was then the district magistrate of 24 Parganas, but had been a *khashmahal* officer in Barisal district of East Bengal before Partition. As a result he was not a complete stranger to Kalabhai, who had been a local celebrity of sorts in Barisal, on account of his participation in revolutionary terrorism and his role as the editor of a literary journal called *Sarathi*.[44] Kalabhai had met Bandyopadhyay at a cultural function organised by the Brahmo Samaj in Barisal, where

[43]For a literary representation of this social distance see Amitav Ghosh, *The Shadow Lines,* Delhi, 1988. Also see MD. Mahbubar Rahman and Willem Van Schendel, 'I Am Not a Refugee': Rethinking Partition Migration', *Modern Asian Studies*, 37, No. 3 (2003): 551–584.

[44]*Sarathi* literally means the charioteer but in this context, the name clearly evoked the role played by Krishna in the epic battle of *Mahabharata* where he had guided the mythical Pandava brothers to victory as the charioteer of Arjun.

he had been extremely impressed by the latter's lecture on Vedic philosophy. Subsequently, he had invited Hiranmoy Bandyopadhyay to be the chief priest at a cultural festival, *Kalidas Janmajayanti,*[45] at the town hall of Barisal. Kalabhai did not hesitate to remind the district magistrate of their previous acquaintance, no doubt in the hope of eliciting sympathy for the squatters.[46]

Bandyopadhyay in turn directed the refugees to seek the help of yet another optee: the officer-in-chief of Tollygunj Police Station, Amulya Bannerjee. He had been a police officer at Keraniganj police station of Dacca district before Partition.[47] The vast majority of the squatters' colonies of south Calcutta, including Bijaygarh, came under his jurisdiction. Refugee reminiscences from Bijaygarh suggest that Amulya Bannerjee secretly helped the residents of squatters' colonies to exploit every possible loophole of the criminal procedure code, while publicly continuing to carry out his duty of evicting illegal squatters.[48] If Kalabhai's account is to be believed, Amulya Bannerjee came to a mutually beneficial compromise with the refugees. He agreed to allow the named refugees to surrender at a pre-determined spot, and to immediately grant them bail. Thus, the refugee leaders were saved the ignominy of being locked up. Mr Bannerjee, in return for his co-operation, was promised a plot or two of the illegally occupied land.[49]

Though the threat of harassment from the police had been averted, the case still had to be fought in court. As the hearing dragged on, the refugees again turned to their more accomplished East Bengali brethren for support. Girin Ray Chowdhury, the lawyer representing the refugees, was from Faridpur district.[50] However,

[45]Literally, this means the birth anniversary of the Sanskrit composer Kalidasa; however, in fact, it was more likely to be the opening ceremony of a literary and cultural festival.

[46]Interview with Dhirendranath Ray Chowdhury, Mukhopadhyay, *Shikorer sandhane,* 77.

[47]Ibid., 113. (Interview with Mani Pal).

[48]Himanghsu Majumdar, a member of the central committee of Bijaygarh colony and its resident since December 1947 makes special mention of his aid. For details see Interview with Himangshu Majumdar in Mukhopadhyay, *Shikorer Sandhane*, 103.

[49]Ibid., 79–80. (Interview with Kalabhai).

[50]Ibid., 115. (Interview of Manindra Pal).

defeat and conviction seemed imminent until the refugees requested Chinta Haran Ray, a famous criminal lawyer from Subidda in Dacca, to argue on their behalf. The colony dwellers could not afford the services of a renowned lawyer. It seems that ties of a lost homeland, coupled with a sense of obligation arising from personal familiarity with one of the refugees, prompted Ray to take up their case free of charge. 'He knew me', explained Manindra Pal, one of the many leaders of colony construction. 'I used to be his brother's classmate at Jagannath Hall in Dacca.'[51] Chinta Haran Ray's expert arguments forced Layalka to drop charges.[52] Thus, the battle with Layalka, which has been mythologised as a militant conflict won by the sheer muscle and grit of desperate refugees, was actually won in court and through deft mobilisation of social connections and cultural capital.

The success of the refugees in negotiating the bureaucratic and legal maze of partitioned Bengal cannot be attributed to successful appeals to well-placed East Bengalis alone. To the colonies they inhabited, many East Bengalis brought a measure of familiarity with associative politics. The founders of the Jadavpur Refugee camp, Shombhu Guha Thakurta, Sushil Sengupta and Ashish Deb Ray, besides being East Bengalis and residents of the small residential complex around Jadavpur University, shared in common their membership of the Jayprakash faction of the Congress Socialist Party.[53] The refugees who took the lead in establishing squatters' colonies usually proceeded only after forming an association or a committee.[54] These committees and associations were invariably registered with the Registrar of Firms, Societies and Non-Trading Corporations of West Bengal under the Society Act of 1886. They conformed to the institutional structure required of registered

[51]Interview with Manindra Pal, Chakrabarti, Ray Mandal, Ghoshal, *Dhangsa-o-Nirman*, 120–21. Also see interview with Manindra Pal in Mukhopadhyay, *Shikorer Sandhane*, 115.

[52]Since the records of criminal cases which do not reach the higher courts are routinely destroyed every ten years, the records of this case have not survived.

[53]Interview with Dr Subratesh Ghosh, Chakrabarti, Ray Mandal and Ghoshal, *Dhangsa-o-Nirman*, 97–98.

[54]Here, Bijaygarh was the exception rather than the rule, as a committee to regulate the day to day life of the Jadavpur Refugee Camp took shape after the abandoned military barracks had already been occupied.

societies, framing a constitution and electing or nominating an executive committee consisting of a president, treasurer and secretary. This indicated not only a high degree of literacy, but also organisational skills typical to a bourgeois public sphere. This knowhow of popular associations provides a far more rational explanation than mere willpower or enterprise, for the ability of a certain section of the refugees to resist official policies of eviction and dispersal.

A significant number amongst the squatters soon came to be employed as clerks or lower level officials in the various departments of the government of West Bengal.[55] This made the colony committees privy to an 'insider's' knowledge of bureaucracy. Often, these contacts succeeded in obtaining government aid for a particular venture of the colony. A number of Bijaygarh's constructive initiatives derived support and stability from such linkages. Shanti Sen was an employee of the government of West Bengal, possibly one of the many clerks employed at Writers' Building, the seat of government in West Bengal. He saw himself as a facilitator of the first meeting between the refugees of the Jadavpur camp and the authorities at Writers' Building. 'I had gone with them (the refugee leaders) since they had never seen Writers' Building before. I guided them and we met the relief minister.'[56] Familiar with the idiosyncrasies of bureaucracy, Shantiranjan came up with an ingenious plan of exploiting the loopholes in administrative procedure in order to derive some official recognition for Bijaygarh.

There were several government employees amongst the refugees at Jadavpur camp who had 'opted' for government service in West Bengal. Sen instructed these men to address an official letter to their

[55]The East Bengali migrants' ability to secure white collar jobs has been highlighted by Joya Chatterji in *The Spoils of Partition: Bengal and India, 1947–67* (Cambridge: Cambridge University Press, 2007) 141–50. Also see Nirmal Kumar Bose, *Calcutta: 1964, A Social Survey* (Bombay, 1968), 34. According to Bose, refugees from East Bengal tended to avoid manual labour and most found jobs as clerks. A statistical survey of refugees in West Bengal conducted in 1955 noted with alarm their high rates of employment in government and other services. For details, see State Statistical Bureau, Government of West Bengal, *Rehabilitation of Refugees—A Statistical Survey, 1955* (Alipore, 1956), 5–9.

[56]Interview of Shanti Ranjan Sen, Mukhopadhyay, *Shikorer Sandhane*, 46–47.

respective departments, asking for some land for resettlement. The letters further requested that if the authorities could not provide land, could they at least forward the application to the Jadavpur Refugee Association, along with a request to that association of a plot of land for the applicant. The point of the exercise was not to actually obtain land, but to trick the respective government departments into indirectly endorsing an illegal seizure of land.

> This strategy of ours paid off. Every department approached in this manner forwarded the applications to our association. They did not know what value these had ... Later on, we could tell the government that they could not deem us to be trespassers, since their administrative departments had forwarded applications to the secretary of our association. This was a great safeguard for us in legal terms. Ten or twelve such applications were forwarded to us.[57]

At other times, Bijaygarh colony enjoyed more direct benefits from having government employees amongst residents. All respondents acknowledged Nalini Mohan Dasgupta as the moving force behind the establishment of the first secondary school for the children of Jadavpur camp. A school named *Jadavpur Vastuhara Banipeeth* was started by local refugee leaders on 6 January 1949. It was later renamed *Jadavpur Vastuhara Vidyapeeth* and with the rechristening of the camp as Bijaygarh colony, it came to be known as *Bijaygarh Vidyapeeth*. At this stage, a permanent committee took over the administration of the boys' section of the school and Nalini Mohan Dasgupta became the secretary of this committee.[58] Dasgupta earned his living as an employee of the Refugee Relief and Rehabilitation Department of West Bengal. 'He was perhaps the office superintendent there', says Gouranga De Chowdhury in his reminiscences.[59] Thus, he was uniquely placed to obtain government recognition for the school, as well as the full package of benefits that refugee students were entitled to.

[57]Ibid., 52.

[58]Datta, *Bijaygarh*, 28.

[59]Interview with Gouranga De Chowdhury, Mukhopadhyay, *Shikorer Sandhane*, 61.

The importance of education in the social geography of the squatters' colonies cannot be over-stated.[60] Almost every colony boasted of at least one secondary school and several primary schools. These schools were not only vital to refugee aspirations of economic rehabilitation through training the next generation for employment, they were also the embodiment of the educated and cultured *bhadralok* identity to which the middle-class squatters clung.[61] These schools also bound the refugee community together at a more practical level. Almost all the teachers of the schools were drawn from amongst local refugees. Manas Ray, in his autobiographical account, noted a large number of school teachers amongst the early migrants to West Bengal.[62] Schools were popular as they provided local employment. Most schools were started by pooling together meagre funds. The teachers depended upon *chanda* or donations for their salary, which was paid irregularly, if at all.[63] Yet, given the high levels of unemployment in contemporary Calcutta, the colony's schools seldom suffered from a dearth of teachers. Moreover, compared to the regularisation of land ownership, which still awaited many refugees, it was comparatively easy to obtain government recognition for the schools. Once a school was registered, which the refugees were quick to organise through their network of connections, it provided regular government jobs to a significant number of refugees. It also became the first step towards gaining legitimacy from the authorities and recognition from the host society of Calcutta.

Not all the residents of the squatters' colonies were middle class or educated. However, the self-image of the squatters was without exception, of the educated *bhadralok*. Literally meaning 'decent people', the term was originally used to describe the landed and

[60]For an analysis of the significance of education in the mind-set of the residents of refugee colonies see Dipankar Sinha's 'Adjustment and transition in a Bengali Refugee Settlement: 1950–1999' in *Refugees in West Bengal*, ed. Pradip Kumar Bose, 147–151.

[61]Manas Ray, 'Growing Up Refugee', ibid., 173.

[62]Manas Ray, 'Kata deshe ghorer khonj' ('The quest for home in a divide land'), in *Dhangsa-o-Nirman*, eds. Chakrabarti, Ray Mandal, Ghoshal, 254.

[63]For a descriptive account of the foundation of numerous schools in Bijaygarh see Datta, *Bijaygarh*, 27–31.

educated Hindu middle class of Bengal. However, with the radical decline of the *bhadralok* in the first half of the twentieth century, the term had increasingly come to represent a claim towards social respectability, bolstered by superior educational qualifications, lineage and cultural pursuits, which may or may not be reflected in economic status.[64] The leaders of the squatters' colonies, irrespective of political affiliations, represented the colonies as *bhadralok* communities, repeatedly stressing education and pursuit of bourgeois culture as markers, which set them apart from the urban poor of Calcutta.

Kalabhai's attempt to elicit support from the district magistrate of 24 Parganas for regularising Bijayagarh colony has been discussed above.[65] In this meeting, he described the squatters of Bijaygarh as 'members of that (East Bengali) erudite society'.[66] Sailen Chowdhury's play on the cultured identity of the squatters was far more spectacular. Once the chairman of Sherpur Municipality of Mymensingh in East Bengal, Sailen had joined the ranks of squatters in West Bengal and had helped to found Deshbandhu colony.[67] He succeeded in eliciting an impromptu meeting with the governor of West Bengal, Dr Katju, through a calculated display of culture. Young refugee girls dressed in saris, blowing conch shells and scattering flowers upon the governor's car as he travelled along the main road bordering the colony proved to be far more effective than a road block. A rudimentary felicitation of the governor in a squatter's shack followed, accompanied by songs and recitations by refugee children. Sailen Chowdhury wrapped up the session with an appeal for help.[68] The display of cultural affinity had the desired effect upon Dr Katju. According to Hiranmoy Bandyopadhyay,

[64]For an exploratory survey of the decline of the Bengali *bhadralok* and their attempts to stem the rot, see Joya Chatterji, 'The Decline, Revival and Fall of Bhadralok Influence in the 1940s: A Historiographic Review', in *Bengal: Rethinking History, Essays in Historiography*, ed. Sekhar Bandyopadhyay (Delhi: Manohar, 2001), 297–315.

[65]Ibid., 159–60.

[66]Interview of Dhirendranath Ray Chowdhury, alias, Kalabhai, Mukhopadhyay, *Shikorer Sandhan*,.78.

[67]Ganguly, *Colonysmriti: (Memories of Colonies)*, 1997, 36–9.

[68]Ibid., 39–41.

who was his companion on this tour, the governor was extremely impressed by the refugees' commitment towards preserving their cultural heritage despite poverty. He showed his appreciation by arranging for the resettlement of Deshbandhu colony on land legally requisitioned nearby. Naktala No. 1 colony, an island of legal settlement within the expanding mosaic of squats in south Calcutta, emerged as a result of Dr Katju's determination to rescue these cultured families from a life of illegality.[69]

From the above discussion, it is clear that much of the enterprise and initiative of the squatters in rehabilitating themselves derived from their social and cultural antecedents. The refugees who built the squatters' colonies came from a socio-cultural milieu where education and white-collar jobs were highly valued. The East Bengali migrants who succeeded in rebuilding reasonably prosperous lives in West Bengal, either as well-paid professionals or as officials in the national administration, remained connected to their poorer 'country cousins' through social ties born of common schools, colleges, socio-cultural forums, or through familial ties perpetuated by marriage. What the squatters around Calcutta lacked in economic means and urban sophistication, they sought to make up through judicious exploitation of social networks and familial ties. However, cultural capital alone was not sufficient to see the refugees through. They turned to politics in order to combat the might of the state, which remained stubborn in its attachment to 'law and order' and reluctant to concede space to the refugees.

The 'infiltration' of refugee associations by the CPI, the relationship between refugee politics and the electoral success of Left parties in West Bengal, as well as the limits of CPI's commitment to the refugee cause has been discussed in vivid detail by Prafulla Chakrabarti.[70] It cannot be denied that Communist support played a crucial role in bolstering the refugees' demand for rehabilitation. But an overt emphasis on confrontational politics obscures the diverse strategies employed by refugees to find a foothold in Calcutta. The vast majority of the refugee families who unleashed the veritable movement of land-grabbing upon Calcutta

[69]Bandyopadhyay, *Udvastu*, 39. Also described in Ganguly, *Colonysmriti*, 36–9.
[70]Chakrabarti, *The Marginal Men*.

had been reduced to bare subsistence levels by circumstances. Desperate to better their lot, they used every possible means, whether legal or illegal. At the microhistorical level, political agitation is revealed to be the most visible of the many strategies of wresting rehabilitation from a reluctant state; not the only, or even the most effective one.

CONCLUSION: SQUATTING AS *BHADRALOK* RADICALISM

Recent research into patterns of displacement from East Pakistan has highlighted how difference in socio-economic background impacted the patterns of migration and resettlement of Hindu refugees from East Pakistan. An enduring paradox that emerges is that those who had the most to lose, in terms of immovable assets, i.e., land and property, were the first to leave East Bengal. These were largely upper-caste, educated Hindus of rural and urban East Bengal, who claimed *bhadralok* status, held white-collar jobs and enjoyed a level of familiarity with Calcutta through work, education or familial ties. Poor peasants and artisans, who were much further down the social scale, left years after Partition and were more often than not pushed out of East Bengal by violent riots during the 50s and the 60s.[71] The squatters of Calcutta came primarily from the first group. Historians have quite rightly highlighted the initiative and enterprise of refugee squatters in order to contest the official stereotype of Bengali refugees as 'an object of derision and contempt', 'a bundle of apathy', 'rebellious' and 'obstructive'.[72] However, there has so far been no attempt at critically analysing what resources enabled the refugees to wrest rehabilitation from a recalcitrant and hostile state. Instead, most accounts indulge in a largely uncritical celebration of the 'self-reliance' and 'resolve' of the architects of the squatters' colonies.[73] Hiranmoy Bandyopadhyay claims that what set the squatters apart from refugees who entered government camps was

[71]See, for example, Chatterji, *The Spoils of Partition.*

[72]U. Bhaskar Rao, *The Story of Rehabilitation* (New Delhi: Government of India, 1967), 141.

[73]See for example, Nilanjana Chatterjee, 'The East Bengali Refugees', 70–77.

their initiative and self-respect,[74] while to Prafulla Chakrabarti, they are no less than partitioned Bengal's '*deux ex machina*'.[75]

This litany of praise simply inverts the official practice of blaming the refugees for the failure of rehabilitation to instead congratulate them for their successes. Both tendencies resist historical analysis and instead turn rehabilitation into a function of the 'character' of the refugees. The microhistorical approach enables this study to move beyond celebratory narratives to reveal the nature and limits of refugee agency. It is clear that the success of refugees in building Bijaygarh derived less from their masculine valour in resisting the goons of Layalka and more from their formidable reserves of cultural capital. Literacy, knowhow of associative politics, ability to negotiate bureaucratic systems of governance and a host of 'contacts' and sympathisers within 'optees', the bureaucracy and various political parties of West Bengal are the resources that the refugees drew upon to consolidate their hold on their illegally constructed homes. In other words, much of the success of squatting derived from the class and caste background of the *bhadralok* residents. It was, thus, a form of politics that was not very accessible to more plebeian populations, such as Calcutta's vast population of urban poor, or illiterate Namasudra peasants who joined the ranks of refugees after 1950. Moreover, the residents of the squatter colonies were extremely eager to maintain their social distance from the urban poor, who were also migrants in acute need of affordable housing. In other words, while the success of the squatters in carving out space for themselves in the face of a hostile government was no mean achievement, it is misleading to celebrate it as a form of radical political intervention by marginalised or subaltern actors.

[74]Bandyopadhyay, *Udvastu*.

[75]Chakrabarti, *The Marginal Men*, 33–66.

CHAPTER nineteen

Becoming a Minority Community: Calcutta's Muslims after Partition

Anwesha Sengupta

I

Calcutta had always been a migrants' city. At various stages of its life, it attracted people from different parts of Bengal, the Indian subcontinent, and beyond. Among such varied groups of settlers, Muslims formed a significant section. Muslims who came to this city belonged to diverse classes, various sects and spoke in different tongues. Bengali-speaking Muslims had come to Calcutta from neighbouring rural districts and they found work in the service sector, especially among street hawkers, weavers, washermen, labourers, and domestic servants. Being the prime centre of education, Calcutta also attracted young men from elite Bengali Muslim families. Since the late eighteenth century and throughout the nineteenth and twentieth centuries, Muslims also came from more distant lands: with the Nawab of Awadh and the ruling house of Mysore came big entourages of court nobles, service men, and intellectuals dependent on royal patronage; traders came from Kathiawar, Delhi, Lucknow, western India and Persia. The court language of the early colonial era being Persian, there were demands in the government services for upcountry Muslims for their language skills. To put it in a nutshell, in the course of colonial rule, certain urban professions of Calcutta were almost exclusively manned by the Muslims: the *khansama*,[1] *darji*[2] and *kasai*[3] being cases in point. Their presence was also significant among the artisans, petty traders, and masons. Similarly, the city housed a world of Muslim intellectuals, journalists, white-collar professionals, and very prominent politicians. Thus, the highly heterogeneous community of the Muslims was, by late colonial times, integral to the city life.[4]

The city could boast of one of the finest Muslim educational institutes namely the Calcutta Madrassah. It was also the birthplace of Urdu journalism in the Indian subcontinent[5] and a specific Urdu dialect, known as Ghulabi Urdu, developed here. Popular Bengali dailies like *Azad* and *Ittehad* that had their clientele primarily among the Bengali Muslims were published from the city. The Mohammadan Sporting, a much admired Calcutta football club that drew the finest of Muslim players from the subcontinent had its fan following not only among the middle-class Muslim population and students, but also among poor Muslims.[6] The city had been home to many Islamic socio-religious movements and in the course of twentieth century, Calcutta became one of the nerve centres of Muslim politics in the subcontinent. Thus, to quote M.K.A. Siddiqui, the involvement of Muslims with colonial Calcutta had been 'fairly deep and systematic'.[7] It was as much of a Muslim city as it was a Hindu one. Naturally, as the partition of British India and the consequent division of Bengal Presidency became inevitable, Calcutta became a major bone of contention between the two communities and the political parties that represented them.

[1]English translation: Principal male servant of an elite household.

[2]English translation: tailor.

[3]English translation: butcher.

[4]See Kenneth Mcpherson, *Muslim Microcosm: Calcutta, 1918–1935* (Wiesbaden: Franz Steiner, 1974), 9–19; to have an idea about the composition of the Muslim community, see Abhijit Dasgupta, 'Muslims in West Bengal', *Economic and Political Weekly,* XLIV(April, 2009): 91–96.

[5]M.K.A Siddiqui, *The Muslims of Calcutta: A Study in Aspects of their Social Organization* (Calcutta: Anthropological Survey of India, 1974), 24; Also, I may mention here, this section is primarily based on the account of Siddiqui, particularly see 18–27.

[6]See Partha Chatterjee, *The Black Hole of Empire: History of a Global Practice of Power* (Ranikhet: Permanent Black, 2012), 319–323.

[7]Ibid., 27.

II

Not surprisingly, the Bengal Provincial Muslim League made a very strong bid for Calcutta in front of the Boundary Commission. Newspapers like *Azad* and *Ittehad,* which sympathized with the Pakistan movement, regularly published maps and statistical charts to establish the League's claim over Calcutta. Rallies and meetings were organized in various parts of the city to mobilize the public in favour of their claim. The student wing of the Muslim League played an important role in organizing these meetings.[8] Economic reasons were put forward to substantiate their position; the Calcutta port was manned by the *Laskars* and much of Calcutta's glory was because of the flourishing jute trade. The *Laskars* were primarily Muslim sailors from Sylhet and eastern Bengal was the major centre for jute production. In other words, Calcutta glittered because of eastern Bengal, which was soon to become East Pakistan. If that was the case, then Pakistan and not India had the stronger claim to the city.[9] In the city itself, Muslims were in a minority in terms of numbers.[10] The Calcutta District Muslim League, however, appealed to the Boundary Commission to ascertain the number of Muslims in the city on the basis of ration cards and not on the basis of the census figures of 1941.[11] Moreover, in a meeting organized by the Calcutta District Muslim League Women's Sub-Committee, an appeal was made to the members of the Boundary Commission and to Lord Mountbatten 'to take into consideration the floating population of

[8]Abul Mansur Ahmed, *Amar Dekha Rajnitir Ponchash Bachhor*, 2nd Edition, (Dhaka: Naoroj Kitabisthan, 1970), 259.

[9]*Anandabazar Patrika,* 19 July 1947. The press clipping is available in N.C. Chatterjee Papers, Volume 2, Press Clippings, Nehru Memorial Museum and Library (NMML), New Delhi.

[10]The 1941 census gives the following figure: Hindus in Calcutta—1,531,512; Muslims in Calcutta—497,535; the census figure is taken from Joya Chatterji, *The Spoils of Partition: Bengal and India, 1947–1967* (Cambridge and New York: Cambridge University Press, 2007), 167; P.C. Mahalonobis too lists Calcutta with the Muslim minority regions of united Bengal, where 23.6 per cent of the total population was Muslim in 1941 and 72.6 per cent was Hindus. See, P.C. Mahalonobis, 'Distribution of the Muslim in the Population of India: 1941' in *Sankhya: The Indian Journal of Statistics*, 7 (1946), 429–434.

[11]*Amrita Bazar Patrika*, 25 August 1947. The press clipping is available in N.C. Chatterjee Papers, Volume 2, Press Clippings, NMML, New Delhi.

Calcutta as well as the permanent residents of the city in this regard.[12] Among other reasons, it was argued that since the major portion of the Bengal Presidency would become East Pakistan, it was only fair that they got the greatest city of Bengal.[13]

If it was impossible to include Calcutta in East Pakistan, the alternative was—according to the Muslim League—to declare it as a 'common' or shared city, belonging to both East and West Bengal, to Pakistan and India. Huseyn Shaheed Suhrawardy, the last prime minister of undivided Bengal, had apparently convinced the governor of the province about the justification for such a demand.[14] A report published in *The Statesman* on 17 July 1947, also quoted Muhammad Ali, the finance minister of United Bengal, as making similar claims. Ali opined that Calcutta should be the seat of both East and West Bengal governments 'until such time as the assets and liabilities were divided' as that would 'obviate difficulties involved in rushing an important matter like the building of a capital for a new province'.[15]

Needless to say, such proposals were vehemently opposed by the Hindu Mahasabha and the Congress. Mahasabha leader N.C. Chatterjee described the League's claim to Calcutta as bizarre and redundant. Calcutta residents were predominantly non-Muslim and *they* owned 91.55 per cent of the residential buildings, they paid the bulk of municipal and other taxes, they owned and operated the major industries and educational institutions of the city—all these points were raised by Chatterjee as he represented the Mahasabha in the public session of the Boundary Commission.[16] Numbers and, more importantly, property, were his justifications for ownership of Calcutta. More interesting was an article by Jatindra Mohan Datta

[12]*The Statesman*, 15 August 1947. The press clipping is available in N.C.Chatterjee Papers, Volume 2, Press Clippings, NMML, New Delhi.

[13]Majid Baksh of South Calcutta Muslim Association made this argument in the Public Sitting of Bengal Boundary Commission. *Amrita Bazar Patrika*, 25 August 1947. The press clipping is available in N.C.Chatterjee Papers, Volume 2, Press Clippings, NMML, New Delhi.

[14]Ahmed, *Amar Dekha*, 259.

[15]*The Statesman*, 17 August 1947. The press clipping is available in N.C.Chatterjee Papers, Volume 2, Press Clippings, NMML, New Delhi.

[16]*Anandabazar Patrika*, 19 August 1947. The press clipping is available in N.C. Chatterjee Papers, Volume 2, Press Clippings, NMML, New Delhi.

published in *Hindustan Standard* on 13 July 1947. He described the plan to make Calcutta a 'common' city as a 'preposterous' one.[17] The idea of a single city forming a part of two sovereign states did not surprise the author as this was not something unprecedented—the Vatican City in Rome was a similar case in point. But then, the Vatican's position was unique: it was above temporal competition among other states and its territory was considered as 'neutral and inviolable'. Pakistan was no Vatican, argued Datta:

> Pakistan to be born is already receiving congratulations from Saudi Arabia and other Arab States; it will surely seek admission into U.N.O ... Pakistan is going to be an Islamic State, but not a spiritual power like the Holy See.[18]

Sharing territory with Pakistan, thus, was out of question.

However, what disturbed Calcutta Muslims most was not opposition from the Mahasabha and the Congress, but the difference of opinion within the League. The position of the 'Nazimuddin faction' of the League vis-à-vis the claim over the city was vague. Abul Mansur Ahmed, a prominent Calcutta-based intellectual and then the editor of *Ittehad,* writes:

> Many leaders belonging to Nazimuddin-group used to come to the *Ittehad* office and tried to convince me against the 'keep Calcutta movement'. They told me that if we did not claim Calcutta, East Pakistan would get Rs. 33 crore as compensation. With that amount of money Dacca could easily become New York.[19]

The promise of 33 crores of rupees was alluring enough to tame the demand for Calcutta. Gradually, pro-League papers like *Azad* and *Morning News* became less insistent about the prospect of possessing or sharing Calcutta.

Perhaps, the League made only a half-hearted attempt, or the reasons for putting Calcutta within India might have outnumbered

[17]The press clipping is available in N.C.Chatterjee Papers, Volume 2, Press Clippings, NMML, New Delhi.

[18]Ibid.

[19]Ahmed, *Amar Dekha*, 260. [Translation mine.]

counter-reasons: whatever the case might have been, with Partition, Calcutta became an Indian city, turning the city's Muslims into a rather vulnerable religious minority, against the backdrop of the communal violence that erupted again and again. With Calcutta being pushed into West Bengal, a new chapter began in the lives of the Muslim inhabitants of the city.

III

On 15 August 1947, shortly after a phase of violence, Calcutta was peaceful and jubilant, to an extent that it seemed almost unreal.[20] The special correspondent of the *Guardian,* reporting from Calcutta, wrote:

> Hindus and Moslems, freely mixing with each other, are in Calcutta tonight wildly celebrating the approach of independence. The former scenes of communal battles are now happy meeting places for crowds of both communities who are shouting and dancing in the streets. No incident has been reported until a late hour tonight.[21]

Andre Béteille, then a school-going child, offers a vivid account of the day:

> In late afternoon, a couple of the boys in our neighbourhood came to our house in great excitement to tell us about what was happening in Rajabazar. The Muslims had come out on the main road in festive clothes and were greeting passers-by from our side with rosewater and flower petals ... we were sent off by my mother to witness and participate in the celebration at Rajabazar.
>
> There was something magical about the transformation that we witnessed and millions of others in other parts of the city also witnessed.[22]

[20]From Tazuddin Ahmed's diary it is evident that in Dhaka too, the day of Independence passed peacefully. Hindus and Muslims joined the Independence day procession in large numbers and there was no news of communal trouble in the city. See *Tazuddin Ahmed's Diary, 1947–48,* Vol-1 (Dhaka: Pratibhas, 1999),37–39.

[21]http://www.guardian.co.uk/theguardian/1947/aug/15/greatspeeches, accessed on 7 December 2012.

[22]Andre Beteille, *Sunlight on the Garden: A Story of Childhood and Youth* (New Delhi: Penguin, Viking and Ravi Dayal, 2012), 125.

For a city that had witnessed the most gruesome communal violence a year back, it was an extraordinary moment. Since 'the Great Calcutta Killing', Calcutta had been the site of sporadic communal trouble. No one was expecting a peaceful Independence Day. Gandhi was staying in the city to pour, in his own words, 'a pot of water over the raging fire that was burning'.[23] Amidst this atmosphere of fear and anxiety, the day of Independence that was all about celebrations and festivities, seemed nothing short of a miracle. Gandhi, however, wrote to Mira Behn,

> the joy of the crowd is there ... but not in me is any satisfaction.... Hindu Muslim unity seems to be too sudden to be true.[24]

There were good reasons behind the peace, albeit transient. After almost two centuries of colonial rule, freedom, for all its terrible costs, did call for a respite, however temporary, and celebration. Also, Hindus, in a majority in the city, must have been relieved as Calcutta remained in India and they celebrated without restraint. Muslims—now a suspect and minority category—could no longer afford to be perceived as trouble makers. Independence, moreover, would have touched all hearts, including theirs. This perhaps explained the 'miracle' on August 15.

Gandhi's apprehensions, however, were not misplaced as the cordial atmosphere proved to be very short-lived indeed. Within a couple of weeks the city was again in flames. Professor Anisuzzaman, a child then, was in Calcutta at that time. He remembers:

> (The Riot) continued for three-four days. Gandhi sat for a fast as long as the violence continued. Suhrawardy toured the riot affected areas of the city. Some of the leaders of the ruling party and of the opposition tried their best to stop the carnage.[25]

People were panicky. Little Anisuzzaman, down with high fever, had nightmares about being attacked by the Sikhs: 'I used to see that the Sikhs were coming along the Bright Street to kill us. I shouted: "The Sikhs are

[23]Krishna Kripalini, *Gandhi: A Life* (New Delhi: National Book Trust, 1968), 179.

[24]Ibid., 181.

[25]Anisuzzaman, 'Amra Pakistan-e Elam' in *Deshbhag: Binash O Binirman*, ed. Madhumoy Pal (Kolkata: Gangchil, 2011), 53. [Translation mine.]

coming, the Sikhs are coming.'"[26] The September riots had traumatized him. His father decided to leave Calcutta and India for East Pakistan.[27]

The city remained a site of intermittent violence against the Muslims for years to come. A general feeling of anxiety was punctuated with moments of intense conflict. Calcutta witnessed brutal communal riots again in the early months of 1950. From late 1949, such trouble in East Pakistan was making headlines in the city newspapers. There was a notable increase in the number of refugees coming to West Bengal and Assam. They brought with them horrid accounts of Muslim violence—accounts that were made by weaving together rumours and realities. It agitated the Indian Hindus. Many of them had relatives and friends living on the other side of the border and for others, it was a threat to their religious community that needed to be redressed. The situation worsened in both East and West Bengal towards early February. Following a chilling retributive understanding of justice, right wing organizations and their sympathisers systematically started targeting Calcutta Muslims. On 6 February, Sheikh Muhammad Rafiq, a member of the West Bengal Legislative Assembly, informed the House that Muslims were facing trouble in areas like Kankurgachhi, Beliaghata, Mirzapur and Bagmari.[28] He described it thus:

[26]Ibid.

[27]Though the communal riots during Partition are almost always perceived as conflict between two communities—the Hindus and the Muslims, the Sikhs too played a very active role in them. During the Great Calcutta Killing, there had been many instances where the members of the Sikh Community, along with the Hindus, actively participated in the riot. Among the victims too, there were Sikhs. See, for instance, *Calcutta Disturbances Commission of Enquiry*, Records of Proceedings, Minutes of Evidence, Government Printing, 1947, Volume VI, 178–179 (Available in Maulana Abul Kalam Azad Institure for Asian Studies, Kolkata). This is only one random example from an eleven volume document. There are numerous similar examples referred to in these volumes. Also, one may mention that in Punjab and Delhi too, the communal riot during Partition was broadly between two groups: the Sikhs and the Hindus on one side, and the Muslims, on the other. It appears that at that moment of conflict, Sikhs were incorporated within the larger Indian community against the Muslims. However, in less than 40 years this 'alliance' would be broken with the Khalistan Movement, Operation Blue Star, and finally, with the most gruesome anti-Sikh riot (1984) under the auspices of the Congress Party.

[28]These areas are located in the north-central part of Calcutta.

> These troubles do not start at daytime; they always take place at night. And as usual it takes time for the police to arrive. The police arrive not only one or two but sometimes three or four hours after the occurrence. Those who live near College Street and Mechuabazaar junction know how certain people, members of certain community, tried to interfere with the Kowali which was being held in the market there, resulting in loss of properties and injuries to members of minority community.[29]

Describing the Muslims of the city as 'nervous and panicky', he asked:

> If anything happens in any part of the [other] Dominion the repercussion is there for us ... Are we responsible for that? Have we not done everything that you wanted us to do, in order that the minority in the other Dominion may be given full protection?[30]

Rafiq had not much faith in the ability or in the goodwill of the city police. So he requested the government to be more liberal in giving arms licences to the 'law abiding and peaceful' members of the minority community so that they could 'at least protect their houses and their women folks'.[31] Despite their secular claims, it seems that the Congress government under Dr Bidhan Chandra Roy in West Bengal had not been able to restore confidence among Muslims.

A proposal like that of Rafiq's, however, was bound to be rejected by the government as it would only establish its inability in protecting the citizens. On the other hand, Muslim members of the Legislative Assembly could only request the government to ensure the protection of the minorities, make suggestions in this regard, and join the ruling party to squeeze some benefits from the government for their supporters or side with the other opposition parties to create strategic pressure on the government. They tried all of these avenues at various stages. But in those anxious days of February, they mostly pleaded with the government for some relief.

[29]'Budget Session', West Bengal Legislative Assembly Proceedings, 1950, 12.
[30]Ibid., 13.
[31]Ibid., 14.

On 7 February 1950, Husan Ara Begum, a member of the West Bengal Legislative Assembly made another desperate appeal:

> At the present moment, the Muslims of Calcutta are living under a pressure, I should say, of fear, specially at Maniktalla and Narkeldanga which I have visited personally ... even last night they were harassed. Many of the Muslims of Paikpara have left their hearths and homes ... I am appealing to the honourable chief minister to protect the life and properties of those citizens who are looking up to him for help.[32]

Despite these appeals, a full-fledged riot broke out in Calcutta on the very next day. Violence first erupted in the Maniktala (in northern part of Calcutta) area. Soon it spread across places that were within the jurisdictions of Beliaghata, Amherst Street, Entally and Tangra police stations.[33] There were numerous instances of stabbing, loot, and arson that systematically targeted Muslims. Inflammatory leaflets and handbills were distributed, posters demanding 'blood for blood' were put up in certain parts of the city. The police proved to be ineffective on numerous occasions. The presence of Rashtriya Sevak Sangha Chief Golwalker in Calcutta in the month of February and the provocative speeches made by Mahasabha leaders like N.C. Chatterjee further worsened the situation. They demanded an immediate exchange of population: that is, an exchange of the Muslim population of West Bengal with the Hindus of East Bengal. The demand implied that there was no space for Muslims in Calcutta or in West Bengal, irrespective of whether they wanted to stay here or to go to East Bengal. The massive influx of Hindu refugees from East Bengal further marginalised Muslims within the city. A large section of refugees coming from East Bengal squatted on abandoned Muslim properties. At times they forcibly occupied, with the help of the Mahasabha and other right wing parties/organisations, the mosques, graveyards, other *wakf* properties and houses where Muslim families lived—thus displacing the minorities.[34]

[32]Ibid., 54.

[33]Sekhar Bandyopadhyay, *Decolonization in South Asia: Meanings of Freedom in Post-Independence West Bengal, 1947–1952*, First Paperback edition (Delhi: Orient Blackswan, 2012), 51–52.

[34]Mridula Sarabhai's Report on the Communal Situation and Riots in Calcutta in 1950 (22 Feburary 1950) in J. Bagchi, and S. Dasgupta (ed.), *The Trauma and the Triumph: Gender and Partition in Eastern India*; Volume 2 (Kolkata: Stree, 2009), 260–267.

Lalbagan Seva Samiti, a voluntary organisation situated in Raja Dinendra Street, Calcutta, for instance, claimed to have rehabilitated about 650 refugee families in 229 houses that were apparently lying vacant in the Lalbagan area. Apart from these 229 houses, there were numerous 'burnt houses' which, too, they allotted to refugee families. The Samiti was assisted by the North Calcutta District Committee of the Congress Party.[35] It is important to mention that Lalbagan area meant the locality marked by Vivekananda Road in the south, Nirodbehari Mullik Road in the north, Canal West Road in the east and Upper Circular Road in the west.[36] It incorporated Maniktala, Amherst Street and Beadon Street[37]—i.e., areas that were the worst affected by the riot of 1950. It is obvious that the vacant and torched houses had had Muslim occupants before February 1950. Some of the incidents that took place here were notorious enough to draw the attention of the prime minister. Jawaharlal Nehru wrote in a letter addressed to Dr B.C. Roy: 'I am informed that Hindus are taking forcible possession of many Muslim houses in Mirzapur area ... I understand that a very large number of houses were destroyed in Maniktola etc.'[38]

One may note in passing that till 1958, the government had received at least 3,176 applications from Muslims reclaiming their properties that were forcibly occupied during the February Riot. At the same time, the government claimed that they already had restored to Muslims 956 houses originally owned by Muslims but which were later forcibly occupied by refugees from East Pakistan in 1950.[39] These numbers together provide an idea about the intensity of the riot.

[35]Sibnath Banerjee Papers, Subject File No-122, Year—1950, NMML, New Delhi.

[36]Ibid.

[37]See P.T. Nair, *A History of Calcutta's Streets* (Calcutta: Firma KLM Pvt Limited,1987), 244, 624–625, 924–925.

[38]Letter dated March 16, 1950. See S.Gopal (Series Editor), *Selected Works of Jawaharlal Nehru*, Volume 14, Part I, Second Series, Jawaharlal Nehru Memorial Fund, 1992, 122–123. The date of the letter proves that though the riot of 1950 is known as the February Riot, the disturbances continued even in March. Actually, the situation improved slightly in April as Nehru and Liaquat Ali Khan (president of Pakistan) met and signed a pact to safeguard minority rights (8 April 1950). The pact is known as Nehru-Liaquat Pact or Delhi Pact.

[39]West Bengal Legislative Assembly Proceedings, 21 February 1958, *23 (admitted question no 25), 174.

People of Calcutta and scholars who write about this city, however, seldom remember this riot.[40] The 'Great Calcutta Killings' of 1946, with Suhrawardy as its main culprit is much more etched in the public memory of the city.[41] The reason behind this selective memory is somewhat obvious. In 1946, the British government had been at the helm of affairs and the Muslim League then ruled in Bengal. In the dominant postcolonial imagining of Indians, both groups were 'outsiders'. Either or both together could be comfortably blamed for the riot without tarnishing the image of the 'nation'. However, the riots of 1950 and 1964 in West Bengal questioned the secular claims of the Congress government and also pointed the finger towards right wing parties like the Hindu Mahasabha.[42] Now the perpetrators of the communal violence were unquestionably Hindu and the victims were

[40]There is one article by Sekhar Bandyopadhyay, 'The Minorities in Post-Partition West Bengal: The Riots of 1950' in *Minorities and the State: Changing Social and Political Landscape of Bengal,* eds. Abhijit Dasgupta, Masahiko Togawa, and Abul Barkat (New Delhi: Sage Publications, 2011), 3–17. Also, in an article by Anasua Basu Ray Chaudhury, the impact of the February Riot in Hooghly has been discussed. See Anasua Basu Ray Chaudhury, 'Remembering the Communal Violence of 1950 in Hooghly', *Journal of Borderland Studies* (2012), 47–59.

[41]A fascinating study is possible regarding the ways in which Suhrawardy is remembered by various sections of the people in both the Bengals. In the memoirs/autobiographies of Abul Mansur Ahmed, Anisuzzaman and others, Suhrawardy is a hero—a saviour of the Bengali Muslim interests in West Bengal after Partition. For the Bengali Hindus, however, Suhrawardy was the principal culprit behind the Great Calcutta Killings, a coward who was saved from the agitated Hindu mob by Gandhi. But there is a lack of scholarly work on this very fascinating figure who stayed put for a while in Calcutta after Partition, perhaps had been involved in the Calcutta Riots, was an aide of Mahatma Gandhi during Gandhi's last stay in Calcutta, had a troubled relation with Nazimuddin and later became the prime minister of Pakistan.

[42]Calcutta was one of the major epicenters of the riot of 1964 that affected both East and West Bengal. The parts of the city affected by this riot included areas within the jurisdiction of Kareya, Beniapukur, Amherst Street, Beliaghata, Entally, Muchi Para, Taltala, Jorasanko, Watgunge, Ekbalpur and Garden Reach. For most of the month of January, 1964, these areas were under curfew. The army was called in to maintain law and order in the city. Also, as a precautionary measure many schools and colleges in the city remained closed during this period. I have found the details of this riot in the *Amrita Bazar Patrika* newspaper of January, 1964. Needless to say, going through the pages of a daily published from Dhaka, like *Azad* or *Morning News*, or the Communist Party paper *Swadhinata* (published from Calcutta)—one will see accounts of the riot that may differ significantly from those found in *Amrita Bazar Patrika.*

Muslim. It was also a total departure from the earlier pattern of violence where both sides were equally pitted against each other. Naturally, moments like these were seldom discussed, often denied and ultimately forgotten by a 'national' community that was very much Hindu.[43]

IV

Numbers, in themselves, did not turn the Muslims into a minority community overnight. Becoming a minority was about a feeling of vulnerability:

> A community begins to perceive itself as a minority when it feels disadvantageous in the context of the nation-state; and the claims of minority rights gets strengthened when a case of discrimination can be convincingly made against the nation-state. The fact that minorities are fewer in number enhances this sense of marginalization and vulnerability but does not constitute in itself a sufficient condition either for the emergence of a minority consciousness or for validation of minority claims.[44]

The fact that the government failed to prevent communal riots and provide security to the lives and properties of the Muslims of the city made the latter feel cornered and helpless. However, in the 'partitioned times' overt violence was but one, albeit major, factor in turning the Muslims into a minority. There were other factors too. Many of the Islamic institutions and symbols were systematically erased from the city landscape. Take the case of the Islamia College. Situated in central Calcutta, it was founded in 1926 by Lord Lytton, then governor of Bengal. This was a premier institution that promoted Islamic education as well as a more 'general' education to Muslim pupils. With Independence, the gates of the college were opened to all students irrespective of their religion. Moreover, the name of the college was changed from Islamia College to Central Calcutta College. The new name indicated its geographic location but attempted to

[43]In West Bengal a significant number of the Hindu Bengalis were originally from East Bengal and many of them were 'refugees'. So they have their own positional politics to shape their memories and understandings.

[44]'Introduction' to *Minority Identities and the Nation-State*, eds. D.L. Seth and G. Mahajan (New Delhi: Oxford University Press, 1999), 8.

erase a certain past associated with the institution.[45] From the Central Calcutta College (today known as Maulana Azad College), it is a five-minute walk to the Calcutta Madrassah, another major institution for Islamic learning. Built in 1781, this institution, too, bore the brunt of Partition. All its moveable properties, including books and manuscripts in the Madrassah Library, were shifted to Dhaka. The Bengal Madrassah Education Board also shifted to Dhaka, leaving behind a number of high madrassahs and the Hooghly Islamic Intermediate College, without any central organization for their control and coordination. Apart from two professors, the entire faculty of the Calcutta Madrassah opted for service under the East Bengal government.[46] The institute survived, but became a shadow of its past. When I went to the Calcutta Madrassah in search of documents related to the transfer of its collection, the librarian showed me a catalogue of the books that were available in the library back in 1927, and lamented that not a single book mentioned in the catalogue was now there in the library. 'Pakistan took it all. They forgot that Islam does not allow its followers to collect booty after any war', said Md. Kased Ali, the librarian. For him, Partition was a war that the League won with the creation of Pakistan. 'People who ruled Pakistan never thought of us, who stayed on in India', said the librarian.

He continued:

> Who knows whether the books reached the Dhaka Madrassah or not. We have heard that they carried the books and the manuscripts on open trucks. It was the rainy season. Many books were probably destroyed due to the rain, people say so.[47]

[45]In 1960, the name of this college was again changed. Now it became Maulana Azad College in honour of the most prominent nationalist-Muslim' leader from the Congress, Maulana Abul Kalam Azad. Azad was a figure that fitted well with the secularist portrayal of Congress—he was a Congress man himself, who though being a practicing Muslim, never supported the Pakistan movement. Later, he became the first education minister of independent India. Thus, he was the 'good' Muslim who could be posthumously accommodated within the nation-space through the construction of statues and renaming of streets, institutions, and localities.

[46]Md. Maniruzzaman, 'Kolkata Madrasah-er 205 bachhor' in *Madrasah College: Bicentenary Celebration Souvenir,* February 1985, pages are not numbered.

[47]Interview with Kased Ali, 10 February 2012.

Partition left Calcutta Muslims bereft of their heritage: old names, institutions, intellectual resources.

Muslims were also losing their grip over their religio-social spaces. Since 1946, every communal clash had resulted in the desecration or forced occupation of mosques, graveyards, and *waqf* properties. The squatter colonies that developed on the southern fringes of the city—Behala, Tollygunj, Kasba, Garia, Santoshpur—often appropriated *waqf* lands.[48] Hindu refugees coming from East Pakistan because of majoritarian violence or for fear of it, saw Calcutta Muslims as 'soft targets' and often selected their properties for squatting. Writing in 1964, Nirmal Kumar Bose noted that many of the Calcutta mosques were then in a 'moribund condition' and some of them were actually used by the refugees for residential purposes.[49]

In this regard, one must specially mention the seminal essay by Joya Chatterji titled 'Of Graveyards and Ghettos: Muslims in Partitioned West Bengal 1947–67'. She has shown how Muslim residents of Selimpur (in Dhakuria, Calcutta) gradually lost their rights over a local graveyard. This was not an exceptional case. To quote Chatterji,

> Calcutta's landscape is dotted with Selimpurs. Most Muslim burial grounds in the city bear similar marks of retreat and defeat. Part of the burial ground for Muslim paupers at Park Circus, which had no boundary wall and no masonry graves, was being used in 1997 as a football ground, despite complaints to the corporation on whose ground it stood. The custodian of the burial ground at Gobra, founded in 1896 by Zillur Rahman on *Waqf* land, told a similar story. The cemetery had originally covered some twenty bighas in the chart of a Muslim dominated locality and close to a mosque on Ashgar Mistri Lane. In 1964 during the Hazratbal riots, scores of Muslims left the area and the locality was occupied by the refugees from East Pakistan ... gradually they occupied more and more area of the paupers' graveyard, which had no boundary wall and no masonry graves, until three quarters of the cemetery had been captured. Appeals to the corporation for permission to erect

[48]See Romola Sanyal, 'Contesting refugeehood: Squatting as survival in post-partition Calcutta' in *Social Identities*, 15, No. 1 (January 2009), 70.

[49]Nirmal K. Bose, *Calcutta: 1964, A Social Survey* (Bombay, New Delhi, Calcutta and Madras: Lalvani Publishing House, 1968), 66.

> a boundary wall were unsuccessful. The new occupants have since then set up a tannery on that ground and also use part of it as a football ground ... [thus] boundaries of sacred and ritual space ... were redrawn in the aftermath of partition.[50]

Economic opportunities, too, progressively diminished for certain sections of Muslims. For instance, in pre-Partition Calcutta, Muslims had dominated the tailoring occupation. Muslim *darzis* who lived mostly in the Metiaburj and Santoshpur area, had nearly monopolized markets for readymade garments in Calcutta and Howrah. But with Partition and the coming of refugees from East Bengal, they started losing their control over the markets. As M.K.A. Siddiqui and S.P. Lala note:

> It is said that these people [i.e. the refugees from East Bengal] are more efficient businessmen than the Darzis of Metiaburj. Moreover they have an extra advantage ... of receiving loans from the government.... Within a short period they have received a sufficient knowledge about tailoring by coming in contact with the tailors of Metiaburj.... The women of these refugee tailors also participate in the business.[51]

One may mention in passing that this was also a time for political compromise. To establish their loyalty towards the Indian state, Muslims who chose to stay put in India, had to sever all possible links with the Muslim League. Joining the Hindu Mahasabha was not possible for its pronounced communal colour. But many erstwhile League supporters joined the Congress. The 'separatist' politics of the pre-Partition Muslim League had no longer any relevance in postcolonial India, as was stressed by many Muslim leaders repeatedly. For instance, in a meeting of West Bengali Muslims held at University Institute Hall, Calcutta, in November 1947, a resolution was passed:

[50]Joya Chatterji, 'Of Graveyards and Ghettos: Muslims in Partitioned West Bengal 1947–67'in *Living Together Separately: Cultural India in History and Politics,* eds. Mushirul Hasan and Asim Roy (New Delhi: Oxford University Press, 2005), 239.

[51]Siddiqui and Lala, 'The Darzis of Metiaburj' in *Aspects of Society and Culture in Calcutta*, ed. M.K.A. Siddiqui (Calcutta: Anthropological Survey of India,1982), 136.

> Existence of a separate political organisation for the Muslims of India in the present set up is not only unnecessary but suicidal.[52]

Some Muslim leaders, who could not bring themselves to join the Congress but were prudent enough to sever their links with the League, formed a new party named the Parliamentary Opposition Party of West Bengal. Janab Abul Hashem declared the fundamental aims of the party in the Legislative Assembly of West Bengal on 26 March 1949: 'namely equality of man, socialistic economy and democratic polity'.[53] He was also careful to mention that the party would be 'non-communal and non-sectarian' in nature.[54]

As it is perhaps evident from the earlier discussion, in several socio-economic spheres of this city, Hindu refugees became the prime contenders against the Muslims. Much of refugee rehabilitation took place at the expense of Muslims as well. It was a very delicate situation for the government. Their secular commitments obliged them to safeguard minority interests. On the other hand, in the context of the Partition, they could not oppose refugees beyond a point as the latter enjoyed immense public sympathy as well as the support of both right and left wing parties. In their much touted attempt to maintain a fair balance, the government repeatedly tried to move refugees from the illegally occupied houses, but promised alternative arrangements According to the West Bengal Act XVI of 1951, refugees, if evicted from the properties where they squatted, were ensured of alternative accommodation and monetary compensation. It was also decided that the compensation amount would be determined by a neutral 'competent authority' (read—high court judge) and the location of the alternative accommodation would be determined keeping in mind the occupation of the refugee. But in 1957, certain amendments were brought in. Compensation was no longer necessarily money *and* accommodation, but now could be only financial compensation. Also, 'competent authority'

[52]*Amrita Bazar Patrika*, 10 November 1947. The press clipping is available in N.C.Chatterjee Papers, Volume 2, Press Clippings, NMML, New Delhi.

[53]West Bengal Legislative Assembly Proceedings, 26 March 1949, Volume 5, No: 2, 259.

[54]Ibid.

no more meant a high court judge but the government. The Bidhan Roy ministry justified the law and the subsequent amendments as necessary steps to free houses once owned by Muslims from illegal occupants and to restore them to their original owners. But, of course, the opposition was vehemently critical of this. The CPI suspected that the real intention of the government was to evict the squatting refugees from the properties of industrialists like Anandilal Poddar and Bangur. Right wing leaders saw the interventions as anti-refugee measures. Whatever be the priorities of the government—industrialists or Muslims—evicting refugees from illegally occupied land was a deeply sensitive issue at the time. It is interesting to note that in the scholarly accounts too, the focus is either on the 'trauma and the triumph' of the refugees *or* on the plight of the minorities.[55]

V

For many of the city Muslims, staying put in Calcutta was no longer an option. Migration started early as some elite Muslims started moving out of Calcutta immediately after Partition. The 'Great Calcutta Killing', the Noakhali riots and the Bihar riots (all in 1946) along with the ongoing communal carnage in Punjab and Delhi, had made them jittery about staying back in West Bengal as a minority. So, when Calcutta became a part of India, they chose to leave immediately. For many others, it was the February Riot that worked as the ultimate push factor. Staying on was no longer a safe option and they had to migrate. Also, as a consequence of Partition, Dhaka became the major centre of Muslim politics of East Bengal, and Calcutta, like the rest of India, had a Congress government. Many of the prominent Muslim leaders therefore left Calcutta for Dhaka to start a new episode of their political career in Pakistan.[56]

[55]I am not saying that all the accounts of the lives of the refugees in West Bengal, demonize the Muslims, but that generally, they maintain a silence about the displacement of the Muslims caused by refugee settlements. Similarly, articles like Joya Chatterji's 'Of Graveyards and Ghettoes' sympathize with the Muslims but in a way forget the desperation of the refugees.

[56]See Mcpherson, *Muslim Microcosm*, 150–152.

Moreover, Dhaka, as the new capital of East Pakistan, had significant employment opportunities.[57] So it drew in the bulk of the elite urban Muslim migrants. Also, accustomed to the Calcutta-life as they were, going somewhere else apart from Dhaka was almost unthinkable for this urban elite group.

But even then, compared to Calcutta, Dhaka was no more than a *muffasil* town. Calcutta had been one of the most magnificent cities of the British Indian Empire, it imagined itself as the London of the Indian subcontinent. To understand the glamour of the city one may quote Andre Béteille, who was originally from Chandannagar:

> Calcutta was the city of every mofussil Bengali's dream ... I thought of Calcutta only in terms of variety and abundance. It had everything that Chandannagar lacked. No doubt London was even more magnificent, but it was out of my reach, even in imagination. Calcutta, on the other hand, occupied a central place in our folklore.[58]

Naturally, leaving such a city was a crushing experience. In their autobiographies and memoirs, many erstwhile Muslim residents of Calcutta remembered the despair and loss they had felt in their early days in East Pakistan. Many also recalled the apprehension among their family members about settling down in Dhaka. Let us go back to the memoirs of Anisuzzaman. He remembered the discussions that his father had with his brothers-in-law. For him, leaving Calcutta for Dhaka was almost like leaving civilisation behind. He repeatedly asked:

> How is this city? Do people get bread and butter there? Is there electricity, tap water? How do people commute from one place to another? Are there trams and buses like Calcutta?[59]

[57]With the majority of the Hindu *bhadralok* leaving East Pakistan for India after Partition, much opportunity for employment was created in the education and health sectors and in government services. The educated Muslim middle class was absorbed in these sectors in East Pakistan. All the Bengal (and Punjab) government employees were given a choice to opt for a job either under the Pakistan government or under the Indian government after Partition. Most of the Hindu officials opted for India and their Muslim counterparts chose Pakistan.

[58]Beteille, *Sunshine*, 71–72.

His longing for Calcutta was so acute that he ultimately did not go to Dhaka. He settled down in Khulna instead. Khulna Town was much nearer the border than Dhaka and hence was closer to Calcutta—one did not have to cross the river Padma to come to Khulna from Calcutta. The proximity to Calcutta gave him some solace: if Pakistan should ever become a part of India again, he could at least easily come back to his beloved city.

Mijanur Rehman, who later became a noted author and cartoonist of Bangladesh, left Calcutta in 1948. He was then a teenager. Leaving Calcutta for Dhaka was a demoralizing experience. As he confessed in his memoir:

> I was very depressed when we came to Dhaka from Calcutta. Dhaka could not claim to be a big city ... it was not even that big in size ... The Dhakuria lake, the Alipur Zoo, theatre halls like Minerva, Srirangam, Star or Natyabharati, cinema halls like Metro, Light House, Globe, New Empire, Elite.... Dhaka had no equivalents. Let me not speak about the College Street book market and the Maidan! Why Dhaka, there were perhaps no such places in the whole world![60]

If Mijanur Rehman missed the grandeur of Calcutta, for Taiyeba Kamal, settling down in Dhaka was more about everyday compromises. She left Calcutta with her parents only two days before Partition. Her father, a supporter of the Pakistan movement, wanted to participate in building the new nation of Pakistan. Like many of his co-religionists, migration to him was the 'natural culmination of one's religiously guided participation in the Pakistan Movement'.[61] Pakistan was the beginning of a much greater task: the nation had to be built from the scratch. Despite all the dedication, ideological commitment and enthusiasm of these Pakistani nationalist elites, however, they could not help but notice the disparities between Calcutta and Dhaka and missed the little comforts that the former

[59]Anisuzzaman, 'Amra Pakistan-e Elam', 54. [Translation mine.]

[60]Mijanur Rahman, *Dhaka Puran* (Dhaka: Prathoma, 2011), 104. [Translation mine.]

[61]Tahir Naqvi, 'Migration, Sacrifice and the Crisis of Muslim Nationalism', *Journal of Refugee Studies*, 25, No-3, (2012), 487.

could offer and the latter could not provide yet. So, Taiyeba Kamal did remember:

> There were too many mosquitoes. Bread was not to be had. We munched *muri* (puffed rice) for breakfast. You see, Dhaka was not as developed as Kolkata, where the British influence was considerable and good quality bread could be bought.[62]

Those who left the city in these years were not necessarily residents of Calcutta by birth. Some of them were originally from areas that were now parts of East Pakistan. But they had grown up in Calcutta, studied in its colleges and universities, and had then started their career in the city. They had participated in its political movements, had joined the city-based literary and cultural organizations and cheered for their favourite football team in the Maidan and so on. Their social lives were intrinsically linked to the city. This was their city of opportunities, hopes, and dreams. For them to leave the city was as tragic as becoming refugees. As Abul Kashem, the noted painter of Bangladesh wrote in his memoir:

> I was born in East Bengal. But I spent the early years of my youth in Calcutta—the great city of the British Empire. I often think of those days. When I think of Calcutta I still get overwhelmed. It is like watching a huge flock of birds, flying in the sky. They compel you to observe them, as long as possible.[63]

To Kashem, the flock of flying birds—the ultimate motif for freedom—symbolized his days in Calcutta. The city had meant freedom and liberty. Born and brought up in a conservative family where painting was taboo, not surprisingly, Calcutta gave the young painter the much needed space to breathe in. The riot of 1950 forced him to leave the city—but the city remained his icon of freedom.

Nonetheless, be it Abul Kashem, Mijanur Rehman, or the family of Anisuzzaman—they all belonged to the upper echelons of society. Migration and relocation was relatively easy as they possessed the

[62]Bagchi and Dasgupta, *Trauma and the Triumph*, 163.

[63]Abul Kashem, *Puber Janala* (Dhaka: Bangalisamagra Jadughar, 2010), 34 [Translation mine.]

necessary 'mobility capital'—i.e., 'the goods of education, land, cash, and gold in varying amounts, as well as local standing, networks of contacts, and the know-how to deploy these assets to make their migrations viable.'[64] Although, in a way, their migration from West to East Bengal could be seen as 'forced', they still had scope for deliberations: their journeys, though traumatic, were almost always preceded by much preparation, debate and discussion within their families, friends and neighbours.

The experience of the city's poor Muslims was significantly different. They literally fled from the riots. Some of them managed to cross the border but most lacked the necessary means for bordercrossing. They searched for security in areas within the city or in the suburbs where their co-religionists had some numerical strength. Scholars of post-Partition Calcutta have, at times, identified—ghettoizing tendencies among Muslim residents.[65] Those who could neither make it to East Pakistan, nor found refuge in Muslim majority areas, were the most vulnerable lot. They were the worst victims during riots. A few who managed to escape from the violence, huddled together in the hastily put-up government relief camps. But as Muslims, they received very step-motherly treatment from the government. For instance, a section of poor Muslims took shelter in the Park Circus Maidan during the 1950 riot. But staying for months on a stretch of open ground, with no proper shelter apart from some tents, was not much relief. The government provided some dry rations to them till mid-June. But then began the attempt to shift them to the Mohishadal Destitute Home in Midnapur as: 'Concentration of so many people in this Park was a danger to public health' and 'Government could not allow the city's parks to be breeding grounds of cholera and small-pox'.[66] Doles were stopped to push them out. Finally, they were forcibly evicted

[64]Joya Chatterji, 'Dispositions and Destinations: Refugee Agency and "Mobility Capital" in the Bengal Diaspora, 1947–2007', *Comparative Studies in Society and History*, 55, No. 2 (2013), 284.

[65]See for instance Joya Chatterji, 'Of Graveyards and Ghettos'; Also see 'Staying On' in Joya Chatterji, *The Spoils of Partition*; Also refer to Gargi Chakravartty, *Coming Out of Partition,* (New Delhi: Bluejay Books, 2005), 118.

[66]Press Note, 13 January 1951, File No–9c1-1/51, Bundle No 4, List 119, Political (C.R.), Archives and National Library, Dhaka, Bangladesh.

from the Park Circus grounds in early 1951.[67] What separated these destitute Muslims from the impoverished Hindu refugees staying in the government camps was the lack of public sympathy towards the former. In the 'partitioned times' forced eviction of Hindu refugees always gave birth to much controversy, public protest and political mobilisation on their behalf. But as Muslims, and, that too, as poor Muslims, dwellers of the Park Circus Maidan, were easily thrown out from their make-shift camps and no public protests followed.

However, it is nearly impossible to have a very detailed idea about the movement or displacement patterns of the poor urban Muslims because of the paucity of material. We know from Legislative Assembly debates and certain ethnographic surveys that there had been significant shifts in settlement patterns of the Muslims within Calcutta. M.K.A. Siddiqui, for example, noted while studying Muslims *Patuas* who primarily stayed in slum areas of Narkeldanga:

> Frequent shuffle in their population has, however, occurred and several families from the locality have immigrated to East Pakistan (now Bangladesh) as well as to the suburban villages of Mallikpur and Sonarpur while several other families have come to stay in the locality from other areas of Calcutta ... and even from suburban villages during last three decades.[68]

Similarly, we come to know from the Legislative Assembly debates that after the February Riots of 1950, many Muslim labourers who worked in Calcutta and Howrah, had to leave their homes and jobs.[69] The riot, according to a government estimate, displaced approximately 30,000 Muslim industrial labourers from West Bengal. Of them, 20,000 returned and were absorbed into their jobs by 1953.[70] One may safely assume that most of them

[67]Ibid.

[68]M.K.A. Siddiqui, 'The Patuas of Calcutta: A Study in Identity Crisis' in *Aspects of Society and Culture,* 55.

[69]See for instance the statement of Janab Lutful Haque in West Bengal Legislative Assembly, 2 March 1953, Legislative Assembly Proceedings, Vol VII, No-2, 19.

[70]West Bengal Legislative Assembly Proceedings, Volume VIII, 24 November 1953, 978. The figures are given by Kalipada Mookherjee, M.I.C., Labour Department.

worked in the industrial belt of Howrah and Hooghly and a sizeable number were from Calcutta. But one has no clue as to the exact or approximate district-wise distribution of displaced labourers who moved 'internally', nor can one guess how many of them crossed the border. Similarly, we do not know why some of them chose to come back and others did not and it is almost impossible to trace the experiences of their migration, let alone of their return.[71]

It is possible to argue that Partition was not just a 'refugee generating process', as another category of migrants—the Internally Displaced Persons (IDPs)—was also born out of it. However, the migration/displacement patterns of the city's poor Muslims were far more complicated than terms like refugee or IDP reveal. A Muslim, facing or fearing communal violence, could temporarily move towards a *mohalla* within the city where Muslims were in a majority. But the *mohalla* might not be safe enough and eventually he would have to leave for Pakistan. To further complicate the picture, moreover, there were significant numbers of returnees who had to be rehabilitated in their original homes. Returnees, IDP and refugees were, therefore, not mutually exclusive or neat categories in the context of partitioned Bengal.

IN LIEU OF A CONCLUSION

Almost a decade after Partition, Ela Sen wrote a letter to the editor of the *Times of India*:

> Calcutta has its own Frankenstein—the four and a half million refugees ... are now holding the city at ransom. It is impossible to enter from any direction without climbing over their heads. They are in possession of the railway stations. Desperate and despairing, this is a classless society. Each one has been ground down to bear

[71]After the February Riots of 1950, a pact known as the Delhi Pact or Nehru-Liaquat Pact was signed between India and Pakistan which though promised smooth passage between East Pakistan and India for migration of the religious minorities, also encouraged return migration of the already displaced population. The pact assured the refugees that they would get back their lands and homes on their return to their countries of origin within a particular date. The pact indeed encouraged considerable return migration.

> an identical face—a face from which all distinguishing marks of education, culture or occupation have been effaced. No longer it is possible to tell the school master from the postman.... At Sealdah station, on the east side of the city, the counter marked 'Reservation' is like some island in a vast sea of ragged filthy destitution. The clerk and his clients are separated by thick masses of humanity. At first the would be traveler looks around a little desperately, then he picks his way over sleeping children, bags full of rags that pass for clothes, before they can possibly arrange their reservations.[72]

Evidently, Ela Sen was at her wit's end. Not every individual shared her feelings so strongly though. Some had deep sympathy for refugees and were disgusted with what they thought was the lackadaisical attitude of the government regarding rehabilitation. But it is almost certain that if one asks septuagenarian or octogenarian Hindu residents of Calcutta about the memories of the city in the 1950s and '60s, they will talk about the massive influx of the refugees, the left politics of protest that rocked the city life and perhaps about the failures and successes of the Congress government, depending on their political orientation. But they will hardly recall that Muslims, once an important and integral part of Calcutta, were either disappearing from the city or were ghettoized in a few areas like Park Circus, Raja Bazaar and parts of Central Calcutta. This selective amnesia is also reflected in much of the scholarly work, as the literature on the impact of Partition on Calcutta's Muslims is surprisingly thin. This article is a very modest attempt in addressing this gap.

[72]*The Times of India*, 14 July 1957.

CHAPTER twenty

I Had a Dream One Night (1929)

Rabindranath Tagore

Translated by Swagata Mazumdar

In the depths of sleep, I heard Binu call
Wake up, wake up, see Calcutta roll
I looked up and found the roof all a shake
Beams and rafters clashing in journey's wake.

Brick and mortar monsters ploughed ahead
Doors flapped, windows took on flight
Roads shook all over like well fed beasts
Helpless tramcars tossed on the troughs and crests.

Shops, stalls, markets—now up, now down
Roof clutching, roof trying not to drown
The Howrah Bridge, a centipede, crawling away
Harrison Road flowing all the way.

The Monument swayed, enraged elephant
Rending the skies with blows from its trunks.
Our school runs off at a smart pace
Maths and Grammar books, too, not to be left.

Maps on walls, all restless for change
Fluttering, as birds do, when they sense a change.
Bells ring, bells ring all through the day
No pause at all, let alone an end.

Millions clamour for an end to the madness
They say how futile is this journey endless
To such prayers, Calcutta pays no heed
But dances on, intoxicated by speed.

I muse, why not head off to Bombay
Delhi, Lahore, Agra—and live in a new way
If perchance, we end up in Albion
Worthy citizens we'll be, dressed up as their own.

Some sudden sound jolted me back to sense
To find Calcutta still the same old place.

CHAPTER twenty-one

Time in Place
Urban Culture in Decades of Crisis

Tanika Sarkar

I

Studies of modern Indian cities generally revolve around the creation and transformation of urban space, propelled by long term historical change. They discuss the uneasy cohabitation between pre modern and modern urbanisms as colonialism imposes its built forms on Indian cities ; as modern planning and sanitation schemes gradually crowd out older landscapes and shove the urban poor to the city margins ; and as neo liberalism envisions brand new corridors and enclaves of power where a postcolonial urban aesthetic can come into play for the urban rich. Sometimes the city is visualized as a stage for specific actors: cultural performers, insurgents, criminals, prostitutes, victims of epidemics. Depending on our inclinations, we can see the modern city as a hard, planned, impenetrable space, created entirely according to colonial and bourgeois interests and plans: or we can see it as 'soft city', malleable and plastic, which even urban subalterns can imagine and indent in their own ways.

The present collection brings to the fore a very different order of urban experience where time becomes a palpable and mighty force, beating against urban space and people, creating, destroying and remaking lives in bewilderingly quick ways. Several momentous histories got compressed into the two brief decades of the 1940s and 50s. Some of them were catastrophic, some were moments of rare ecstasy and promise. The promise and the limits were, moreover, intertwined intimately.[1]

The book begins with a later poem by Rabindranath: of Calcutta of the poor clerk and of the rich and fashionable artist, of a moribund lane and of deathless classical music, which, nonetheless, exist within the same alley space which is a metaphor for the city itself. Both the romance and the misery appear enduring.

In the middle of this collection, however, the slow rhythms of an older urban life are sharply fractured by a very different kind of poem by Samar Sen. The Second World War came very close to Bengal and, for the first time, Calcutta experienced modern warfare as Japanese bombs fell on the city, creating panic. Along with war came a killer famine, scattering rotting corpses all over city streets. It was followed immediately by a violent communal holocaust which, in its turn, presaged a cataclysmic partition—when the rivers and villages of the first poem were lost to the people of Calcutta. If the famine was of colonial making, the savage communal killings that followed were a quicksand that Hindus and Muslims devised for themselves. The second poem recalls the city before the riots: the squalor and slog of quotidian lives, the occasional poetry of certain special places and times. All are now lost and all are recuperated as intense longing for the ordinariness of humdrum urban existence.

Yet, these were also the best of times. Long awaited Independence came sooner than expected and it exceeded the urban everyday as well as the urban cataclysmic. It was a day of pure joy, of tumultuous celebration, such as never seen in the city before. Enmities were forgotten—though only too briefly—and freedom was greeted with a renewed sense of bonding that overcame a savage history of strife. It was a moment out of time.

The third poem, with which the collection ends, is another one by Rabindranath. Written much earlier, it still responds to the acceleration of senses and experiences that urban change involves. It creates a dream-fantasy about the city that seems literally to hurtle through space. The present collection similarly recalls times when all that is solid melts into air: as does space itself in the poem.

[1]For an excellent overview of the times, see Sri Manjari, *Through War and Famine: Bengal 1939–45*, Orient BlackSwan, Delhi, 2009.

II

Times which put the very survival of lives and norms at stake also threw up an immensely diverse and creative cultural world. Obviously, the work that comes down to historians belongs predominantly to the literate middle classes who alone possess the resources to preserve their experiences. However, we do find occasional traces of cultural activism of the urban poor in our period. In this postscript, I will very briefly touch on just a few aspects of the many cultural developments of these years. So much happened in these years that the essay will, unfortunately, read like a catalogue or an inventory. The Calcutta cultural scene was significantly shaped by political engagements of different kinds. Some of the leading intellectuals came to advocate non political art. They, too, however, had initially been involved with anti fascist activities. Second, the forties were definitely dominated by a broadly leftist cultural understanding. If the dominance receded somewhat in the fifties, leftist culture continued to set some of the terms of the debates. Third, even though all through the two decades, communal politics and rightwing political groups exerted strong and even hegemonic sway over much of Bengali political imagination, they could not mark the cultural horizon in any significant way.

Debates about culture were dominated by three strands: the left, non left liberals, and leftists who abjured Stalinism and who therefore distanced themselves from the Communist Party of India (CPI) line. Non left cultural liberals were sometimes strikingly experimental in their imaginaries about personal lives and choices, about new kinds of gender relations. They were concerned with questions of poverty—though they, as well as the leftists largely ignored caste—and they were secular and anti communal to a remarkable degree. There were, of course, uncertainties about the desired degree of liberal values, especially as older moral norms had tumbled not because of a deliberate new social consensus but because of new material circumstances which forced change. At the same time, rapid changes simultaneously created social anxieties, an intense longing for older figures of female nurture at home, an idealization of joint families and rural lives.

As historical processes became more and more turbulent, political partisanship grew intense. The Congress still enjoyed hegemony as the bearer of the freedom struggles, a reputation enhanced by its eventual decision to oppose the war effort, to resign from all ministerial positions and to launch the Quit India Movement. Calcutta, though affected by the upsurge, was, however, not one of the strongholds. When the Congress was banned, the political field was largely left to communal politicians of the League and the Mahasabha who continued to enjoy the spoils of government and who intensified mutual hate campaigns. The Congress also faced a formidable rival in Subhas Chandra Bose whose celebrated Great Escape from house arrest in 1941 made him a Bengali icon. The subsequent formation of the Azad Hind Fauj with Axis support endowed him with a romantic-militarist aura and created a soft spot for anti British Fascist powers in many Bengali minds.

Communists enjoyed a rare spell of freedom from repression in the early and mid-forties when their anti-War line changed overnight into support for the People's War as Nazis attacked the Soviet Union. There was, consequently, a brief period of collaboration with the British war effort. They put the reprieve to good use with energetic famine relief; with peace activism during the Great Calcutta Killings which cost them several young cadres ; and by sending out young men and women to join the rural uprising on the Tebhaga issue. The 'anti national' anti Congress politics was, nonetheless, a time of considerable growth and influence, especially among rural sharecroppers, urban intelligentsia and factory workers.

Communists of the 40s took culture very seriously.[2] That did not mean that they crudely fictionalized, dramatized, painted or versified political dogma. They experimented with creative forms to add rich nuances even to propaganda art. Their representations of subalterns and class struggles—especially in the fiction of Manik Bandyopadhyay and in the political journalism of the poet Subhas Mukhopadhyay—were filled with a raw energy and passion, a staccato and jagged prose, and bitter irony as well as detailed and vivid descriptions of subaltern lives which were, of course, idealized as a contrast to so called middle class decadence. So, even

[2]The best account of leftist cultural production is in Sudhi Pradhan, ed and compiled, *Marxist Cultural Movement in India: Chronicles and Documents, 1936–47*, National Book Agency, Calcutta, 1979.

if the themes were predictable, the forms created a new expressive language. In the next decades, some leftist women novelists like Sabitri Ray and Sulekha Sanyal imparted other, more complex and delicate tonalities to the range. At the same time, there were far more towering non left authors too, especially fiction writers who represented a liberal nationalist politics: Bibhutibhushan Bandyopadhyay, Tarashankar Bandypadhyay and, increasingly, Ashapurna Debi, among others. Their writings on rural lives and on wartime Calcutta also used social realism and an acute sense of fast changing times. The narrated worlds were often larger and more layered than in leftist fiction.

Major debates about poetry accompanied new poetic forms in the post Rabindranath era. While a self conscious modernism and boldly transgressive themes and words characterized the works of Buddhadeb Bose and Sudhindranath Dutta, Jibananda Das struck out a lonely path with poetry steeped in a haunting melancholy about spectral rural landscapes and pasts. Communist poets, Subhas Mukhopadhyay and Sukanta Bhattacharya, wrote with a simple and strong diction and critical energy. Samar Sen's leftism, however, produced a very different order of poetry: instead of strident hope, it was dark, angry, mocking, almost nihilistic, laced with a doom laden beauty. It was poetry at the limit of itself and he stopped writing it after Independence.

It was, in many ways, a culture produced by young people. Many were students in their twenties, sometimes working closely with teachers, scholars, artists who were in their thirties and forties. In the new sociabilities of the times—the informal yet regular *addas*[3] that were held in the 'drawing rooms' of literary figures or in rooms rented by journal editors or political activists—discussions were undirected yet deeply intellectual and often political. They were also multi generational as students and very young literary or political activists received a warm welcome at the homes of senior intellectuals: a major one being located at the Rashbehari Avenue

[3]For the concept of the new Calcutta *addas*, see Dipesh Chakrabarty, 'Adda, Calcutta: Dwelling in Modernity', *Public Culture*, Duke University Press, 11(1) 1999, pp. 109–145. I have borrowed much from an elaborate discussion of the new sociabilities from Sumit Sarkar, *Modern Times*, forthcoming, Permanent Black, Ranikhet.

residence of Buddhadeb Bose which also doubled as Kabita Bhawan for the journal of poetry, *Kabita*, and which continued to be a hub in the fifties.[4] Though these meetings did have a central figure who set the tone, civil arguments and disagreements were not uncommon.[5] In the forties, however, these were still all male gatherings and the women of the families who hosted them would appear as providers of refreshments or as rather silent listeners. Young women became much more visible and audible in the intellectual and political discussions at coffee houses and tea shops in the fifties. Another group of people who sometimes joined the *adda* were European and American soldiers serving in India, usually with a strong left leaning—some were veterans of the International Brigade during the Spanish Civil War—or academics and visiting literary figures who sought out their Indian counterparts.

Rather than a conventional taxonomic labelling of this enterprise as a typical manifestation of bourgeois civil society practice, Dhritikanta Lahiri-Choudhury's word for the gatherings—*goshthibhittik bandhusamaj* or association of like minded friends—tells us more about their shape and content as well as about new sites of literary-political friendship.[6] There were quite a few of the *addas*: the leftist circle around the journal *Parichay*, gatherings at the homes of Budhhadeb Bose and the leftist poet Bishnu Dey, and so on. The discussions flowed from and contributed to journals and publications.

Since the twenties, or even somewhat earlier, groups of Bengali writers had tried to turn the literary focus upon subaltern lives and struggles and had experimented with incorporating the speech patterns and idioms of workers, peasants and tribals, breaking away from the chaste classicism of Rabindranath. These writers of the so called *Kallol* era continued to write. On the other hand, a new generation of poets struggled to find their own diction which would take literature beyond the overwhelming power of Rabindranath's language.

[4]Buddhadeb Bose, *Amader Kabita Bhaban*, Calcutta, 1976.

[5]Sunil Gangopadhyay, *Ardhek Jiban*, Ananda Publications, Kolkata, 2002, pp. 154–5.

[6]Dhritikanta Lahiri Choudhury, *Jibaner Indradhanu*, Ananda Publications, Calcutta, 2012, p. 115.

On the eve of the war, at a three days' Calcutta meet at the All India Pragatisheel Lekhak Sammelan, the trends briefly came together. Buddhadeb Bose, who later founded the memorable *Kabita* journal, devoted entirely to poetry and literary criticism, declared in a speech: 'The age of Rabindranath is over'.[7] To mark the new age of poetry, he and Abu Sayyid Ayyub collaborated in bringing out a collection of self consciously modern poetry by new poets. *Kabita* also introduced new poets: ranging from Jibananda Das to Samar Sen.

At first, anti fascist sympathies brought liberals and communists under a joint literary front but dissensions soon appeared. Bose was alienated by the monolithic political line of communists. And, ironically, he was repelled by their total break with Rabindranath's representational modes and their aspirations to restrict literary sensibility to representations of class struggles alone. He took his own class seriously, and saw more in it than mere food for criticism. The leftist literary journal, *Parichay*, on the other hand, moved steadily in a pronounced communist direction and, gradually, poets like Sudhindranath Dutta who were critical of Stalinism, withdrew their association with it. They pursued a more ironic stance towards the world, complex experiments with poetic language and with aesthetic, emotional and erotic experiences. The left, in its turn, found their opponents' commitment to art for art's sake, their insistence on the autonomy of the aesthetic, and their endless probes into the endless facets of love tedious, if not socially and politically irrelevant.[8] At the same time, personal friendships and mutual respect survived across political difference and the entire spectrum continued to share certain common liberal values. Outside this complex literary horizon, and pitting itself against it, stood the conservative, anti communist and anti avant garde literary journal, *Shonibaarer Chithi* which lampooned both.[9]

[7]Buddhadeb Bose, *Amader Kabita Bhaban*, Calcutta, 1976, p. 149.

[8]Hiran Kumar Sanyal, 'Fascibaad, Samaj O Shilpa': Paper read at All Bengal Fascibaad Birodhi Sammelan, December, 1942, and a review of *Kabita*, nd, in *Chhoriye Chhitiye*, Papyrus, Calcutta, 1991, pp. 25, 127–9.

[9]See for example, Shrikrishna Dey, 'Dhanasamyabaad' in *Shonibaarer Chithi*, cited in Sipra Sarkar and Anamitra Das, eds, *Bangalir Samyabad Charcha*, Ananda Publishers, Kolkata, 1998, pp. 171–3.

Much of the initiatives for institutionalizing cultural activism came from the Communists in the late 1930s when they founded, in quick succession, the Pragati Lekhak Sangha (1936), the Youth Cultural Institute (1939), the Fasci Birodhi Lekhak O Shilpi Sangha (1943) and the Bharatiya Gananatya Sangha (1943). The Youth Cultural Institute, formed by students of the Calcutta University, coined the concept of Ganasangeet or people's songs—a new combination of folk and radical political music which would, some day, bring subalterns and middle class cultural activists within a shared left rubric. At first, traditional folk songs were used but Jolly Kaul wrote a new song one day which was set to tune by Nikhil Sen: 'Mazdur mazdur hai hum/sari duniyaki raja hai hum' (we are workers, we are the kings of the world). This was followed by a spate of new songs about contemporary political and material problems of workers.[10]

This was, possibly, an anticipation of the Indian Peoples' Theatre Association (IPTA) movement of the famine years when the Communist Party, under the General Secretary P.C. Joshi's broad initiative, developed remarkable departures in Indian musical and folk theatre practices. Troupes of communist cultural activists experimented with songs, dance and drama and took them to different cities and villages in India to raise funds for famine relief in Bengal. They brought back a newfound closeness with lives of the rural poor. Songs were composed in many Indian languages, perhaps the most emblematic being 'Bhukha Hai Bangal' or Bengal Goes Hungry. They synthesized folk and varieties of traditional Indian musical compositions as well as western ones. The Bengali composer of the political-folk, Salil Choudhury, broke with the modal structure of standard melody form in his 'Dheu Uthechhe' or Waves Rise High, and used a series of modal melodies, each accompanied by its own harmonic orchestration, so that each section sounded like a different song. The world of songs composed a new musical-national as all regional languages participated: and also a new musical-international which drew upon a knowledge of and fluency in world music.[11]

[10]Anuradha Ray, *Challish dashaker Banglai ganasangeet Andolan*, Papyrus, Calcutta, 1992, p. 42.

[11]Sumangala Damodaran, 'Singing Resistance: Understanding the Musical Tradition of the IPTA' in Gargi Chakravartty, ed, *People's Warrior: Words and Writings of P.C. Joshi*, Tulika Press, Delhi, 2014, pp. 428–446.

Famine themes were taken to famine struck villages by young urban enthusiasts who improvised open air performances, new stage techniques, script and theatrical conventions in a matter of days. Bijon Bhattacharya's play, *Nabanna*, was one of the best known IPTA productions. The enthusiasm and the confidence were, perhaps, somewhat overdone and even leftist critics complained that the play was not an adequately realistic portrayal of peasant lives, the construction was weak and melodramatic and the use of rustic language was often amateurish. At the same time, they proudly congratulated the troupe's acting talent and its commitment which made it respond to immediate needs and not wait till the perfect play could be produced.[12]

Jamini Ray recreated older *patachitra* from rural and urban folk art traditions to produce serene and earthy figures painted in deep, primary colours. They made his urban studio a haven for urban avant garde intellectuals and artists, who paradoxically imagined the Calcutta based artist to be a sure route to an authentic rural cum mythological world and culture, and to people's art which represents timeless figures in times of change. Love for his paintings was shared by non communist and communist intellectuals and literary figures. But communists gradually evolved a new art form. They combined the bold and minimal lines from Ray and the spare black and white woodcut tradition that Nandalal Bose had perfected in the *Sahaj Path* primers in the thirties. This resulted in a new people's art or propaganda art for the Party. A communist youth, Somnath Hore, travelled to rural Bengal to compose a pictorial diary of his encounters with peasants during the Tebhaga movement: depicting in small woodcuts, their labour, details of their everyday lives and homes, the lined faces of old men and women bending to their tasks: familiarizing and endearing the historical subjects of peasant insurrection to urban viewers, rather than representing struggles as such.[13] Chittaprasad, whom P.C. Joshi recruited into the Party in 1940 to work as propaganda artist, created striking posters, cartoons, portraits of leaders, documentary images as well as calligraphic texts, focusing on details of bodies at work. Later he

[12]Hiran Kumar Sanyal, *Chhoriye Chhitiye*, Papyrus, Calcutta, 1991, p. 109.
[13]Somnath Hore, *Tebhagar Diary*, Subarnarekha, Calcutta, 1991.

drew a Hungry Bengal series in the Communist newspaper, *People's Age*: linocuts that showed with clinical brutality starving, dying and dead bodies of famine victims.[14]

Political differences sharpened in the fifties, as communists dismissed Independence as illusory. Under the leadership of B.T. Ranadive and an overall direction from a changed Soviet line, they began an insurrectionary phase of action: unleashing a series of exemplary single actions, strikes as well as minor acts of violence against government properties, which would, hopefully, herald a mass revolution. At the same time, the sharp change in political line led to fratricidal tensions within the Party: a situation that Sabitri Ray's contemporary novel, *Swaralipi* portrayed vividly. There were major strikes in the fifties: tram workers' strike in 1953, schoolteachers' strike in 1954 and the food movement of 1959 against steep prices. Teachers' strikes were a new development and the sight of schoolteachers sitting on a dharna on public streets was unprecedented. The Congress government hit back with a formidable arsenal of repression. The Party had already been banned in 1949, and the ban was later lifted just before the first general election. There were firings on protest demonstrations, including on women, lathi charges and tear gases. Police firing killed four Communist women—Latika, Pratibha, Amiya and Geeta: perhaps, for the first time, middle class women activists stopped bullets in the city.

Young students, even when immersed in cultural preoccupations, found the daily confrontations exhilarating. Sunil Gangopadhyay, one such young man, describes the 1953 tram workers' strike:[15] 'Every day we would hurry to Wellington Square, the hub of the movement. Then began hand to hand fights with the police. We would be pushed back into alleyways and then again come out to join the fray and throw brickbats at the police. We faced lathis and teargas and once I lobbed a teargas shell back at a policeman'. The spectacle of fights with longstanding symbols of repression was too tempting to stay away from: even for a budding poet who

[14]Rajarshi Dasgupta, 'The People in people's Art and People's War' in Gargi Chakravartty, op cit., pp. 446–8.

[15]All translations from Bangla passages are mine.

frequented the Kabita Bhawan and who spent the rest of his time devouring Dostoevsky, Mallarme as well as Mir Musharraf Hussein. It was also the time when he first met Sankha Ghosh who had started a movement for bringing poetry to the streets: young poets reciting poems in front of pedestrians. They planned to bring out a collection of poetry written by the very young. Sunil Gangopadhyay met the best known illustrator of the times—Satyajit Ray—and the proprietor of the remarkable Signet Press which brought out a large and extremely beautiful collection of significant literary works. He was also entering a new world where romances with young women became a distinct possibility for these young social radicals and, what was more significant, romances were now an end in themselves, without thought of marriages to follow. It was, indeed, a time when many worlds—old and new—overlapped.[16]

The same mingling of literary, academic and political activism is recalled by Dhritikanta Lahiri Chowdhury, a regular habitué of Bishnu Dey's home gatherings and a communist student of English literature, active in discussions on Greek drama at the university. He participated in the tramworkers' strike and has left a hilarious account of his activism. 'Biren was chosen to explode a bomb at the junction of the Jagubazar corner, right on the tramline ... we reached Ground Zero at the intersection of Ashutosh Mukherjee Road and Puddapukur. We stood at a distance, surrounding him. But he had to be visible and be seen by the masses while in action. Biren got the bomb out of his sling bag and then discovered that he could not light a match with a single hand Undeterred, he squatted on the ground and placed the bomb right on the pavement. Then he brought out his sweat soaked matchbox from his pocket and rubbed the matchstick till the wick of the bomb was lighted... In the meantime, a few hundred pedestrians had gathered around and were watching him avidly. Now arrives a tramcar, ringing its bell and Biren hurls the bomb at it. The tram was untouched but there was a lot of smoke. Reactionary passengers came down shouting abuse at us and we shouted back revolutionary slogans...'[17] Lingering

[16]Sunil Gangopadhyay, *Ardhek Jiban*, Ananda Publishers, Kolkata, 2002, p. 154.

[17]Dhritikanta Lahiri Chowdhury, *Jibaner Indradhanu*, Ananda Publishers, Kolkata, 2012, pp. 91–2.

smoke as the only trace of a full scale insurrection plan—something like a metaphor for the communist experience?

Independence and the recovery of the national homeland had left millions homeless: at Sealdah Station, at rudimentary camps, in colonies. The struggle for land was led by the communists among refugees. Though it led to a heroically determined struggle for survival through everyday battles with owners of vacant properties which refugees occupied, the struggle had its dark side as well. Land hungry, dispossessed refugees often encroached on land owned by Muslims with greater ease.

Out of strife and pain, great art was born. As the new cinema of the fifties portrayed the intensity of loss of more immediate homelands in Rithwik Ghatak's many partition based films, Satyajit Ray's *Pather Panchali*, also replayed the loss on a different register: displacement from a rural home as an impoverished rural family leaves the ancestral home for large cities. Shambhu Mitra's Bohurupee troupe enlarged possibilities of a new modernist public theatre and cinema flourished at art and at popular levels. The radio made folk songs of Salil and Nirmalenu Choudhury and of Abbasuddin accessible to many more listeners and Pankaj Mallik introduced and popularized Rabindrasangeet which, in this decade, found notable renderings by Suchitra Mitra, Kanika Bandyopadhyay and Rajeshwari Dutta. Classical music joined with more popular musical forms on radio and gramophone records and all night soirees at rich urban households were memorable urban occasions.

The world of art saw older figures experimenting with very new art forms: Abanindranath with his small wooden toys, Nandalal Bose and woodcuts, Binodebehari Mukhopadhay who extended the Shantiniketan art training in new directions, and the popular art of Asit Haldar. New figures emerged: Ramkinkar Baij with his breakthrough paintings and monumental sculpture, perhaps, partly influenced by the Soviet art. Older poets and novelists, men and women, probed new themes and forms: Sudhindranath Dutta and Amiya Chakravarty, who were joined by a new generation of iconoclast poets, bent on breaking expressive codes and conventions: Sunil Gangopadhyay, Shakti Chattopadhyay and their associates in the Harbola Club and in the new journal, *Krittibas*. Popular entertainment, organized sports and art forms flourished and widened: football, cricket, public dance performances. Original scientific research also bloomed as Satyendranath Bose left Dacca University and moved to Bengal, Meghnad Saha founded his institute and the Indian Statistical Institute bloomed under P.C. Mahalanobis. Universities supported very different pedagogical models and academic approaches: of historians and teachers as varied as Jadunath Sarkar, Rameshchandra Majumdar and Susobhan Sarkar.[18]

Yet, something perhaps was missing from the vibrant, indefatigable, ever widening cultural scene. In the forties, Jyotirindranath Moitra's revolutionary songs—Nabajibaner Gaan (Songs For a New Life)—and the tradition of political songs written for the cause of People's War—Janajuddher Gaan (Songs for the People's War)—were taken via song squads to working class suburbs of Calcutta. These were inhabited by largely North Indian Hindu and Muslim workers, and composers, therefore, used Urdu, Hindi and North Indian musical traditions, especially Bhojpuri songs. Binay Ray led one of the squads and communist women had three of their own. They did not just sing to workers but workers also sang and taught them new songs. There was such overwhelming audience reception and so catchy were the tunes and words that on one memorable occasion in February 1943, even the police joined in loudly. Debabrata Biswas, Binay Ray and Jyotorindra Moitra went among jute workers and tramworkers to sing together and the factory guard and officers sang along with them. Of course, this was a time when communists supported the British war effort and did not preach strikes or work stoppage. So mill owners did not obstruct them. The squads began to throw up singers and composers from among workers themselves. At Metiaburz, worker-poet Gurudas Pal, better known as Santiram Mondol, became a front ranking singer at the squad. When first asked to sing before the middle class left audience, he was unnerved: 'I lost my communist identity for a moment and became a rustic.' His clumsy movements evoked laughter from the audience till it was rebuked by leaders, Then a silent and admiring audience listened to his own compositions on the famine. Later, Joshi urged to make him a member of the IPTA.

[18]See Sunil Gangopadhyay, op cit.

From the shared music that came out of this brief cross class cultural collaboration, we get a glimpse of the songs that the workers were already familiar with: 'upcountry' forms like *Kawali, tarja, kajri, chaiti*. In course of the union meetings, some workers revived the *tarja* singing competition and song based performances that they had brought from their villages. The submerged and unknown world of working class culture surfaced as squad leaders tried to compose in the musical-performative modes workers knew. But workers, too, composed in the new mode. Dasrathlal made a name for himself among tram workers as a wonderful drum player. He also wrote new songs: a very well known one being *kekera kekera naam batau/is jag me bara lutera hai* (whose names shall I disclose/ from among those who are among the worst looters?).[19] In October 1943, jute mill worker Bipad moved among mills and sang his own songs about daily life in factories: *Mera chatkalke bhitar/kya kya hota dinbhar*: inside my jute mill what happens the whole day long. They made their own life experiences the stuff of cultural activity.

Sometimes they wrote songs about what communists had taught them: worker-poet Ershad Ali, for instance, wrote about *Stalingrad ke kahani*. Sometimes, the songs reiterated what mills needed at war time—increased production: a need that was also endorsed by the new communist line. At Metiaburz Gurudas Pal wrote songs about this that became highly popular. Calcutta Corporation workers sang and danced with their tools of trade—brooms and brushes—as they pledged to work and keep the city clean: an ironical change as communists had led major strikes among them in 1928.[20]

The times had unleashed a new creativity among workers, so far totally invisible on Calcutta's cultural radar, either as producers, or as consumers of culture. The middle class city, so immensely proud of its cultural traditions, suddenly glimpsed—all too briefly—a class of urban cultural producers, of whom it had known nothing so far. For that moment, it became a much larger city.

[19]Anuradha Ray, *Challish Dashaker Banglai Ganasangeet Andolan*, Papyrus, Calcutta, 1992, pp. 40–65.

[20]Sipra Sarkar and Anamitra Das, eds, *Bangalir Samyabaad Charcha*, Ananda Publishers, Kolkata, 1998, pp377–9.